T0385356

Exterminate / Regenerate

Also by John Higgs

I Have America Surrounded

The KLF

Stranger than We Can Imagine

Watling Street

The Future Starts Here

William Blake Now

William Blake vs the World

Love and Let Die

Exterminate / Regenerate

The Story of Doctor Who

JOHN HIGGS

First published in Great Britain in 2025 by Weidenfeld & Nicolson,
an imprint of The Orion Publishing Group Ltd
Carmelite House, 50 Victoria Embankment
London EC4Y 0DZ

An Hachette UK Company

The authorised representative in the EEA is Hachette Ireland, 8 Castlecourt Centre,
Dublin 15, D15 XTP3, Republic of Ireland (email: info@hbgi.ie)

1 3 5 7 9 10 8 6 4 2

A CIP catalogue record for this book is
available from the British Library.

ISBN (Hardback) 978 1 3996 1477 1
ISBN (Ebook) 978 1 3996 1479 5
ISBN (Audio) 978 1 3996 1480 1

Typeset at The Spartan Press Ltd,
Lymington, Hants

Printed in Great Britain by Clays Ltd,
Elcograf S.p.A.

www.weidenfeldandnicolson.co.uk
www.orionbooks.co.uk

For my Whovian family

CONTENTS

Ever the dim beginning
Ever the growth, the rounding of the circle,
Ever the summit and the merge at last, (to surely start again,)
Eidólons! eidólons!

Walt Whitman (1819–92)

'You don't have to be real to be the Doctor.'

The Doctor, *Extremis* (2017)

INTRODUCTION

One of my favourite memories is of a moment that happened around 2007, when I went to the pub with Tom Baker, the actor best known for playing the fourth Doctor Who.

I was the director of a pre-school animated television programme at the time, and Tom was the programme's narrator. It was a cheap, hastily made little series, and it would have been wiser to spend more of the budget on the animation and less on the voice talent. Being sensible, however, was very much a secondary consideration when the possibility of hiring the extraordinarily charismatic Tom Baker arose. After recording the actors in a Soho sound studio, I would usually retire to the nearest pub with my producer colleague Adam, and sometimes Tom could be persuaded to join us. As I remember it, he didn't need much persuasion.

The pub was the Yorkshire Grey, a small, traditional boozer in Fitzrovia, London. A favoured drinking spot of the poet Ezra Pound, its façade is painted a regal green and the interior stuffed with period details. It is owned by the old Yorkshire brewery Samuel Smith's, which meant that it only served their own brand of beers. As a result, getting a round of drinks usually took a bit of conversation, as familiar brands were absent and the merits of the less familiar Sam Smith's equivalents needed to be debated.

So it was that I was standing at the bar with Tom Baker with a ten-pound note in my hand, discussing which of the unfamiliar beers he would like. At that moment, I happened to look up. The end of the bar turned a corner, and this gave me a view of a man in his forties who was leaning on the bar, intently studying a pint of lager. It just so happened that I looked at this man at the exact moment that he casually glanced up and saw Tom Baker standing there. I think about the expression that crossed his face at that moment often.

It was not a reaction that said, 'Oh look, there's that man who used to be on the telly!' It was not a gentle smile and raised eyebrows, as you might expect from a person when they recognise someone famous. This man was not excited, happy or pleased to see Tom Baker. He was – and I use this word literally – awestruck. This may have been the only time in my life that I have seen a genuinely awestruck face. It was not the reaction you would expect to see when someone has a surprise encounter with a 1970s children's television actor. It was the expression you would expect to see when someone walks into a wardrobe and finds themselves in Narnia.

The man at the bar appeared to be a similar age to myself, so I assume that Tom would have been 'his Doctor'. The concept of 'Your Doctor' is something *Doctor Who* fans understand on a very deep level. They may argue at length about the various merits of different actors, but they understand that, when it comes to the Doctor you first watched as a child, rational critical arguments fail completely. They cannot compete with the nostalgic, magical association that you have with that version of the character. This was *Doctor Who* encountered in its purest form, with no concern about whether it was better or worse than it had been before. This was the version of the character that burnt into your mind, imprinting itself so deeply that it can never really be forgotten, even decades later when you pop out for a quick drink in Fitzrovia. Viewers would come to understand that *Doctor Who* was a series of constant change, but that was not the case during our first encounter. It simply was exactly what it should be, and we were never quite the same again.

For the typical British child in the 1970s, your world was small. You would know your own house, and your garden if you were lucky enough to have one. You would know the route to school, and maybe a friend's house in the street, plus the home of any nearby relatives. Beyond a park or a nearby shop, that was basically it – that was your world. There were occasional cartoons on the TV, which you would look forward to, but most of television back then consisted of boring old men in grey suits talking to themselves behind desks. There was no YouTube or video game consoles to take you off into different worlds whenever you wished. Films about science fiction, fantasy or superheroes were rare. Yet on Saturday evenings Tom Baker would arrive on BBC One with his long scarf, his huge mad grin and his delighted eyes, and take you potentially anywhere in time and space. He made the world you knew and understood suddenly appear tiny. The programme was, in these circumstances, mind-blowing.

My earliest memory of watching *Doctor Who* was a 1975 gothic horror story called *Pyramids of Mars*. Tom Baker's time-travelling Doctor and his companion Sarah Jane Smith are trapped in an English manor house in 1911, hiding from robotic Egyptian mummies and the terrifying Sutekh, an alien god of Death. At one point Sarah asks one of those questions that television characters should never ask – why didn't they just leave? They could jump into the Doctor's time machine and escape to the present day. To explain why they had to stay and fight the ancient awakening Egyptian evil, the Doctor does indeed take Sarah back to the modern day. On arrival, he opens the doors. Outside is not the welcoming English countryside she was expecting, but a hellish, lifeless wasteland. Terrible events that were happening in the past, the Doctor explains, had the potential to prevent the world we lived in from ever existing. I was four years old when I watched that. It broke my little mind. There I was, just beginning to grasp the basics of dull normality, when an innocent-looking television programme showed me that there was far more interesting stuff in the wider universe beyond.

Fast-forward to the early twenty-first century – and a man stood at a bar, minding his own business, drinking a pint and mulling over his middle-aged concerns. One casual glance upwards revealed that a white-haired old actor had entered his everyday world, and suddenly long-suppressed memories of what it was like to be a child took him by surprise. They momentarily banished his sense of a limited, predictable world, and allowed all that intoxicating wonder to flood back. It would take Olympian quantities of cynicism to fail to see the value in moments like these.

A few years before this trip to the pub, I had been talking to my friend Brian Barritt about the lack of male role models in my childhood. My father had died when I was three and I had no male teachers until secondary school. While I was familiar with old, retired men like my granddad, working-age men were largely a mystery to me. I remember watching the dads of my friends in an attempt to figure them out, but these men didn't seem to do anything. They just sat around in armchairs. Looking back at this, I realised with something of a shock that the most significant adult male figure in my childhood was the carefree bohemian wanderer that was Tom Baker's Doctor Who. This was a man unconcerned with ambition or status and unimpressed by authority. He had a moral compass that saw him prepared to fight for the greater good when needed, but was otherwise content to bumble about the universe, enjoying himself. I told Brian about this realisation. He nodded, looked thoughtful and then replied, 'You were very lucky.' I didn't tell Tom Baker any of this, of course. But you can imagine why it meant so much to me to buy him a pint.

It's easy to dismiss the role of fictional characters in our lives. We assume that things that are not real don't matter in the way that real things do. Yet seeing the man at the bar's face makes it hard to agree with that sentiment. If something can have an impact like that, then it clearly does matter. It's hard to think of real things that would have affected him to quite that extent. There's not a huge amount of awe in the modern world.

The arrival of a new fictional character in our culture is, of course, hardly unusual. Not a day goes by without a newly imagined figure arriving on your television or cinema screen, being introduced in a paragraph in a book, or walking out onto a theatre stage. The life cycle of such fictions can vary considerably. Typically, they are not with us long, performing the role in the story they were designed for before slipping away, never to be seen again. The Doctor, in contrast, behaves in a way quite unlike the vast majority of invented people.

Some fictional characters make repeated appearances in different stories, particularly if they are a hero or a detective, and sometimes if they are a villain. Characters that survive over decades are far rarer, but they do exist. Sherlock Holmes has been featured in stories for over 135 years. Tales have been told about the adventures of Robin Hood since at least the fourteenth century. If a character outlives their creators and their original storytellers we grant them a new status which recognises that they have achieved something rare and remarkable. We see them as more than just a fictional character. They become a folk hero. If they live for long enough, like Robin Hood, then they become classed as a legend. In time, a character can go beyond the status of folk hero or legend, and become a myth, such as King Arthur.

Over the past sixty-plus years, Doctor Who has gone from being just another fictional character to becoming the British folk hero of the television age. Whether further promotions in status await them remains to be seen, but there are reasons to consider this likely. In particular, the Doctor has an almost unprecedented ability to step into more new stories than almost any other fictional character. There are 884 episodes of *Doctor Who* to date. That impressive mountain of narrative is dwarfed by the thousands of other stories the Doctor appears in outside of television, in the mediums of officially licensed novels, audios, comics, stage plays or video games. It is unlikely that anyone has consumed every single official *Doctor Who* story. When we include unofficial fan fiction, that number expands beyond all hope of counting.

No television-created character has appeared in as many stories as the Doctor. Only long-established comic characters like Superman or Batman can compare, and even then, those characters often retreat to retelling their origin stories, rather than continuing onwards in a single narrative like *Doctor Who.* As fictional characters go, the history of the Doctor is uniquely expansive, rich and complex. If the imagination does matter and if fictional characters do mean something in our lives, then this mountain of narrative suggests that there is no stronger candidate to illuminate us about this phenomenon than the Doctor.

When we think of fictional characters, we tend to assume that behind them stands a single creative individual who dreamt them up – an imaginative writer like Arthur Conan Doyle, J.K. Rowling or Ian Fleming. With the Doctor, this isn't the case. There was no one person who had the idea of a regenerating alien time traveller exploring the universe in a box that is bigger on the inside than the outside. Instead, the character emerged from the space between many minds, crawling up into our world as if self-willed and determined to exist. Most writers spend their careers hoping to create a character who can live on after their work, if only for a few years. Very few manage to achieve it. That such a character can just turn up, unbidden, can seem a little unsettling.

Perhaps the unauthored origin of *Doctor Who* is why the show is so strange, bewitching and ridiculous. A single creator would have focused on plausibility and believability. They would have defined what the character was, and therefore what they were not. They would be too professional to offer up the messy explosion in an ideas factory that defines the programme at its best. As the current showrunner Russell T Davies has said, no one has ever tried to copy *Doctor Who* – unusual for a successful genre show – 'because it's nuts. Because it's strange. It is eccentric. It is absolutely unique, and I think that calls out to you when you are eight years old and beginning to realise that you're unique.'

Although the Doctor does not have a single creator, they are continuously being created by the imaginations of decades of cast and crew. Many writers, actors, producers and directors gave part of themselves to the character. Aspects of their history, beliefs and personality became imprinted in the fiction, where they will continue onwards and outlive them. As we shall see, some people arguably gave too much of themselves. After the Doctor had finished with them, they never seemed quite complete.

For a long while, it looked like Tom Baker had suffered this fate. He stayed in the role much longer than any other actor, and as a result he was more typecast by the part than his peers. His difficult relationship with the show after he left saw him attempting to distance himself, unsuccessfully, from the role. With his excessively long scarf and wild grin, Baker remained the archetype of Doctor Who in the public's mind for the next three decades, regardless of who the incumbent actor in the role was – a situation that proved detrimental to his career. The Doctor, it seemed, was someone he could never escape from.

Yet around the time I bought him a drink in the Yorkshire Grey, things were starting to change. Tom was being replaced as the archetypal Doctor in the mind of the public by the current incumbent, David Tennant. It seemed to me that this development was a weight off Tom's shoulders. It left him able to enjoy his association with the programme once again. I remember him turning up at recording sessions delightedly gossiping about the nature of the characters that Derek Jacobi and John Simm were playing in an upcoming story. He seemed thrilled that the public had once again fallen in love with that strange show. I think he never quite shed the idea that the programme was special, even through the long years when the press and public thought otherwise. It was at this point that he agreed to record BBC audiobooks in character as the Doctor once again, a decision that would eventually lead to him returning to the role in a range of full-cast audiobooks. Playing the Doctor again in his later years brought Tom a great deal of pleasure. As he said in 2023, at the age of eighty-nine, 'I think being Doctor Who has done me a bit of good after all these years. It's made me happy, otherwise I wouldn't have stayed with it so long. It's become part of me, and I've become part of it [. . .] Because it makes me so happy I think about it most of the time, really. It's just a wonderful thing.'

The person I bought a drink for was Tom Baker, not Doctor Who. Tom Baker is a wonderful character who is every bit as charming and entertaining as you would hope. Like many charismatic, talented older men, he was not really looking for a conversation. What he wanted was an audience. This was fine by me, and sitting in the pub listening to his tall tales was an absolute joy. But although Tom was not the Doctor, he had helped animate something larger than himself. As a result, there is an aspect of Tom Baker that seems set to live forever. As he charmed and entertained me that day, Tom was an ordinary mortal man finally at peace with his immortal aspect.

Forty-nine years after I watched Tom defeat the evil Sutekh in *Pyramids of Mars*, that Egyptian-styled god of Death returned to our screens in a sequel to that half-century-old story. In the build-up to Sutekh's reveal, the Doctor – now played by Ncuti Gatwa – repeated the moment that had so affected me as a child. He took his companion to the present day and showed her that events in the past had destroyed the world she knew. I could not help but wonder how children in 2024 reacted to this scene. In forty years' time, when a middle-aged man or woman enters a bar and sees Ncuti Gatwa standing there, I feel certain they will experience a moment of simple, unforced awe.

PRE-TITLES

The Conception (1962–63)

1. Verity Underground

On 30 November 1958, the Welsh actor Gareth Jones died off-camera during the transmission of an episode of *Armchair Theatre*, ITV's flagship weekend drama anthology series. It was, as usual, being filmed and broadcast live.

The production was partway through the second act when Jones suffered a fatal heart attack. According to the director Philip Saville, Jones was 'a very exciting actor', similar to a young Charles Laughton or Simon Russell Beale. His character was important to the story because he had betrayed the rest of the cast and was going to be unmasked as a traitor at the end of the play. With bleak irony, the script called for his character to die of a heart attack in the dramatic finale.

The story, titled *Underground*, was about survivors from a nuclear war living in the remains of the London Underground. Jones had complained about feeling unwell in make-up but had then returned to set, which was a grim series of tunnels and rubble, to take his next cue. As fellow cast member Peter Bowles recalled, 'I was in this little group and the character played by Gareth Jones was supposed to join us and share dialogue. We saw him coming down the tunnel towards us and then we saw him fall. We presumed he'd tripped up and we could see people apparently tending to him. So we had to carry on and extemporise to cover it.' Bowles and the other actors did not realise that he had died. Jones was only in his early thirties.

In the early decades of television, it was usual for dramas to be performed live – it was much cheaper than committing a programme to expensive videotape. Actors had typically learnt their craft in the theatre, so performing a teleplay from start to finish was a natural way of working for them. Indeed, television drama was originally understood to be much the same as theatre, except with cameras for an audience. That idea, however, tends to underplay how complicated making television drama was, from a production point of view.

A typical production would involve around three or four cameras, mounted on heavy moveable pedestals. The camera movements would be carefully planned out by the director. Those movements would be limited by the cables leading from the camera pedestals to the various outlets, because it was vitally important that the cameras did not become tangled up in, or trapped by, each other's cables. The sound team also needed to know in advance the positions of the cameras and which size of lenses they would be using at any one time, so that they knew where they could position the microphones, and how close they could be to the actors, without them appearing in shot. For a programme to run smoothly the movements of the cameras had to be accurate, timely and follow the camera script methodically. Any deviation could throw off not only the shot being broadcast, but the shots that followed as well.

The camera scripts and the associated camera cards were typed up by the production assistant. The PA was historically a female position, and one that demanded unflappable reliability with a sense of natural authority. They would typically sit on the director's left in the control room, with their paperwork in front of them and a stopwatch in their hand. It was their voice that counted down to the beginning of the live broadcast, usually in a clipped, received pronunciation accent. During the broadcast they would call out the shots for those in the control room and for the camera crew on the studio floor. If the PA found this responsibility stressful, it was imperative that this wasn't betrayed in their voice. The PA kept the programme running and to time, and their calm, controlled voice was an indication that everything was going to plan. The production assistant for the live broadcast of *Underground* was a young ex-boarding school pupil named Verity Lambert, who had celebrated her twenty-third birthday only three days earlier.

The production team learnt that Jones had died when the programme went to a commercial break. If something similar happened now, of course, it would be abandoned and the channel would broadcast an emergency repeat to fill the air time. Early television drama, however, was still rooted in theatrical attitudes. As the crew instinctively understood, the show must go on. 'It was one of these things where nobody knew what to do,' Lambert recalled later. 'Nobody could prepare for it. You had to think on your feet. I don't know, rightly or wrongly, we just ploughed on with it.' The story would have to change even as it was being told. Another character would have to be unmasked as the traitor at the end of the story, and Jones's expected actions and dialogue would have to be improvised around.

The cast were not informed of Jones's death. They were told that he was ill and unable to appear in the rest of the play, and they performed incredibly well in this unprecedented situation. The actor Andrew Cruickshank, for example, was due to give a big speech that reacted to questions thrown at him by Jones's character, such as, 'How are you going to lead us?' Cruickshank ad-libbed dialogue such as 'Now, you might ask, how am I going to lead you?' before delivering his original dialogue as best he could.

The director of *Underground* was Lambert's boyfriend, a 27-year-old Bulgarian-Canadian named Ted Kotcheff. He realised that he would have to take the script and go down to the studio floor, where he could change the play on the fly. By reading a few pages ahead of the scene being broadcast live, he would hopefully be able to see problems coming and, somehow, solve them in time. He turned to Verity and told her that, for the rest of the programme, she would have to take over the director's role in the control room. She would now be responsible for vision mixing and cutting between shots. Quite what those shots would be were, at this stage, as yet unknown. So it was that Verity Lambert, who had never directed multi-camera studio drama before, found herself directing ITV's high-profile weekend drama as it was being broadcast live to the nation, with no real knowledge of where the story was going or how it would end.

There was little hope that it would go smoothly. Lambert was unprepared and knew that the cast were going to start improvising their parts in a way that would throw out her existing camera script. Still, she rose to the challenge, took charge of the studio gallery and directed the rest of the play, whatever it might be.

The extent to which the show was a chaotic mess is not entirely clear. Television reviewers, who filed their opinions before news of Jones's death broke, generally found the programme unsatisfying, but they didn't seem to have noticed the extent of the production chaos. For those more intimately involved in producing television drama, however, it was apparent that things weren't going well. The young director Christopher Morahan recalls watching at home, fascinated, as the programme winged its way towards a conclusion. The programme would cut to cameras that were in the wrong place, filming other cameras and crew rather than the actors. 'Every time someone went to a door, there was a camera there. So I said, "I think we're watching a live disaster!"' One person who did realise that something unusual had happened was Jones's fiancée. She was watching the programme at her home in London, and she could not understand why Jones had suddenly disappeared from the drama.

The death of an actor during a live play must be, in television production terms, as big a nightmare as it is possible to imagine. Yet when the young Verity Lambert was thrown into this unthinkable position, she kept her head and she didn't panic. She did what was needed to be done to keep the programme on the air. Her impressive response did not go unnoticed by the programme's experienced producer, a 41-year-old Canadian named Sydney Newman.

2. What It Thought Was Good for Them

The unique corporate culture of the BBC was originally forged by its first Director General, John (later Lord) Reith. The youngest son of a Presbyterian minister in Kincardineshire, Scotland, Reith was a stern, serious individual who believed he was destined to be a great man in history. His hero was Oliver Cromwell. In his diaries, he claimed that he wasn't drawn to political parties for their policies. What mattered, he wrote, was whether they advocated for 'righteousness in every department of human activity' and demanded 'an unqualified, deliberate, manly and aggressive adoption of the principles expounded by Christ'. His interpretation of Christ's principles was a very right-wing one. In the early 1920s, he worked as a political secretary for a group of Conservative MPs, to fight what he called 'the Labour menace'.

In an earlier job at a gun factory, he regularly sacked employees who asked for a pay rise or better conditions and claimed that he 'enjoyed doing it'.

Under the guiding hand of Reith and the other founders of the BBC, the corporation saw improving the British population, intellectually, spiritually and morally, as its solemn duty. They took it for granted that they knew best. The British people, the BBC believed, would be improved by making them think more like Reith. It was its duty, therefore, to spread his values and worldview throughout the viewing public. Aspects of culture that Reith disapproved of such as jazz, regional accents and anything remotely connected to modernism were therefore conspicuously absent from the airwaves. The early BBC's elitist attitudes were nicely illustrated in the expectation that presenters in London were, for a time, expected to dress in formal evening wear when broadcasting on radio.

The Reithian culture of the BBC lingered long after Reith had left. The post-war BBC was, in the opinion of the screenwriter Dennis Potter, 'paternalistic and often stuffily pompous. It saw itself in an almost priestly role.' It tended to assume that its audience was upper-middle class, like the people that the BBC employed. When independent television began broadcasting in the mid-1950s, this gulf between the corporation and the British public quickly became evident in the viewing figures. According to the BBC's own research for 1957, the new ITV channels had an audience share of 72 per cent in regions where viewers could receive both BBC and the independent channels. 'When commercial television started, it absolutely knocked the BBC for six, because the drama was so good,' recalled Betty Willingale, who worked in the BBC's script department at the time. 'It just made the BBC [seem] ridiculous.'

This was the situation that Hugh Greene inherited when he

became Director General of the BBC in 1960. Greene knew that he had to engage with the tastes and lives of the British public, now that they had a choice of what to watch. The BBC could no longer get away with giving viewers what it thought was good for them. As he said in 1962, 'One must get away from the middle-class "Who's for tennis?" type of drawing-room drama to show the problems of poverty, lack of housing, what have you.' It was for this reason that he poached Sydney Newman from ATV that year as his new Head of Drama. The disastrous *Underground* episode aside, Newman had proved his popular touch as producer of *Armchair Theatre* and his earlier work in his native Canada. This was thought by many to be a great improvement on the type of plays shown on the BBC.

Newman was very different to the typical public-school-educated BBC employee. His habit of putting his feet on the table and swearing in meetings was considered shockingly uncouth. In the eyes of long-term BBC drama staff, he was an overpaid outsider and his position of power was a constant reminder of their failings. They knew that he had been employed as their boss because he understood viewers and could speak to them in a way that they couldn't. All this did not make him popular. Internal resentment did not make his job easier.

When Newman arrived at the BBC, he realised that he had a lot of work to do. 'I'll be perfectly frank,' he said later. 'When I got to the BBC and I looked my staff over I was really quite sick, because most of the directors there were people whose work I just did not like. I thought it was soft and slow and had no edge. Believe me, I had a bad Christmas, because I didn't know what to do – how to change those people who were stuck in their old ways.'

His solution was to restructure the old script department and create separate departments for series, serials and stand-alone plays. He split the original role of producer into two separate jobs, producer and director, and he gave individual productions their own script editor, rather than leaving that responsibility with the department as a whole. He also had to radically scale up both staff and productions, in preparation for the launch of the BBC Two channel in 1964. Among all this high-level restructuring, there was still the issue of individual series to attend to.

Around March 1963, Newman was called to a meeting with Chief of Programmes Donald Baverstock and Joanna Spicer, the Assistant Controller of planning, to discuss a hole in the schedules. This was the space between *Grandstand*, the hugely successful sports programme on Saturday afternoons, and *Juke Box Jury*, a music programme with a big teen audience that typically aired around 6 p.m. In between these two staples was something of a scheduling wasteland, and a variety of cartoons, repeats and American imports had been tried to fill it. What the corporation really wanted was a series which would keep families tuned to the BBC for the duration of Saturday evening. What this should be, however, was tricky. *Grandstand* and *Juke Box Jury* were very different programmes that attracted very different demographics. As Newman defined the problem, 'We required a new programme that would bridge the state of mind of sports fans and the teenage pop music audience while attracting and holding the children's audience accustomed to their Saturday-afternoon serial [. . .] The problem was, as I saw it, that it had to be a children's programme and still attract adults and teenagers. And also, as a children's programme, I was intent upon it containing basic factual information that could be described as educational – or, at least, mind-opening for them.' But what type of programme, exactly, could appeal equally to sports-loving dads and music-crazy teens?

3. 'Mad Scientists and All that Jazz'

Newman decided that the answer was science fiction, a genre that he was very fond of. 'Up to the age of forty, I don't think there was a science fiction book I hadn't read,' he said in 1988. 'I love them because they are a marvellous way – and a safe way, I might add – of saying nasty things about our own society.'

Although Newman's enthusiasm for science fiction was not something that most BBC employees shared, the notion of making something in that area had been discussed in the years before Newman joined the corporation. In March 1962, for example, Eric Maschwitz, the Assistant and Adviser to the Controller of Programmes, wondered if there was any merit in adapting science fiction stories for television. Maschwitz was then coming towards the end of a long, varied and successful career in the entertainment industries. As a screenwriter, he had been nominated for an Academy Award for his work on *Goodbye, Mr Chips* (1939), and as a lyricist his work included songs like 'These Foolish Things' and 'A Nightingale Sang in Berkeley Square'. Maschwitz, therefore, was the sort of person whose queries were worth paying attention to. Donald Wilson, the head of the BBC script department, duly commissioned a report to examine the matter. The fact that Wilson had to commission a report to answer this question nicely illustrates the status of the science fiction genre in the eyes of the BBC. When the script department turned its attention to comedies, historical dramas or thrillers, they did not first research those genres to confirm that they had value.

Contemporary attitudes to science fiction, and the prejudices of BBC staff, are readily apparent in the finished report. It was not enthusiastic. Science fiction, they said, was 'not itself a widely popular branch of fiction'. The authors of the report, Alice Frick and Donald Bull, were deeply unimpressed by science fiction and fantasy authors, and they were forthright in their opinions. C.S. Lewis, for example, was described as 'clumsy and old-fashioned [. . .] There is a sense of condescension in his tone, and his special religious preoccupations are boring and platitudinous.' Frick and Bull saw little merit in existing British science fiction writers, who were not welcome at the BBC. 'We must admit to having started this study with a profound prejudice – that television science fiction drama must be written not by SF writers, but by TV dramatists. We think it is not necessary to elaborate our reasons for this.' Still, they did hold out some hope for what they called the 'Threat and Disaster school' of stories, which they neatly summed up as 'mad scientists and all that jazz'. Ultimately, though, their conclusion was 'we cannot recommend any existing SF stories for TV adaptation'. It was from within this dismissive analysis that the spirit that would become *Doctor Who* first twitched.

To read this report now, you would assume that the idea of developing science fiction drama would have immediately been abandoned. That would almost certainly have been the case at other media organisations. The BBC, however, is governed by very different assumptions than other companies, and it had always been something of a contradictory beast. Although it unconsciously believed that it knew best, it also saw itself as independent, neutral and universal.

This neutrality was debatable, and tended to fluctuate with events. During the General Strike of 1926, for example, the BBC remained on air and – initially at least – attempted to report events neutrally. Statements from trade union leaders and Labour politicians were dutifully reported alongside government spokesmen. Soon, however, government pressure caused the corporation to reassess this neutrality. After the Archbishop of Canterbury requested a platform to broadcast an official Church opinion on the strike, the BBC was informed by the government that the archbishop's words should not be broadcast. It was felt that they contained a certain amount of unacceptable empathy for the strikers.

Reith made the decision to cede their neutrality to the government, and duly complied with the politicians' wishes. As the strike dragged on, any pretence of neutrality evaporated. This was acceptable, an internal BBC memo argued, because 'our news was "doped" only by suppressions, not by fabrications'. With this incident, a template was set for how the BBC would operate in the years to come, during periods of intense political pressure. The BBC would be a proudly neutral broadcaster, except for when it wasn't.

The government could put pressure on the BBC like this because, after it ceased being a private company in 1927, they ultimately controlled how it was funded. After the BBC was granted corporation status by royal charter, it was pointedly not funded out of general taxation. That would have defined the BBC as a government mouthpiece rather than an independent broadcaster. Instead, it was funded by a licence fee, which had to be paid by every household with a radio and then, after 1946, a television set. Non-payment would result in legal action and a fine. The royal charter, however, needed to be renewed regularly, and the government had the ability to alter the price of the licence fee. For this reason, the corporation remains eternally nervous about political pressure, and acutely aware that the source of its funding remains its Achilles heel.

The licence fee system was relatively uncontroversial when the BBC was the only broadcaster in the country, but it became harder to defend after commercial channels, satellite broadcasting and streaming took up an increasingly large share of British viewing. The system does not survive because it is easy to defend, but because it is generally seen as the least-worst option. The best defence of the compulsory nature of the licence fee is that the BBC – unlike independent competitors – is duty bound to provide programming for everyone. Sydney Newman, for example, was looking for a child-friendly family drama, and a show like that was unlikely to be developed at a commercial channel. The 'family' demographic is of little interest to broadcasters funded by advertising, because advertisers want to target their products at specific sections of the population. There is little point in paying to reach a large audience that includes children, mothers and grandparents when only a small section of that audience is interested in your products.

As long as the BBC provides programming for all demographics and interests, the argument goes, commercial competitors have to compete on quality. The net result of this is a better, healthier broadcasting ecosystem in the UK. For these reasons, when the 1962 script department report concluded that science fiction was not particularly suitable, Wilson did not scrap the idea. He knew that a section of the audience did enjoy the genre, regardless of what the BBC thought. It was necessary to serve this audience because ultimately the defence of the licence fee, and the very future of the BBC, required it.

It was not as if there hadn't been successful science fiction on television before. The 1953 serial *The Quatermass Experiment* was hugely popular and is now viewed as a major landmark in the evolution of post-war television. More pressingly, the fledgling young commercial ITV channel had just begun broadcasting *Out of This World*, a science fiction anthology drama series which adapted the work of writers including Philip K. Dick and Isaac Asimov. Knowing that the BBC was duty bound to provide something similar, Wilson commissioned a second report. This ignored the question of whether science fiction was something they *should* do, and assumed instead that it was something that they were *going* to do. It asked what type of science fiction stories might be made to work on television.

Wilson received this second report on 25 July 1962, six months before Sydney Newman arrived at the BBC. It had several recommendations. The first was that any proposed series should not include any 'Bug-Eyed Monsters'. The second was that 'The central characters are never Tin Robots (since the audience must always subconsciously say "My goodness, there's a man in there and isn't he playing the part well").' Stories about telepaths, it thought, were possible. But the concept that its authors thought was 'particularly attractive in a series' was time travel. This, they felt, would allow a variety of scriptwriters to work on different plots in a serialised format. Time travel, they declared, could be 'the *Z-Cars* of science fiction'.

This proved to be a prophetic description. *Z-Cars* was then a new series, having launched in January 1962, but it lasted for 801 episodes and became one of the longest-running police procedural series in British TV history. A time travel series that matched *Z-Cars* in longevity would be a remarkable hit indeed.

4. 'Somewhat Pathetic'

The following March a meeting was called in Donald Wilson's office, room 5078 at Television Centre. Wilson was now Head of Serials, following Sydney Newman's arrival and reorganisation of the drama department. After Newman had decided that a science fiction series would fill the gap between *Grandstand* and *Juke Box Jury*, Wilson had been tasked with working out what it should be.

Wilson summoned Alice Frick and John Braybon, the authors of the second report into science fiction, and the writer Cecil Edwin Webber, known to all as 'Bunny'. This nickname was the result of the odd way that Webber ran, which was said to be like a rabbit. It is fitting that a person who ran strangely was present at the birth of *Doctor Who*. The various actors who have played the role over the years are very different people, but there is one characteristic that unites them – they usually have a slightly silly run. Many people involved in creating the Doctor gifted parts of themselves to the character, and not always intentionally. Bunny Webber would make an invaluable contribution to *Doctor Who* by writing the first draft of the first episode. It would be irrational, but also pleasing to think that his strange physical quirk somehow imprinted on the character as well.

In Wilson's office, the four creatives began suggesting ideas. These were varied and wide-ranging, covering notions such as telepathy, a team of scientific troubleshooters, the nature of human thought and the use of a flying saucer. As Webber saw the developing series, here was 'a fine opportunity to write fast moving, shocking episodes, which necessarily consider, or at least firmly raise, such questions as: What sort of people do we want? What sort of conditions do we desire? What is life? What are we? Can society exist without love, without art, without lies, without sex?' Speculation along such lines suggested a series that was far more serious, adult and potentially intellectual and ponderous, than the one that would eventually emerge. Newman would continually steer the developing idea back in a more populist, child-friendly direction.

One key idea was established at this point, however. Webber's post-meeting memo starts, 'Envisaged is a "loyalty programme", lasting at least 52 weeks, consisting of various dramatised S.F. stories, linked to form a continuous serial, using basically a few characters who continue through all the stories.' Here the very first piece of *Doctor Who* DNA falls into place. Before anyone knew what the series was, there was intention that it would run for a long time. Everything that was to come would be built on this idea. Longevity was the foundation stone of *Doctor Who.*

A second piece of the series can also be glimpsed in Frick's memo. This follows on from Wilson's earlier report, which recommended time travel. According to Frick, 'Donald Wilson suggested if [a time machine] were used, it should be a machine not only for going forward and backwards in time, but into space, and into all kinds of matter (e.g. a drop of oil, a molecule, under the ocean, etc.).' This was something far stranger and more fantastical than the time machine imagined by H.G. Wells. Here, in embryonic form, was the birth of the TARDIS. Webber suggested that the machine should be invisible, but Newman scotched this idea. He insisted that a 'tangible symbol' was needed, whatever that would turn out to be.

But who, exactly, was this series about? That was the question that remained unanswered at the end of the meeting. Webber's memo speaks of characters in only the vaguest terms. The 'first character' is described only as 'THE HANDSOME YOUNG MAN HERO', while the second character is 'THE HANDSOME WELLDRESSED HEROINE AGED ABOUT 30'. There was no deeper attempt at characterisation. As Frick's report concludes, 'The major problems in format are, how to involve a part of a permanent group in widely differing adventures, and how to transport them believably to entirely disparate milieux.'

During April 1963 the ideas gradually developed into the programme that would be broadcast that autumn, largely through the interchange of ideas between Wilson and Newman, supported by Webber, the story editor David Whitaker and the eventual screenwriter of the first serial, Anthony Coburn. The question of which person created which aspect of the finished format remains opaque, and we can't be certain exactly who suggested key ideas such as the programme's name, or that the time machine would take the shape of a mundane police box. A BBC memo dated 9 May 1963 refers to the series as 'Mr. Who?', but subsequent paperwork quickly corrects this to 'Dr. Who'.

Newman wanted a young teenage character added to the cast, someone who could cause trouble and get into scrapes. This character was originally given the name Bridget or Biddy, before she was renamed Sue and finally Susan. She was originally described by Webber as 'A with-it girl of fifteen, reaching the end of her Secondary School career, eager for life, lower-than-middle-class.' The phrase 'lower-than-middle-class' is a telling insight into the culture of the BBC at the time. Newman corrected this wording, changing it into the avoided phrase 'working class'. Despite this, when the programme was finally broadcast all the main cast were firmly middle class and spoke with received pronunciation accents.

Another character appeared in Webber's memo, imagined only in the vaguest of terms – 'THE MATURER MAN, 35–40, WITH SOME "CHARACTER" TWIST'. Webber offered no suggestions of what this twist would be. As character descriptions go, it was as vague as it is possible to be. If anything, it was less of a character, and more a desire for a character. Yet it was around this desire that the shape of the Doctor would coalesce – in much the same way that a pearl only forms inside an oyster if there is a piece of grit for it to form around.

As the birth of a major fictional character, this was a long way from J.K. Rowling having a vision of Harry Potter while daydreaming on a train, or J.R.R. Tolkien pausing while marking exam papers to scribble 'In a hole in the ground there lived a hobbit'. Many thousands of character descriptions circulated on documents in the BBC's drama department during the 1960s, and most were far more inspired and promising than this one. This character sketch lacked intention, imagination and vision. Yet the great majority of those intended characters never left the page, while this desired character would outlive everyone who dealt with those documents. This sentence was the piece of grit within the shell of the BBC around which Doctor Who formed.

In a now lost memo, Newman developed this character into something resembling the role that William Hartnell would shortly play. In a programme format document dated 16 May 1963, we discover that 'Dr. Who' is:

> A name given to him by his three earthly friends because neither he nor they know who he is. Dr. Who is about 650 years old. Frail looking but wiry and tough like an old turkey – is amply demonstrated whenever he is forced to run from danger. His watery blue eyes are continually looking around in bewilderment and occasionally a look of utter malevolence clouds his face as he suspects his earthly friends of being part of some conspiracy. He seems not to remember where he comes from but he has flashes of garbled memory which indicate that he was involved in a galactic war and still fears pursuit by some undefined enemy. Because he is somewhat pathetic his three friends continually try to help him find his way 'home', but they are never sure of his motives.

So there he was – Doctor Who, a fictional character who would behave and evolve in a way quite unlike the thousands of other fictional characters invented for television each year. He was built around the concept of longevity, yet he was frail and somewhat confused. He is the title character, yet he only appeared in the format in order to grant the hero and heroine their adventures. His most positive attribute was the ability to run away, and he was capable of utter malevolence, yet he was destined to become a hero to millions for decades to come. Given the extent to which the Doctor would become a powerful, almost godlike figure in the twenty-first century, the fact that he was originally conceived of as being 'somewhat pathetic' should give hope to us all. The Doctor has been steeped in contradictions from the very start.

5. A Certain Lack of Enthusiasm

Even as the concept of the programme was being developed, plans were under way for the practical aspect of producing it. A memo from the Drama Group Administrator on 26 April 1963 states that the budget for each episode would be £2,300. Adjusted for inflation, this would be around £40,000 in 2024, and it was clear from early on that money was going to be tight. Writers were advised that they should 'work to a very moderate budget'. There was an extra £500 granted to build the set of the 'space/time machine', which would then be used throughout the series. The final cost for the TARDIS's interior turned out to be somewhat more expensive, at £4,328. Overall, this did not seem to be a budget suited to a series with the ambition to explore all of time and space. With this seemingly crippling restriction on what the programme could put on screen, another integral part of its long-term DNA clicked into place.

Another concern was the studio allocated to the production, Studio D at Lime Grove. At 73 by 55 feet, excluding fire lanes, it was tiny compared to the modern studios that had recently opened at Television Centre. Its technology was also increasingly out of date, and it was immediately clear that, for a series that needed to be ambitious in storytelling, Studio D was going to cause major difficulties. When the fledgling production team raised their concerns, Ian Atkins, the Controller of Programme Services for Television, agreed that the old-fashioned lighting equipment and other issues made Studio D 'virtually the worst possible studio for such a project'. The allocation, however, remained. Programmes assigned to newer, more suitable studios had precedence over this nascent children's programme. *Doctor Who* was not a high priority for the corporation.

Several departments which would be crucial to the making of the programme were firmly against it. James Murdie, the Head of Scenic Servicing, the department responsible for building and striking sets, saw the programme as excessively ambitious. He wrote to the Senior Planning Assistant urging them to 'think twice before proceeding with a weekly series of this nature'. Richard Levine, the head of both the design department and the visual effects department, sent a memo to Assistant Controller Joanna Spicer, saying that *Doctor Who* 'is the kind of crazy enterprise which both Departments can well do without'.

A certain lack of enthusiasm for the show within the BBC can be detected in Newman's efforts to find a producer to make it. Initially, the director Rex Tucker was hired as a caretaker producer, but he did not want the role permanently. 'I did not particularly want to work on it,' he said, 'but as I was due to go on holiday I decided to help out with the initial casting sessions.' Shaun Sutton, who would later become involved with *Doctor Who* when he became first Head of Serials, and then Head of Drama, was also offered the job. He turned it down. Newman began looking outside the BBC because, as he said in 1984, 'I didn't feel that I had anyone on staff who seemed right for the kind of idiocy and fun and yet serious underlying intent.' Newman tried Richard Bates, who was then the script editor on *The Avengers* and who went on to produce landmark series including *The Prime of Miss Jean Brodie*, *The Darling Buds of May* and *A Touch of Frost*. He wasn't interested. The director Don Taylor claims that he was also asked. Writing in his biography, he recalled that he turned down Newman by saying that he'd 'never had the slightest interest in science fiction, and if I wanted to do plays about the past, I didn't need a time traveller to take me there'.

What Newman needed was a producer who didn't think the show was beneath them and who wouldn't just begrudgingly take it on until something better came along. He needed someone who would take control of the programme and fight for it within the corporation. He wanted someone who was, as he memorably defined it, 'full of piss and vinegar'.

Having seen how Verity Lambert had dealt with the crisis of an actor dying during a live broadcast five years earlier, Newman knew she had the qualities he needed. Though she had no experience as a producer and no interest in children's science fiction, she was ambitious, driven and eager to move up in television. He liked the way that she was prepared to argue with him when she felt that he was wrong. Lambert, Newman felt, was exactly the sort of talent that was overlooked by the industry but who deserved to be given a chance.

At this point, Lambert had already become disillusioned with television. She was ambitious and wanted to direct, but directing remained an almost exclusively male domain. The BBC had ended its 'marriage bar', which prevented the hiring of married women, in 1944. Yet there was still a lingering belief that there was little point in training women for complex jobs, such as directing, because they would leave the workplace to raise children after they married. Such attitudes were certainly present at the independent ABC Weekend TV, where Lambert was then working. She knew that she was just as capable as her male colleagues in those roles, but she saw little hope that she could progress, given the attitudes of her industry. 'There were no means of really complaining in 1962. There wasn't a sexual discrimination board,' she has said. 'I decided that if I couldn't move up somewhere within a year, I would forget about television and do something completely different.' She was considering a career in the antiques trade.

This was the point, in early 1963, that Newman called her from the BBC and asked if she would produce a new children's science fiction series called *Doctor Who*. According to her friend Linda Agran, her immediate response to Newman was 'I don't know any children, I don't want children, I don't fucking like children!'

But Newman was offering her a chance to move up in television. That was exactly what she had been hoping for. And if it meant that she had to care about science fiction and children, then Verity Lambert would do exactly that.

6. The Three Musketeers

When it came to recruiting the rest of the crew, the lack of enthusiasm for the programme within the BBC was clear. Betty Willingale, who had worked with Wilson in the former script department, was offered the role of story editor. 'I nearly died, I fell over laughing,' she recalled. 'I can't bear *Doctor Who* [. . .] I said, "Oh God, that's the last thing I want to do!"' The director James Cellan Jones recalls that he turned down *Doctor Who* because, 'I was a frightful snob and said, "No, I don't direct that class of material."' The director Alvin Rakoff also declined, believing that, 'It was way beneath me; it was a kids' series.' Even Terry Nation, who would become incredibly wealthy by inventing the Daleks, admitted that 'I remember feeling vaguely insulted at being asked to write for "children's hour".'

Like Lambert, Waris Hussein, the director eventually allocated to the first story, was also relatively inexperienced. He had completed the BBC's directing traineeship and took the job because he was eager to prove himself. 'Nobody wanted to touch *Doctor Who*,' he recalls. 'Nobody thought it was going to get made. They thought it was crap. The attitude was, "If it's going to fail, it might as well fail with this young Indian."' In his diary, he wrote that 'The more I think of "Dr Who", the more it depresses me and I can't bear the thought of it. I hope it never happens.' His concern was that the first story took the time travellers back to the Stone Age. 'The discovery of fire was not my idea of directing something after my Cambridge days where I studied Shakespeare. And I didn't want to be laughed at – directing actors in skins.'

Because so many established BBC faces thought that working on the series was beneath them, the final production team varied significantly from the corporation's norm. This very British icon was created by a strikingly international team. Newman was Canadian, Hussein was Indian, the designer of the TARDIS Peter Brachacki was Polish, the first script was written by the Australian Anthony Coburn and the theme was composed by his fellow Australian Ron Grainer. Many in the team were also unusually young, and their hiring was progressive in other ways. Verity Lambert was still only twenty-seven. This made her the youngest producer at the BBC and the only female producer in the drama department. Waris Hussein was even younger, at twenty-four. He was the BBC's first Indian-born director and he was also gay, although as homosexuality was illegal in Britain in 1963 he was not 'out' in the modern sense.

'We were like the Three Musketeers,' Hussein has said. 'We were the aliens fighting the establishment. Sydney was Canadian Jewish, Verity was an upper-middle-class Jewish princess and I was an Indian. How much more can you be outsiders?' For

Hussein, their difference was a constant issue during the working day. 'I was very conscious of my ethnic background – of walking on the studio floor and having these redneck crews looking at me askance and wondering when I was going to stumble and fall. I knew I would have to be absolutely prepared, my camera scripts immaculate. For Verity, the whole attitude to women was that they don't do this job, they were secretaries or PAs – it was a testosterone-driven thing.'

These were the experiences of the first people to actively shape the character of the Doctor, and they had an impact. As Lambert said, the Doctor was 'sometimes dangerous or unpleasant, sometimes kind, sometimes foolish. But, most importantly, he was never a member of the establishment. He was always an outsider.'

That Lambert and Hussein were the programme's first producer and director is now seen as symbolic. The programme, at its very start, came from a team that was progressive and diverse, and those attitudes are now championed by the showrunners of the modern series. On one level, however, both Lambert's and Hussein's backgrounds *were* similar to typical BBC staff. They both came from wealthy families and were privately educated. Lambert's father bought her a house in Belgravia, complete with a cleaner and a car, and she was in a position where she was able to spend far more than she earned. She got her first job in television, at Granada, because her father was friends with Sidney Bernstein, the company's co-founder, and asked him to find her a position. She got a later television job, she has claimed, because someone misread the reference to the elite boarding school Roedean on her application and thought that she had gone to RADA.

Hussein, meanwhile, had been educated at Clifton College in Bristol and Queen's College, Cambridge. His entry to television came about because 'I went to the Cambridge Appointments Board and I said to them I wanted an interview with the BBC.

They got me one.' Hussein's privilege was particularly noted by Douglas Camfield, his PA. Camfield was desperate to direct and believed he was better qualified, but he felt he was overlooked because of his working-class background. Camfield, happily, did eventually become a director and went on to direct many classic *Doctor Who* stories.

Pre-production did not go smoothly. The launch date was pushed back twice. The pilot episode had to be rerecorded after Newman felt that the tone was too strange and off-putting. More seriously, the programme was very nearly scrapped due to concerns about feasibility and cost. Lambert fought the internal BBC politics behind this decision and was granted a stay of execution, but only for a run of thirteen episodes. This would not be the last time that the series faced cancellation, but this threat came when the programme was at its most defenceless. If it was to face internal opposition like this again it would need external help to defend itself, in the shape of an audience or fanbase. At this point, it was protected by nothing other than Lambert's piss and vinegar.

Despite the issues of budget and the indifference of many of the corporation's staff, scripts were written, actors were hired and the time machine was designed. Soon it was time for actors to perform and cameras to roll. The BBC was not expecting much to come from *Doctor Who*. What the British public would make of it remained to be seen.

OPENING TITLES

At 5:16 p.m. and 20 seconds on Saturday, 23 November 1963, the first episode of *Doctor Who* was broadcast on BBC TV – as the only BBC channel was then called. The channels BBC One and BBC Two – or BBC1 and BBC2 as they were styled until 1997 – would not launch until the following year.

The opening shot of the title sequence is predominantly black except for a striking white line shooting upwards from the bottom of the screen. It looks like a rocket ship blasting upwards into the vast heavens, straight and direct and powerful. For a split second it appears to be a purposeful, masculine representation of the coming future – a perfect symbol of the thrilling, brave Space Age we were on the verge of entering.

But almost immediately, things begin to change. The rising line seems to hesitate and stall. It twists and distorts as misty echoes thicken on each side. The one line becomes two, and then three, and then many. What had been linear, rational and neat devolves into something unpredictable and abstract. The screen becomes full of strange swirling patterns, pulsing with energy. From the firm white line comes chaos.

This pulsing chaos was achieved through an experimental technique called 'howlaround'. This is the visual equivalent of the howling feedback generated when a microphone is placed too close to a speaker. A camera was pointed at a monitor displaying the picture from that camera. The swirls and patterns that emerged were a by-product of the fraction of a second delay in this feedback loop. These first howlaround shots had originally been used for the BBC's 1960 production of the opera *Tobias and the Angel*, directed by Rudolph Cartier. There is no shame in reusing offcuts when money is tight.

Then a word appears – but only for a few frames. In bold capitals, the archaic exclamation 'OHO' appears in the centre of the screen, like a cry of alarm a few centuries out of date. The use of this word was a fudge, a clever trick to make something otherwise impossible appear on the screen. The desired word 'WHO' was not symmetrical, and as such would not produce the symmetrical howlaround effect that the designer Bernard Lodge wanted. To solve this problem, he used the symmetrical word 'OHO', then quickly superimposed the correct title over it. Its inclusion was both practical necessity and an act of inspired experimental ingenuity. There would be a lot of this in the programme's future.

At this point the title of the programme reveals itself: *Doctor Who*. It is a silly name, if we are honest – a name that fitted the children's programme that the BBC originally thought this series would be, before Verity Lambert and the desire to attract a family audience created a programme that was harder to classify. Still, it is a title with the same direct, no-nonsense, self-explanatory power that superhero names have, like Spider-Man or Batman. There would be a Doctor, and he would be a mystery. Such names work well, provided that you don't think about them too deeply.

These strange visuals are accompanied by what would have been, for the majority of the 1963 audience, a piece of music quite unlike anything they had heard before. It was written by the Australian composer Ron Grainer, who was then the unchallenged king of television theme tunes. His work includes the themes for *Steptoe and Son*, *Maigret* and *That Was the Week That Was*, all of which are still familiar to many six decades later. Grainer's fame was such that, two days after these titles were first broadcast, he was the guest on BBC radio's *Desert Island Discs*. That a composer like Grainer wrote the *Doctor Who* theme, then, explains why the tune is memorable. But his melodic reputation did not prepare the audience for what this piece of music sounded like.

Grainer's theme was arranged and performed by the electronic music pioneer Delia Derbyshire. Only twenty-six at the time, Derbyshire was motivated by the desire to create sounds which had never been heard before. She joined the BBC's Radiophonic Workshop after being told, when she applied for work at Decca Records, that they did not employ women in recording studio jobs. The Radiophonic Workshop, in contrast, was an odd, over-looked department which was grateful for anyone who wanted to help, regardless of their gender.

A year after joining the Radiophonic Workshop, Grainer had handed Derbyshire a torn-off section of manuscript paper on which he had written down his new score. As Derbyshire recalled, the music description had 'abstract things on like "wind clouds" and "sweeps" and "swoops" and "wind bubble" – all beautiful descriptions, but with a carefully worked-out rhythm. It was very, very subtle, the way he wrote the rhythm.'

Over the course of three weeks, Derbyshire created the finished theme without the use of anything we would recognise as a modern synth or sequencer. She worked with oscillators and white-noise generators recorded onto analogue tape, which she cut with razor blades and laboriously spliced back together until it howled and hissed and sang. The Radiophonic Workshop's Brian Hodgson, who assisted her in the task, recalled that, 'Ron came to hear it and said, "Jeez, Delia, did I write that?" Delia said, "Well, most of it, Ron."'

There were precedents for the unearthly sound of Derbyshire's arrangement, but these were in the world of *musique concrète* and early experimental electronic music. Very few people who tuned in to watch *Doctor Who* would have been familiar with them, and never before had those strange alien sounds been used for a tune quite that memorable. To the ears of the audience at home, this startling, frightening sound was unprecedented. It could only be music from the future.

When Verity Lambert played Sydney Newman the finished title sequence, he didn't like it. He thought that it was too weird and frightening for the broad family audience he hoped to reach. Displaying the judgement and strength of character that Newman had originally hired her for, Lambert's response was, 'Well, I just think you're completely wrong, Sydney!' She did not change the titles.

The title sequence comes to an end as the words 'Doctor Who' reduce in size and the screen fades to black. It lasted for just twenty-five seconds, but it had been a perfect crystallisation of what was to follow. It was futuristic but built with elements that were archaic, like the cry 'Oho!' It had been created with ingenuity, on an unhelpful budget, on the edge of what was technologically possible. It was inspired, visionary and gently bodged together. It demanded your attention, and it was a little frightening. It was touched by genius and also a bit daft. That title sequence not only introduced that first episode perfectly, but it also described every one of the episodes that have followed. Considering the extent to which the programme has evolved over the following sixty-plus years, that is quite an achievement.

I
The Exiled Wanderer (1963–64)

1. Out of the Shadows

Twenty-four hours after the assassination of President Kennedy, and twelve minutes into the first episode of *Doctor Who*, the title character stepped on screen and entered, for the first time, the minds of the British public.

Emerging out of the shadows of a derelict, seemingly abandoned junkyard and surrounded by outdated, worn and discarded oddities comes an old man, frail and coughing, dressed oddly in pre-war clothes. It is as if part of the junkyard had come to life.

This man is clearly no hero. His entrance is deeply sinister. It is observed by two teachers, Barbara Wright and Ian Chesterton, who are investigating the strange behaviour of one of their students. Ian and Barbara suspect that this suspicious figure has kidnapped their teenage pupil, fifteen-year-old Susan Foreman, and is holding her against her will in a wooden police box. Susan is indeed in the box, but she is in there willingly. The frightening Doctor is her grandfather, not her kidnapper, but the teachers' fears about the old man are otherwise not far wrong. It turns out that he is the type of person who would kidnap innocent people and hold them in that police box against their will. They just don't realise yet that they are the people he is going to kidnap.

When we look back at this first appearance of the Doctor now, we project a lot of contemporary ideas and backstory onto that mysterious character emerging from the shadows. We don't think he is sinister, because we know he is the Doctor. The Doctor is a Time Lord from the planet Gallifrey who fights for the oppressed against the cruel and unjust. We know he has the ability to regenerate – to physically turn into a different person, including changing gender and ethnicity. He has lived for thousands of years and travelled through space and time in a stolen or 'borrowed' time machine, fighting evil and righting wrongs. He has two hearts and a scientific magic wand called a sonic screwdriver. He is a hero – never cruel or cowardly, a friend to children, someone who would risk their life to save others. When Ncuti Gatwa was cast as the Doctor in 2022, the actor made a video explaining who the character was for the benefit of a new young audience. 'The Doctor is full of optimism and hope, with a fierce sense of right and wrong,' he said.

None of this was true, back in 1963. The actor, writer or director of the programme would not have recognised any of those descriptions of the Doctor. They did not describe the mysterious coughing figure who walks on screen and upends Ian and Barbara's lives.

For the audience in 1963, the character of Ian Chesterton, played by William Russell, would have been seen as the hero. Russell was then best known for playing the title role in the 1956 ITV series *The Adventures of Sir Lancelot*, so viewers were primed to see him as a dashing archetypal lead. He was the person that the early development documents described as 'THE HANDSOME YOUNG MAN HERO' – the series' 'first character'. Barbara Wright, played by Jacqueline Hill, was the heroine and the programme's second lead. Barbara was a history teacher and Ian was a science teacher, so they were both authoritative, knowledgeable and trustworthy. They could explain to the viewing audience relevant facts about the history and science which the stories explored. The Doctor, in contrast, was a troubling and slightly scary figure who was unsuitable for the delivery of exposition because he was emphatically not to be trusted.

The Doctor of 1963 was often petulant, childish and pig-headed. His eyes would dart back and forth, leaving you unsure what he was thinking. He could be quite foolish, as likely to hinder Ian and Barbara as to help them. At times, he could be cruel. In the third episode, the Doctor wants to return to the safety of his ship even if this means leaving an injured man to die. Susan, Ian and Barbara are appalled by this, and insist on helping the wounded figure. In response, the Doctor picks up a rock, seemingly intent on killing the injured man in order to solve the problem and get his own way. He is only stopped by a horrified Ian, who realises just in time what he was about to do.

The Doctor could also be a danger to his travelling companions. In the third story, he threatens to throw Ian and Barbara out of his ship during a fit of paranoia, despite not knowing whether the ship was in space and whether this would result in their death. He makes a similar threat again at the end of the seventh story. These were not necessarily idle threats, as he would later abandon his granddaughter Susan in the ruins of a future Earth, despite her pleading to be let back on board his ship. According to the actor Maureen O'Brien, who played his later companion Vicki, Hartnell invested the character with his own personality, and his performance 'used his dangerous nasty qualities as much as his benign grandfatherly qualities [...] You feel that danger, even if you don't see it, even if he doesn't actually show it – you know that it's there.'

The backstory of this strange character was a mystery. The teachers only knew that he was a doctor, and Susan's grandfather.

He wasn't even given a name. Because Susan claimed that her surname was Foreman, Ian assumed that his name was Doctor Foreman. Yet when Ian called him this he just muttered 'Doctor who? Who's he talking about?' Susan, we then realised, had adopted the name 'Foreman' from a sign at the junkyard. Nor did we know what type of doctor he was. As he confessed to Ian in a later episode, 'I'm not a doctor of medicine.'

'He was a mystery. That's why he was Doctor Who,' Verity Lambert explained to the later showrunner Russell T Davies in 2006. 'Had he stolen this thing called a TARDIS? He didn't know how to work it – was he an absentminded professor? Was he a criminal? Was he on the run?' Hartnell initially asked the production team for firm details of his character's backstory, but those details didn't exist. Lambert simply told him that, 'You know where you're from, but you never let on. And the fact is we don't know if you're a criminal. Maybe you are a criminal.' Lambert wanted a Doctor 'who didn't have a background, who was just there, and could have been anything, and that was actually more interesting than trying to give him a background. At that point we wanted him to be a mystery. If he'd stolen the ship, were [Ian and Barbara] in the hands of some lunatic?'

The nearest thing we are given to an explanation came after Ian and Barbara forced their way into the police box in the junkyard, and discovered that the box was bigger on the inside – a machine that travelled in time and space, which the Doctor simply called 'the ship'. Susan explained that she had given this craft the name TARDIS, an acronym for Time And Relative Dimension In Space – which, for a physicist, conjures up far more questions than it answers. 'Have you ever thought what it's like to be wanderers in the fourth dimension?' the Doctor asked. 'To be exiles. Susan and I are cut off from our own planet without friends or protection. But one day, we shall get back. Yes, one day.'

The question of why the Doctor and Susan were exiled and cut off from their own planet is one that the original programme was not prepared to answer, and also a question that subsequent writers and producers have largely kept away from. It is still not answered to this day. The situation implies a further mystery – one which the TV series has also not acknowledged or explored. If the Doctor was in exile with his granddaughter, then where were Susan's parents, one of whom would likely be the Doctor's son or daughter? Were her parents alive, and did they know where she was? Had the pair run away to protect Susan, or to protect the Doctor?

The mystique of the Doctor would lose something if an explanation was given. It may simply be that Susan was orphaned due to accident or ill health, but because this is never established the mind is free to imagine other, more melodramatic alternatives. To be unfixed and partly unknown, then, was the essence of Doctor Who from the very start. Definition and backstory are limiting. Mystery can lead anywhere.

2. A London Urchin

Doctor Who – as the character was then commonly called – was originally portrayed by the experienced screen actor William Hartnell. The performer and the character had much in common. Both kept their origins a mystery and Hartnell, in particular, was rarely truthful about the circumstances of his birth.

Hartnell often falsely claimed that he was born on a farm in Devon. According to his granddaughter and biographer Jessica Carney, however, he was born in 1908 in the run-down area of London surrounding St Pancras. Hartnell was illegitimate, and he never discovered the identity of his father. His mother, Lucy

Hartnell, was a domestic servant. It was not uncommon for young women in service during the Edwardian era to feel they could not name the father of their child on the birth certificate, and the prevalence of coercive and abusive sexual relations between the wealthy and their servants is an under-discussed part of British history. There is no way of knowing for sure, however, if this is the reason for Hartnell's fatherless upbringing. As a child, he was bullied by other children for being a 'bastard'. From his evasiveness around his origins, it seems that this remained a source of shame for him.

When he was fifteen, Hartnell wrote a 52-page journal that gave an account of his life so far. It was written in the third person about a boy called 'William Fenn', but the events described are an exact match for Hartnell's own life. At some later point he wrote 'The story of my life – WH' on the back. It was called *The Life of a London Urchin*.

In this journal, Hartnell recounts his life living with a foster family, the Harrises. His foster father was stern and often beat him, because Hartnell was constantly stealing and getting involved in petty crime, including running errands for a corrupt bookmaker and forger. For a time, his birth mother returned to London, and he lived with her and her new boyfriend, a policeman. In his journal, he described how his mother was a violent woman who beat both him and her partner. This policeman, however, tried to protect Hartnell from his mother's attacks. This seems to have been one of the few positive relationships in his young life, and Hartnell saw the policeman as a surrogate father. Sadly, he did not remain in Hartnell's life for long. As he wrote in his journal: 'No one seemed to love me only my policeman father. It almost broke my heart to think mother was so cruel to me. I shall never forget that man I called dad he was not really my father I found that out later on. I haven't a father because I am illegitimate. That's why mother hated me so much I suppose.'

Hartnell was constantly hungry, short of clothes and was regularly beaten. As Carney wrote, 'He never used his own difficult childhood to get sympathy; he simply internalised it. I believe it was this which was largely responsible for the "chip" many people said they felt he had when he was older.'

Being a child during the First World War, when most young men were away fighting, meant that there was a lack of positive father figures or male role models in his life. By good fortune, however, one did enter his life when he was sixteen. This was Hugh Blaker, a wealthy art collector in his early fifties, who befriended Hartnell and encouraged him to take an interest in artistic pursuits. *The Life of a London Urchin* was written at his request, and it is possible that he paid Hartnell to write it. It was Blaker who encouraged Hartnell's interest in acting, and he supported his enrolment into the Italia Conti Academy. If Blaker hadn't befriended him when he did, Hartnell may have been heading for a life of crime and imprisonment, or worse. As he wrote in the journal, 'If he had not come along when he did I could not have carried on [with] no food and hardly a rag to my back.'

The pair met at a boxing club that Hartnell used to attend. Blaker liked to watch young boys fight, and also to sketch them. To modern eyes this relationship might sound suspect, but there was a tradition of wealthy patrons supporting poor and neglected children in the days before the welfare state. Certainly, whenever Hartnell spoke about Blaker later in life he always expressed deep gratitude for all that he had done for him. He never hinted that there was anything predatory about the relationship.

After drama school, Hartnell began a long and distinguished acting career, initially in the theatre. In 1928 this took him on a tour of Canada. He was part of a troupe of actors that included the 21-year-old Heather McIntyre, who came from a wealthy Scottish background. Heather soon became pregnant, and the pair married after they returned to England. It was a relationship that had its difficulties, for Hartnell was frequently unfaithful and at times Heather came close to divorcing him, yet the marriage was solid enough that the pair stayed together for the rest of their lives. *Doctor Who* paid tribute to the couple in 2017, when the companion Bill, played by Pearl Mackie, fell in love with a character called Heather. The romance between the fictional Bill and Heather did admittedly differ from the story of the Hartnells, as Heather was possessed by a sentient space puddle and Bill was converted into a Cyberman. Yet these difficulties were overcome and, in the fiction of *Doctor Who*, Bill and Heather are still out exploring the stars together.

Hartnell moved into film, where, under the name Billy Hartnell, he specialised in comic performances. His career was interrupted by the Second World War which, for Hartnell, proved to be difficult. He suffered a minor nervous breakdown and was discharged from the army after nine months, regarded as unfit for military service. Despite the reality of his war record, he started to specialise in playing tough soldiers and hard men. He was cast in the lead of *Carry On Sergeant* (1958), the first of the *Carry On* films. Despite his background in comedy, he played the straight man while the rest of the cast got the laughs, and he played a nearly identical part in *The Army Game*, ITVs first sitcom. He was also cast as brutal villains, such as Dallow in *Brighton Rock* (1948), alongside Richard Attenborough. For serious roles like these he went by the name 'William Hartnell', rather than 'Billy'. The press began referring to him as 'the British James Cagney'.

This led to the role that many still consider the greatest performance in his career, the washed-up rugby coach in *This*

Sporting Life (1963). It was a role that should have lifted his career onto another level and led to a deeper appreciation of his talents as an actor. Instead, the phone stopped ringing. Hartnell found himself in one of the rare periods of his career where he had no work. His personal reputation may have played a part in this. According to his granddaughter, 'his nerves were certainly never the same after his breakdown', and his drinking increased after the war. He became more bad-tempered. Hartnell was a perfectionist, both professionally and personally, and this caused others to regard him as prickly and awkward. The stresses and insecurities of a career in acting impacted on a personality formed through neglect as an unloved child. His bigotry was often remarked upon, and it did not take much for him to explode in anger.

It was at this point that Verity Lambert had the inspired notion to cast him as Doctor Who. She had seen him in both *The Army Game* and *This Sporting Life*, and was impressed by his range and his ability to 'combine being lovable and touching some of the time, and rather irascible and difficult other parts of the time'. Hartnell was invited to lunch by Lambert and Hussein, where he was as bemused by their descriptions of the proposed series as he was by how young they were.

He needed the work, but the role was fascinating. He was being offered the lead, title character on a BBC Saturday weekly serial. It would combine his talent for comedy with his spikier, more threatening persona, allowing him to develop a character with depth and nuance. Perhaps the most exciting thing about the character was that, as the world moved towards the Space Age, it felt modern and original, yet it still had its roots in the age-old archetype of the wizard. It had the potential to make him a beloved and nationally known character, both for children and the wider family. It was a role that would put him in touch with, and perhaps help to heal, his inner child.

As Lambert recalled, 'He read the script and just loved it. He felt that the part had almost been written for him.' From the very start, William Hartnell knew that this part was everything he had been looking for.

3. The Portal

The final shot of the first episode shows the TARDIS standing at a slightly canted angle in a desolate prehistoric landscape. The TARDIS, we learn during that episode, was the Doctor's time machine, disguised as a mid-century British police box. The Doctor has kidnapped Ian and Barbara in his unearthly blue box and taken them, against their will, away from 1960s London, across time and space, and into unknown dangers. A shadow of a mysterious and threatening figure then moves into the foreground, as the end theme and rolling credits appear. It was the series' first cliffhanger ending.

To the audience watching at the time, it was a disturbing and uncanny image. Back then, a police box was a familiar and unremarkable sight on the streets of Britain. They were primarily built to allow an officer on the beat to contact their station, in the days before police radios or mobile phones. They contained a fire extinguisher, a first-aid kit, a stool, a table and an electric heater, and they also allowed members of the public to contact the police in an emergency. The box had a light on top which flashed when the station needed to contact an officer on the beat. A policeman could temporarily restrain a suspect by locking them in the box, or in bad weather they could also use it for shelter. As an object, they were functional and utilitarian.

It was strange, then, to see one in a junkyard, where it was discovered in the first episode. Police boxes were typically constructed of concrete with teak doors, and hence were not readily moveable. That the box had somehow left the junkyard and now stood on prehistoric Earth was a whole different level of weird. The programme had taken something familiar and placed it in an unfamiliar context, and the result was profoundly disturbing. The imagery of the TARDIS has become comforting and familiar over the years, yet it always retains something of the uncanny. It is always in a place where it should not be. In context and appearance, the TARDIS is always wrong.

The image of the TARDIS, a (then) familiar object situated in a place where it shouldn't be, is the only piece of the programme's history and imagery that has remained constant over the years. The main actor changes, the theme tune is rerecorded, backstory about Time Lords and Gallifrey are added to the mythos, Daleks change colour and Cybermen change design, but the exterior of the TARDIS remains resolutely recognisable. The blue box has received only the most minor of tweaks over the decades. Those inviting blue doors are the heart of *Doctor Who*, the fixed icon of this ever-changing series. They lead to anywhere and everywhere. They are the promise of endless surprise and potential. To step in and out of those doors is to leave the normal everyday world behind and find yourself somewhere strange and different – the Otherworld.

Those doors are part of a long tradition of British and Irish storytelling. They are the equivalent of entering a wardrobe and finding yourself in the magical land of Narnia, or falling down a rabbit hole and entering Wonderland. They are a portal that takes you from the real world and into imagined realms, much like passing through a stone arch at King's Cross station to find platform nine and three-quarters and the train to Hogwarts. They are the Scottish mists parting on one day every hundred years to reveal the village of Brigadoon.

Stories of the Otherworld are central to ancient British and Irish myth. The Otherworld was given names such as Tír na nÓg or Mag Mell in Ireland, and Annwn in Wales. In later English stories it became the land of Avalon – the Isle of Fruit Trees. The ways to the Otherworld are unpredictable and varied. Entering a cave or ancient burial mound might take you there, or a supernatural being might transport you. The Otherworld might be found underwater, or by crossing the western sea. Sometimes a fog will fall, and a weary traveller will get lost. Simply accepting the gift of a silver apple could be enough to transport you there.

According to our myths and stories, the Otherworld is a wonderous place of joy and beauty that exists alongside our own, should we be able to find our way into it. Time, however, works differently there. A visitor might stumble into it for a day, only to discover that a hundred years had passed when they returned home. It is a terrible fate to long to return, and yet never be able to find your way back. The Otherworld is a realm of delight and imagination – but darkness and danger are part of it too. Usually it is only gradually that this darker side is revealed. As J.R.R. Tolkien wrote to a friend in 1937, 'A safe fairyland is untrue to all worlds.'

As central as the idea of an Otherworld is to British and Irish myth, it is relatively unusual. More commonly myths and legends, particularly in northern Europe, talk not of an Otherworld, but of an Underworld – the place where the dead reside. The Underworld is one of three realms – a Mount Olympus-like realm of the gods above us, the land of the dead below us and our everyday world in the middle. For this reason, J.R.R. Tolkien set his stories in a place he called Middle-earth, and Norse myths call our world Midgard. Christian ideas of Heaven and Hell are an evolution, or perhaps a devolution, of this concept. The

Otherworld, however, is significantly different to the Underworld. It is not the realm of the dead. It is the Land of the Ever Young.

This is not to say that the Otherworld is a uniquely British or Irish phenomenon. The land of Oz in the books of L. Frank Baum is a distinctly American equivalent. The idea also appears in Japanese folk stories, such as the fairy story about the fisherman Urashima Tarō. In this story, Tarō is taken by a turtle under the sea to a fabulous Dragon Palace, where he meets a beautiful princess. When he returns to his home village, he discovers that he has been gone for a hundred years. The Japanese refer to the genre of stories about being transported to an Otherworld as Isekai. But while the Otherworld is not unique to British and Irish storytelling, it is unusually central to it. It reappears constantly across the centuries, from the Celtic myths to the legends of King Arthur, and from Shakespeare's *A Midsummer Night's Dream* to *Alice in Wonderland*.

In most countries, myths are divorced from contemporary culture. They took place in the far distant past or, in the case of the Norse myths of Ragnarök, at the end of time. They are complete and finished, and it is not usual for them to remain contemporary. The myths of the Otherworld, in contrast, are still ongoing. We are not beyond them. We are inside them, recreating them anew during every age. It was probably inevitable, then, that British television would continue this tradition when it arrived in our homes during the second half of the twentieth century.

When Ian first encountered the TARDIS, he struggled to accept that the box he had walked into was bigger on the inside. The Doctor described the problem in terms of television. 'You say you can't fit an enormous building into one of your smaller sitting rooms,' he said to a baffled Ian. 'But you've discovered television, haven't you? Then by showing an enormous building on your television screen, you can do what seemed impossible, couldn't you?'

In 1963, the concept of the TARDIS was initially explained by saying that it was just like television. Ian may have scoffed, but on one level it was true. A television set in the 1960s was a wooden box which seemed bigger on the inside. Despite its small dimensions, it contained whole worlds. The TARDIS is also a wooden box famously larger on the inside. It lived inside the television set, echoing it by also being a portal to infinite worlds. The TARDIS was a portal within a portal, a perfect reinvention of the entrance to the Otherworld for the television age. And it was now to be found in almost every living room.

4. 'A Mild Curiosity'

The idea that the Doctor was Susan's grandfather was not present in any of the documents detailing the development of the series. It appears to have been introduced by Anthony Coburn, the writer of the first episode. Coburn was a devout Catholic who may have wanted to define the relationship of the young girl and the old man in an uncontroversial way. Newman was extremely unhappy about this change. 'They pulled that thing on me and I was livid with anger,' he said in 1986. He felt that normative family ties made this enigmatic mystery character too domestic.

If there was a clear, literary inspiration for the archetypes of an unnamed, untrustworthy grandfather and his young granddaughter becoming exiles and wanderers, then it is Little Nell and her grandfather in Charles Dickens's *The Old Curiosity Shop*. At the start of the novel, Nell is a young girl, 'nearly fourteen', who lives with her grandfather at the junk shop of the novel's title. Her grandfather is never given a name, which was unusual for a prominent character in a Dickens novel; one of the great joys of his work are the evocative character names, such as Ebenezer Scrooge, Uriah Heep or Mr Pumblechook.

In the illustrations that were included in the novel, Nell's grandfather looks remarkably like Hartnell's Doctor – frail, dressed in period clothing and with white or grey hair worn long to the collar. He walks with a stick or a staff, like the Doctor, and talks in similar voice patterns. In the Doctor's remark that, 'It all started out as a mild curiosity in a junkyard,' it is tempting to see a nod to *The Old Curiosity Shop*.

In Dickens's novel, Nell's grandfather loses the shop, and all he owns, in circumstances that he refuses to explain, but which have a sense of shame or scandal about them. Nell and her grandfather are then forced to become exiles, 'two poor adventurers, wandering they knew not wither'. The fate of the rest of Nell's family remains a mystery, although there are hints that a great tragedy has occurred.

Nell is the only significant person in this nameless grandfather's life. His one wish is to protect and look after her, but he is becoming increasingly weak. It seems likely that he will die and leave the child unprotected, alone, homeless and penniless in a frighteningly cruel world. Viewers of those early episodes could easily have assumed that the fate of Doctor Who would follow a similar path to that of Nell's grandfather. They both wander in exile with their granddaughter, homeless and in constant danger, for reasons that remain a mystery. Later *Doctor Who* fans may assume that those reasons would be noble and heroic, if we were ever to uncover them, but there was no reason to think that back in 1963. The exile of Nell's grandfather is eventually revealed to be the result of gambling debts. William Hartnell also had a great love of gambling. It was highly plausible that the Doctor's inability to return home was the result of a similar weakness or scandal.

After Doctor Who arrived on screen frail and coughing, his health was a constant source of concern and anxiety. He was often exhausted and frequently needed to rest, due to problems such as radiation sickness, heat exhaustion or altitude sickness. For those familiar with *The Old Curiosity Shop*, a frail grandfather on the run with his young granddaughter seemed set to end in tragedy. The weak old man could only protect his granddaughter for so long.

The other principal cast were necessary for the ongoing drama. Susan was the teenage audience identification figure who needed to be protected, given her youthful ability to repeatedly get into danger. Ian and Barbara were there to do just that, while also providing the necessary exposition to explain the problems they encounter. The Doctor's role had been to lure Ian and Barbara into an uncontrollable time machine, in order to throw them into a series of wild, imaginative adventures. Having done that in the first episode, it wasn't entirely clear if he was really needed any more. Given the format of the show in its first year, it's easy to imagine it continuing without him. It would have featured Ian, Barbara and Susan travelling the universe in a time machine they could not control, hoping that one day they might return to modern-day Earth. When Hartnell had a week off to take a holiday, the programme worked just as well without him.

This, of course, was not the path that the show would take. The format may not have needed this 'somewhat pathetic' character, but William Hartnell invested him with so much of his personal charisma that audiences fell in love with him. It helped, of course, that the programme was named after him. The title *Doctor Who* may be silly, but it safeguarded the title character in a way that may not have happened if the programme had been called, for example, *The Time Machine*.

Hartnell loved the character and hoped that it would go on and on. At the start, he predicted that the show would run for five years – a wildly ambitious claim for any weekly programme. He told journalists that he allowed the character 'to hypnotise' him, believing fully in the fantastical stories that followed. As Lambert recalled, 'He absolutely loved the part – he was endearingly proprietorial about it, and he simply became the Doctor. Some actors do envelop themselves with the part and when they are not acting there's this person waiting to be invaded, rather like a workaholic who is rather lost outside their work.'

Although it's hard to imagine that William Hartnell would have ever voluntarily retired from the role, he did not, of course, continue forever. Signs that his undiagnosed arteriosclerosis was affecting his stamina and his ability to learn his lines were becoming apparent. After three years, the production team felt that they had to replace him with a different actor.

A strange echo of Hartnell's fate can be found in the 1978 BBC production of *The Old Curiosity Shop*. This was produced by the later *Doctor Who* producer Barry Letts. *The Old Curiosity Shop*'s primary antagonist is a malignant villain called Quilp and Letts cast Patrick Troughton, the man who would ultimately replace Hartnell as Doctor Who, in the role. The production started by shooting all the location filming and, in the opinion of Letts, Troughton 'was going to be the definitive Quilp of our time'. But Troughton then suffered his first heart attack and was unable to continue with the upcoming studio recordings. Out of necessity, the role was recast. The actor and songwriter Trevor Peacock played Quilp for the rest of the production. There was no budget to reshoot the scenes already shot with Troughton but it was hoped that, in costume, the two actors looked sufficiently similar that the audience wouldn't notice.

As a result, William Hartnell's Doctor and Little Nell's exiled wandering grandfather proved to have identical fates. Quilp was the character responsible for the downfall of Nell's grandfather and, in Letts's production, the actor portraying Quilp kept changing. The ultimate fate of Nell's grandfather was to be doomed by a man who started off as Patrick Troughton, and who then kept changing his face.

2

The Unlikely Hero (1965–66)

1. Enter the Daleks

During the development of *Doctor Who*, Sydney Newman issued a strict edict to the production team: there must be 'no bug-eyed monsters'.

Science fiction 'B-movies' of that era were stuffed full of strange alien monsters, flying saucers, ray-gun battles and other sources of thrills and adventure. The BBC, however, saw itself as different to the producers of pulpy science fiction. Their stated mission was to 'inform, educate and entertain', quite possibly in that order. They did want their new programme to excite children – but only to a point. It also should be educational and informative, particularly about science and history, so that parents would approve of it as well. When the BBC thought about the interests of parents, they always imagined upper-middle-class ones.

Most of the writers of that first series took Newman's instructions to heart. Even when the time travellers journeyed into space and met aliens who initially appeared frightening, they were quickly revealed to be civilised creatures rather than actual monsters. Our first glimpse of a Sensorite – a telepathic alien from a planet called Sense-Sphere – is truly terrifying. In one of the most memorable cliffhangers in the history of the series, the travellers are trapped on a stranded spacecraft, adrift in a far-off galaxy, when the face of an alien, crawling on the hull of the spaceship, appears outside the window. With its noseless, hairy face and its large-domed head, it is unlike anything that the viewing audience has ever seen before. The knowledge that it is crawling about on the outside of this threatened, damaged ship is truly chilling. As the story continues, however, the Sensorites are revealed to be a bureaucratic, slightly dull race, who are struggling to fix issues with their water supply. The initial thrill of an unknown monster is quickly replaced by discussions about hydrological engineering.

There was one writer, however, who paid no attention to Newman's 'no monsters' rule. This was Terry Nation, a Cardiff-born screenwriter who had previously written for the comedian Tony Hancock and would go on to create adventure series like *Blake's 7* and *Survivors*. He also wrote exciting, action-based programmes including *The Avengers*, *The Persuaders!*, *Department S* and *The Saint*. Nation's focus as a writer was firmly entertainment first, and a format like *Doctor Who* was, in his eyes, crying out for monsters, regardless of what the bosses thought. He added a warlike, sinister aquatic species called the Voord to two episodes of the series' fifth story, but he is best known for the monsters he created for *Doctor Who*'s second story: the Daleks.

During the first episode, the likeable, sensible teachers Ian and Barbara are taken away from 1960s London against their will by the sinister and mysterious Doctor. They find themselves stranded in prehistoric times and are taken prisoner by a tribe searching for the secret of fire. Ian and Barbara have fallen out of their comfortable 1960s English lives and landed in a terrifying savage world. They had been deliberately created to be trustworthy figures capable of explaining relevant historic and scientific information to a young audience, yet the show begins by placing them in a world with no history or science, where their talents were entirely useless. They are not heroes who arrive in a strange new world and bring justice or liberate the oppressed. Instead, they are horrified victims trying to escape from brutality and violence.

This adventure set the format which the other writers followed during *Doctor Who*'s first season. The travellers arrive at some dangerous point in time and space and become in some way separated from the TARDIS. They face great peril and struggles before eventually managing to get back to the safety of their time machine. The worlds they visit are not societies to get involved with, but places to escape from. In stories like this, no one is saved, and no great wrongs are righted. Getting out alive is all that matters.

Terry Nation's first story sees the travellers land in a petrified forest on a radioactive alien world. It seems, at first, to be as bleak as the prehistoric episodes that preceded it. Exploring the dead wasteland, the travellers discover a seemingly deserted metal city. The Doctor lies about a TARDIS component, which he claims is broken, in order to trick Ian and Barbara into exploring the mysterious city. The Doctor is not someone his companions, or the viewers at home, can trust.

The first episode of Nation's story, broadcast on the winter solstice in 1963, ends with Barbara screaming in terror. She has encountered a horrific creature, but viewers see only a point-of-view shot, taken from this mysterious creature's perspective, which focuses the audience's attention on Barbara's reaction and the sheer horror she experiences at the sight of this unknown thing. The only clue that viewers at home have makes the hidden monster seem more bewildering and mysterious – out of the bottom of the shot, they see that Barbara is not being menaced by a claw or a hand but is being threatened with, of all things, a sink plunger. The viewers then have to spend Christmas week waiting to see what that monster is – during which time, their imaginations can only run wild.

When the creature is finally revealed a week later, it could easily have disappointed. It could have been a man in a cheap, unconvincing monster suit. Instead, it is unlike anything the viewers have ever seen before. It isn't humanoid. It is a small tank containing a mutated, hate-filled soldier, that glides around the metal city in a manner both graceful and sinister. We finally get to see a Dalek and it is an inspired piece of design.

The person originally tasked with designing these creatures was the Hollywood director-to-be Ridley Scott. At the time, he had just started working at the BBC as a trainee set designer. A scheduling conflict, however, passed the job over to the Lambeth-born BBC staff designer Raymond Cusick. His finished design was greatly constrained by budget, which led to details such as the sink-plunger arm and flashing lights on the dome of its 'head' made from ping-pong balls. Sometimes, however, it is in such restricted circumstances that true creativity thrives.

The finished creature was entirely original and looked like no other monster before or since. Even if a child drew a Dalek badly, it still looked like a Dalek. With its distinctive circular bumps on its skirt, the design of those evil Space Age monsters had a strong mid-1960s Pop Art feel. Better still, the Daleks had a near-hysterical, electronically distorted voice which would be a key factor in their appeal. The Daleks sounded like panicked children on the verge of a murderous tantrum. This was great fun to imitate.

Such was the undeniable iconic appeal of Cusick's design that it has remained remarkably consistent over the decades. Attempts to refresh or upgrade it are usually unsuccessful. The larger, colourful, race of 'New Paradigm' Daleks introduced in

Victory of the Daleks (2010), for example, were quickly accepted as a mistake and quietly dropped. The quality and budget of the actual Dalek props have improved over the years, but no one has been able to stray far from Cusick's original design in a way that improved upon it. As a result, aspects of the design that were imposed by the original low budget, such as the sink-plunger arm, remain to this day. That such a technologically advanced race can only interact with the world via a rubber plunger is obviously ludicrous, yet it remains a vital part of the design's innate alchemy.

2. The Ultimate Evil

That the design of the Daleks is borderline ridiculous is, on one level, appropriate. Daleks, Nation's script made clear, were space Nazis. No matter how horrific the actions of fascists are, there is always something about them that remains unintentionally absurd and ripe for mockery.

The Daleks were created at a very specific point in time, when memories of the Second World War mingled with Cold War nuclear paranoia. The age of nuclear missiles was difficult for Britain. It had, for centuries, based its identity around the idea that it was a global superpower protected by the world's greatest navy. The moment nuclear weapons arrived, that identity became irrelevant. Given how difficult this was to face, it is perhaps not surprising that the country preferred to look back to the certainties of the Second World War.

The conflict still coloured Nation's imagination as he sat down to create a futuristic race of monsters. The war had only ended eighteen years earlier, and Nation's childhood had been shaped by the global fight against the Third Reich. The war and the impact of fascism had also affected the rest of the cast and crew, often in wildly different ways. The designer of the TARDIS interior Peter Brachacki, for example, had been a member of the Polish resistance. He was captured by the German Army in 1944 and sent to the infamous concentration camp at Dachau. The actor Peter Butterworth, who played the Meddling Monk, had helped organise the 'Great Escape' from Stalag Luft III, and sent coded messages to British Intelligence while a prisoner of war. Butterworth famously auditioned for a role in a 1950 film version of the story, but was told by producers that he didn't appear convincing. The associate producer Mervyn Pinfield, in contrast, came close to joining Oswald Mosley's British Union of Fascists in the early 1930s, although he ultimately decided against it.

Nation's early scripts were not subtle about the fascist nature of his creations. His Daleks would line up and raise their plunger arms in an imitation of a Nazi salute, while chanting about the superiority of the Dalek race. They used the word 'exterminate', which is still their catchphrase to this day. This is a word used to refer to the indiscriminate killing of animals or people viewed as being less than human, and it was associated with the Holocaust during the Second World War. During the 1964 story *The Dalek Invasion of Earth*, Nation went as far as referring to the 'final solution'. In Nation's scripts, the Daleks' authoritarian, murderous actions were justified by their belief in racial superiority. When people on the planet Skaro were attempting to understand why the Daleks were intent on killing them all, Ian explained that 'There is a reason. An explanation might be better. It's stupid and ridiculous, but it's the only one that fits . . . A dislike for the unlike.' For the Daleks, their desire to kill followed logically from their belief that all others were inferior to the Dalek race.

The Daleks may have become less explicitly fascist over the following half-century, but their Nazi roots have never been entirely hidden. *Genesis of the Daleks* (1975) leant heavily on Second World War iconography and uniforms in its depiction of their creation. In *Remembrance of the Daleks* (1988), a Dalek faction was working with a 1960s white supremacist organisation with links to the British military. The design of the Dalek conference room in *Mission to the Unknown* (1965) was inspired by the Nuremberg rallies. Other references were more subtle. In 1932, the aristocrat and politician Oswald Mosley formed the British Union of Fascists. Adolf Hitler thought that Mosley had failed to understand the British character when he named this organisation. As Hitler saw it, the British people would reject anything that explicitly described itself as fascist. His suggestion, which he passed to Mosley via their mutual friend Unity Mitford, was that he name his party the Ironsides, after the parliamentarian cavalry in the English Civil Wars. With hindsight, Hitler's insight was probably quite astute, but Mosley was not one to admit the failings of his own judgement and kept the original name. The incident was referenced in the 2010 *Doctor Who* story *Victory of the Daleks*. Set during the Second World War, it featured scheming Daleks seemingly supporting Winston Churchill during the Battle of Britain. Not knowing their true nature or identity, Churchill named them his Ironsides.

Even before the war was over, people started to notice that words like 'fascist' were being used in a broader, less clearly defined context. Writing in 1944, George Orwell noted that he had heard the word 'fascist' being used to describe conservatives, Catholics, communists, socialists, war resisters, war supporters and many others. He attempted to nail down a definition for the word as it was then being used and decided that it had become a synonym for 'bully'. 'That is about as near to a definition as this much-abused word has come,' he wrote. According to the classical historian Tom Holland, the meaning of words like fascist, Hitler and Nazi took on a darker meaning than 'bully' in the global cultural imagination after the war. They became our standard personification of ultimate evil. In doing so, Holland believes, they took over the role held for centuries by the Devil.

Throughout history, people condemned their enemies as being in league with the Devil – or perhaps even being the Devil himself – to frame them as being as bad as it was possible to be. When the 'other' was defined as diabolical in this way, waging war against them was not only good, but necessary, and many a crusade, witch-hunt or violent invasion was justified on the grounds that the people being attacked were in some way linked to the Devil. During the increasingly secular late twentieth century, however, this framing began to break down. It was hard to convince yourself that those you disliked were in league with the Devil if you didn't truly believe that the Devil was real.

After the war, Hitler and the Nazis replaced the Devil as our modern ultimate evil. They had the advantage of being real, as well as undeniably evil. As a result, people no longer claimed that those they violently disagreed with were the Devil. Instead, they were said to be fascists, Nazis or 'literally Hitler'. It did not matter if the politics involved differed from those found in Germany or Italy during the 1930s. Of course, this situation is complicated by the fact that actual fascists, who believe in racial supremacy and the use of violence for political ends, are still with us. What muddies things further is that modern fascists also recognise that Nazis are the ultimate evil in our culture, to the extent that genuine fascists condemn anti-fascist campaigners on the grounds that they are fascists. To give another example, the mercenary organisation the Wagner Group were supposedly named after Hitler's favourite composer, left neo-Nazi graffiti behind on the battlefield and had a leader, Dmitry Utkin, whose tattoos are said to include a swastika, a Nazi eagle and SS lightning bolts. Yet when they took part in the invasion of Ukraine, they justified the operation on the grounds that they were going to 'de-Nazify' the neighbouring country. This is clearly a deeply confusing situation.

All this serves to illustrate the extent to which, when Terry Nation created a race of space-fascists in the second half of the twentieth century, he was tapping into powerful and heavily loaded archetypes. With such a conceptually potent monster portrayed in a striking Pop Art design, it is perhaps not surprising that the Daleks made an instant impact on the country's psyche. As soon as the first Dalek story hit the screen, the programme's ratings shot up, moving from 6.9 million viewers for the first episode to 10.4 million for the last. Suddenly, unexpectedly, the arrival of the Daleks had made the BBC's strange little time-travel programme one of their biggest hits.

This came as a great surprise to the BBC drama department. Newman had not read the Dalek script before it was filmed and was furious with Lambert when he saw what she had made. He thought she had blatantly flouted his instructions about there being no 'bug-eyed monsters'. One person who read the script was Donald Wilson, who then called Lambert and script editor David Whitaker into his office. 'We assumed he was going to say it was terrific,' Lambert recalled. 'He looked at us and said, "I think this is one of the worst things I've ever read. It's utterly appalling. It can't go out."' It's possible that his reaction to the Daleks was influenced by his service during the war. Wilson was present at the liberation of Bergen-Belsen concentration camp and had to arrange burials for the bodies found there. His daughter Holly has said that he used to get angry at people who casually described others as fascists. He would say, 'If you knew what real fascists do, you would never say that.'

Despite Wilson's opinions, however, the Dalek serial had to

go into production. None of the other scripts were ready. *The Daleks* was originally intended to be the fifth story in the series but problems with the other scripts moved it forward. The only reason why the scripts for *The Daleks* were ready and available so early was because writer Terry Nation had churned out all seven episodes in a week.

Nation had not initially been interested in taking the job. The comedian Tony Hancock, who Nation worked for as a joke writer, told him that being asked to write for such a programme was an insult to his talent. But Hancock sacked Nation shortly afterwards, and he took the job because he needed money. 'I suppose [the Daleks] were born in a flash of inspiration,' he said, 'except that makes it sound altogether too poetic. I was sitting at a typewriter, doing a job of work for money, and I needed a monster. And that's when they were born.'

Had Nation cared more about the project, and worked on the scripts up until his deadline, it would not have been available as an emergency replacement for the second serial. In those circumstances, Wilson would probably have cancelled it outright, and the history of *Doctor Who* would have been very different. Just like evolution, the story of *Doctor Who* is often propelled by the potent force of blind chance.

3. The Wandering Exile Was Reimagined

Early in *Doctor Who's* second season was a two-part story called *The Rescue*. This introduces a resourceful space orphan called Vicki – the character that is, as the title implies, in need of rescuing. After meeting the Doctor, Vicki says, 'It's funny, but as soon as he walked in, I felt that you could trust him.' To modern ears, this feels like a reasonable appraisal of the Doctor as we have come to know them. Her impression, however, was strikingly different to that of the viewers who had first encountered him, shifty and untrustworthy, in a shadowy junkyard. After only a year on screen, the Doctor changed.

Up until that point, the Doctor had been frail. In his first series he was often suffering from some debilitating condition that forced him to sit down and rest. When his character echoed Little Nell's grandfather in *The Old Curiosity Shop*, his frailty made his attempts to protect his granddaughter more dramatic. It emphasised the age difference between them, and hinted that he would not be around to protect her for long. Susan's presence helped shape the original unheroic character of the Doctor, because a man attempting to protect a granddaughter should not be constantly rushing into danger.

After a year of playing Susan, however, Carole Ann Ford became the first actor to leave the series. She had become disillusioned with the series and her character. She was used to reading each script as it came in and finding little of interest for her character to do. When she took the role, she had been promised that the character would be more physical, alien and intelligent. When it became clear that her role was basically getting captured and waiting to be rescued, she decided to move on.

Susan's final episode was the last part of *The Dalek Invasion of Earth*. In the story, the Doctor realises that she is no longer a child, and that she has fallen in love with a brave resistance fighter. But he also knows that she will never leave him to start her own life somewhere, regardless of how much she hates their endless wandering and longs for somewhere to settle. He therefore makes the decision for her. He gives a noble, self-aggrandising speech and leaves her behind, with only one shoe, on a destroyed planet with an older man she barely knows. The travellers then encounter the orphan Vicki immediately after abandoning Susan, and she joins the regular cast as her replacement. She is another teenage character, intended as someone who the child audience can identify with, but she is not, crucially, a member of the Doctor's family. It would now become extremely rare for the programme to reference the Doctor's status as a grandfather.

Vicki's initial impression of the Doctor was a fair description of the reinvented character. As well as becoming more energetic and gleefully getting into fights, the Doctor had become wiser, more loveable and more willing to listen to the concerns of others. Hartnell was able to apply the skills he had acquired during his days as a comedian. His Doctor was still irascible and quick to temper, but he was now on the side of good rather than the side of chaos.

The cause of this change in his character had been his second meeting with the Daleks. When the Doctor first encountered the metal fascists, he was genuinely shocked to learn they were planning the total extermination of the Thals. 'That's sheer murder!' he exclaims, with barely suppressed anger, as if he had not previously known that such levels of evil existed. Fury could often be glimpsed bubbling under the surface of Hartnell's performance, but rarely did it erupt with such moral clarity.

The Doctor had been ready to fly away in the TARDIS and leave the threatened Thals to face the Daleks alone. 'Our fate doesn't rest with the Thals, surely,' he tells Barbara as they prepare to depart. 'Let's leave well alone. We have ourselves to worry about.' It is only after he realises that he has left a crucial part of the TARDIS behind in the Dalek city that he is forced to become involved in the events on Skaro, because there is no other way that he can leave the planet. For his own selfish reasons, he persuades the previously pacifistic Thals to attack their enemy.

In his second Dalek story, Nation connects his Space Age fascists to the greatest fear of the wartime British – that their island would be conquered by the Nazis. The TARDIS lands in London around the year 2164, two centuries after Ian and Barbara's time. They discover the city destroyed, the population enslaved, and that the all-conquering Daleks have already become the masters of Earth. From the opening scenes of the first episode, we find ourselves in a bleak, despairing world. It begins with a figure in a strange helmet staggering past a poster on a bridge by the Thames which reads, 'It is forbidden to dump bodies in the river.' With a cry of pain, he collapses into the Thames and drowns.

When the Doctor sees a Dalek appearing out of the dirty river, he immediately knows what he has to do. 'I think we'd better pit our wits against them and defeat them,' he tells Ian. With those words, the format of the series changes. No longer would *Doctor Who* plots be about just trying to make it back to the TARDIS alive. The Daleks had dragged the Doctor into a universe containing an evil more powerful and reprehensible than the production team had originally planned. The darkness that these metal creatures represented was so profound that even an amoral enigma like the Doctor could not help being shaped by it. He had no choice but to fight. He was forced to grow and evolve in order to balance the sheer symbolic weight of those metallic horrors.

Previously, the time travellers had tried to avoid getting involved in the events of places they visited. 'You can't rewrite history!' the Doctor had told Barbara when she attempted to make humane changes to Aztec culture. 'Not one line!' With the arrival of the waterlogged Dalek, however, the voyeurs suddenly became active agents in history. From now on, they would battle evil and attempt to save the people that they encountered. On the face of it, the deceitful, crotchety figure of the Doctor seemed an unlikely candidate to become a hero, but such is the extent that people are changed by exposure to evil as dark as fascism. The wandering exile was reimagined. Doctor Who had been radicalised.

4. Dalekmania

The Daleks arrived at a potent time. In the years following the Suez Crisis of 1956, the old sense of Britain as a place of empire and class deference was increasingly rejected. The British public wanted a new, modern sense of themselves, to replace that outdated and unworkable past. The public flocked to films like *Goldfinger* and *A Hard Day's Night* because they were forward-looking and modern. They offered new visions of who the British were and what type of people they could be. In this atmosphere the Daleks, Cusick's and Nation's Space Age, Pop Art, child-friendly repackaging of the ultimate evil, were an immediate phenomenon. 1964 was the year of Beatlemania and Bondmania. In 1965, the press began reporting on a third new obsession to grip the British public, which would in time be called Dalekmania.

This was, significantly, not *Doctor Who* mania. On a cultural level, the Daleks had become far larger than the programme that introduced them. The first book inspired by the series, for example, was *The Dalek Book* (1964). Aside from a photomontage of scenes from their first television appearance, it made little reference to the Doctor or his adventures. In later Dalek books, he was not mentioned at all. Terry Nation owned the rights to his creations, and he became the only person to ever become seriously wealthy through *Doctor Who*. 'I don't know to this day what the enormous appeal of the Daleks was,' Nation has said, 'I've heard all sorts of ideas about it, but they were slightly magical, because you didn't know what the elements were that made them work.' Dalek comic strips, games and candy cigarettes arrived on shelves, along with records such as 'I'm Gonna Spend My Christmas with a Dalek' by The Go-Go's. By 1965, over a million toy Daleks had been sold. Toys featuring the Doctor or the TARDIS, in contrast, were rare indeed.

Attempts to merchandise later alien monsters from the series, such as the Zarbi or the Mechonoids from series two, fell flat. Only Daleks sparked the public's imagination. It was Daleks that children drew and imitated, allowing them to explore disturbing ideas and dark archetypes. Some were alarmed by this playful embrace of power, aggression and slaughter. The conservative Christian campaigner Mary Whitehouse, for example, claimed that the Daleks would incite children to murder. Here she displayed an accurate understanding of what the Daleks represented, if perhaps a lesser grasp of children themselves.

When Dalekmania took off, the original Dalek story was quickly adapted into a full-colour feature film. Peter Cushing was cast as the cinema 'Dr. Who', and he played essentially the same character as Hartnell, a doddery old man with a twinkle in his eye. There was no thought of new incarnations of the Doctor at this point. The film was called *Dr. Who and the Daleks* (1965), although the words 'Dr. Who and the' were considerably smaller on the poster than the word 'Daleks'.

The film was an immediate success, so Terry Nation's second Dalek serial, *The Dalek Invasion of Earth*, was green-lit and adapted into a bigger-budget sequel called *Daleks' Invasion Earth 2150 A.D.* (1966). The words 'Doctor Who' did not appear in the title or anywhere in the trailer. Audiences were only told that 'leading the resistance fighters is Peter Cushing, in his most thrill-making role'.

Verity Lambert and the *Doctor Who* production team launched the series knowing that many inside the BBC looked down upon it and expected it to fail. They had felt like outsiders, unaccepted and patronised. But *Doctor Who* turned out to be a huge hit – and not only in terms of ratings, audience appreciation and critical reaction. It impacted society in ways that very few television programmes ever achieve. Words like 'Dalek' and 'TARDIS' were added to the dictionary and political cartoonists had a new set of cultural iconographies to play with. It became a cultural touchstone and reference point, to the extent that it would later become used to help justify the continued existence of the BBC. That this had been achieved by a group of outsiders – people who were not considered to be 'the right sort' in terms of nationality, gender, ethnicity or age – inevitably led to resentment. For Lambert in particular, the runaway success of the Daleks was a great vindication. She was always going to be belittled and dismissed, she knew, but it was easier to put up with when it came from a place of jealousy.

Despite their initial rejection of the concept, Lambert now found her immediate bosses eager for *Doctor Who* to tell more and more Dalek stories. This led to lengthy adventures such as the twelve-part epic *The Dalek's Master Plan* (1965–66), which meant that Daleks were on television every week for three months. They were also on stage at the same time, in matinee performances of David Whitaker and Terry Nation's play *The Curse of the Daleks* at the Wyndham's Theatre in London's West End. By this point, the market for Dalek-branded merchandise had become thoroughly oversaturated, and Dalekmania peaked in 1965. *Daleks' Invasion Earth 2150 A.D.* was released in 1966, after the bubble had burst. It disappointed at the box office and plans for future Dalek movies were scrapped. Those two films remain the only *Doctor Who* feature films to this day.

Terry Nation, in response, decided to try and launch a standalone Daleks series in America, where his creations were still largely unknown. For this reason, he denied the BBC permission to use them in future *Doctor Who* stories. His creations were dropped from the series following what was described as their 'final defeat' in *The Evil of the Daleks* (1967). They would not be seen again for another five years, after it was clear that American television had no interest in these Space Age monsters.

The Dalekmania bubble may not have lasted long, but its impact on *Doctor Who* was permanent. The Daleks had propelled the series into its first Golden Age, a period of huge ratings success where it became part of the national conversation. Before the first Dalek story was broadcast, the BBC had scaled down their initial plans for a year-long series and had only committed to thirteen episodes. Following the success of the Daleks, the programme was commissioned to run for all but a few weeks every year. The Daleks had not only changed the character of the Doctor. They were also responsible for the continuation of *Doctor Who* itself.

5. Season Three

The second season ends with something a little unusual. As the theme music plays, we are shown a vast galaxy of endless stars. The faces of the Doctor's new companions Steven and Vicki appear out of these stars, each looking upwards in wide-eyed wonder. These are followed by the face of the Doctor, with the slightest of smiles on his lips and a hint of mischief in his eyes. The credits then start to scroll. The season ends with a sense of confidence, ready for the future.

At the time, it seemed like there was much to be confident about. Having navigated the difficult loss of three quarters of the original cast, the series had successfully introduced the characters of Vicki and Steven to replace the hole left by the departure of Ian, Barbara and Susan. Steven was tall, strong and quick to anger, while Vicki was elven, quick-witted and able to manipulate Steven with ease. There was great chemistry between the pair, and all the ingredients were in place for series three to build on these strong foundations. In actuality, what followed was turmoil. Change was painful and constant, and very few members of the cast or crew were unaffected. The tone and format were violently stretched, twisted and fought over, but the programme that emerged at the end was infinitely stronger. In the fires of season three, the modern show was forged.

Perhaps the single most destabilising change was Verity Lambert's departure, after the first five episodes of series three. Hartnell did not take to her replacement, the South African John Wiles. 'Bill was feeling very insecure,' recalled the script editor Donald Tosh, 'and he didn't behave well when he was afraid. Bill and John absolutely did not hit it off.' Lambert had understood the importance of keeping nervous actors flattered and reassured, but Wiles had little interest in treating adult professionals with kid gloves. Hartnell, by now the only surviving member of the team that had launched the show, felt that his status as the heart of the programme was threatened. 'I think [Hartnell] wanted to be part of our team on *Doctor Who*, but he wanted to be the captain,' said Tosh. 'And he wanted everyone to acknowledge that, because somehow I think he felt that other people wanted to take the captaincy away from him.'

Wiles's vision was to take the show in a more adult, sophisticated direction. As he explained in 1983, he and script editor Donald Tosh 'wanted to develop the programme and get it out of the somewhat childish rut it was in. It was the boundaries I think we wanted to extend the most – to push it, if you like, a little bit more towards adult science-fiction.' This was a source of many clashes with his lead actor. As Hartnell saw it, the programme existed primarily for children. If they got bored and lost interest, the show would be in serious trouble. The question of whether *Doctor Who* should grow up with its audience or target a new generation of children was one that the programme makers would struggle with many times over the following decades.

The most immediate result of these changes was that stories became richer and more mature. They also, however, became incredibly bleak. Here the tone was set by *Mission to the Unknown*, the only stand-alone single-episode story of the original run, which featured none of the regulars. It tells the story of astronauts on a dangerous jungle planet attempting to warn Earth authorities of an impending Dalek attack. This they fail to do. Every human character is killed by the end of the episode. Lambert was still credited as producer, but Wiles was already taking over her role and making his presence felt. The episode set the tone for the relentless, bleak slaughter that marked the stories to come.

In the Trojan War-era story that followed, *The Myth Makers*, the Doctor gives the Greeks the idea for the wooden horse. As such, he is responsible for the massacre of the Trojans in the final episode. This is a historical story which builds to a terrible act of mass slaughter in which the characters we have met are senselessly murdered by a rampaging army or mob, while the Doctor and his crew barely escape with their lives. This story structure is repeated in that season's fifth story, *The Massacre of St Bartholomew's Eve*, which is set in the sectarian religious conflict of sixteenth-century Paris. It leads terribly and inevitably to the slaughter of thousands of Protestant Huguenots by Catholic mobs in the final episode – serious stuff, but not what many would have described as child-pleasing.

The expectation of a solid Steven–Vicki partnership did not come to pass. The first story of the season was originally written for Ian and Barbara, and their lines were given to Steven in a way that often seemed out of character. In their second story together, the pair were split up and, in the final episode, Vicki was written out of the series. This came as a surprise to the actor Maureen O'Brien, who only discovered that she was not continuing in the role when she read the final page of the script and learnt that her character was to be left behind in Ancient Greece. 'As I recollect it, when I came back [from holiday] there was just one set of scripts, and normally there would have been more than one set of scripts. I thought that was a bit odd,' she recalled. 'I was quite put out because I hadn't been asked or told in any way.' O'Brien had been unprepared for the fame that the programme brought and longed for more challenging roles, so she came to see her dismissal as a blessing in disguise. 'I was absolutely fed up with it,' she said. 'I was doing it because it was a job and it's better to have a job than not, but I wasn't happy.'

As a new producer taking over and shaping the show to his own vision, Wiles was simply doing his job when he decided to refresh the principal cast. It's not clear, however, that he had a clear idea of how his replacement cast should work, or quite what their characters should be. Vicki was replaced in the TARDIS by an ancient Greek handmaiden called Katarina, played by Adrienne Hill. Confronted with the otherworldly miracle of the TARDIS, Katarina believed that she had died and that the TARDIS was a temple transporting her to the afterlife. She only lasted five episodes before Wiles decided that this wasn't working. Katarina was duly flushed out of an airlock, where she died in the vacuum of space. Her replacement was Sara Kingdom, a glamorous Space Security Agent from the fortieth century. Sara lasted eight episodes before being aged to death in a sequence that is still one of the most horrifying in the series' history.

That two of the Doctor's companions died in such quick

succession shows how dark and threatening the series had become. As Wiles later commented, 'One of the things I wanted to do was redefine our attitudes to death on screen [. . .] I asked the whole production team to look at the event with more responsibility.' Death became a constant theme, and loss of life central to the drama. It was not treated in the off-hand inconsequential way in which a lot of television action programmes kill characters. There was no hint of the idea that beloved characters were safe with the Doctor around.

Wiles seemed to have particular problems with female cast members. As bleak as Katarina and Sara's fates were, they were at least more dignified than that of Sara's replacement Dodo, who didn't even get an on-screen goodbye. The programme explained she had 'gone into the country' for a few days to recover from being hypnotised, and she was never mentioned again. Even when she had been on screen, her character wasn't treated with much respect. Wiles originally imagined her as a working-class Mancunian, and as such she spoke with a broad Manchester accent during her first episode. Wiles was then informed by his BBC superiors that this was unacceptable. Dodo's regional accent was dropped, and she suddenly started talking with a received pronunciation accent. By the time of her third story, *The Gunfighters*, she had become incredibly posh.

Wiles's desire to change the cast was not limited to the companions. He wanted to replace William Hartnell as well. After three years of a punishing schedule of one episode per week, the programme was taking a toll on Hartnell's health. He struggled to learn his lines, and Wiles was not sympathetic. The writer William Emms recalled a script read-through turning into a stand-up shouting match, after Hartnell repeatedly attempted to simplify his lines. 'You do it the way it is,' Emms recalls Wiles telling Hartnell, 'or I'll sack you.' Hartnell's memory issues gradually led to more complicated dialogue, particularly that which included exposition or technobabble, being given to the character of Steven.

Suffering from decreasing energy and frustrated by his memory issues, Hartnell became increasingly quick to anger. As Maureen O'Brien recalls, 'He'd go off into these terrible rages several times a day. It was my job to laugh him out of it.' At moments like these the worst of Hartnell's prejudices would be revealed. 'He was a terrible racist and homophobic and all these terrible things,' O'Brien has said. 'Bill said the most terrible things [about West Indians] you just wouldn't believe it. He'd be arrested now, and quite rightly.' Despite these outbursts, she remained fond of him, on the grounds that 'When you're brought up as a Catholic, you're taught to hate the sin but love the sinner.' Hartnell's granddaughter Jessica Carney acknowledged his antisemitism in her biography of him. 'Bill often came out with xenophobic comments,' she wrote. 'His so-called dislike of Jews was based on the fact that he believed the film industry had been taken over by them.' The actor Nicholas Courtney, who played Brigadier Lethbridge-Stewart in *Doctor Who* in the 1970s and 1980s, also appeared in a 1965 Hartnell story. He wrote that Hartnell 'could be unnerving, when his bigotry was allowed to surface. During a break from rehearsals one day, he whispered somewhat confidentially in my ear: "You see that actor sitting over there, Nick? You know he is a Jew." I just froze and murmured something like, "Ah."'

Increasingly convinced that Hartnell wasn't up to the job and having no sympathy for his outbursts, Wiles wanted to sack him and replace him with a less problematic actor. He intended to do this in the fantastical story *The Celestial Toymaker*. The Toymaker, played by Michael Gough, was a godlike amoral being who wished to use the Doctor and his companions in his games. Near the start of the story, he turned the Doctor invisible, meaning that Hartnell could enjoy a couple of weeks' holiday while his role in the story was confined to a floating, disembodied hand and a few lines of pre-recorded dialogue. Wiles's initial plan, however, was that when the Doctor became visible again, he would have changed into a different actor. This radical idea, however, was vetoed by Wiles's bosses. The idea of *Doctor Who* without William Hartnell was still unthinkable.

Wiles, frustrated by this and seeing no way of making the programme as he felt it should be, resigned. 'I'm one of the few producers ever to resign from the BBC,' he said, 'and it was simply because I was heading very rapidly for a nervous breakdown. And I decided that if I was going to have a breakdown, it might as well be in something for which I had respect, rather than this programme which, at that stage, I didn't like.'

Hartnell remained difficult when the new producer Innes Lloyd took over. As Lambert described him, 'He could be quite intimidating if you didn't know that under this spiky exterior he was very sweet – marshmallow in fact. He could be cutting, but I think it was a defensive thing. He was rather like the character – sometimes he was nice, sometimes he wasn't. He was frustrated with himself, and with his failing memory, and he reacted by lashing out and blaming others for his difficulties.' It became increasingly apparent that Hartnell would have to be replaced. Wiles may have failed when he attempted to recast the Doctor, but he crucially left behind the idea that it could be done. As strange an idea as the Doctor being played by a completely different actor was, Wiles had shown that the fiction of the series could find a way to explain it.

Losing the job that he loved more than any other was hard for Hartnell. He was drinking heavily, and the stress affected his health as he neared his final appearance. He had to be written out of his penultimate episode when he developed bronchitis, which required penicillin injections. In the end, the in-fiction explanation for why he suddenly changed into a different person was simply that his old body was 'wearing a bit thin'. Perhaps because there was truth to this in real life, it was all the explanation that was needed.

Hartnell would never really recover from losing the role. In a letter to a fan, he claimed that he suffered another 'breakdown' after giving up the part. He had given so much of himself to the character, but it had emotionlessly marched on without him when he was too frail to give any more. He may have been the first to be treated like this by the Doctor, but he would not be the last.

That, however, is not how history will remember William Hartnell. One Sunday, Hartnell was being driven back from the pub when they were stopped by a police roadblock. 'Leave this to me,' he told the driver, and swept out of the car shouting, 'Don't you know who I am? I'm Doctor Who, Doctor BLOODY WHO!' That is William Hartnell as generations as yet unborn will know him. He was the first, the original and the initial imprint of the Doctor, gifting him his mercurial temperament with its mass of contradictions. He was Doctor Bloody Who and, in keeping with the time-mangling nature of the character, he always will be.

3

The Trickster (1966–69)

1. 'I Need Change'

In 1955, Patrick Troughton and his wife Margaret moved into a new north London home, in Uphill Road, Mill Hill. They had just welcomed their third child, Michael, who was born in March, and they needed somewhere larger to live. Patrick was getting regular acting work on television and outwardly all appeared well with the Troughton family.

Michael, however, was to see very little of his father as he grew up. While he was still a baby, Patrick set up a second home in south London, near Kew, with his girlfriend Ethel 'Bunny' Nuens. Patrick and Bunny would go on to have three children together, but Patrick and his wife Margaret never announced a separation. The couple kept up the pretence that they still had a normal marriage. Patrick's long absences from the family home were explained away as his having to work away from home, due to the nature of the acting profession. When Patrick's mother died twenty-four years later, in 1979, she was still unaware of the separation. Patrick and his original family had kept up the façade by visiting her every Christmas Day and pretending that nothing had happened. She never knew she had three more grandchildren.

This was a situation that could, perhaps, only have happened in the 1950s. The fact that the couple preferred to keep up the appearance of a happy marriage, rather than simply separating or divorcing, illustrates the pressures that came with the social attitudes of the day. It seems even stranger to us now when you consider that Patrick was also a highly regarded stage and television character actor, who became a public name when he was cast as the second Doctor Who. The values of the British press were very different then. A famous person could spend his days going back and forth between two families and get away with it.

Patrick's two families were only part of his complicated network of romantic relationships. He met the actor Ann Morrish in the early 1960s on the set of the publishing-based soap opera *Compact*. The pair began a relationship which lasted up until 1966, just before he was cast as the Doctor. Morrish recalled being 'astonished at his family arrangements and I was introduced to Bunny fairly early on. Whether she knew that we were lovers or not I don't know.' To further complicate matters, Morrish had three children of her own, who became close to Patrick's wife Margaret and her three children. The two families looked forward to holiday visits, and would go on outings to places like Corfe Castle together.

Patrick and Bunny's relationship lasted for two decades, until he began a relationship with another woman, Shelagh Holdup. It was only after Patrick got together with Holdup that he finally asked Margaret for a divorce, which was granted. Holdup and Troughton married in 1976 and remained together until Troughton's death in 1987.

When he was a young man, Patrick's relationships had been more traditional. He married Margaret in 1943 when he was twenty-three years old, and their marriage had initially been very strong. Cracks started to appear in 1952 after Patrick returned home from a five-month run of theatre in New York, alongside

Laurence Olivier and Vivien Leigh. Margaret would later say, 'Ever since Pat's return from America he was different. Nothing that you could put your finger on but there was a change in his affections towards me. It was slight but it was definitely there.' Patrick struggled with what he saw as the competing demands of, as he put it in his diary, 'The Artist and the Family Man.' After returning home from America on the RMS *Franconia* and docking in Liverpool, he wrote that the 'Trip has changed me I think. I want more of the bright lights but feel guilty I have to sacrifice family. Instinct tells me one thing and brain tells me another. I am confused.'

After his time in America, Troughton abandoned his attempts to remain monogamous. His son Michael later became an actor and recalled how 'many mature actresses whom I have worked with in the past have often shuffled up to me in rehearsals with a wicked twinkle in the eye and quietly whispered, "I knew your father very well, an adorable creature!"' Those words are typical of accounts of Troughton's womanising. He was never described in terms that make him sound predatory or creepy. Instead, he was a charismatic and well-loved figure. Many were drawn to him, but his inability to maintain a monogamous life caused a great deal of emotional hurt. Today, Troughton would be described as polyamorous, or possibly even a sex addict. In the mid-twentieth century, however, his behaviour was so taboo that there was no simple label for it. This may have been what allowed such a famous figure to maintain two families, plus mistresses, for so long. People are slow to spot what they can't imagine.

When Michael Troughton was in his twenties, he got to spend time with his largely absent father on a boating holiday on the Norfolk Broads. During their time together, he was able to ask his father why he had left his mother and siblings, and why he behaved the way he did. Patrick's reply was simple. As he told his son, 'I need change. Things have to change all the time for me I'm afraid, that's the way I am made. I am sorry if I hurt you.'

Change may be necessary, but it is difficult. When it happens, we are profoundly aware of what we have just lost, and what will never return. The value of what the new situation brings, in contrast, isn't immediately apparent. It has not yet become part of our lives and identities, and as such we have no real affection for it. It takes time for its importance to be revealed.

Troughton feared the status quo. He could not bear the thought of being in a rut. In his eyes, things got stale after a certain amount of time, and that scared him. Patrick Troughton was by nature an avatar of change. This would be his great gift to *Doctor Who*.

2. 'They Must Be Mad'

The 1966 story *The Power of the Daleks* begins with the Doctor's companions Polly and Ben attempting to come to terms with what has happened to the Doctor. He entered the TARDIS looking like William Hartnell, yet inside they find only the disorientated figure of Patrick Troughton lying on the floor. Initially, Ben denies that this shorter, younger, scruffier figure is the same man that he had travelled with. Finding the original Doctor's ring on the floor, he tries it on the stranger's finger and discovers that it is too large for him. If the Doctor's ring doesn't fit, Ben theorises, then this new man can't be the Doctor.

The stranger's response is cryptic. 'I'd like to see a butterfly fit into a chrysalis case after it's spread its wings,' he says.

'Then you did change!' exclaims Polly.

'Life depends on change and renewal,' the Doctor tells her.

With those words, the actor Patrick Troughton and the character of the Doctor became one.

Hartnell did not want change. He wanted to continue in his beloved role long into the future, even after his deteriorating health meant that this was not possible. If the Doctor had not been recast, then the series would have come to an end and, in the eyes of both Head of Serials Shaun Sutton and the producer Innes Lloyd, Troughton was the perfect replacement. 'The producer and I were absolutely determined to have Patrick Troughton', Sutton recalled in a 1992 interview. 'I had actually been a drama student with Patrick Troughton many years ago, before the war. And even back then, Patrick had those deep lines on his face – he had the look of a thousand-year-old leprechaun. I remember saying to him once, before the war, "Patrick, you have the secret of eternal age," and I thought that was a very good quality for *Doctor Who*.' From Lloyd's perspective, Troughton had a reputation for being a very good actor with probably more experience of television than any of his peers. He had found that he enjoyed television far more than theatre and had specialised in it earlier than most. Replacing a leading man was risky, but Troughton was undeniably a safe pair of hands.

Troughton was first contacted about the role when he was on location in Ireland, filming a Hammer historical adventure film called *The Viking Queen* (released in 1967). This was a curiously named film, considering that it contained no Norse Vikings at all. Unusually, Patrick was with his wife Margaret at the time, rather than his partner Bunny. The couple were attempting a rare reconciliation, but this was short-lived, causing more hurt to the long-suffering Margaret and her three children.

After receiving the call from the BBC, Troughton's immediate response was that the idea was 'Quite preposterous'. As he told Margaret, it was the 'Quickest way to make [*Doctor Who*] die a death, casting me in the part! They must be mad. They must be absolutely stark raving mad!' Yet the BBC was persistent and the money, together with the lengthy contract, was hard to resist for long. Troughton had six children by this point and was attempting to have them educated privately. From a financial point of view, the opportunity to play the Doctor was not something he should turn down.

But how, exactly, would he play the role? The usual method of replacing a leading man was to hire someone physically similar and accept their take on what was essentially the same character. That the BBC did not take this approach was creatively brave. As Christopher Barry, the director of *The Power of the Daleks*, said in a 1987 interview, Troughton 'couldn't have done an imitation of Hartnell because, as those dreadful Peter Cushing movies had shown, there was just no substitute for the real thing'. The original actor had made the part his own. No one could out-Hartnell Hartnell.

British culture had changed radically in the three short years since the programme had first appeared on our screens. Hartnell's stern patrician figure made sense in 1963, before the impact of Beatlemania had worked its magic on the British public. In the aftermath of the Fab Four, however, Hartnell's Doctor seemed even more out of his time than originally intended. This was particularly apparent in *The War Machines* (1966), when the TARDIS landed in contemporary London. The sight of Hartnell's Doctor visiting a hip youthful London nightclub called the Inferno made him seem far more lost in time than any of his previous adventures.

A new Doctor could be more contemporary in his values and thoughts. He could also be a bit more fun and welcoming. In keeping with the zeitgeist, Troughton played the role with his hair longer and swept forward in the Beatles 'mop top' style – a look that would have been unthinkable for Hartnell in 1963. This style, however, wasn't the result of a considered choice. Troughton had wanted a curly wig, not dissimilar to that worn by Harpo Marx. 'I'd had a lovely wig fitted which had loads of mad thick curls,' he recalled. 'I put it on and took a look in the mirror, and I thought, "That looks lovely!"' His co-stars Anneke Wills and Michael Craze, and probably the rest of the crew, thought otherwise. Possibly acting under instruction from Innes Lloyd, the pair staged an intervention and refused to act opposite the ludicrous wig. The curls were abandoned and make-up designer Gillian James removed the wig. As Troughton recalled, she 'started doing things with my hair. This was about five minutes before transmission. The next time I looked in the mirror I saw a Beatle! I looked like Ringo Starr! But it was too late to do anything about it. I was stuck with it and I stayed the same through the whole series.'

Although a decision had been made to change the Doctor's character, the question remained of what, exactly, his new character should be like. This was an issue that Troughton had great difficulty wrestling with. At home with his original family, he tried out many wildly varying characterisations, including a mutton-chopped character similar to the Victorian prime minister William Gladstone, an Arab character in a turban and a spiky-haired mad scientist. He showed his sons sketches of potential costumes including a pirate and a Mississippi river-boat captain. It's hard not to detect a little desperation in these ideas. Troughton was looking for a disguise that he could hide behind.

Eventually, a scruffy, Chaplinesque costume was settled on. The new Doctor was said to be a 'Cosmic hobo'. This was not a huge distance from Sydney Newman's original ideas about the Doctor, which was that Hartnell should 'be like the upper-class Steptoe'. Even so, Newman had his doubts that the new characterisation and costume would work. After a costume fitting for Troughton's outfit, he told Shaun Sutton that 'I still don't see it, but if you and Innes say it's okay, okay, go ahead.'

Along with the Harpo Marx wig, Troughton wanted his Doctor to wear an absurd tall hat. Despite the best efforts of Craze and Wills, the hat lasted longer than the wig. It appears in Troughton's first three stories, before it was eventually discarded. Indeed, the new Doctor as he appeared in his first three months of stories had something of a fixation on hats of all different styles. He even had a catchphrase – 'I would like a hat like that!' This did not catch on and was, perhaps fortunately, soon abandoned.

3. The Trickster

The character of a new Doctor rarely appears fully formed. They often take a little time to settle. The period before the actor has brought enough of themselves to the part to really bring it alive, and before the writers have grasped how the actor is playing the role, often allows us to glimpse a side of the Doctor that is normally hidden. In the uncertainty of the post-regeneration period, there is usually a moment when the true nature of the Doctor is revealed. This is not the character as a hero. Beneath that heroic mask, the character is fundamentally a trickster.

A trickster is a character archetype that appears in myth and folklore throughout the world. Tricksters have almost supernatural intelligence and wit, and a transgressive ability to not fit into the structures of the world. They enjoy disguises and the playing of roles. They mock authority, question power, and they can disrupt society so that it is remade differently. They are often found at boundaries, which they can cross with ease – in the Doctor's case, this includes the boundaries of time and space. They sometimes steal objects of otherworldly power from the gods – or a TARDIS from the Time Lords. Like the Doctor, they have the ability to change gender. Loki, Coyote, the Greek god Hermes, the West African spider god Anansi and Bugs Bunny are all examples of tricksters. Crucially, they are considered neither good nor evil. Instead, they act in the moment as a force for change, and they rarely pay attention to the consequences of that change. In the first months of Troughton taking over the role, the character of the Doctor was at their most tricksterish.

A classic example of a trickster story concerns Eshu, the trickster god of the Yoruba people of West Africa. Like Troughton's Doctor, Eshu was very fond of hats. One day he walked through the village wearing a hat that was white on one side and black on the other. The villagers looked on in amazement. 'Did you see that?' one said to his neighbour on the other side of the street after Eshu had gone. 'A god walked through our village wearing a white hat!' 'I did see it,' his friend replied, 'only he wasn't wearing a white hat. He was wearing a black hat.' 'No, you're mistaken,' said the first man, 'it was a white hat. I saw it clearly.' Soon the village descended into increasingly vitriolic argument, with those who saw a white hat convinced that those who saw a black hat were in the wrong – and vice versa. In this way, Eshu changed the village from a place of harmony into a place of discord.

There are many different and often contradictory versions of this myth, which are all considered to be as valid as each other. In some versions, Eshu returns and shows them his hat, and the villagers become enlightened about the limited nature of their perception. In other versions Eshu is never seen again, and the village descends into warfare. The intention and outcome of Eshu's actions – enlightenment or destruction – were not the point. Eshu is simply a divine agent of transformation, regardless of consequence.

The tricksterlike nature of Hartnell's Doctor was apparent on many occasions. In the 1965 story *The Romans*, for example, the Doctor assumes the identity of a murdered lyre player called Maximus Pettulian. This was something he did in a spirit of mischief, only for his own amusement, with no concern about what the consequences would be. This was in keeping with the character of the Doctor as it was then written – in an earlier story he had boldly assumed the identity of a Regional Officer of the Provinces during revolutionary France, for example.

The Doctor was unable to play the lyre, however, a problem that came to a head at a feast where he was expected to play for Emperor Nero himself. The disguised Doctor solved this problem in a quintessentially tricksterish way. He told the assembled audience that his composition 'is so soft, so delicate, that only those with keen perceptive hearing will be able to distinguish this melodious charm of music'. He then silently pretended to play. Nero could not admit to not hearing this music, so he had to pretend to enjoy it. 'He's all right, but he's not that good,' was his considered response. Because Nero claimed that he could hear the music, the rest of the audience then had to pretend as well, and they responded with applause and admiration. The Doctor had outwitted the crowd by using their vanity to his advantage. This was textbook trickster behaviour. As he confessed to Vicki, 'It's the old fairy story, child. The Emperor's New Clothes. Yes, I gave it as an idea to Hans Andersen.'

Troughton's Doctor, like those who followed him, eventually settled down into a different archetypal form. By *The Moonbase* (1967), the Doctor had developed a most un-tricksterlike sense of morality. 'There are some corners of the universe which have bred the most terrible things,' he says, referring to the Cybermen. 'Things which act against everything that we believe in. They must be fought.' With these words, the trickster presented as a hero.

The trickster is supposed to be beyond good and evil, an agent of change who acts in the moment with no concern for consequences. A hero, in contrast, has clear understanding of good and evil, and acts in the service of good. This change helped the audience accept Troughton's Doctor and proved to be a positive thing for the long-term survival of the character. In mythology, however, tricksters are supposed to remain tricksters, never learning from their actions or developing empathy or intention. What they do like, however, is a disguise. It would be quite in keeping with the trickster archetype if they hid behind the mask of the hero, for their long-term advantage and out of a sense of mischief. If mythology is to be believed, this is far more likely than a trickster genuinely changing into a hero.

It may be that tricksters are compelled to disguise themselves as heroes in this way if they want to exist on television. The character of Loki relished his trickster nature when he was introduced in the Marvel superhero films. When he was granted two seasons of a television series, however, that was jettisoned for a standard hero persona. We suddenly saw Loki behaving in implausibly heroic ways, such as forming friendships and sacrificing themselves for others. Even an arch trickster like Bugs Bunny behaves in a noble way if you take him out of short cartoons and put him in a feature-length film like *Space Jam*.

If these mercurial characters are to continue on centre stage, they can only unsettle the audience for so long. Yet beneath their heroic disguises, their true nature can never be entirely overwritten. We can never erase that which the writer Alan Watts called 'the element of irreducible rascality'.

4. Monsters

When actors who played the Doctor are asked about their predecessors, they frequently cite Troughton as the one they most admire. This is the safe, uncontroversial choice. In part, it recognises Troughton's importance in the continuation of the role. As Colin Baker noted, 'If it wasn't for Patrick, the rest of us wouldn't have got the part.' By this, he means that the series would not have continued if Troughton had failed and that it only continues through the decades because he proved that recasting could work. 'For me, he was the "guvnor" among Doctors,' said Baker.

In a 2013 documentary, David Tennant said that 'I think Patrick Troughton created the Doctor as he is now. William Hartnell created something that was unique and brilliant. But actually the Doctor we recognise today is much more Patrick Troughton's Doctor. We've all sort of done our version, kind of, of what Patrick Troughton did.' Such a statement might initially appear unfair on Hartnell. After all, his Doctor was every bit as brilliant and mercurial as his successors. He could be charming and, occasionally, tender, so you can't claim that those elements originated with Troughton. Yet Troughton did bring something new to the character, which has been an integral part of the role ever since. Hartnell could be frightening. He was rash and quick to temper, and he was as likely to get you into danger as to get you out of it. Yet while Troughton's Doctor often appeared out of his depth, you still felt safe with him.

This sense of the Doctor as an unconventional protector was not part of the production team's conception of this second version of the Doctor. BBC paperwork described the intended character as having 'humour and wit' but also 'an overwhelmingly thunderous rage which frightens his companions and others [...]

He enjoys disconcerting his companions with unconventional and unexpected repartee.' Here was a more forceful Doctor, one who would take charge of the situation and display his superiority. Troughton, however, did not see the Doctor in those terms. He resented the producers circulating their vision of the character before he had fully developed his own. He complained that they wanted 'A very long-winded and complicated autocratic Sherlock Holmes type who never stopped talking. Well, that was no good to me!'

Troughton did not want his Doctor to grandstand. He wanted him to listen. His Doctor would be acutely aware of what was going on around him, even as he played down his intellect and acted the fool to disarm authority figures. Hartnell liked to be centre stage, ready for his close-up. Troughton was more likely to hang back in the scene, allowing the other characters to reveal themselves while events played out. The audience trusted the Second Doctor because he didn't miss anything.

One side effect of this choice was that the character retained his mystery. In the original drafts of *The Power of the Daleks* script, the more talkative Doctor was set to reveal a lot about his backstory. It was 'over seven hundred and fifty years since I left my own planet', he tells Ben and Polly, although he confusingly later claims to be 750 years old. There was the suggestion that the Daleks may have destroyed his own planet. 'I don't know. Perhaps I'll never know,' he tells Polly when she asks about this. 'You see, we left in the TARDIS, Susan and I – before the end.' Taken on face value, these comments suggest that the Doctor left his home planet as a baby – but in the company of his granddaughter. This sounds rather like the starting point of a Steven Moffat script.

This dialogue about the fate of his home planet echoed the producer's description of the new Doctor, which declared that 'He is the eternal fugitive with a horrifying fear of the past horrors he has endured (these horrors were experienced during the galactic war and account for his flight from his own planet).' The idea that there had been a war between the Daleks and his own people directly contradicted what we had seen in the Hartnell years, but in the fullness of time these discarded attempts at backstory would turn into prophecy.

All these glimpses into the Doctor's past were cut when the script was rewritten for the character as Troughton wanted to play him. His desire to have his Doctor listen and be fully aware came in part from his concern about the children watching, who he saw as the primary audience. The series could get away with scary stories, he felt, if the children felt safe and secure with the Doctor. Michael Troughton believes that his father was behind the special trailer shown ahead of *The Web of Fear* – a 1967 story that saw the return of the Yeti, who had been redesigned to appear less cuddly and more terrifying. The trailer featured Troughton on set and in character, addressing the young audience directly. The Yeti would be, he says, 'just a little bit more frightening than last time. So, I want to warn you that, if your mummy and daddy are scared, you just get them to hold your hand!' It was a line that captured both Troughton's Second Doctor, and his concern for the audience, perfectly.

Verity Lambert, who was not overly interested in children or in making programmes for them, had always had an older audience in mind. 'I was fairly confident that if I, as an adult, accepted what was on screen as being right, valid and interesting, then it would be the same for the child,' she said. As Waris Hussein wrote in his diary a month after the programme had started, 'Nobody in the corporation is quite sure whether it's now an adult programme and varied complaints have come in about the violence in some of the episodes.' Lambert's philosophy was that 'children today are very sophisticated and I don't allow scripts which seem to talk down to them'. For Troughton, not talking down to children wasn't enough. He wanted to talk to them directly.

Lambert did, of course, consider how the programme would impact the younger audience. When the 'howlaround' video effects were being recorded for the title, there was some thought about including the Doctor's face in the sequence. Tests were made, but the idea was dropped as a face looming out of that strange abstract chaos was deemed too frightening. The idea was reused when a new title sequence was made for the Patrick Troughton series. Hartnell's face would have pushed the sequence too far and made it terrifying for the young. Troughton's kindly face, in contrast, made it reassuring.

The Web of Fear was part of season five, which Troughton described as his 'year of monsters'. It offered two Cybermen stories, two Yeti adventures, a seaweed monster and the Ice Warriors. For variety's sake, it also included a Mexican dictator from the far distant future of 2018, who just happened to be Patrick Troughton's doppelgänger. But for most of the episodes, *Doctor Who* was now a series that told monster stories. The original format of a mix of historical stories and no bug-eyed monsters had been discarded. Pure historical stories had been dropped after *The Highlanders*, Troughton's second story, and a 'base under siege' type of story had fallen into favour. These were stories set primarily in one key, isolated location, such as a moon base, a Tibetan monastery or a space-tracking station at the South Pole. Here the TARDIS crew encounter a cast of key characters, usually including a dangerous security officer and a mentally unhinged base commander. The base will then be attacked by some form of monster and, cut off from the wider world and unable to get help, our heroes must use all their wits to survive.

This is a format that works well both dramatically and

practically. It requires a smaller number of sets, so these can be larger and more ambitious. What the story does need, however, is good monsters – something that series five had in spades. Fortunately for the child audience, it also had the reassuring presence of Patrick Troughton who, by changing himself, had changed the programme with him. The safer we felt with him, the scarier the monsters could be.

5. 'You Will Become like Us'

The monsters which defined the Troughton years were the Cybermen – scientifically advanced humans who had replaced their humanity with technology. They first appeared in the 1966 story *The Tenth Planet*, in which Hartnell was 'renewed' into Troughton, and returned for four more stories between 1967 and 1969. While they have never supplanted the Daleks as the premier monster of the series, they have taken the silver medal as the Doctor's next-best monster. This is apt, given their metallic or silver appearance, which looked particularly striking in the black-and-white era of *Doctor Who*.

As the Daleks are essentially space fascists, it is tempting to define the Cybermen as space communists – a race of identical people stripped of their individuality in the name of an inhuman ideology, whose terrifying threat was not 'Exterminate' but, 'You will become like us.' But the Cybermen are not quite that easy to define. Every time they appear, they have been changed in some way, as if the series is always trying to nail down exactly what they are and how they should behave. While the silver bodies, blank faces and the 'handles' on their helmets – which run from the ears to the top of the head – are always present, all other elements of their costumes are in flux. Almost every time they appear, they look different.

It is not just their physical appearance which keeps evolving. Sometimes they are an aggressive, invading empire, while at others they are a small band engaged in a desperate struggle for survival. Sometimes their stories lean into the body horror of humans being forcibly converted into machines, while others portray them as little more than murderous robots. Sometimes their lack of emotion is emphasised, while in other stories Cybermen exclaim 'Excellent!' and clench their gloved fists in a highly emotional manner. Their weaknesses also change over time. They are usually defeated by an immaterial power, the exact nature of which becomes more refined and elevated over the years. Depending on the story, Cybermen can be killed by radiation, gravity, nail polish remover, gold, emotions or love.

The Cybermen were originally the creation of story editor Gerry Davis and Kit Pedler, a medical scientist who had become a scientific advisor to the *Doctor Who* production team. Pedler was fascinated by current advances in medical surgery. The first successful kidney transplant had taken place in Boston, Massachusetts, in 1954, and by the end of the 1960s liver, heart and pancreas transplants were occurring. Pacemakers and other technological advances suggested that human organs could be replaced by more efficient cybernetic parts. If this process continued through to its logical end, Pedler mused, at which point would the patient stop being a human? When would they become a machine? With that question, the Cybermen were born.

For all that Pedler was commissioned to bring scientific plausibility to the series, *The Tenth Planet* is one of the strangest and most mystical stories in the history of the show. Its plot centres on the arrival of a new planet in the heavens, called Mondas, which is an inverted version of Earth. It appears on the scanners as our planet but upside down, with the south pole at the top. Whereas our planet orbits the warmth of the sun, Mondas had been travelling through the dark and cold of the interstellar void. The bitter struggle to survive led to the population of Mondas turning themselves into Cybermen, and in doing so they lost their humanity. Mondas, essentially, is the anti-Earth, a planet equal but opposite, where humans became anti-humans.

Mondas is, in some unexplained way, draining Earth of its energy. The Cybermen attempt to empower themselves by draining the planet of the humans, only to discover that the energy of humanity is poison to its inhuman occupants. The one thing that anti-humans cannot survive, it seems, is humanity. After the destruction of Mondas, the Earth recovers its energy and is unharmed. The impact of these strange events on the Doctor, however, is more dramatic.

As it drained this undefined energy from the Earth, Mondas was also draining energy from the Doctor. All other people, it seemed, were unaffected. While everyone was celebrating the destruction of the Cybermen, Hartnell's Doctor knew that, 'It isn't all over. It's far from being all over.' Collapsing onto the TARDIS floor, the Doctor then physically changed into a different person, clothes and all. The Mondasian apocalypse was the chrysalis in which the old Doctor died and a new Doctor was born. The reaction caused by the combination of Earth and anti-Earth, or humanity and the inhumane, was not a zero-sum equation. Here was a clash of opposites which brought change and evolution, and ultimately moved the world onwards. This was a worldview you would expect to find in the writings of William Blake, but not a rational scientific advisor like Kit Pedler. Just as the Doctor is a trickster who dons the disguise of a hero, *Doctor Who* is a show that claims to champion science and logic to disguise its innate mysticism.

The Tenth Planet not only created a new Doctor, it created a new blueprint for the series. It was the first 'base under siege' story, with our heroes trapped inside a South Pole base awaiting attacks by visiting Cybermen. With this story structure, the programme finally accepted that monsters were the driving force of its narrative. *The Tenth Planet* not only gave us Troughton's Doctor and his arch enemy the Cybermen, it showed us how the coming stories would work.

The backstory of the Cybermen very quickly became a contradictory mess. In the 1967 story *Tomb of the Cybermen* we learn that the home planet of the Cybermen was Telos, and not Mondas after all. In *Rise of the Cybermen* (2006), we see a near-identical race of handle-headed horrors evolve in a parallel universe, before making their way to our world to fight Daleks at Canary Wharf. In *World Enough and Time* (2017), the Cybermen evolve again from scratch in a gigantic spaceship trapped by a black hole. By this point, the programme viewed Cybermen as an inevitable product of parallel evolution – beings fated to reappear whenever humanity has the skills to invent cybernetic technology but lacks the wisdom not to use it.

The Cybermen, therefore, were the perfect monster for Patrick Troughton's Doctor. On a personal level, Troughton needed change. Change brings the birth of something new, just as it brings what we had to an end. It is necessary, because a lack of change leads to stasis, decline and irrelevance. This was the guiding principle of both his personal and professional life. It was why he, after three years, walked away from the lucrative role of the Doctor, in a way that his predecessor William Hartnell never would have done.

But who, ultimately, can know what the result of change will be? Here again is the spirit of the trickster, bringing change where the outcome is unknown. Troughton personified the importance and the positive side of change, turning *Doctor Who* into a show that would live for decades. His nemesis the Cybermen, in contrast, personify the horrors of change. They are the nightmare that happens when change makes things worse – much worse – rather than better. The opposing aspects of change were the drama that the Troughton years were built on.

6. Prison in Space

Season five, the 'year of monsters', was a success. It halted the gradual decline in viewing figures since the peaks of Dalekmania, and even generated a small but welcome rise. The programme did, however, start to get repetitive. The TARDIS crew kept landing in a string of 'base under siege' stories that were, fundamentally, quite similar to each other. Troughton, as you might expect, was troubled by this. As he told his son at the time, 'We need something new . . . something creative to happen. The programme's tired and predictable.' Troughton, as always, was acutely afraid of stasis.

Concerns about his finances and multiple school fees proved sufficient to convince Troughton to sign on for a third year, but his fear of repetition gave him doubts. He discussed his concerns with the new producer Peter Bryant, who accepted that future stories needed to be more original and varied. Accepting that change is required, however, is very different to defining a new goal. The new stories for series six were more experimental, but they varied considerably in quality. Stories like *The Invasion*, *The War Games* and *The Mind Robber* are usually rated among Troughton's best, while stories like *The Krotons*, *The Dominators* and *The Space Pirates* tend to be dismissed as his worst.

This was a fertile time for experimental television. *Doctor Who* was now competing with strange and groundbreaking shows like ITV's *The Prisoner*. In those rapidly changing times, the boundaries of acceptability were often blurry and confusing – and it was easy to go quite horribly wrong. So it was that, in an effort to stretch the format and experiment with different types of narratives, *Doctor Who* very nearly produced a farcical sex comedy.

The story in question was called *The Prison in Space*. It was written by the seasoned sitcom writer Dick Sharples, who would become better known for series like *In Loving Memory* and the film version of *George and Mildred*. Sharples's idea was to take the TARDIS crew to a future where women had seized power and ruled as a harsh dictatorship. This was an idea that seemed to fascinate many male writers in the late 1960s, and Sharples was not the only person to explore that scenario. The playwright Joe Orton, for example, used it in his script for a proposed Beatles movie, *Up Against It*, in 1967, although the Beatles were unimpressed and passed on the script. The idea would eventually resurface in 1980 as a serialised comedy story on *The Two Ronnies* called 'The Worm That Turned'. While the idea of inverting societal norms to explore gender inequality could have worked, all of these writers used the idea to express their belief that women were unsuitable for positions of leadership.

In *The Prison in Space*, society is ruled over by a harsh dictator called Chairman Babs, who rules with the aid of a leather-clad, all-female militia called the Dolly Guards. Men are referred to as 'inferiors' and are treated accordingly. From the start of episode one, the Doctor and his companion Jamie display a remarkable level of chauvinism which was not in keeping with their regular personalities. In the first minutes of the first episode, for example, Jamie tells the new companion Zoe that making food is her job, because a woman's place is in the kitchen. Jamie was an eighteenth-century Highlander so you might not expect him to hold particularly progressive views, but it was still a very different characterisation to the one we were used to. The Doctor, meanwhile, discusses his 'natural protective instincts towards women', who he refers to as 'the gentle sex'. Other male characters express similar views, such as the prisoner Albert who sings about 'Those dear dead days beyond recall – when women knew their proper place and didn't know-it-all'.

The Doctor explains that the matriarchal dictatorship was 'The inevitable result of giving women the vote. They were bound to take over sooner or later.' Albert agrees, telling him that 'The rot really set in when women got a parliamentary majority.' Previously, *Doctor Who* had frightened viewers by claiming that developments in medical technology would inevitably lead to Cybermen. Now it was claiming that female suffrage and political representation would inevitably lead to the subjugation of men.

From the perspective of the twenty-first century, *The Prison in Space* is an undeniably outdated piece of work. In 1992, however, Sharples remained insistent that it was perfectly acceptable when it was written. 'On re-reading the story, it's amusing to see what was generally deemed humorously acceptable in the sixties, in the days before rampant feminism,' he said. 'If the story was produced today, the Writers Guild Women's Committee would doubtless demand that I be stripped of my [word processor].'

In his script, Sharples described the Dolly Guards outfits in detail. These included belted micro-skirts and black calf-length boots, in a tight black material. The front of the uniform 'could be much more obviously (blatantly) feminine – and show both cleavage and bare midriff, if so desired'. Zoe, who is brainwashed by the matriarchy, ends up wearing this uniform. So too does Jamie, who dons it in an attempt to escape from the titular prison. Jamie is chosen for this cross-dressing escape after the

Doctor argues that, being used to wearing a kilt, he would walk more naturally in a micro-skirt.

By the end of the story, the regime of Chairman Babs has been overthrown. She has fallen hopelessly in love with the Doctor, because his defiance showed her that he was 'A real man. The first real man I've ever met.' Initial talk of equality in this brave new world fizzles out quite quickly. The men take the defeated Dolly Guards to the kitchens 'where they belong', because 'It's about time the lads had a proper meal'. Jamie then has to free Zoe from her brainwashing, which he does by putting her over his knee and spanking her. The script specifies that this should be a 'really hard' spanking. It's a scene which coincidentally echoes the moment that Zoe and Jamie met. Zoe, who was born centuries after Jamie and so was unfamiliar with kilts, laughed at him for wearing 'female garments'. In response, Jamie threatened to put her 'across my knee and larrup ye'. According to the *Prison in Space* script, Zoe comes round after her good spanking, and starts to see sense again. At this point, the TARDIS team continued on to their next adventure.

The Prison in Space was not a vague idea that was kicked around but quickly discarded. It came very close to being made. Scripts were commissioned and accepted, a director was assigned, casting began and work was started on sets and costumes. It was only while the third episode of the preceding story was being filmed that Bryant came to his senses and scrapped it. The story was intended to be a farce, in which Jamie accidentally stumbles into a women's shower room for comedic purposes, and the Doctor is chased by an amorous Chairman Babs. The series had experimented with this story style before, in the Hartnell story *The Romans*. That story also had elements that seem misjudged now, in particular a scene in which the Doctor chuckles to himself about Emperor Nero's attempts to rape a handmaiden, unaware that this handmaiden was really his friend Barbara. *The Romans* did show, however, that the *Doctor Who* format could be stretched sufficiently to accommodate an out-and-out comedy. But by writing a sex comedy Sharples had gone too far. He had discovered the limits to the format.

In theory, the programme was limitless. It could take us to all of time and space. It was a portal to the Otherworld of unfettered imagination, and as such it was more varied and versatile than any other format. It did, however, have one constraint. It could never bore children. It needed to tell stories that engaged the imaginations of its youngest viewers. Children were not the entirety of the programme's audience, of course, which the viewing figures made very clear. The programme could still include adult elements which resonated with older viewers, so long as the story still worked for the little ones. It could tell stories about politics, corruption and mature relationships, provided there was always a monster about to pounce. *The Prison in Space*, in contrast, was entirely about adult concerns. There was nothing in there for children to enjoy, with the possible exception of Frazer Hines's Jamie in a micro-skirt and boots – a treat for all ages. But there were no monsters, aliens or scenes that would grab a child's imagination. It was a failed experiment that served to reveal what the programme wasn't.

7. Call for Help

Change was coming once again. By the end of the sixth season, all the principal cast, the companions as well as Troughton, had decided to leave. So too had the producer and script editor. Ratings had started to decline again, and the quality of the more experimental stories was patchy. Cancelling the series, however, doesn't seem to have been seriously considered, even though it might have seemed justifiable in the circumstances. If the show had ended then, it would have run for six years and 253 episodes, which was highly respectable. *Doctor Who* had created the wild years of Dalekmania, however, and very few TV shows ever had an impact like that. This alone was reason for another roll of the dice. A seventh series would go into production with an all-new cast and production team. It would be recorded in colour for the first time. It would also relax the exhausting pace of nearly one episode recorded every week, by dropping the episode count down to around twenty-six episodes a year. Alongside this, plans were put in place to develop a replacement series, if this new style of *Doctor Who* didn't work out. Few were confident that the series had a long-term future.

This still left the question of how to end the Troughton years. The decision was made to go epic. One final ten-part story was commissioned to round off the sixth series. This huge story was the chrysalis in which the caterpillar of 1960s *Doctor Who* would be transformed into a new, currently unimagined 1970s butterfly. Before he could leave, the series required one final act of change from Patrick Troughton.

This final story was *The War Games*. It took the TARDIS crew through battles across all of Earth's history. For the first time, the Doctor was faced with a situation that he was unable to solve and an adversary that he was unable to defeat. This was unprecedented territory. As the Doctor saw it, he had no choice but to call for help. He telepathically placed his thoughts in a glowing white cube and dispatched it to his home planet. For the first time, he was calling on his own people to rescue him. This was the only way he could free soldiers trapped in a never-ending invented war.

What is remarkable about *The War Games* is the way in which this dramatic plot choice was handled. Beautifully, it removed part of the character's mystery, but it did so in a way that kept him as mysterious as before. Over the previous six years, the programme had gradually settled on the idea that the Doctor was not a human being from the future but an alien from some unknown species. At Troughton's swansong, we were finally told something about his alien nature. The Doctor, it transpired, was a Time Lord. And yet, the story didn't tell you what this meant. It was clearly a grand name, but then a culture that could build a TARDIS was always going to be an impressive one.

We saw three new Time Lords, in matching elegant black-and-white robes. They appeared rather serious and austere, quite unlike the Time Lords we had previously met – The Doctor, the Meddling Monk and, possibly, Susan. We saw them standing in front of a black background and we did not get a good look at their location or their city. We did not learn their names, and we did not discover the name of their home planet. The one thing that did register was their sense of overwhelming power. The Time Lords were portrayed as omnipotent gods, able to exert their will throughout time and space at ease. They were able to end the war games and punish those responsible. They effortlessly wiped the memories of Jamie and Zoe and returned them to their own times, tragically unaware of their travels with the Doctor. Finally, they put the Doctor on trial. He was accused of stealing a TARDIS and breaking the Time Lords' law of non-interference with the rest of the universe. He was quite clearly guilty of these charges, yet they took into account the Doctor's defence – that his 'meddling' was morally justified.

The Time Lords' sentence was to forcibly change the Doctor's appearance and exile him to the backward planet Earth. It was a sentence that doesn't make a huge amount of sense, if you think too long about it. As the Doctor's crime was to interfere with events in the wider universe, it would have made more sense to confine him to his own planet. Changing his appearance was said to be because Troughton's Doctor was already known on Earth, but he was known by very few people, and after being exiled there his new incarnation would soon become known by many. If he was guilty of stealing a TARDIS, it is strange that he did not have that TARDIS taken from him.

The ultimate purpose of the Time Lords' actions came from outside the fiction of *Doctor Who*. The Time Lords acted as they did in order to set up the new format for the returning series. They changed his face because a new actor would soon take on the part. They let him keep the TARDIS because it was too iconic for the series to remove. He was exiled to Earth for reasons of budget and increased location filming, plus the desire to appeal to a broader, more mainstream audience. The nameless Time Lords, then, were the will of the BBC, imposing itself into the fiction of the series.

These godlike beings from a higher plane of existence would return to the programme in the future. Just as in their first appearance, their actions would usually be focused on fulfilling the wishes of the BBC rather than serving the logic of the story, as we shall see. This wasn't a problem, however, and it did not negatively affect those stories. If there is one thing that the long tradition of myth tells us, it is that the actions of higher beings are rarely comprehensible to us poor humans.

So it was that Patrick Troughton, an agent of change both on and off screen, moved on from *Doctor Who* like Eshu walking away from the village. The politics of the real world and the narrative of the fiction combined, acted as one and, for good or ill, changed *Doctor Who* forever.

4
The Action Hero (1970–74)

1. A 'Boy's Own' Feel

Certain stories, such as allegories and parables, have a definitive meaning which can be traced back to the intentions of their author. This intended meaning is so central to the story that it would not make much sense without it. Characters in these kinds of stories tend to be relatively fixed. They need to fulfil their part in the intended narrative and can't be changed too radically. Winston Smith in George Orwell's *Nineteen Eighty-Four*, for example, exists to express Orwell's horror of the nature of totalitarianism. You couldn't take Winston Smith out of that book and use him to help tell a completely different story.

Other fictions, however, are a lot more flexible. The category of fiction loosely classed as 'myth' is an extreme example. Mythic characters can be endlessly reinvented and reinterpreted, in ways that differ wildly from, and may even contradict, their original values. The use of Norse gods like Thor and Loki as Marvel superheroes is an example of this. Another example is King Arthur, who started life as a post-Roman British warrior leader on a doomed quest to defeat Anglo-Saxon invaders. This did not stop medieval and Victorian writers from reinventing him in ways that had little in common with his original ancient Welsh stories. Arthur represents an ideal leader, a useful and flexible concept that different eras can interpret in their own way – in this example, by adding elements of medieval Christian mystery or romantic codes of chivalry. Over the centuries, the character of King Arthur was changed to support the same kind of aristocratic rulers that the original Arthur would have fought to the death.

The Doctor has a similar flexible quality. They are an outsider, an alien who will show you the wonders of the universe and also defeat the monsters. They are a representative of what lies beyond the known world. Like the ideal leader, the Doctor is an archetype who can be placed in endless different stories – a character mythic enough to support regular reinvention.

The move from Patrick Troughton to Jon Pertwee was probably the most radical change in the history of the show. As the 1960s gave way to the 1970s, the programme moved from black-and-white space adventures to Earthbound colour action. The entire cast was replaced, apart from a couple of soldiers, played by Nicholas Courtney and John Levene, who had appeared in Troughton stories but who were now elevated to the regular cast. The downside was that the number of episodes per series fell dramatically, from forty-four in Troughton's final series to twenty-five in Pertwee's first. This was the first significant drop in yearly episode count. It would not be the last.

The Doctor was now exiled to Earth and his knowledge of time travel had been removed by the Time Lords. This made him unable to travel the universe in his TARDIS. Unless, of course, the Time Lords had need of him, in which case the rules of his exile could occasionally be bent. For the production team, this Earth-based focus was a practical decision. It made filming a weekly series easier, meant that they rarely had to build alien worlds, and it allowed them to increase the amount of attractive location filming. They were also, however, discarding a key part of the original format. The Doctor was now more likely to travel in his bright yellow vintage roadster 'Bessie' than in his time machine. The appeal of *Doctor Who* in the 1960s was meeting beloved characters and watching them as they journeyed across time and space. For most of Pertwee's run, we watched beloved characters journey around the Home Counties. To discard the key strength of the format was a shockingly bold creative decision, one as bold as recasting the main character had been three years earlier. That it worked suggests that the Doctor's travels were not the heart of the series. How we humans reacted to the character of the Doctor was what really mattered.

Now that the Doctor was stuck in England, unable to whizz unwary strangers across the cosmos, it became necessary to find new ways to mark him out as different. For the first time, the programme leant into his recently confirmed status as an alien. He spoke vaguely of being several thousands of years old. This was considerably older than the Second Doctor, who told Victoria that he was about 450 years old, in Earth terms. He identified as a Time Lord, not as a human, though we still knew little about what a Time Lord was or where they came from. In his first story, we learn that he did not have human blood and, more strikingly, he had two hearts.

This alien physiology was new. There had been no indication of two hearts when Troughton's Doctor was examined with a stethoscope in *The Wheel in Space* (1968), or when Ian listened to the chest of an unconscious Hartnell's Doctor in *The Edge of Destruction* (1964). Official spin-off media would also refer to his heart as singular, such as the 1966 *Dr Who Annual*, which tells us that 'his heart is big enough to respect every one of the countless forms life has taken in all the ages and all the worlds'. Perhaps the Time Lords altered more than just his external appearance when he was sentenced. In the twenty-first century, the Doctor's two hearts would be used to emphasise his humanity – implying that he loved like we did, only more deeply. But the original idea was intended to imply the opposite and define him as definitely alien.

During his Earthbound exile the Doctor worked as a scientific advisor for UNIT, a military organisation first introduced in *The Invasion* (1968). UNIT's brief was to investigate strange or extra-terrestrial threats. As a result of this army setting, the programme took on more of a 'boy's own' feel, with lots of gunfights, soldiers and explosions. It now required the skills of a regular team of stuntmen, called HAVOC, and relied for the first time on a recurring cast of characters who did not travel with the Doctor, most notably the UNIT officers Brigadier Lethbridge-Stewart, Sergeant Benton and Captain Yates. The Third Doctor's relationship with his military colleagues started off spiky and uncomfortable, but soon softened into something more akin to a family. Rather than travelling the cosmos with a group of up to three others, the Doctor now had one female companion, designated his 'assistant' – a change that would mostly stick for the rest of the 1970s.

When the original producer Verity Lambert looked at the show in the 1970s, she barely recognised it as the same programme she had created. That the Doctor now worked for the military was particularly surprising to her. 'Jon Pertwee was definitely a more straightforward establishment figure,' she argued. 'And for me didn't have the quirkiness.' After a decade on air, the programme had repeatedly ejected what seemed to be its core strengths and had fallen into a cavalier, almost reckless relationship with its past. The hope was that it didn't matter what was dropped – as long as what replaced it had a magic of its own.

2. Pertwee, Jon Pertwee

The Doctor is a role that actors reinvent in their own image. As Jon Pertwee's wife Ingeborg neatly summed up his Doctor, he 'created a flamboyantly dressed character, a dashing, fearless man of action with a love of supersonic gadgets, fast cars, helicopters and speedboats'. It was a portrayal that had little in common with Troughton's Chaplinesque 'cosmic hobo'.

Pertwee's era was influenced by the popularity of secret-agent stories, and in particular the James Bond film series – an appropriate reference for Pertwee, as he had worked in Naval Intelligence during the Second World War alongside Bond's creator Ian Fleming. There have been claims that Pertwee was one of the inspirations for the character of Bond, and he was later considered for the part of Indiana Jones's father in *Indiana Jones and the Last Crusade* (1989), only to lose out to Sean Connery. This heroic image of Pertwee would have sounded absurd during his pre-*Who* career as a broad comedian, when he was best known for the *Carry On* films and radio comedy. Back then he was loved for his skill at silly voices and funny faces, and was not known for heroic alpha-male qualities. *Doctor Who* would repeatedly have great success casting comedians in serious roles, from Catherine Tate to Matt Lucas and John Bishop. Pertwee, like many of the other actors who took on the role, probably would never have been cast as a leading man or hero had it not been for the innate oddness of the Doctor.

Inside the BBC, Pertwee had first been suggested for the part by Peter Bryant, the producer of Patrick Troughton's Doctor from 1967 to 1969. Bryant's initial idea was that the new Doctor should be a song-and-dance man, with songs and comedy being added to the show. Though that idea was soon dropped, Head of Drama

Shaun Sutton was an old friend of Pertwee's from his days as a stage manager in pre-war theatre and he found the suggestion appealing. He knew that Pertwee had other qualities which his broad, crowd-pleasing comedy tended to obscure.

Pertwee served in the Royal Navy during the Second World War. He was an Ordinary Seaman aboard the HMS *Hood* – known to its crew as the Mighty Hood. His transfer to the Naval Intelligence Division in 1941 came as a complete surprise, and also saved his life. It meant that he left the *Hood* a matter of days before it was sunk by the *Bismarck*, killing all but three of the 1,418 men on board. Losing so many friends and colleagues like that 'was a terrible, shocking thing,' he later admitted, 'and I've never really got over it'.

Naval Intelligence suited Pertwee well. 'I did all sorts, [such as] teaching commandos how to use escapology equipment – compasses in brass buttons, secret maps in white cotton handkerchiefs, which only showed when you urinated on them. Pipes you could smoke that also fired a .22 bullet. All sorts of incredible things. Now that suited me perfectly, as I have always loved gadgets.' Pertwee's new role meant that he would join Ian Fleming and sit in on security staff meetings with Winston Churchill himself. He would pocket the prime minister's used cigar butts and sell them to friends afterwards, for a few shillings each.

Like Bond, Pertwee championed dressing well. He was a founder member of the Waistcoat Club, an organisation established to counter the drabness of male clothing. Peter Cushing, who played the Doctor in the two 1960s feature films, was a fellow member. A 1954 British Pathé newsreel shows Pertwee at a gathering of members, wearing an embroidered waistcoat that originally belonged to King George III. The slender Pertwee had had the historic waistcoat cut down to fit. Pertwee was descended from French aristocrats who, like Christopher Lee, traced their lineage back to Charlemagne. His surname was an Anglicisation of 'de Perthuis de Laillevault.'

Pertwee's dandyish attire of velvet jackets, capes and frilly shirts has received approval from Ncuti Gatwa, who in 2023 celebrated what would have been Pertwee's 104th birthday with an Instagram post. Over a particularly stylish-looking photograph of Pertwee as the Doctor wearing a dark blue velvet smoking jacket, light blue ruffled shirt and large bow tie, Gatwa wrote, 'I mean . . . drip UNPARALLELED! 💧'. This message may have initially appeared bewildering to older Whovians, but it was a sentiment they approved of once younger family members had translated it for them. 'I love Jon Pertwee, the Third Doctor's, outfits,' Gatwa told *Rolling Stone*. 'Lovely velvet jackets and frilly shirts. I feel a connection to him. Our Doctors are the only two who dress like sluts.'

In the same interview, Gatwa talked about how he felt a personal connection to the role of the Doctor, declaring that 'I *am* the Doctor. The Doctor is me.' Gatwa's declaration that 'I *am* the Doctor' echoes Jon Pertwee, who used that exact phrase for the title of his final autobiography and as the refrain in a single he released in 1972. The single was quite a notable shift in style from his remarkable 1962 album, the perfectly titled *Jon Pertwee Sings Songs for Vulgar Boatmen*.

Pertwee was offered the role during a lunch with Shaun Sutton. 'All right, I'll have a whirl,' he said after an initial hesitation, 'but I'm very concerned about how I'm going to play it.'

Sutton replied, 'Play it as Jon Pertwee.'

This advice may sound simple, but Pertwee struggled with it. His response was, 'That's very difficult. I don't know what me is.' Pertwee was the type of actor who was drawn to the profession because he felt he lacked a clear sense of himself in real life.

Acting allows people to dress themselves in different identities, and certain actors can feel more real on stage than they do off it.

Among actors, issues with their sense of identity are common, and can have serious consequences. An extreme example occurred in the mid-2010s. The Ninth Doctor, Christopher Eccleston, was hospitalised following a severe mental breakdown after the death of his father and the break-up of his marriage, which impacted on his long-held struggles with body dysmorphia, anorexia and depression. His psychotherapist later told Eccleston that he knew he'd gone beyond his help, because he could see he no longer had a sense of self. As Eccleston later wrote in his autobiography, 'That's a frightening thing to hear.'

The difficulty in bringing your insubstantial sense of self to the role is something that other *Doctor Who* actors have talked about. As Peter Davison has said, 'You have a grand scheme about how your Doctor is going to be an amalgamation of all those previous Doctors plus your own personality. But actually, who knows what your own personality is? I've no idea. That's the one thing as an actor you shy away from.'

By the time Pertwee was recording his second story, his producer Barry Letts thought that Pertwee had found his approach to the part. 'Surprisingly, it was his own personality. The elegance of the dandy, the air of authority and, yes, the charisma, all these were facets of himself.' From Pertwee's perspective, however, the situation was more complicated. After playing the Doctor, Pertwee realised that he had not only found the character – he had discovered himself. As he said, 'I hadn't really found myself before *Dr. Who*. I was always scared of myself.' The act of being the Doctor on camera caused his sense of identity to suddenly click into place both on stage and off. From this point on, Pertwee's identity and that of the Doctor's became, to some extent, inseparable. Here Pertwee was like his successor Tom Baker, who has said, 'It's become part of me and I've become part of it [...] I can't tell the difference between me and Doctor Who.'

Katy Manning, who played Pertwee's companion Jo Grant, has suggested that the reason why the Doctor has two hearts is because one comes from the character, and one comes from the actor playing him. Pertwee was the first actor to play the Doctor with two hearts, so it is fitting that he never stopped identifying as him.

3. The Sea Devil

Fiction and reality blur throughout Jon Pertwee's life. As a child, his playwright father Roland took him to tea at the house of his friend A.A. Milne. It was here that young Jon met Milne's son Christopher Robin, who was dressed in a suit of shining armour. Christopher introduced Jon to his toy animals Piglet, Owl, Kanga, Roo and a teddy bear called Winnie the Pooh. Jon was then given a ride on Eeyore, the family's pet donkey. Later in life, Christopher Robin Milne would also struggle with the way his identity had been merged with a fictional counterpart. It seems right that the Doctor has met Winnie the Pooh and Christopher Robin, yet it is strange to think that it happened in reality, rather than fiction.

A good example of the extent to which Pertwee's life and the role of the Doctor merge into each other is his iconic 1972 *Doctor Who* story *The Sea Devils*, an adventure set around a navy sea base in Portsmouth under attack from an aquatic reptilian invasion force. Here Pertwee's Doctor was at his most Bond-like. He was in the thick of the action, utilising his skill at an otherworldly martial art then called Venusian Karate, and later known as Venusian Aikido, to fight off the invading monsters.

These were the titular Sea Devils, turtle-headed monsters dressed in blue netting who had been sleeping under the ocean since the dawn of time. Like Daleks before them and Haemovores and Marshmen afterwards, they were filmed dramatically emerging from the water – one of the programme's most iconic and distinctive monster reveal shots.

This story was the exact midpoint of Jon Pertwee's five-year run playing the part. It somehow captured not only the essence of his heroic action-hero Doctor, but also the story of Pertwee himself, as if his entire life was compressed into this one shining jewel of a story. Thirty years earlier, Pertwee had been stationed at that exact same naval base in Portsmouth where *The Sea Devils* was filmed. There had also been an episode of his radio comedy *The Navy Lark* titled *Pertwee Posted to Portsmouth*, just to blur the line between fiction and reality a little further. The outfit that Pertwee wore in that story also had echoes of his own past. When he was a student at RADA in the 1930s, he was known as quite an outrageous dandy. He used to carry his father's ivory-knobbed Malacca cane and wore his grandfather's Inverness cape, with a scarlet lining – the same cape he would later utilise as part of his *Doctor Who* outfit. Pertwee loved speed and vehicles in all forms, reflected in the variety of motorbikes, hovercraft, gyrocopters and off-road trikes that his Doctor would drive on screen. In *The Sea Devils*, Pertwee's love of vehicles resulted in a dramatic speedboat chase, along with the use of hovercraft, a diving bell and a submarine.

Back in the 1940s, when he was known as PJX178358 Ordinary Seaman Pertwee, he had risked his life to defend that same naval base, just like the Doctor. An airborne invasion was expected, and a call had gone out to look for enemy parachutists. Pertwee was on fire watch in the attic of G Block when he realised with horror that it was not a German parachute squadron that was falling towards the base – it was parachute mines. With a terrifying crash, an incendiary bomb came through the roof of G Block and landed just in front of him. Thinking quickly, he threw a sandbag on top of it, but it dropped through the attic floor and landed in the hammock nettings in the room below. These ignited and soon the room was an inferno.

Pertwee was halfway down the ladder trying to escape when a second parachute bomb hit the Chiefs and Petty Officers Block opposite. The force of the explosion, as he recounted the situation, 'sucked me off the ladder and dropped me in the actual shell hole, where the bomb had gone off. I was picked up by the rescue squad who naturally assumed that I had been in the building. I had a sort of triangular shaped head and looked very dead indeed. And they put me in the larder of the officers' mess opposite, thinking that I was a corpse.'

When he came to sometime later, the deafened and confused Pertwee turned to the people around him to find out where he was, only to discover that he was locked in a room with a multitude of mutilated dead bodies. He shouted and screamed until someone came in, amazed that he wasn't dead. A similar situation would occur in the Doctor's future, when Paul McGann's newly regenerated Eighth Doctor would also wake up in a morgue, startling the mortuary assistant as he forced his way out.

While Pertwee lay in his hospital bed, recovering from his significant injuries and hazy from morphine, 'an angel flew down out of the sky with a red cross on her bosom'. As he would later recall the incident, 'I was almost deaf from the blast but she somehow got through to me and asked what my name was.' When he told her she burst into tears. The nurse was a girlfriend of his that he had last seen ten days earlier in London. He was so badly injured she had been unable to recognise him.

Although Pertwee had appeared in a long list of films before

Doctor Who, including comedies like *Carry On Screaming!*, *Carry On Cleo* and *A Funny Thing Happened on the Way to the Forum*, he was most famous for being one of the leads in the hit radio comedy *The Navy Lark*, which ran from 1959 to 1977. Pertwee's character was conveniently named Chief Petty Officer Pertwee. He also voiced several minor characters, including one curiously called the Master. During the production of *The Navy Lark*, the scripts were regularly vetted for accuracy and 'suitability' by Commander Mervyn Ellis, a representative from the Admiralty. When Ellis read one potential script concerning an anti-submarine device, he turned white. The fictional device described in the script, he knew, was identical to one of the navy's top-secret weapons. The Admiralty assumed there must have been a leak, so the producer Alastair Scott Johnston was interrogated by security officers. Johnston and the scriptwriter Lawrie Wyman then found themselves being followed around by two intelligence officers in dirty raincoats for the next three weeks.

A strikingly similar incident occurred after the broadcast of *The Sea Devils*. The director Michael E. Briant was in his office at the BBC, when security called and informed him that officers from MI5 had entered the building and wanted to interview him. A surprised Briant met with 'two rather ordinary looking blokes from Naval Intelligence, looking nothing like Sean Connery at all'. They asked him where he got the plans for the nuclear submarine shown in the programme. Briant explained that they had bought a model submarine kit from Woolworths. Visual effects designer Peter Day had bought the plastic submarine from the high-street store, put it together and painted it black. Given the limited effects budget for *Doctor Who*, practical short cuts like this were common.

After departing to investigate the range of model kits available in Woolworths – not the sort of intelligence activity usually depicted in the James Bond films – the MI5 officers returned. They proceeded to interrogate Day about why he had made changes to the model's propeller. Day explained that he had thought that the propeller which came with the kit didn't look very good. As a conscientious and talented effects designer, he had replaced it with something that was visually better. Day's new propeller was actually a part he had taken from the inside of a hoover, but it happened to have the same number of propeller blades as real nuclear submarines. The exact number was top secret, because knowledge of it could be used to calculate the specific sonar signature of the British nuclear fleet. 'By sheer chance,' Briant admitted, 'we'd actually told the world the sonar signal of British nuclear submarines.'

It was a very Jon Pertwee-esque situation, and not just because it involved those great loves of his life – *Doctor Who*, *The Navy Lark*, the sea, Naval Intelligence and vehicles. To be under investigation by the security services for revealing submarine-based national secrets on one of the country's most popular programmes is an unlikely scenario, but when it happens twice it becomes quite farcical. As those involved in real intelligence will admit, the work is often far more absurd and ridiculous than Ian Fleming's fiction suggests. The dashing spy archetype, like any character who takes themselves seriously, is a front that disguises something inherently comedic.

In Pertwee's portrayal of the Doctor, the light-hearted comedian supposedly hidden underneath the earnest action hero remained just about visible. While Matt Smith would later play the Doctor as an ancient soul in a young man's body, Pertwee appeared like a child disguised as an old man. For all his attempts to play the part with deadly seriousness, he could never quite hide the sparkle in his eyes.

4. 'Something for the Dads'

Barry Letts, a former actor from Leicester, was the new producer of *Doctor Who* from 1970 to 1975. He was a thoughtful, sometimes inspired programme maker who benefited greatly from his strong relationship with his script editor, Terrance Dicks. The pair tackled the task of turning the show around with determination and a sense of professionalism that had perhaps been lacking in recent years. 'One of the reasons we were in such a state,' Dicks thought, 'was because [previous production team] Bryant and Sherwin spent as much time in the bar as the production office.'

By reimagining the programme for a contemporary 1970s audience, Letts and Dicks probably contributed more than anyone to the long-term survival of the show. In doing so, they also added 1970s ideas and attitudes to the programme. With the benefit of fifty years of hindsight, those 1970s perspectives are something of a mixed bag.

Like Pertwee, Letts had served in the Royal Navy during the Second World War and was familiar with military stories and characters. He focused the new Earth-based format on the military organisation UNIT, a format change that meant there could be plenty of fist fights, shoot-outs and explosions. In doing so, the programme became skewed more towards boys and men. One consequence of the amount of male military roles in the series was the relative lack of speaking female characters in the stories that followed.

Perhaps because the first producer had been female, *Doctor Who* had originally included strong female characters, such as Barbara and Vicki, who helped the show attract a mixed, family audience. It is true that the male-written scripts did not always give a lot of depth to these characters. It often fell to the actor themselves to bring the part to life, but fortunately that was something that actors such as Maureen O'Brien, who played Vicki, were capable of doing. After 1970, the regular team of characters travelling with the Doctor were typically replaced by one single, attractive woman. This character was described not as the Doctor's friend or equal, but as his assistant, companion or just 'the girl'. They went from being audience identification figures for young and female viewers to being openly described by the production team as 'something for the dads'. When Letts discussed this approach to casting the 'Doctor Who girl' in his autobiography, he justified it by writing, 'Obviously, she had to be attractive (am I being sexist here? No, just pragmatic).'

In the days before the role of showrunner was introduced, the creative responsibility for the programme was shared between the producer and the script editor. After Verity Lambert left, both of those roles remained male for the rest of twentieth-century *Doctor Who*. One hundred and fifty-five stories were produced during that time, but only four female directors were hired. Despite the use of a few female pseudonyms on some scripts, only three female writers are believed to have scripted or co-written episodes. It was not unusual for entire seasons of *Doctor Who* to be made by an entirely male team of writers, producers and directors.

This behind-the-scenes gender imbalance naturally affected the characters depicted on screen. According to the writer Simon Fernandes's 'Doctor Who Bechdel Project', more Jon Pertwee stories fail the Bechdel Test than any other Doctor. The Bechdel Test is considered passed when a story includes two named female characters who have a conversation about something other than a man. This is a blunt tool and something of a low bar, of course, but it is still informative in its way. During the 1960s, about 32 per cent of stories failed the test. During Pertwee's era, that rose to an all-time high of 54.2 per cent. The scores improved noticeably in the late 1980s. The only Sylvester McCoy story to fail the test was *The Greatest Show in the Galaxy* (1988), which failed more for quirks of its structure than because of an absence of interesting female roles. Indeed, the McCoy results are noticeably better than the 21st-century Christopher Eccleston, David Tennant and Matt Smith eras.

When Fernandes analysed the results for different producers, rather than different Doctors, he found that Verity Lambert, unsurprisingly, scored far better than any of her successors. 'What Verity did was launch a brand-new series with two men and two women, a phenomenon for the time,' Russell T Davies has observed. 'She was well ahead of the curve. I'm struggling to think of other series at that time which could equal that.' This on-screen representation masked entrenched sexism in the BBC, however, where there was a widespread belief that Lambert had only got the job by sleeping with her boss Sydney Newman. Both have denied this, and it is implausible that Newman would have given Lambert the job if he hadn't thought she had the rare talent needed to make a success of it. Still, Lambert had to put up with constant belittlement from male colleagues. 'Verity arrived with a great deal of sniggering,' the director Richard Martin has said. 'She had enormous boobs and once, by mistake, I called her "Very-titty" to her face.' As Lambert summed up those days, 'As a woman I did have to work twice as hard. You really had to be good.'

In the 1960s, patriarchal attitudes were so entrenched in British society, and considered so unremarkable by those that subscribed to them, that television drama foregrounded those attitudes relatively rarely. With the growth of the second wave of feminism in the 1970s, however, the patriarchy felt under threat and an openly patronising attitude to women became far more prominent in our culture. If the attitudes shown in contemporary television programmes are any guide, the 1970s witnessed an extraordinary growth in chauvinism. This became more common than in the 1960s, before a notable decline began in the mid-1980s.

It's not that the male production crew were unaware of sexism. It was occasionally addressed on screen. *The Web of Fear* (1968), for example, contains a scene in which the soldier Captain Knight attempts to chat up the scientist Anne Travers. 'What's a girl like you doing in a job like this?' asked Knight. Travers shuts him down by calmly replying, 'Well, when I was a little girl, I thought I'd like to be a scientist. So I became a scientist.' In other stories, however, the sense that sexism was being explained from a male perspective is hard to avoid. The scientist Dr Ruth Ingram in *The Time Monster* (1972), for example, repeatedly complains about how she is treated as a woman in the workplace, only for this to be typically met by eye-rolls from her male colleagues, along with remarks like 'Here we go . . .' After Ingram complains about a 'bland assumption of male superiority', her male colleague dismissively quips, 'May God bless the good ship women's lib and all who sail in her!' In *The Monster of Peladon* (1974), Jon Pertwee's Doctor told his new companion Sarah Jane Smith, played by Elisabeth Sladen, to have a conversation with the Queen of Peladon, because he hoped that Sarah Jane would help the Queen develop a more feminist perspective. As Sladen later wrote, 'The irony of male writers getting a male character to "order" a woman to talk about feminism wasn't lost on me.'

The character of Sarah Jane Smith, probably the most well-loved of all *Doctor Who* companions, was a deliberate attempt to improve the portrayal of women on the show. Sarah was created as an explicitly pro-feminist character with a successful journalism career, but despite this Sladen initially found her working environment difficult. 'As the new girl on the *Doctor Who* set in 1973 I have to admit to initially being intimidated by Jon's off-screen macho bravura,' she wrote. '*Doctor Who* in those days could be a bit of a boys' club, I think it's fair to say.' An extreme example of this 'macho bravura' occurred after she suggested that the bawdy tales Pertwee used to tell about his days at sea weren't always entirely true. 'One day I made the mistake of referring to one of his tall tales when we were both sober,' she wrote in her autobiography. 'That was it – his hand went *smack* across my face! Well, he got a slap straight back.'

The script editor for most of Sladen's stories was Robert Holmes, who was asked in 1978 whether the predominantly male casts of his stories meant that he was against using female characters in *Doctor Who*. 'I suppose it's basically true,' he replied. 'Women don't usually have major roles in action-adventure shows [. . .] it's more difficult to show a woman coming to a sticky end (convention's against it) and as characters in *Doctor Who* are always coming to sticky ends, my feeling is that female characters, generally speaking, have less value.' Attitudes weren't much better in the 1980s, as can be seen from the character description written by John Nathan-Turner for the companion Mel in 1985: 'Melanie is one of those annoying young ladies who is a women's libber at all times, except at moments of great stress when she relies on playing the hard-done-by, downtrodden, crocodile-teared female.' As Janet Fielding, who played the companion Tegan from 1981 to 1984, summed up the culture of the production team, 'Nobody gave a shit about whether girls were watching it or not.'

Such attitudes were far from unusual in the BBC and the broader British culture at the time. Nicola Bryant, who played the companion Peri from 1984 to 1986, recalled her experience of walking around the curved corridors of BBC Broadcasting House, which had wooden swing doors dividing different parts of the building. 'One in three times that I went through a door, someone would pat my behind,' she said. 'That's not the weird bit. The weird bit was that you would turn back and sort of smile as if you were saying "thank you", because you just did not make any trouble.'

Perhaps the most notorious *Doctor Who*-related example of the industry's sexism occurred after Pertwee had left the role. Around 1981 he appeared in character as the Doctor in a corporate video for Zanussi – an Italian manufacturer of kitchen appliances – aimed at kitchen appliance salesmen. The Doctor explained to a nicely dressed couple that he had just returned from the planet Zanussi, and that he had brought back news of a five-year breakdown-cover scheme which the advert existed to promote. 'It's the biggest thing to hit white goods in years!' Pertwee promised the couple as they admired the Zanussi range of washing machines. At the end of the video, the woman approached Pertwee and said, 'Doctor, before you go – one question. Where in the galaxy is Zanussi?' To which the Doctor replied, 'Show us your tits and I'll tell you.' The advert then ended with the Zanussi corporate logo. The video reveals much about attitudes in the British workplace during the late 1970s and early '80s. For anyone who grew up watching Jon Pertwee's *Doctor Who*, and looked up to him as a stylish, confident force for good, it is a very hard thing to watch now.

5. 'The Old Man Must Die'

Increased chauvinism was not the only value that Barry Letts added to the programme in the 1970s. Letts was, in the words of Katy Manning, 'an early eco-warrior', and a story like *The Green Death* (1973) is remarkable for its environmental awareness. While a lot of Patrick Troughton stories were content to be an exciting adventure with monsters, Letts and Terrance Dicks understood that the programme needed to be more than this. Nearly 60 per cent of the audience were adults and somehow they had to keep them interested while also making a programme that worked for children.

Rather than dial down the adventure, imagination and scares, their solution was to inject themes and morally interesting situations. 'No matter what the theme, it would never be up front, lecturing the audience,' Letts wrote, 'but it would be there as a unifying subtext to inform the structure.' Letts's tenure, for example, included stories that thematically criticised apartheid and colonialism. Given his interest in environmentalism, it was perhaps unsurprising that he used this as his theme when he came to co-write the season finale for the tenth series. *The Green Death*, he later said, 'was explicitly planned to call attention (in Who-ish terms) to the pollution that uncaring big business can bring about.'

It was a story that made a lasting impression, not least because of the horrific giant maggots which were the adventure's primary monsters. Constructed from condoms with moulds of fox skulls used for their vicious, sharp mouths, they lingered in the memory, and in nightmares, long after the programme ended. In the story, these giant maggots are first discovered down a coal mine in South Wales, where a chemical company is secretly dumping waste. The Doctor arrives in Wales to investigate the mysterious death of a miner, accompanied by Jo Grant and the Brigadier. They team up with an ecologist, Professor Clifford Jones, who runs a hippy-ish commune officially named the Wholeweal community but locally referred to as the Nut Hutch. Here the staid, establishment figure of the Brigadier discovers a whole range of counterculture ideas. He is amazed, for example, to enjoy a vegetarian meal in which meat has been substituted for mushroom-based protein. At a time when whole aisles in our supermarket are dedicated to similar meat-free foods, it can be hard to recognise just how radical this then was. Environmental ideas rarely made it onto mainstream television back in 1973, and *The Green Death* would have been, for a sizeable part of the audience, their introduction to environmental thought.

That the programme makers approved of these ideas was evident from the portrayal of Professor Jones, a young, idealistic scientist. He had much in common with the Doctor himself, with his natural enthusiasm, intelligence and charm. The main difference between the two was that, rather than adventuring through all of time and space, Jones's priority was the protection of natural life on Earth. The audience could understand, in this context, why Jo Grant decided to leave the Doctor for Professor Jones at the end of the story. The scenes of a stoical, silent Doctor slipping away from the couple's engagement party are some of the most touching and emotional in the original series. Jo adored the Doctor, but she had found a younger, handsome human version of him who managed to be both idealistic and grounded at the same time.

Environmentalism was not the only one of Letts's interests to be added to the programme. Having struggled with Catholicism in his early life, Letts had gone on to become a committed Buddhist and saw no issue with introducing Buddhist thought into the programme, or giving those ideas to the Doctor himself. 'The sort of "religion" that I can find acceptable is one that could be discovered anywhere in the universe, being based on evidence and experience, rather than the interpretation of myth,' he wrote. 'And "anywhere in the universe" would of course include Gallifrey, if it existed.'

The clearest Buddhist impact on *Doctor Who* occurred in the final Jon Pertwee story, which Letts both directed and co-wrote with Robert Sloman. The finale of *Planet of the Spiders* (1974) would see Jon Pertwee regenerate into Tom Baker. Before this story, the concept of regenerating Time Lords did not quite exist as we think of it now.

Planet of the Spiders was the first story to use the word 'regenerate' to describe how one Doctor changed into another. That the word had never been used during the programme's first decade seems surprising, given how central it now is to the format. A change of lead actor was handled differently in the early years, compared to how it is presented now.

The first time regeneration occurred, no real explanation was given for what happened. Hartnell's Doctor complained that his body was 'wearing a bit thin' and then returned to the TARDIS, where he collapsed. At this point, both his body and his clothes changed. In the logic of the story, the change of form appeared to be the strange after-effects of Mondas, the Cybermen's home planet, draining energy from the Doctor. There was no indication that what happened would ever – or could ever – happen again. It was simply a story event that happened for production reasons, rather than plot ones. The series seemed eager to move on from it quickly, rather than lingering to justify or explain it.

The story circumstances that saw Jon Pertwee take over from Patrick Troughton were very different. Troughton's final story saw him tried by his own people, the Time Lords. The Doctor was sentenced to be exiled on Earth, and his knowledge of time travel was removed from his mind. His appearance was also forcibly changed. The reasons for this were never really explained. It was presented as a form of punishment, although being made taller and more dashing does seem an odd form of chastisement. Still, the important point was that it was something which was done *to* him, against his will. It was not something that he did himself.

Ten years into the show, then, the concept of 'regeneration' as we now know it had yet to be used to explain away the recasting of the programme's lead actor. Such an explanation was then far from inevitable. It could have been established that changing faces was always a punishment inflicted on the Doctor. Instead, Letts's interest in Buddhism came to define the process. The Buddhist belief in reincarnation clearly has strong parallels with Time Lord regeneration, but Letts's thinking ran deeper than this.

Planet of the Spiders is partly set in a meditation retreat somewhere in the Home Counties. The story's theme is established in the first episode, when a Tibetan monk called Cho-je explains the purpose of meditation. 'The old man must die and the new man will discover to his inexpressible joy that he has never existed,' he tells Sarah Jane. The first part of this statement appears to be preparing the viewer for the Doctor's coming regeneration, but the rest of Cho-je's words need a little unpacking.

To experience 'inexpressible joy' upon the realisation that you have never existed refers to the Buddhist understanding of the self – or rather, the non-existence of the self. What Letts was referring to with Cho-je's enigmatic dialogue was that recognition of change is fundamental to the Buddhist worldview. We are not the same person at fifty that we were at fifteen, for example. On a physical level, the great majority of the cells that form our bodies will have died and been replaced, often many times. Our opinions, interests and values will be different, and we will physically not look like our younger selves. And yet, we still tell ourselves that we are the same person – an individual who sustains and exists over time. In Buddhist thought, this fixed 'self' is just a delusion created by our mind. It is our ego speaking, and our ego is nothing more than an illusion. The real truth is that nothing is persistent, and that everything changes. Our ego refuses to accept this, however, because to do so would bring the realisation that it isn't real. The resulting struggle is the cause of much of our suffering. The purpose of Buddhist meditation is to transcend the ego, and – as Cho-je was explaining – to realise to your inexpressible joy that the illusory fixed self never really existed.

Cho-je's words are given further meaning when we learn, later in the story, that Cho-je himself doesn't actually exist. He is a mental projection of K'anpo Rimpoche, an old Buddhist abbot who is eventually revealed to be another Time Lord. He was the old hermit who became the Doctor's guru back when he was a boy, long before he stole a TARDIS and ran away from his home planet. K'anpo would also later leave Gallifrey to live peacefully in a Tibetan monastery. Here Letts was expressing his belief that Buddhism was 'universally true' by making Gallifreyan thought essentially Buddhist.

Planet of the Spiders is about the Doctor achieving this realisation. It is not just about this, of course, for it is also a *Doctor Who* story and it needs to excite younger viewers who are, perhaps, less enthused by discussions of Eastern concepts of no-self. As such it features memorable monsters – huge talking spiders from the planet Metebelis Three, who cling to people's backs and promise them power in the material world. On Letts's thematic level, these spiders are the demons of the mind, which seduce us in order to protect and strengthen the ego. The story also has plenty of action. The bulk of episode two is an extended vehicle chase that includes a vintage car, a gyrocopter, the Whomobile, a police car, a hovercraft and a motorboat. There was no profound thematic reason for this, admittedly. It was simply Jon Pertwee's final story, so they wanted to give him the most Pertwee-esque, Bondian send-off they could.

At the finale of the story, the Doctor voluntarily goes into a cave flooded with dangerous radiation, knowing that it will kill him. This is a plot point that doesn't really make a huge amount of sense if it is considered separately to its thematic meaning. He explains his actions by saying that it is more important to face his fears than to go on living, and that he has to atone for his sins. The sin in question was taking a blue crystal from Metebelis Three during a previous visit, long before the spiders had evolved on the planet. Yet on the scale of the Doctor's crimes, taking a crystal from an uninhabited planet must rank very low. It is surely far below stealing a TARDIS or kidnapping Ian and Barbara, and it is in a completely different league to his failure to prevent the Brigadier from blowing up a colony of Silurians. In this context, it doesn't make sense that this particular 'sin' should be sufficient to cause him to voluntarily end his life. But the final episode of Letts's story is operating on the level of spiritual metaphor, rather than simple adventure. By the end of the story, we have left the hovercraft chases a long way behind.

The theft of the crystal from Metebelis Three, the Doctor tells us, was caused by his greed for knowledge and information. His great sin is his pride. This was, historically, often considered the greatest sin of all, and the sin from which all others derive. It was pride that caused Satan's fall from heaven, for example. Pride is the ego believing in its own greatness. Seeing it for the delusion that it is was the Doctor's greatest fear – or more specifically, his ego's greatest fear.

Once inside the radiation-flooded cave, the Doctor encounters the Great One – a spider of giant proportions, giddy with its own immense power. It is able to manipulate the Doctor, causing him to turn in circles like a puppet. The Doctor has come face to face, on a thematic level, with his own ego, the thing that has been controlling him. It demands from him the one thing that it lacks, the perfect blue Metebelis Three crystal that symbolises the Doctor's pride. By surrendering this, the Doctor is symbolically surrendering his greed and pride and divesting himself of the very qualities that the ego needs to survive. This made the crystal fatal to the Great One. As a result, the Great One is destroyed, in the obligatory end-of-story huge explosion. The destruction of his ego, however, meant the end of the Jon Pertwee Doctor also.

The Doctor is saved from this explosion by the TARDIS, which returns him to UNIT headquarters on Earth. It is here that Jon Pertwee collapses to the floor and, in the company of the Brigadier and Sarah Jane and helped by a spiritual visitation from his old guru, regenerates into Tom Baker.

On a surface level, the Doctor has destroyed the tyrannical spiders of Metebelis Three and been injured in the blast. On Letts's thematic and spiritual level, however, he has done far more. He has come face to face with his own ego, surrendered the pride and greed which sustained it, and come to understand it for the illusion that it was. He has seen himself not as a fixed self, but as an expression of eternal change. Reincarnation is then defined as a Buddhist process – not a simple analogy for reincarnation, but as the process of transcending the delusion of the self.

As Cho-je had prophesised at the start of the story, 'The old man must die, and the new man will discover to his inexpressible joy that he has never existed.' No wonder, then, that Tom Baker grinned so wildly as he sat up.

5

The Bohemian Traveller (1975–77)

1. The Monk

The beaming grin on the curly-haired man now dressed in Pertwee's clothes belonged to someone who would, in later life, describe himself as a 'sort of Buddhist'. By this he did not mean that he was a serious student of that religion, like Barry Letts. By the time he became the Doctor, Tom Baker had already suffered a crisis of faith and become deeply irreligious. He meant that, like Jon Pertwee, his sense of identity was ill formed and fragile – or at least it was, when he was not acting. He had, he felt, an 'incomplete personality'. Like Buddhists, he recognised that his sense of self was not fixed and solid. It was defined by change and impermanence.

As a young man, Tom Baker had a deep relationship with faith. He was raised as a Liverpudlian Catholic and was, from an early age, extremely devout. The theatricality, high stakes and inherent drama of the Catholic worldview overwhelmed him as a child in a way that few other things could match. This marked him out as different. As he later recalled, 'Even at the age of eight I was an embarrassment to everyone because of my preoccupation with God.'

At school, Baker failed his eleven-plus exams and was dismissed by his teachers as 'thick'. It seems likely that he was neuro-divergent and lived with some form of undiagnosed disorder. 'All my life I have had learning difficulties and been unable to grasp the point of what everybody else sees clearly,' he has said. Physically, he was a gangly, awkward child, and has claimed that he was already six foot one by the time he was nine years old. Baker is not the most reliable of sources about his own life, given his love of exaggeration and embellishment, but it is true that he was strikingly tall. This was just one of the ways he didn't really fit in with the other boys. He was preoccupied with sin, redemption and death while his classmates were more interested in football, comics and bicycles. As he memorably began chapter one of his autobiography, 'My first ambition was to be an orphan.'

More than anything, Baker wanted to be good. Or, more specifically, he wanted to be seen as good in the eyes of God. His ultimate dream was to be declared a saint. When he left school at the age of fifteen, he entered a monastery, took vows of chastity, poverty and obedience, and became a novice with the Brothers of Religious Instruction of Ploërmel. In the order, he chose a monastic name fitting for a future Doctor Who – Brother Sylvester. As he memorably described his attitude when he arrived in the monastery, he was 'randy for martyrdom'. He lasted six years.

Despite being surrounded by his fellow novices twenty-four hours a day, Baker suffered from feelings of isolation. The forming of friendships or any worldly attachments was strongly discouraged. It was considered unacceptable for novice monks to go round in pairs, so they had to congregate in groups of three or more. This forbidding of friendship was one of the factors that caused Baker to start questioning his beliefs. 'Does He really not want us to have a pal?' he wondered. His previously solid faith began to weaken.

To demonstrate their modest and humble natures, novices were expected to look down at the floor and not at the faces of their fellow monks. On one occasion, Baker inadvertently looked at the face of the novice who sat opposite him at mealtimes. 'He'd been sitting there for at least six months because I recognised a broken button near his throat, but I'd never looked past that broken button and into his face,' he later wrote. 'As I looked at him (in my weakness), I was quite shocked at how beautiful he was [. . .] I longed to lay my head in his lap. I wanted to be in his lovely lap forever.' To Baker's mind, the novice was not only beautiful, but 'interesting, too, in the way I imagined the devil might be interesting if one could only catch a glimpse of him'.

Being modest, humble and obedient was difficult for Tom Baker. He suffered from intrusive thoughts, such as his desire to break the silence of the breakfast hall by suddenly standing up and shouting, 'Everybody get his dick out!' He developed an intense desire to break every one of the ten commandments, and found that his resentment of monks in positions of authority gradually coalesced into outright hatred. Initially, he was gripped by the desire to kick them. It is tempting to see his struggles with those urges as the inspiration for the morbid and disturbing children's book he wrote in 1999, *The Boy Who Kicked Pigs*.

The more Baker tried to ignore his intrusive thoughts, the more powerful and darker they became. Eventually he found himself contemplating killing the older monks. Troubled by these thoughts, he confessed them to a visiting brother, Father Bernal. A lengthy discussion about his fading faith followed, and Father Bernal came to the conclusion that Baker was not cut out for monastic life. Baker's admission that he had put rabbit droppings in the soup a couple of days earlier was no doubt a factor. Baker was taken to the train station, given four pounds and abandoned. He was now alone in the civilian world. Although he found much to enjoy in his new-found ability to commit sins, he would never shake the feeling that, by losing his faith, he was in some way a failure.

Baker was claimed by another form of institution shortly afterwards, when he was called up for national service. He desperately hoped to find the friendships that he had so longed for in the monastery but, having lived in near silence for six years, he lacked the social skills to fit in with army banter. He never did find the friend he hoped for. 'I think, looking back, I tried too hard,' he later wrote, 'and though people quite liked me, there was something about me that also disgusted them.'

Yet for all his social difficulties, Baker discovered that he did have the ability to project incredible charisma and charm. He was different to other people, and standing out could be an asset if he pursued a career as an actor. After his national service he enrolled at the Rose Bruford College of Speech and Drama. After all his difficulties fitting into school, monastic life and the army, he had finally found a life that he was suited to.

Baker may not have been able to connect with people on an equal level, but he could perform at them. 'Actors don't have friends,' he would later say. 'They have acquaintances.' This isn't to say that he was unsocial. To compensate for his inability to chat, he would entertain. He was a great storyteller and raconteur. 'I think that to be a good actor you have to prefer strangers,' he later wrote. By 'strangers', he meant the audience. The people you performed for were more important than people that you knew. 'I'm afraid I have no gift for friendship,' he admitted, 'I quickly get tired of people and off they go.' Tom Baker always struggled to grasp how a genuine long-lasting deep-rooted relationship worked, but the fleeting approval of an audience was something he understood immediately.

While at drama school, Baker met his fellow student Anna

Wheatcroft and in 1961 the pair married. Baker worked a series of odd jobs to support his new wife, but his lack of wealth caused Wheatcroft's wealthy family to look down on him, and to refer to him as a burden. The couple had two children together, but divorced after five years. Baker's mental health grew increasingly poor during the marriage, as he struggled with the guilt he felt over his loss of faith, his inability to start a career, his failing marriage and a period of impotence. He began stockpiling his father-in-law's anti-depression tablets, in the belief that taking an overdose of those pills would cause him to die happy. He did not leave a suicide note, but just swallowed the lot in the late afternoon when he knew no one would return to the house for many hours. He grew drowsy and blacked out, before waking half an hour later, severely constipated but otherwise unharmed.

Baker didn't hide his demons or his strangeness. He was able to talk about them in an entertaining way that delighted people rather than disturbed them. In a *Sunday Times* interview from 1978, conducted while he was still playing the Doctor, he talked about starting his day waking up in a strange room in Soho, not knowing where he was. It was an article that he tried to hide from his partner Marianne, after it was published. 'I was hit by terrible waves of anxiety,' he recalled in the article. 'The feeling of loneliness that smacks of self-pity [. . .] The anxiety persisted and I thought suicide is the answer. I got out of bed and looked at some electrical flex. The ceiling was too low. How could I have hanged myself in a room only 5ft. 10in. high?' It's hard to imagine any present-day Doctor speaking in this way to the press. The interview should have rung alarm bells concerning Baker's mental health, but instead it was interpreted as Tom being outrageous and hilarious. It still regularly does the rounds of social media to this day, where it is seen as an example of why people love Tom Baker so dearly.

In the late 1960s, he started to get work as an actor. He played a number of small roles at the National Theatre, in part because he amused Laurence Olivier. These led first to small television parts and then to films. Acting was a way of putting aside all his own problems and becoming someone else. That character would experience their own difficulties, of course, but those were the concern of the writer, not the actor, so they didn't trouble Baker unduly. 'All my life I have felt myself to be on the edge of things,' he wrote. 'All my life I have suffered from bad dreams. All my life I have had difficulty in knowing whether I am awake or in a nightmare [. . .] It is only in the enclosed asylum of a play that I have any assurance at all, and then not much. So, naturally, I have evolved a strategy of always being in a play.'

Roles in films like *The Golden Voyage of Sinbad* (1973) and *Nicholas and Alexandra* (1971), in which he played Rasputin, helped to increase his profile, but he was still having trouble making a living. Like many actors, he fell back on part-time manual work to get by. A combination of heartbreak from another failed relationship, illness and periods of poverty pushed him into a deep depression. During 1973 he was very fragile and, as he wrote in his autobiography, 'I kept bursting into tears and once I deliberately cut myself deeply in my left breast.'

Tom Baker was saved by the arrival of *Doctor Who* in his life at this point. It's not only in fiction that this happens.

2. 'I Was the Doctor and the Doctor Was Me'

Baker was working as a labourer on a building site when he was cast as the fourth Doctor Who. This was still considered sufficiently unusual that publicity shots were taken of him making tea for the rest of the workers on the site, which were then printed in the *Daily Express*.

Barry Letts's decision to cast Baker to replace Pertwee was one of the truly inspired decisions in *Doctor Who* history. Baker may have had considerably less experience than any of his predecessors, but it was immediately apparent that this was the role he had been born for. Baker had the ability to seem utterly alien and absolutely lovely at the same time. He grew the strong audience figures that Pertwee had built up and brought the programme into its second Golden Age. The mid-seventies was a period in which the programme transcended the children's or science fiction audience, just like the Dalekmania period of 1965. It became a shared reference, and a bedrock of British culture.

Baker was, and remains to this day, the longest-serving on-screen Doctor. He played the part for seven seasons, which is longer than the Sixth, Seventh, Eighth and Ninth Doctors combined. His long service means that he was the first Doctor for a larger cohort of children than any of the other Doctors. This demographic bump helped to make him – for the next thirty years, at least – the archetypal Doctor Who in the public imagination. His carefree, bohemian dress redefined him, separating him once again from the establishment, and his overlong stripey scarf became as much an icon of the show as the TARDIS and Daleks. More significantly, this evolution fundamentally changed the motivation and identity of the character. The Doctor was no longer an exile, or a wanderer with no agency over their fate. For the first time, he was not a victim of events outside his control. Instead, he became an intentional, joyful and carefree traveller. As he explained himself in *The Nightmare of Eden*, 'I don't work for anybody. I'm just having fun.'

During the Pertwee years, the extended guest cast became much-loved recurring characters. Because of the chemistry and the close relationship between both the actors and the characters they played, they became affectionately known as the 'UNIT family'. The Third Doctor's relationships with this group ensured that, after the Time Lords had lifted his exile, he still stayed on Earth. As soon as he regenerated into Tom Baker, however, he couldn't wait to get away. Had it not been for a security scare caused by a sentient robot, the Doctor would have left them all behind at the start of his first episode, without saying goodbye or giving them a second thought. This was also what Tom Baker would have done.

'I didn't consciously try to be different from Jon,' Baker has said, 'because I didn't know anything about the series. I was younger, of course – but, having been brought up a Catholic, the idea of disappearing and reappearing, of miraculous events, strange voices and all the other mad things about *Doctor Who* seemed totally natural to me.' From the start, Baker seeded aspects of his unusual personality into the character of the Doctor, just as his predecessors had done. Baker was a sociable loner. He showed great interest in people, but not over an extended period of time. Acting had turned the lonely monk into a transient professional who wandered from job to job without putting down roots or developing emotional ties. It was a lifestyle that worked for him. The pleasure Baker took in this impermanent and evanescent existence transferred seamlessly to the heroic time traveller as he left Earth behind and actively travelled.

When *Doctor Who* started, Hartnell's Doctor was extremely touchy over any suggestion that he could not control the TARDIS. The question of whether the machine was malfunctioning, or whether the Doctor was simply unable to pilot it, remained an open one. During Troughton's years, it was finally confirmed that he was unable to operate his ship, and that the travellers had no control over where it would take them next. For much of

Pertwee's era, the TARDIS was unable to even leave Earth. With Baker at the helm, for the first time the Doctor could take charge and intentionally fly the TARDIS from one place to another. He did not always get it right, of course, for the TARDIS was still temperamental when it suited the scriptwriters. But – in theory at least – the Doctor was finally in control of his destiny and exploring the universe out of choice.

A great strength of the early Baker years was the rapport he struck up with Elisabeth Sladen, who had remained with the show in the role of Sarah Jane Smith. The Doctor and Sarah were already established as great friends, so her presence in the series gave Baker the pal he had always wanted. In *The Seeds of Doom* (1976), the Doctor introduces Sarah to a villain by saying, 'Have you met Miss Smith? She's my best friend!' This ad lib by Baker perfectly captured the relationship between the two characters.

Baker and Sladen clearly adored each other. 'Tom has such an energy, a genuine impish delight in the absurd; always playful, always alert to the possibility of a punchline – a treasure,' Sladen has said. 'He's one of the funniest people that I've ever met.' This is not to say that the pair had the easy, natural friendship that is common between ex-Doctors and their companions, such as Sylvester McCoy and Sophie Aldred, or David Tennant and Catherine Tate. Those are deeper relationships that go beyond the category of typical 'actor friendships', but Baker never did manage to maintain relationships on that level. Sladen recalled that, 'We were so unused to seeing each other outside of the BBC's walls that on the rare occasions when we did bump into each other it got quite awkward.' She recalled once running into Baker and his partner Marianne on Regent Street, at which point Baker tried to buy her a pint of Guinness and a fur coat, rather than casually chatting like a normal person would.

The Doctor was, Baker knew, the best role that he would ever have. It made him famous, and loved. It also opened up British society to him in a way few other roles could. As the children's hero who all adults loved, he found he was able to go anywhere in the country and be accepted. On one occasion in November 1976, Baker was returning from the *Doctor Who* exhibition in Blackpool, accompanied by Terry Sampson from the BBC promotions department, when he decided that he wanted to watch the episode of *Doctor Who* that was just about to be broadcast. Having failed to find a television shop willing to remain open to watch the programme, he knocked on the door of a random house and asked the surprised homeowner if he could come in and watch *Doctor Who* with them. In the house was a father who was indeed about to watch *Doctor Who* with his two young children. Tom Baker was welcomed in.

Baker entered the living room and sat quietly as the two children sat glued to the television. 'They watched with terrific intensity as a bit of the drama unrolled,' he recalled, 'and then, as someone else took up the plot, they lost interest slightly and glanced up at their dad and then at me. Just as they did so, I reappeared on the screen and they looked at me there. Their amazement was simply amazing! They were utterly gobsmacked as the two images jostled in their heads. They could not grasp how I could be in two places at once and then, to the delight of their dad, they couldn't believe Doctor Who was in their house. What a wonderful hour or so that was.'

Like Jon Pertwee, Baker found himself unable to untangle the role from what passed as his sense of self. 'I began to get into the part and then the part got into me and oh! I was the Doctor and the Doctor was me. From then on, we were one. I could do nothing else.' By becoming Doctor Who, Baker was overjoyed to find that he was now universally loved and accepted. Being a children's hero had put him in a unique position. The Doctor was recognised everywhere as a force for good. Tom Baker may have failed to become a saint, but becoming the Doctor more than made up for that.

3. 'He Liked Doing What He Did'

The episode that Tom Baker watched in the house of a stranger, part three of *The Deadly Assassin*, was not a normal, everyday episode. It was one that, both intentionally and unintentionally, would change the course of *Doctor Who* forever. It is telling that Baker thought it was important to watch.

In 1976, after three and a half exhausting years, Elisabeth Sladen decided to leave the show. Baker was greatly saddened by this. He thought Sladen was irreplaceable and didn't want to work with another companion. It would be better, he told the production team, if the Doctor travelled through time and space alone. Or possibly, he suggested, with a talking cabbage. The talking cabbage idea was not taken seriously, and the production team knew that the show would not work without another recurring character – not least because the Doctor would have nobody to talk to or explain what was happening to. But perhaps one story with the Doctor travelling alone couldn't hurt? If nothing else, it might demonstrate to Tom why he needed a co-star.

The companionless story that followed Sladen's departure comes roughly halfway through the original series. In many ways, it is the story upon which the classic series pivots. The Doctor's past had been kept a mystery for the first thirteen years of the show. Now we were about to see his home planet and learn about his background. We were about to lose mystery; in return, we would be given lore.

The Deadly Assassin was heavily inspired by Richard Condon's psychological political thriller *The Manchurian Candidate*. The Doctor travels alone to his home planet of Gallifrey in order to stop the assassination of the President of the Time Lords, only to seemingly carry out the murder himself. Tonally, it was surreal and paranoid, with a cynical view of establishment power. It fitted in well with the mid-to-late 1970s zeitgeist, but it was very unusual for *Doctor Who*. Tom Baker was only briefly dressed in his regular costume and spent most of the story without his long scarf, which was so unusual it was immediately unsettling. Uniquely, the episode began with portentous scrolling text. 'Through the millennia, the Time Lords of Gallifrey led a life of peace and ordered calm, protected from all threats from lesser civilisations by their great power,' it began. 'But this was to change. Suddenly and terribly, the Time Lords faced the most dangerous crisis in their long history.' This was a year before the first *Star Wars* movie opened, which would also begin with similar scrolling text – another example of how often the series either mirrored wider culture or was slightly ahead of the curve.

The Deadly Assassin was written by Robert Holmes, perhaps the most revered of all the original series writers. Holmes's huge contribution to the series saw him writing for the Second, Third, Fourth, Fifth and Sixth Doctors. His stories introduced the Master, Sontarans, Autons, Romana, Jo Grant, Sarah Jane Smith and the Third Doctor. It was Holmes who named the planet Gallifrey, gave the Doctor two hearts and, in *The Deadly Assassin*, decided that Time Lords could only regenerate twelve times. More importantly, Holmes was a gifted storyteller with an exceptional ear for dialogue. In a 2007 *Daily Telegraph* interview, Russell T Davies urged the interviewer to watch the first episode of Holmes's 1977 *Doctor Who* story *The Talons of Weng-Chiang*. 'It's the best dialogue ever written. It's up there with Dennis Potter. By a man called Robert Holmes. When the history of television drama comes to be written, Robert Holmes won't be remembered at all because he only wrote genre stuff. And that, I reckon, is a real tragedy.'

In the opinion of Barry Letts, 'Bob suffered, as they say – this terrible cant expression – from low self-esteem. Which was surprising, for a man who was as assertive as he was. He didn't realise how good he was.' This opinion was seconded by the writer and script editor Terrance Dicks. 'I think the thing about Bob was that he never really appreciated how good he was,' Dicks observed. 'He limited himself. He would say, "Okay, I'm just a hack scriptwriter, I take the job that comes along."' When it was suggested that he consider writing for more prestigious series like *The Wednesday Play*, he 'sort of pooh-poohed the whole thing. "I'm not one of your superior cultural writers, I do *Doctor Who*, or the latest cop show, or whatever's going," he would say.'

Holmes's background and values were strikingly different to the Oxbridge culture which was so prominent at the BBC. Born in Tring, Hertfordshire, he left school in 1942 and lied about his age in order to join the army, which he entered at the age of sixteen and a half. He claimed that the Commission Board realised his deceit, but were impressed by it. According to Terrance Dicks, 'Some old General on the Board said, "Well done, my boy – I did the same thing myself in 1914!"' and signed him up regardless. In this way Holmes became, according to Dicks, the youngest commissioned officer in the British Army. After the war he worked as a policeman, before moving from journalism and magazine editing to writing for television. His values were that of a talented craftsman, for whom doing a job well drove him more than a desire for status. Such an attitude was unusual at the BBC at the time, and many interpreted it as a lack of ambition rather than a challenge to their own values. 'I don't think there is a much better class of television than *Doctor Who*, but [Holmes] could have done more serious things, or had a different sort of reputation if he wanted to,' said Dicks. 'But he didn't. He liked doing what he did.'

In *The Deadly Assassin*, Holmes took the Doctor to Gallifrey for an adventure with his own people, the Time Lords. This was only the third time that they had appeared in the programme, and once again they were depicted as entirely male and living on a female-free planet. Given the Doctor was not travelling with a female companion, there is not a single woman on screen in the entire story.

In other aspects, however, Holmes's script portrays the Time Lords as strikingly different to the awe-inspiring omniscient space gods of their earlier appearances. He thought the original Time Lords 'were a snooty, too-good-to-be-true lot', so he decided to change them. In his story, untold millennia of prestige and power have turned them into arrogant, pompous relics, cut off from the realities of the universe and absorbed in their own empty self-importance. We now see them as ancient and doddery, complaining of difficulties with their hearing and trouble with their hips. For all that the plot pointed towards American politics, Holmes reinvented Gallifrey as Space Oxbridge. Gallifreyan society was divided into academia-style chapters, and the Time Lords casually talked about tutors and classmates as if they had never left school or embarked on their adult lives. 'People have often asked whether I based the Time Lord society on religious grounds, rather like the Vatican with Cardinals etc.,' Holmes later explained, 'but I saw it as more scholastic. I mean you have colleges of learning with Deans and all that.'

As we noted earlier, the Time Lords occupied a unique position in the fiction of *Doctor Who*. Outside of the programme's narrative, their inclusion in stories was a way for the BBC to alter the nature of the series. They first appeared when the programme makers wanted to replace Patrick Troughton with Jon Pertwee and base the series on Earth, and needed a way to make this plausible. When the series had reached its tenth anniversary, the producers wanted to celebrate by bringing Hartnell and Troughton back to share a story with Pertwee. Since this was beyond the established rules of the fiction, it was necessary for the Time Lords to step in so they could give the scenario some form of plausible justification. The Time Lords were the BBC itself, pressing itself into the fiction of *Doctor Who* and shaping the programme to its own ends. That identification, as we shall see, would become most explicit in the mid-1980s.

In this context, Holmes's mocking of the Time Lords reveals a lot about his views concerning the BBC and its culture. When Holmes arrived at the BBC, he found a corporate culture that was, to his outsider's perspective, often blind to its absurdities. Many at the BBC saw themselves not unlike the original depiction of the Time Lords – as a powerful benevolent elite worthy of the utmost respect. To outsiders like Holmes, this self-image could only seem delusional and foolish, which was how he portrayed the Time Lords of Gallifrey. To his writer's imagination, BBC culture was a rich source for absurdist material.

Holmes had a history of hiding his thoughts on the BBC within scripts. His 1977 *Doctor Who* story *The Sun Makers*, for example, is typically interpreted as an attack on the Inland Revenue, but he revealed its true meaning to its star Louise Jameson. 'The story is that it was about the tax man,' she said, 'but actually I have it on first-hand authority that it was actually about the BBC.' An earlier story by Holmes, *Carnival of Monsters* (1973), is a meta-commentary on *Doctor Who* itself. It features a flamboyant, strangely dressed alien called Vorg, who travels the universe with his much younger attractive female assistant and a strange machine, which is bigger on the inside and which he doesn't really know how to operate. Vorg's machine was called a miniscope, and it entertains young people by showing them thrilling scenes of monsters. Vorg and his assistant, however, attract the ire of grey-faced bureaucrats, who feel that their monster show is a bad influence on its audience. 'Our purpose is to amuse, simply to amuse. Nothing serious, nothing political,' protests Vorg, justifying his scarier monsters on the grounds that they were 'great favourites with the children, you know, with their gnashing and snapping and tearing at each other!'

Carnival of Monsters was written after the press had attacked Holmes's previous story, *Terror of the Autons* (1971), on the grounds that it was too frightening for children. The debate had even reached the Houses of Parliament. In a February 1971 debate on mass-media communication in the House of Lords, Baroness Bacon asked, 'I wonder what has happened to *Doctor Who* recently, because many children must have gone to bed and had nightmares after seeing the recent episodes.' Given this, it is hard not to suspect that Holmes wrote *Carnival of Monsters* as a deliberate commentary on *Doctor Who* and its critics. As his biographer Richard Molesworth notes, if this was the case, 'it seems that by being hidden in plain sight in his script, it went completely unnoticed by the cast and crew'. Given Holmes's sense of humour, it is tempting to imagine him enjoying this situation immensely.

In *The Deadly Assassin*, Holmes's script gave the Time Lords a computer system, containing the sum of all Time Lord knowledge, which took the form of a virtual world called the Matrix. This idea is a familiar one to us now, thanks to the somewhat shamelessly named 1999 movie *The Matrix*, yet it was a radical concept to put before a mainstream television audience in 1976. The Doctor enters the Matrix and discovers a virtual world that feels just as convincing as reality. Here he is chased, attacked and hunted by a variety of beasts and by one of the story's villains. It is exciting, nightmarish and imaginative. The Matrix, in other words, is very much like an episode of *Doctor Who*. If the Time Lords are a reflection of the BBC, then it is only logical that they would also possess the ability to create *Doctor Who* episodes – because that's what the real BBC does. The Time Lords, like the BBC, recognise the importance of creating a good story. As the Time Lord Cardinal Borusa says, 'If heroes don't exist, it is necessary to invent them.'

If Holmes did consciously introduce a version of the programme into its own fiction in the form of the miniscope, then the idea that he did it again in the form of the Matrix seems plausible. Indeed, it would also explain why such a strange idea was used in the first place, because it really doesn't follow logically or thematically from the rest of the *Manchurian Candidate*-style plot. That Holmes's Oxbridge-style Gallifrey is a dig at the BBC's heavily Oxbridge culture was entirely in keeping with his sense of humour. Holmes was, after all, revealing the Doctor's origins, and the Doctor could only have come from the BBC.

4. 'Teatime Brutality for Tots'

When producer Philip Hinchcliffe and script editor Robert Holmes took over from Terrance Dicks and Barry Letts, they naturally looked for ways to grow and improve the show. 'The programme was already being watched by, probably, the maximum number of younger viewers that could be attracted to it,' Holmes said. 'So we set out to try and make it popular with the family audience.' As Hinchcliffe explained, 'I had decided, and Bob agreed, that we would try to make *Doctor Who* appeal a little bit more to adult viewers, to make it a bit grittier and stronger in the areas where it was performing more as a children's adventure story.' While the programme remained the lurid, monster-filled romp of the Pertwee years, the new team put more emphasis on character, drama and dialogue. The stories became darker and scarier, edging closer to the world of horror.

For this, they would attract criticism. Not from the general audience, who flocked to the programme in record numbers, but from the press and campaigning groups who became increasingly critical of a show they now considered traumatising for young children.

Questions about the suitability of *Doctor Who* had plagued the programme from the very beginning. An early episode in 1964 which showed Susan threatening Ian with a pair of scissors caused a great deal of internal BBC problems. It clearly broke the rules against household objects being used as weapons in programmes aimed at young audiences. The production team accepted that this was a mistake, and the incident was seen as a sign of their inexperience. In July 1965 Verity Lambert was invited onto BBC Two's *Late Night Line-Up* programme to discuss whether *Doctor Who* was too frightening for children. Her fellow guest was Nigel Kneale, the writer and creator of *Quatermass*, who argued strongly that *Doctor Who* was irresponsible and unsuitable for young children. Kneale never warmed to *Doctor Who* and sadly never accepted any approach to write for it. Given the extent to which the series would shamelessly plunder Kneale's ideas and stories over the years, his antagonism to the show was perhaps not surprising.

More problematic for the BBC, however, were external attacks, particularly from Mary Whitehouse's National Viewers' and Listeners' Association. Whitehouse was a Christian campaigner who had criticised the programme since the days of Dalekmania. This was part of her general campaign against the BBC and its 'propaganda of disbelief, doubt and dirt [. . .] promiscuity, infidelity and drinking'. In Whitehouse's opinion, the BBC's then Director General Sir Hugh Carleton Greene was 'the devil incarnate'. Her complaints against *Doctor Who* increased in the early Tom Baker years, as the programme became more successful, and Hinchcliffe and Holmes moved the programme more towards gothic horror. She memorably described *Genesis of the Daleks* (1975) as 'teatime brutality for tots'.

The debate about acceptable levels of violence in children's programmes came to a head over *The Deadly Assassin*. It was certainly a brutal and horrific production. It saw the return of Pertwee's nemesis the Master, who had not appeared in the programme since the tragic death of Roger Delgado in a car crash in 1973. The character was now presented as a rotting, glistening, skinless corpse. His face was essentially a skull, except for two large bulging eyes. The Master had used up all his regenerations, but his hatred kept him alive, in constant pain. As Holmes's biographer Richard Molesworth notes, 'It has to be said, both Bob and Hinchcliffe were starting to give critics such as Mary Whitehouse and the NVLA a fair amount of ammunition.'

Yet it was the Doctor's adventures in the Matrix which proved to be too violent for the public decency campaigner. 'I write, in anger and despair, following last Saturday's episode,' Whitehouse wrote in another letter of complaint to the BBC, referring here to the finale of the third episode. This was set in the Matrix and featured the Doctor and a hunter fighting for their lives in a misty lake. The fight sequence was shot in a brutal, savage style, and ended with the Doctor being held underwater and drowned. In Whitehouse's mind, this was a 'sequence that could only have been described as sadistic'. As she later said, 'I think it's extraordinary that people with the brilliance, in many ways, to make a programme of that kind, couldn't have extended their awareness, not only to their cameras and all the rest of it, but to the effect of what they were doing upon the children who were receiving it. That was almost as if they were a bit... dumb.'

Hinchcliffe did indeed worry about what level of violence was suitable for the programme, and what would be acceptable to the general viewer. It was just that his conclusions differed from those of Whitehouse. 'I felt that the drowning sequence, the cliffhanger, was perfectly acceptable, as far as we took it,' he said later. Tom Baker, however, felt enough concern about this sequence that he knocked on a stranger's door and asked if he could watch that particular episode go out. 'In *The Deadly Assassin* there was a scene where I was being held under water and where I had to appear genuinely afraid of death,' he recalled. 'It wasn't too hard for me to do this because I really am very afraid of water and I suppose this fear made me overdo the terror. [Director] David Maloney said it was very powerful and this made me faintly ill at ease.'

Whitehouse's letter provoked a defensive response from the BBC Director General Charles Curran. 'I am indeed aware of the previous letters that you and your association have written about "Dr Who",' he wrote. 'In general I have been rather out of sympathy with them, and I think that this has been the view of a very large section of the public.' Curran proceeded to accuse Whitehouse and her viewing panel of failing to have understood the programme, and in particular the concept of that Gallifreyan show within the show, the Matrix. She had not realised, Curran argued, that the violence she objected to was a dream sequence. 'This particular adventure is extremely popular and being watched by a very large number of viewers, millions of whom seem to understand the conventions of the programme,' he cuttingly added. The rest of the audience, Curran was telling her, understood that what they were watching wasn't real.

Despite this official show of support, Whitehouse's attacks did trouble the BBC. British society had changed radically since *Doctor Who* first appeared, and it was a constant challenge for the corporation to balance the views of permissive and traditional viewers. As Hinchcliffe notes, 'There was a slightly febrile atmosphere within the BBC as a whole, I think, about violence and how graphic you could be.' The BBC tradition of bending to attacks, rather than arguing for the work that programme makers were doing, would ultimately result in Hinchcliffe being turned into a scapegoat. Although he had previously informed his boss, Bill Slater, of his intention to stay on and produce the next series of *Doctor Who*, Slater took the decision to remove him from the programme. Hinchcliffe found himself swapping jobs against his will with the new producer Graham Williams, who had previously been in charge of the police show *Target*.

Williams was given clear guidance about how he was to shape the programme. During his time on *Doctor Who*, he later recalled, he worked under 'one of the strongest dictates I ever had: that the violence for which the show had been so heavily criticised the year before I took over had to be got rid of in no uncertain terms'. Or to put it another way, he was to no longer do the things that Hinchcliffe and Holmes did that made the show beloved and extraordinarily successful.

Doctor Who had changed many times by this point, of course, but those changes had always come from within. They were the production team shaping the series to keep it fresh and contemporary. This was a change imposed from the outside, for political reasons. It was an attack, and it knocked the show off its stride. This is not to say that the changes Williams made were unpopular. To make the show more child-friendly, for example, he introduced a robot dog called K-9. Serious science fiction enthusiasts, older viewers and the growing *Who* fandom may have rolled their eyes at this, yet the young and the young at heart loved K-9. In the late 1970s, he was as much an icon of the show as the TARDIS, Daleks or Baker's overlong scarf.

The Hinchcliffe and Holmes era had been remarkably consistent and strong. There are many who still consider it the gold standard for the series, and the premature removal of Hinchcliffe is something that, with hindsight, can be seen as a great loss. It marks the point when the programme started to change from something that was fairly universally respected, to something that could at times be seen as a bit of a joke. Such was the extent of the fallout from the episode which Tom Baker watched in the living room of those two delighted young fans. It is significant that this occurred when the Doctor finally returned home, and lost part of his mystery. A collision with the Time Lords rarely leaves the Doctor unchanged.

6

The Tom Baker Show (1978–81)

1. 'What Has Happened to the Magic of *Doctor Who*?'

The Deadly Assassin also triggered another attack on the series. This came from a more unexpected source – the world of *Doctor Who* fans. The 1970s saw the rise of organised fandom, a movement of people who came together to share information and enthusiasm about the show. They were driven by an awareness that the show had bewitched them in a way that they couldn't quite understand, but wanted to explore. Trying to define what it is that you love, however, can bring what you don't like into focus, and fans can hate and attack their interests as fervently as they celebrate them.

The Deadly Assassin was roundly condemned in the first edition of the fanzine *TARDIS 77* by Jan Vincent-Rudzki, president of the Doctor Who Appreciation Society. His review ran for three and a half scathing pages and concluded, 'Once, Time Lords were all-powerful, awe-inspiring, capable of imprisoning planets forever in force fields, defenders of truth and good (when called in). NOW they are petty, squabbling, feeble-minded, doddery old fools... WHAT HAS HAPPENED TO THE MAGIC OF DOCTOR WHO?' The message was simple: the people making *Doctor Who* were doing it wrong, and they needed fandom to correct them. The despairing histrionic tone would become familiar to those in *Who* fandom over the coming decades.

Holmes had believed that he was free to reimagine the Doctor's origins to create an exciting, entertaining story. Honouring the integrity of earlier episodes didn't hugely factor into this. *Doctor Who* stories had, after all, been ephemeral. They were shown once and, because of union rules, rarely repeated. Before the BBC changed its archiving policy in 1978, tapes of old episodes were routinely destroyed, after their potential for overseas sales had ended. Continuity became, as Terrance Dicks has explained, whatever it was that people could remember on any particular day. Writers were not confined by what had happened years earlier, because there was no expectation that the viewing audience would remember it. For this reason, the home planet of the Cybermen was Mondas except when it was Telos, and the Daleks were genetically engineered from people called Dals, until they became Kaleds, and for the first decade or so of the show no one really minded.

In 1973, the children's publishing imprint Target Books was launched by Universal-Tandem Publishing. It reissued the three *Doctor Who* story novelisations first published during the Dalekmania years of the mid-sixties and, encouraged by healthy sales, commissioned new novelisations of more recent *Doctor Who* adventures. The range grew into one of the publishing success stories of the seventies and eighties, selling over 8 million copies in total. It expanded from dozens to hundreds of different titles, as young *Doctor Who* viewers showed a seemingly unquenchable appetite for the Doctor's earlier adventures. For those kids who delightedly pounced on these books in the school library, or saved their pocket money for another thrilling story, the Doctor became a character who now had a past.

Owning these books made the stories permanent, in a way that the episodes themselves didn't. As the actor Matthew Waterhouse, who would play the Fourth and Fifth Doctors' companion Adric, memorably described past episodes in the pre-home media age, they were as 'irrecoverable as dead pets'. Before the Target range properly began, he recalled lying in bed as a small child, praying to God to send one of his angels to Earth with a *Doctor Who* book. He imagined an angel with a glowing halo hovering in his room, holding out a thick, gold-bound, cobwebbed book, over a thousand years old, containing richly illustrated accounts of all the Doctor's previous adventures. He fell asleep believing that he would find this book at the foot of his bed in the morning. The book did not arrive, alas, but when he discovered a copy of *Doctor Who and the Crusaders* by David Whitaker during a family holiday in Devon a few weeks later, it seemed full of magic and significance.

The invention of rich, complex and consistent fantasy worlds is relatively common among young children, and psychologists call these paracosms. These worlds are imaginary, and yet can feel to the child as real and important as the everyday world. When fantasy authors create believable detailed invented worlds for their stories, such as J.R.R. Tolkien's Middle-earth or J.K. Rowling's Wizarding World, they are continuing in adulthood a practice that even the most imaginative children tend to drop before their teenage years. Younger minds are unusually capable of believing in paracosms, so when those minds encountered the ever-growing range of Target Books, they became engrossed in the *Doctor Who* universe in a way that adult minds are not always capable of. *Doctor Who* became not just the story that was shown on television last Saturday, but the greatest of all paracosms, one that stretched to the far corners of the universe, and to all points in time. There was an endless universe of imaginary wonder and danger within that range of books, and all it took to unlock was taking one playful and charismatic time traveller seriously. Young readers quickly learnt all they could about the Doctor's past, and the details of his earlier adventures. They knew about the people he had travelled with, and what his earlier incarnations had been like. It was intoxicating, but it did mean that the image of the Doctor as an enigmatic, unknowable mystery started to wither.

The stories were often novelised by their original writers or, when this wasn't practical, by a few trusted authors – most notably the Pertwee-era script editor Terrance Dicks, whose clean, brisk prose welcomed cautious readers into this world of thrilling imagination. The authors of these books were often able to add a few improvements to the original television stories, perhaps by adding more backstory or fixing a few plot holes. In the imaginations of young readers, these written adventures had sets and production values far in advance of what the BBC could afford. There were no ropey effects shots in the books, and invading armies weren't limited to three individuals because of constraints in the costume budget. For many, the Target novelisations are the greatest versions of these stories. When old adventures were later released on VHS and DVD, a number of stories failed to live up to the versions in the minds of readers.

This increasing awareness of the Doctor's past from the mid-seventies onwards coincided with, and helped to catalyse, the birth of *Doctor Who* fandom. The love of cult or genre television may play a large role in contemporary culture now, but it was highly unusual at the time. Typically, it was treated with a considerable amount of derision.

Certain fandoms, of course, are publicly accepted. Following a sports team, obsessing over a favourite band or caring about what the monarchy get up to are usually considered socially acceptable, even when the particular choice of team or band is an issue. Fandoms like these can be admitted without too much ridicule. They are usually portrayed as normal in the media and it is considered uncontroversial when they become part of people's identities. We understand that a cup final defeat, or the death of a singer or minor royal, can leave their fans emotionally bereft, regardless of how irrational this may seem to others. Other fandoms, however, were not granted this level of acceptance back in the 1970s. People who participated in them were typically dismissed as obsessive, mad or just sad.

It's not that fantastical stories of heroes and monsters were unacceptable in themselves. A knowledge of Greek myths, for example, was considered by many to be a hallmark of a good education. But those stories had the benefit of age and tradition, and were considered an acceptable subject for academic attention. *Doctor Who*, in contrast, was contemporary monster stories which did not need academia to justify or explain them. Lacking this establishment approval, the cultural commentators of polite society kept their distance.

To be actively engaged in *Doctor Who* fandom in the twentieth century, then, left you open to mockery and derision. *Doctor Who* was for children, the thinking went. It was acceptable to watch it because people tended to sit through whatever was on in the days when there was less media around, but expressing that you cared about it left you open to accusations of being emotionally stunted and the worst type of nerd. In the twentieth century the geeks had not yet inherited the Earth, and were routinely socially ostracised. And yet, most people were fans of *something*. The urge to enthuse is universal, regardless of what it is focused on.

For all that an interest in *Doctor Who* could be framed as immature, there was still much to admire about it. Here was a celebration of wild imagination that was wrapped in a strong moral core, an escapist sense of adventure and a healthy enjoyment of absurdity and camp. Its innate silliness was one of the programme's great strengths, as it kept the self-important away and prevented them from claiming it for themselves. That it kept adults in touch with their inner child was also a strength, not a weakness. 'Maturity is not an outgrowing, but a growing up,' the American author Ursula K. Le Guin has argued. 'An Adult is not a dead child, but a child who survived.' Our childhood selves are part of us, and an adult cut off from their inner child is lost and incomplete.

Left to its own devices, *Doctor Who* can thread itself through British culture and inspire and influence countless people. There are many subjects, surely, much less deserving of our enthusiasm.

2. 'I Wish the Daleks or Someone Would Exterminate Him'

To be a part of a fandom is psychologically healthy, it is believed. An active engagement with, and an enthusiasm for, an aspect of life is vitally important for our mental health. The benefits mainly come from engaging with others who share similar interests. With sports or music fandoms, like-minded people are easy to find at sports stadiums or music venues. Fans of a television series in the pre-digital world, however, found it much harder to find each other. From this impulse came the rise of fanzines and fan clubs.

The world of *Doctor Who* fanzines was a cottage industry of worn typewriter ribbons, Letraset, postal orders, stamped addressed envelopes and archaic copying machines. It coincided with the rise of punk fanzines such as *Sniffin' Glue* or *Ripped and Torn* and had a similar grass-roots DIY attitude. The golden age of *Doctor Who* fanzines ran from the mid-1970s to the mid-1980s, and produced titles such as *Skaro*, *Celestial Toyroom*, *TARDIS*, *DWB* (*Doctor Who Bulletin*) and *Shada*. They typically contained fan art, fan fiction, reviews, contact details for local fan groups and factual information about the programme's history, all crammed onto staple-bound sheets of A4 or A5 paper. Over three hundred different fanzines and well over a thousand different individual issues were produced during this time, and no other British TV programme caused anything like this level of creative activity. While the originators of *Star Trek* fandom and fanzines were largely female, the initial burst of *Who* fandom was overwhelmingly male. Several people involved in the scene would go on to work on the programme, including Chris Chibnall, the *Doctor Who* showrunner from 2017–22, and a teenage Peter Capaldi, who would be cast as the Twelfth Doctor forty years later.

The first *Who*-related fan club was established as early as 1965. Originally called The Official William (Dr Who) Hartnell Fan Club, it changed its name to The Official Dr Who Fan Club when Hartnell left. Initially operating from a bedroom in Hanley in Stoke-on-Trent, it advertised in teen magazines and gained permission from the *Doctor Who* production office to call itself 'official'. Throughout the seven years it lasted, it was run by a series of teenage enthusiasts, the youngest of whom was just thirteen. In the days of expensive brand management and global marketing, the idea of a thirteen-year-old schoolboy volunteer being trusted by the BBC to run an official fan club is a window onto a more innocent time.

In 1972, fourteen-year-old Peter Capaldi wrote to production secretary Sarah Newman, suggesting that he take over the fan club. She sent him a polite dismissal. In a subsequent letter to the real Fan Club secretary Keith Miller, who had apologised for his constant letters, she revealed a more honest insight into the production team's attitude to pestering fans. 'No, no, no, you're not by any means worse than Peter C. I had a very sad letter from him today [. . .] I wish the Daleks or someone would exterminate him, or something to that effect.'

Even at this early stage, there is evidence that production staff viewed fans as an ever-present annoyance. Over the decades, different slurs were used to refer to over-enthusiastic fans. In the 1980s, they were called 'barkers', implying that they were barking mad, or that they endlessly snapped around their heels like barking dogs. In the 2000s, they were called 'mosquitos', in a reference to their persistent annoyance, or 'ming-mongs', about which the less said the better. A common description in the 1970s was 'anoraks', a reference to the unstylish winter coats that fans would typically wear. When the BBC made *Resistance Is Useless*, a 1992 documentary about the show, it was presented by a talking anorak with a Birmingham accent. Charitably, it's possible to see this as an attempt to reclaim a term of abuse but, given that the programme was made by the BBC rather than the fan community, the choice does seem barbed.

To the cast and crew, this level of fanatical interest could seem strange. They wanted people to like what they had done, of course, but *Doctor Who* was usually just a job to them, and a quick and cheap one at that. They had often done many other programmes which they considered more prestigious and worthy of respect. They had not watched the programme through a child's eyes, and so were unable to appreciate it on that level. It was surprising and a little unsettling for them when, in time, their work on *Doctor Who* became the one job in their long careers that anyone showed any interest in.

In fandom, an interest in *Doctor Who* did not stop with what was shown on the screen. The behind-the-scenes story of how the programme was made was equally interesting. The names of BBC staff who featured in the credits quickly became familiar to fans, who shared information about writers, actors, producers and directors, as well as their critical evaluations of the stories, creators and production eras. This made an interest in *Doctor Who* richer and more multifaceted, but it also eroded the suspension of disbelief needed to become lost in the stories. If you were watching a scene and admiring the production design of Roger Murray-Leach or the directorial flair of Graeme Harper, your mind wasn't fully absorbed in the narrative. The deeper your interest in *Doctor Who*, then, the harder it became to keep hold of what made you love it in the first place.

Rather than causing them to disengage, this sent fans hunting for new information and a deeper understanding of the programme, in the hope that they would be reminded why it mattered so much to them. In these circumstances, the relationships and community of fandom could become more important to people than the show itself. Indeed, detailed, rich fandoms can almost be separate entities to the subjects they are built on. They can be created around almost nothing, such as the massive fan community which grew around the Marauders, the group of friends surrounding Harry Potter's parents. The Marauders are hardly mentioned in the books, but the few snippets of information given about them were enough to build a passionate and engaged community.

Interest in *Doctor Who* can be defined in terms of different levels. At the bottom end of the spectrum are people with zero interest in the programme, who don't watch it or care about it in any way. Above them there are casual viewers, who may enjoy it if they happen to catch an episode but who don't actively think about it otherwise. In terms of numbers, these have historically been the most important type of viewers, and the programme can be in trouble if it fails to entertain this casual audience. Then there are people who think of it as one of their favourite programmes, who make an effort to watch every episode. These people might talk about the programme, to friends or on social media. They would probably describe themselves as 'fans' of the show, but not to the extent that they participate in active fandom such as attending conventions or collecting memorabilia.

Above these people are many more different levels of fans. They are actively engaged in fandom, even if they vary in the extent to which their lives are taken up by the programme. They are part of a world that includes books, magazines, audios, comics and conventions. In this world there are exponentially more *Doctor Who* stories available than you have ever dreamt. There is also an encyclopaedic level of factual information about the programme's history and creators, the sharing of which builds relationships and communities. At this level, the fan and their interests have begun to merge. *Doctor Who* has become part of their identity. They have become like sports fans who refer to their team as 'we' rather than 'they'. They no longer see themselves as supporters of a team – they are the team. How the team is performing is therefore extremely personal. Sports fans like this are more likely to change their job, home, spouse or even religion than change their team. They participate in what psychologists call BIRGing, or 'basking in reflected glory'.

According to the American academic Daniel Wann, who specialises in the psychology of sports fandom, identifying with a team at this level is usually a psychologically positive experience that leads to an increased level of self-esteem and happiness, a lower risk of depression and higher levels of mental energy. Even when a team is doing badly and following them feels like a form of communal suffering, the social connections made and the sense of being part of something larger than yourself are still psychologically beneficial.

Fandoms outside sports also appear to offer similar benefits. But just as sports fans communally suffer when their team is not doing well, so too do sci-fi fans struggle with periods when their beloved show is, in their opinion, underperforming. At times like these, their own personal status is at risk. Fans want the show they feel part of to be as successful or prestigious as possible, fearing it reflects badly on them otherwise. When the object of enthusiasm is a quite mad sort-of children's programme made quickly on a tiny budget, the watching of which does not feel quite the same as it did when you discovered it as a child, then the current iteration of the programme can expect a considerable amount of fan criticism. The rise of organised fandom in the mid-1970s, just when pressure from conservative Christian networks convinced the BBC to stop the atmospheric, gothic horror tone and lean into the programme's innate silliness, was therefore always going to cause arguments.

In this context, it wasn't surprising that a high-profile fan like DWAS president Jan Vincent-Rudzki might attack the programme he was so invested in. He wanted the world of Gallifrey to remain consistent over the years because the paracosm of *Doctor Who* becomes harder to believe in when it contradicts itself. The problem was, as he explained in a later interview, 'These aren't the Time Lords we've seen before.' From Vincent-Rudzki's perspective, Robert Holmes's decision to turn an awe-inspiring race of space gods into doddery bureaucrats damaged the believability of the extended history of the show.

The story, however, proved to be a huge success with the mainstream audience. Viewing figures for the notorious part three reached 13 million, which was nearly a quarter of the UK population at the time. Baker and Holmes, in particular, were at the top of their game. The story was original, inventive and risky, and from the perspective of the production team it must have seemed like they had done exactly what they were hired to do. Yet Vincent-Rudzki's criticisms struck a nerve in early fandom.

In a 1976/77 DWAS season poll, fans voted it the worst story of the year. What the mainstream audience wanted and what fans wanted, it seemed, could prove to be very different things.

3. 'I Thought I Could Do Anything I Liked'

In 2007, when Tom Baker was recording narration for a Channel 5 pre-school cartoon, the commissioning editor of children's programmes, Nick Wilson, visited the recording studio. During the late 1970s, Wilson had worked at the BBC and directed episodes of its long-running pre-school series *Play School*. This programme featured a number of toys, including Jemima the doll, the teddy bears Big Ted and Little Ted, and, perhaps the most famous of all, a large green egg-shaped cuddly toy called Humpty. Wilson had been attempting to get his programme shot under tight time constraints when Tom Baker entered the studio, in full *Doctor Who* costume, picked up Humpty, and walked off with him. Years later, Wilson confronted Baker about this.

'You stole my Humpty!' he said.

Baker humbly apologised. 'I'm terribly sorry,' he said. 'It's just that, at the time, I thought I could do anything I liked.'

The success of *Doctor Who* turned Baker, in his own admission, into something of a monster. The initial years working alongside Elisabeth Sladen had been productive and harmonious, but after she left he became increasingly difficult. He was so identified with the role in the eyes of the public by this point that his ever-increasing sense of importance was easy to justify. He was the Doctor, so it followed that he was the programme and what he wanted was what *Doctor Who* needed.

Baker was cold and unwelcoming to Sladen's replacement, Louise Jameson, who played a tribal hunter called Leela. Although he has since apologised and the pair have become friendly, his behaviour was a factor in Jameson leaving the series after nine stories. Other actors have reported similar stories about Baker's difficult behaviour. Sarah Sutton, who joined the show as Nyssa near the end of Baker's run, recalls that by the time she arrived 'the atmosphere [surrounding the programme] had got quite heavy. Tom's a wonderful character but I was absolutely terrified of him.'

Matthew Waterhouse, who played Adric, said that, 'It was fun more than it wasn't, but it was a situation where the leading actor decided how good your day is going to be, or otherwise.' Baker had been a hero to Waterhouse before he joined the show, so discovering what he was like in real life was a shock. During his first day in rehearsals, Waterhouse was confused because he was listed on the rehearsal schedule, yet he did not seem to be in the scene being worked on. Too young and nervous to ask what he should be doing, he stood around awkwardly until Baker turned to him and snapped, 'Why don't you just piss off?'

It was not just the cast who struggled working with Baker. The director Alan Bromly had previously directed *The Time Warrior* in 1973, where he introduced both Sarah Jane Smith and the Sontarans. When he returned for *Nightmare of Eden* (1979), however, he clashed repeatedly with his star. At one point, Baker stood under the microphone and declared loudly enough that all the crew could hear, 'I thought we were supposed to have a director in the gallery, not a commentator!' Bromly resigned halfway through the production, overcome with stress.

The question of Baker's behaviour was discussed by BBC management, with Head of Series and Serial Graeme MacDonald conceding that he had become 'flippant and unmanageable'. The writer Chris Boucher, who wrote three well-regarded stories in the Tom Baker years, once attended a cast read-through in which Baker cruelly savaged the quality of the scripts. 'It was a horrendous experience as far as I was concerned,' said Boucher, 'and I conceived the notion that I would like to see Tom Baker die in a cellar full of rats.'

Baker was leading an increasingly bohemian lifestyle, bouncing back and forth between the studio and his favourite pubs. The Colony Room in Soho was a great favourite, where he became part of the hard-drinking social group surrounding the artist Francis Bacon. His alcohol consumption was considerable, which no doubt contributed to his uncontrollability and meanness even if it didn't affect his performance. In his autobiography, Matthew Waterhouse recounts an incident when Tom Baker was being sick in a car park. 'Halfway through, a little boy came up to him and said, "Are you Doctor Who?" "Hang on a moment," said Tom, and finished vomiting. Then he pulled from the inside pocket of his sick-splashed raincoat a photograph of himself which he signed and inscribed to the child, who walked away blissfully happy.'

Baker had treated the previous producer Philip Hinchcliffe with respect, but this was not a courtesy he extended to his replacement, Graham Williams. As Baker saw it, he was *Doctor Who*. No one understood the programme as well as he did, and this young upstart had no right to come along and tell him what to do. Where Hinchcliffe was able to doggedly pursue his own vision for the programme, Williams's job was more concerned with firefighting and keeping the peace.

Louise Jameson remembers Williams as more of a 'charmer' than Hinchcliffe. 'In a way, he was too gentle to be a producer,' she said later. 'Philip would wear a suit and jacket and Graham would wear a cardigan. Graham was much softer.'

'He wasn't the sort of person that you'd expect to be a producer of *Doctor Who*,' said John Leeson, the actor who voiced K-9.

'I think Graham's strength was in keeping the peace.' Leeson primarily worked in the studio but, he recalled, 'On occasions I would be taken out on location simply to keep Tom happy. I think that Graham realised that Tom liked having me around.'

Making a show like *Doctor Who* work as a lighter, family-friendly comedy would have been an incredibly challenging brief at the best of times. When it worked, such as in *City of Death*, the story Williams co-wrote with Douglas Adams, the results were wonderful. At other times, however, it could be embarrassing, such as the sequence in *Nightmare of Eden* when Baker was being attacked in a bush and ad-libbed the dialogue, 'Argh! My arms! My legs! My everything!' That this sequence remained in the edit can give the impression that nobody making the programme cared about it or took it seriously. In actuality, it was more a consequence of how impossible it had become to work with Tom Baker. Following a blazing row, director Alan Bromly quit halfway through production. Williams stepped up to direct the rest of the story, but the experience convinced him that he too should resign. Looking back on his behaviour in 2023, Baker reflected, 'I regret that I made Graham unhappy. It's not an easy thing for me to say but [. . .] I regret that very much, and I'm sorry for my selfishness there. Very sorry. It's too late now, but I admit it.'

Williams's problems were far more extensive than just dealing with the ego of his star. During his era, inflation was rampant and by his reckoning the budget for his third and final season was, in real terms, half of that for his first. At a time when the success of the first *Star Wars* film had changed viewers' expectation of what science fiction should look like, the budget-stricken late-1970s *Doctor Who* stories appear visibly cheap and slapdash. When Robert Holmes took the Doctor to Gallifrey in 1976 for *The Deadly Assassin*, the design team were able to build sets that did this almost-mythical planet justice. A large ceremonial centre called the Panopticon was realised with strange gleaming green metals running upwards at odd angles. Corridors reached into the living rock deep underneath the planet, and the Doctor was imprisoned in a cell suspended in a dark underground abyss. When the programme returned to Gallifrey two years later, the office of the Lord President of Gallifrey looked like a couple of walls covered in hubcaps painted grey.

Williams kept the ship afloat through a challenging period but, as he later admitted, '*Doctor Who* drove me crackers – it nearly killed me – the hardest work I've ever done in my life.' Having suffered with depression for decades, his life would prove to have a tragic ending. A decade after he resigned from *Doctor Who*, at the age of forty-five, he took his own life, leaving behind a wife and three young children. It says much about Williams that what he gifted *Doctor Who* was not melancholy, but fun in the face of adversity.

The next producer, John Nathan-Turner, was an internal promotion from the ranks of the production team. He would go on to become one of the most significant figures in twentieth-century *Doctor Who*, overseeing four Doctors and remaining in the post far longer than any of his predecessors. He ultimately produced nine seasons – over a third – of classic *Who*.

Nathan-Turner had many qualities that the show desperately needed. He was hard-working and a master of detail, especially with regards to production and costs. 'He was very young to be a producer at the BBC, so there was a lot riding on it,' Janet Fielding has said. 'You could tell he wasn't Oxbridge, and the BBC was still very Oxbridge then. But he was shrewd.' He could find ways to make the most out of a tiny budget. He was focused on promotion, always looking for ways to get the programme in the newspapers and engage with the fan community. He also had qualities which would come to be problematic for the programme, both personally and professionally. He was not a story person and had a poor grasp on the importance of character. An intuitive understanding of the interior of a character is supposed to drive casting and costuming, but that would not be how Nathan-Turner worked. As Peter Davison has said, 'Celebrity always trumped acting ability in John's book.'

John Nathan-Turner's first season would be Tom Baker's last, and the actor seems almost a different person in those last stories than in the Williams years. His clowning and excesses had been tightly reined in. Baker was said to have 'despised' Nathan-Turner for coming into his show and stamping his authority on it. It is to the producer's great credit that he was able to do this. Very few people could have stood up to the fractious, unreasonable force of nature that was late-1970s Tom Baker. Nathan-Turner was not a person who would back down from pursuing his vision. He possessed a much-needed inner steel, although this would, in the fullness of time, mark him as inflexible and unwilling to delegate.

There was a sombre, funereal tone to Baker's final season, as if the Fourth Doctor knew that his time was up. He looked gaunt and appeared swamped by the new burgundy costume that had been made for him. He was suffering from an undiagnosed illness which made the curls fall out of his hair, to the extent that he had to have a perm in order to look like the Doctor. Many have assumed that this illness was a consequence of his hard-drinking lifestyle. It's possible, however, that knowing he had to leave the greatest job imaginable also had a psychological impact on his health. Baker and his co-star Lalla Ward, who played his companion Romana, married during this last season. They were clearly incompatible, and few were surprised when they divorced eighteen months later. Marrying Romana, it's tempting to speculate, suggests a man trying to cling to the Doctor even as he knew his time was up.

He knew he had stayed too long. After seven seasons, he had played the part longer than Hartnell and Troughton together. Tom Baker, ultimately, had become typecast. Whenever the British public saw him on the screen afterwards, they saw him as Doctor Who, not as the role he was playing. This led to a strained relationship with his legacy. Baker declined future invitations to return to the role, such as the twentieth-anniversary celebration story *The Five Doctors*, and he kept his distance from other actors who played the Doctor. Fortunately, he finally did manage to achieve the deeper, long-lasting relationship that he always craved, when he married former *Doctor Who* assistant editor Sue Jerrard in 1986. But when the time came to leave the programme, he seemed horribly aware of how much he was giving up.

When his departure was announced, he appeared on the BBC magazine programme *Nationwide*. He was interviewed by Sue Cook while leaning against the TARDIS in a pin-striped double-breasted suit, being either incredibly charming, slightly creepy or very drunk, depending on your point of view. He suggested that his successor should not necessarily be a man, before telling Cook that the role 'threw up for me lots of pleasures that changed my whole life. It's been fun being Doctor Who, it's been the happiest time of my working life.' When Cook asked him what he would do next, he answered as honestly as he could. 'I'm going into oblivion, I suppose.'

7
The Reckless Innocent (1982–84)

1. 'It's Stopped Being Fun, Doctor'

On 23 November 1963, twelve-year-old Peter Davison was perched on a sofa in the upstairs living room of his family home in the village of Knaphill, Surrey. The adults were still trying to come to terms with the assassination of President Kennedy, but young Peter's attention was elsewhere. The family had just installed a new state-of-the-art television, and he was eagerly awaiting the first episode of *Doctor Who*. It turned out to be more of a mystery programme than the science fiction he had been expecting, but he was still hooked. He would continue to watch regularly throughout the 1960s, as he entered his teenage years. The Patrick Troughton era was a particular favourite.

The first four actors to play the Doctor came to the role with all the baggage that came from dramatic, difficult lives. Hartnell had an almost Dickensian childhood of neglect. Troughton had a secret second family. Pertwee was blown up during the war, while Baker spent years in a monastery. Davison, in contrast, had what he called a 'lower-middle-class, walk-in-the-park life'. He grew up in a stable, financially secure home in an affluent part of England during peacetime. Even better, he lived in a world in which a young boy could watch *Doctor Who* every Saturday. He didn't have the psychological damage or personality issues of his predecessors. As much as he likes to play up to a grumpy persona now that he is older, he was, ultimately, a likeable, stable, normal type of guy.

In 1980, when Nathan-Turner was trying to decide how to replace Tom Baker, he happened to glance at a photograph on his office wall. It showed the cast of the popular television series *All Creatures Great and Small*, a veterinary drama set in the Yorkshire Dales in the 1930s that he had worked on a few years earlier. Nathan-Turner's eye was drawn to the young, innocent face of Peter Davison, who had played the role of the young vet Tristan. The part had made Davison a big star, and he was much in demand. He was then starring in the sitcoms *Sink or Swim* and *Holding the Fort*, as well as making cameo appearances in series such as *The Hitchhiker's Guide to the Galaxy*, where he played a talking space cow. The popular stereotype of Davison on *All Creatures Great and Small* was that he always seemed to have his hand up a cow, so casting him as one was something of a gag in itself.

If Nathan-Turner wanted to get as far away from a 'Tom Baker type' as possible, the kindly, smiling face of Davison on his wall would do just that. At twenty-nine years old, Davison was the youngest Doctor by a considerable distance. Nearly thirty years later 26-year-old Matt Smith would take that honour and become the youngest actor to play the role, but Davison was arguably the more surprising casting as there was then no precedent for the idea that the Doctor could be young. While previous Doctors had all been a little mad in their own ways, Davison was pleasant. You could take him anywhere. He was also far more famous, on television at least, than any of his predecessors. Early in his *All Creatures* years, Davison had been chased down the street by a gang of young girls while out exploring Richmond in Yorkshire. 'I felt like I was in a scene from *A Hard Day's Night*,' he later wrote, 'although, I admit, there wasn't that much screaming.' When he married the American actor Sandra Dickinson, his profile was boosted by tabloid interest in the celebrity couple. To cast Davison as the Doctor was incredibly bold and radical and yet also, thanks to his innate likeability and obvious acting talent, something of a safe bet at the same time.

The most noticeable immediate change in the Fifth Doctor era was that the programme leant into an upper-class southern English aesthetic. The regenerated Doctor now had a great love of cricket and dressed in an outfit inspired by Edwardian cricketers. Stories like *Enlightenment* and *Black Orchid* had Edwardian period settings, with a large part of the latter given over to the Doctor playing his beloved game. The story *Mawdryn Undead* was predominantly set in an English public school and introduced a new companion, Turlough, played by Mark Strickson, who was an alien disguised as a boarding-school pupil. Nathan-Turner's sole direction to Strickson was to play the part posher. Strickson assured him that he was playing it as posh as he could.

Davison now looks back at interviews from early in his career with some embarrassment, due to the public-school accent he adopted after drama school. 'I don't know who that person is at all,' he told journalist Benjamin Cook in 2016. 'It's not me. I don't even know where that person came from. I think it was from fear of being me.' In his autobiography, he talks about how accidents of casting in his early career saw him rapidly rise through the social classes as he played posher and posher characters. 'The problem was, in my everyday life, in the face I presented on those interviews, I bought into this so completely, in accent and manner, that I was living as my alter ego.' Davison's new-found accent fitted perfectly with Nathan-Turner's upper-class evolution of the programme. While this was appealing to some, it did make the character harder to identify with in many parts of the country.

Having grown up with older Doctors, Davison was concerned he was too young to play the role. To counter this, he included aspects of Hartnell's and Troughton's performances in his Doctor, particularly Hartnell's spikiness and Troughton's innocence. He would play relatively neutral lines as if he was angry and trying to keep a lid on his temper, before switching unexpectedly to wide-eyed wonder. It says much for Davison's talent as an actor that he could make this seem natural. It allowed him to suggest that the Doctor was an ancient alien being, despite what the lack of lines on his face said.

This unpredictable approach was important for the success of the Fifth Doctor, a characterisation which Davison has described as a 'reckless innocent'. On the page, the scripts often presented the Doctor as powerless and vulnerable, a trait his youthful appearance brought into focus. He spent much of his debut story, for example, being carried around in a box suffering from regeneration trauma. After seven years of Tom Baker's active confidence, this was a clear indication that Davison would be a very different portrayal.

The sense that the Doctor was now out of his depth was solidified in a story in Davison's first season, in which the Doctor failed to rescue his companion Adric. At the finale of the last episode of *Earthshock*, Adric was killed when a space freighter crashed into prehistoric Earth. His death was more disturbing because the character was supposed to be a child. Matthew Waterhouse, who played the role, saw him as being around fifteen years old. The episode ended with silent credits.

Apart from during the brief John Wiles-produced era in the last William Hartnell season, no *Doctor Who* companions had been killed off like this before. The audience believed that they would always be saved by the Doctor, because the Doctor was understood to be a hero. Davison initially approved of this move, thinking that it would increase the sense of jeopardy in the stories that followed. With hindsight, however, he came to see it as a mistake. The failure to rescue his companion, he wrote, was a 'deeply flawed notion [that] traumatised millions of children'.

The Fifth Doctor was often emotionally untroubled by death. In *Arc of Infinity*, a gardener is killed by the villain Omega, who takes the gardener's overalls as a disguise. Upon discovering the body, the Doctor shows no concern for the murdered man and cheerily remarks, 'Well, at least we have some idea of what [Omega's] wearing!' The Doctor's response to the death of Adric, as scripted, was to display the 'stiff upper lip' attitude commonly associated with the English public-school system. In the episode immediately following Adric's death, Nyssa and Tegan attempt to talk about how much they miss him. The Doctor immediately closes down their conversation by telling them that Adric 'wouldn't want us to mourn unnecessarily'. It was an exchange typical of the emotional repression that characterised the Fifth Doctor and this era of the series. That the Doctor never nipped back in time to rescue Adric from the freighter before it crashed is something that has troubled fandom ever since.

The writer of *Earthshock*, the story which killed off Adric, was Eric Saward, who became the programme's new script editor shortly afterwards. Saward's sensibilities were bleaker and more nihilistic than earlier script editors, a sensibility which seemed to fit with the crueller and more individualistic spirit of the 1980s. Saward was fond of violent, cynical space marines fighting their way through a meaningless universe. In this he was ahead of the curve of popular culture, as stories like *Earthshock* and *Resurrection of the Daleks* appeared a few years before the movie *Aliens* (1986) brought very similar attitudes and characters to the mainstream. The question of whether Saward's bleak, hopeless universe remained in the spirit of *Doctor Who*, however, continues to divide opinion.

A typical Saward story would introduce a host of new characters who were struggling against the odds in a dangerous world, only for almost all of them to be coldly gunned down dead at the finale of the last episode. The Doctor would often be a minor figure in Saward's stories, but he was the one left standing at the end. 'There should have been another way,' he said at the end of *Warriors of the Deep*, after every single character in the story except the TARDIS crew lay dead. With earlier Doctors, there almost certainly would have been another way. They would have saved the lives of *someone*.

This bleak universe took its toll on his companions. The second episode of *Enlightenment* ended with the Doctor's companion Turlough attempting suicide. The story *Snakedance* ended with Tegan traumatised and crying. She eventually ran away from the TARDIS after three years in the series, haunted by the death of so many characters. Her explanation was that, 'It's stopped being fun, Doctor, goodbye.' Given that part of the role of the companion was to be an audience identification figure, Tegan departing seemed like an ominous judgement on the programme itself. Wasn't being fun an important part of *Doctor Who*?

During the 1970s, the Doctor was the centre of attention. He owned the room and would march into any situation brimming with charisma, moral righteousness and good humour, and use his wits and bravery to save the day. Davison's Doctor, in contrast, dressed in beige and looked worried or vulnerable. The 1970s Doctors typically had a single companion, but the Fifth Doctor returned to the format of the Hartnell years and travelled with two or three others. His crew was more fractious, constantly squabbling and arguing with each other. The idea that travelling in the TARDIS was an amazing experience was notably lacking.

There was also an unusual lack of humour in this era, something that Davison fought against. 'I was always battling to put more jokes in,' he has said, 'but I wasn't allowed.' This seriousness seems to have been as much John Nathan-Turner's taste as it was a conscious move away from the silliness of late-era Baker. In his autobiography, Davison recalled being taken out to lunch by Nathan-Turner when he was deciding whether to take the role. 'It's the first time this has happened to me,' he wrote, 'a producer shelling out for lunch before I've said yes to a job, and I joke that it's proof he's serious. He tells me that he never jokes, which I realise later might well have summed up his approach to the show.'

This more serious tone was evident in the different type of titles that *Doctor Who* stories were given. Previously, story titles had been joyously lurid and melodramatic, such as *The Hand of Fear*, *The Seeds of Doom*, *The Invasion of the Dinosaurs* or *Horror of Fang Rock* – all immensely appealing to a young 1970s audience. After Nathan-Turner took over, we got stories called *Frontios*, *Meglos*, *Castrovalva*, *Kinda* and *Logopolis* – titles that took the science fiction elements of their stories seriously. To intelligent early-teenage boys, this more cerebral approach was appealing. To the rest of the viewing public, the show did not seem quite so inviting, fun or entertaining as before.

Despite Nathan-Turner's attempts to make *Doctor Who* older and more serious, the programme's innate absurdity couldn't entirely be removed. It always managed to make its way back on screen, no matter how hard people tried to repress it. In the case of the Peter Davison era, it manifested in one of the most random costume details in television history. On the lapel of his cream-coloured frock coat, the Doctor wore a stick of celery. Such was the confidence with which Davison played the role that few people questioned this choice. Tonally, it felt like a nod to the absurdist Dada art movement, which emerged around the First World War and refused to take the attitudes of that time seriously. It was a very *Doctor Who* touch that a hint of Dadaist mischief sat largely unnoticed in the heart of the Edwardian trappings of the Fifth Doctor's era.

2. 'The Platonic Ideal of the Doctor'

John Nathan-Turner knew *Doctor Who* inside and out. He had originally worked as a floor assistant during Troughton and Pertwee stories, and he had risen to become the unit production manager during the Williams era. He understood that the show had fallen into a rut – with Baker working so well in the role, there had been little pressure to evolve or change. For many people in the late 1970s, the idea that there could be *Doctor Who* without Tom Baker seemed faintly implausible. As the UK elected a new Conservative government led by Margaret Thatcher, Nathan-Turner was determined to drag the programme into the 1980s.

The version of *Doctor Who* that Nathan-Turner inherited featured Tom Baker in his long scarf, offering people jelly babies, clutching his sonic screwdriver and travelling with a younger female assistant and his trusty robot dog K-9. Over his first couple of years, Nathan-Turner went about replacing every single element of this, as well as rerecording the beloved theme music and creating flashy new titles for the show. Just like Barry Letts before him, he was going to change everything, trusting that viewers would still consider it the same show.

That Nathan-Turner changed every detail of the character and the show, and yet we still view them as being the same, gives us a rare insight into the elusive nature of identity. Just like the fictional character of the Doctor, we too are a process of constant change. Physically, our older selves look nothing like our childhood appearance, as weight, height and hair colour all vary over time. The original cells that first made up our bodies die and are replaced, often countless times, gradually changing and distorting over the years. Yet we still consider ourselves to be the same person. Identity is not in the atoms that form us. It can't be found on a material level.

Like the Doctor, our opinions, beliefs, character and personality also change over time. As the writer Jamie Mathieson has said, 'What's interesting about the Platonic ideal of the Doctor is that there isn't really one. There's no one character that everyone writes. I kind of think of them as like a gigantic graphic equaliser, where there are all these different aspects to *Doctor Who* which different writers can turn up or turn down however they wish. You might turn up the "godlike being" fader and turn down the "excited little boy" fader. You might turn down the alien awkwardness and turn up the charm. They are all *Doctor Who*, but there isn't one definitive setting that is the archetype. It's such a broad brief that it can be paralysing.'

Fictional characters are often identified with the world they are active in – the locations, friends, enemies, weapons or props we associate them with. When we think of Sherlock Holmes, King Arthur or Robin Hood, they come with a lot of baggage. We expect to find them alongside Moriarty, Excalibur, Sherwood Forest, a deerstalker hat, Merlin or a long bow, to give a few examples. Yet it is easy to find stories in which these iconic things are absent, and the character is still recognisably themselves. We associate the Doctor with their sonic screwdriver, TARDIS, Daleks and Gallifrey, but we still recognise them as the Doctor when these items are absent.

In discussions of identity politics, it is often claimed that a person's gender, religion, sexuality, class or nationality define them. Yet people can change all these attributes during their lifetime, and they still consider themselves to be the same person. In recent years the Doctor has enthusiastically changed gender, race and sexual orientation, and they are still very much the Doctor. It can seem like the only fixed candidate to define an identity is someone's name, yet an individual may take on a new name. Actors often take on a new name for professional reasons – neither Peter Davison, David Tennant nor Sylvester McCoy went by those names as children.

Although none of these attributes is sufficient to form someone's identity, they all contribute towards it. This is because our identity, ultimately, is a story. It is the tale of a person over time, built from experience, circumstance and memory, and refined into the narrative that we mistake for ourselves. It is understandable, in these circumstances, why the right to define our own stories is so fiercely fought over.

Like all good stories, our identities change and evolve over time, sometimes with shock twists and genre shifts. Yet as long as they remain continuing narratives, they still form the same identity. Perhaps this was the realisation that Jon Pertwee's Doctor achieved in his final story, when he confronted the illusion of self from a Buddhist perspective and made peace with the story continuing without him.

Framing identity as story helps to explain why fictional characters can matter to us as much as, and sometimes more than, some real people – because they are all stories, our minds process real and fictional characters in the same way. It also explains why so many actors have difficulty with their own identity. Because they leave their own personal narrative behind when they inhabit another character, their sense of themselves is weaker than someone who is always the same story. After all, the bigger, richer and more interesting our stories get, the greater our sense of identity. This is why Nathan-Turner was able to change the Doctor so radically and they were still accepted as being the same person. *Doctor Who* was, by this point, a story far longer and richer than most fictions. It was also, for the first time, about to engage with this fact.

3. Longleat

The year 1983 was one of celebration for *Doctor Who* as the series turned twenty years old. Very few programmes enjoy such longevity, and even fewer can reach that milestone while still feeling fresh and creatively inspired. For those celebrating the programme's birthday, the idea that it would last for another twenty seemed plausible. The notion started to circulate that perhaps it might even last indefinitely.

Yet the stories in *Doctor Who*'s twentieth anniversary year were troubled by this notion of longevity. Five of the seven stories broadcast that year featured villains struggling with immortality. In *Enlightenment*, a race of superior beings wrestled with the boredom of eternal existence. In *Mawdryn Undead*, a group of scientists tortured by continuous eternal regeneration longed for their own death. In *Arc of Infinity*, the Time Lord Omega had been driven insane by eternal formless life in a universe of anti-matter and was desperate for vengeance. The year's celebrations culminated in a feature-length anniversary special called *The Five Doctors*, in which the Time Lord President Borusa attempted to gain immortality. The Doctor, then present in four of his five incarnations, declined it on the grounds that immortality was a curse, not a gift. At the point when the series started to appear as if it might go on forever, the stories it told reacted against the idea with horror.

A programme is changed by the awareness that it has a past and will have a future. During the first four Doctors, the programme was seen as something transient. It was rarely repeated, and the tapes of many episodes were junked on the assumption that there would never be any interest in watching or broadcasting them again. *Doctor Who* was just whatever was broadcast that particular week, and within the series references to older stories were infrequent. When a letter from the Third Doctor's assistant Jo Grant arrives in Pertwee's final story, broadcast a year after Grant left the series, it came as a real surprise. The programme was over a decade old at the time, but back-references like this were incredibly rare. In the seven years between *Earthshock* and the previous Cyberman story, *Revenge of the Cybermen* (1975), the only returning elements in any story had been Time Lords, Sontarans and a single Dalek story. In contrast, *Earthshock* kicked off a run of ten stories which all featured returning elements. At this milestone anniversary the programme's past became part of its present.

For fans, conversing via fanzines, swapping audio tapes of old stories, and endlessly rereading the Target paperbacks, an understanding of the series' history had started to become normal. Names of old companions – such as Ben, Polly, Jamie, Vicki, Steven, Barbara or Victoria – had meaning, even to people who were not old enough to have seen them on screen. An awareness began to form as to who followed who, in a similar way to how the timelines of monarchs or presidents are studied in history lessons. The more this sense of the past expanded, the more it made the current story seem smaller. *The Dalek Invasion of Earth* (1964), for example, was the tenth story to be broadcast. In narrative terms, it then made up one tenth of all of *Doctor Who*. *The King's Demons* (1983), in contrast, was the 128th story. It formed less than 1 per cent of the series, and hence it had much less overall significance.

During the first four Doctors, the series continually introduced new elements that became iconic, and which are endlessly reused to this day. Hartnell's Doctor gave us the keystones – Daleks, the TARDIS and regeneration. Troughton introduced Ice Warriors, UNIT and Time Lords. Pertwee gave us Autons, Sontarans and the Master, while Tom Baker added Davros, Zygons and K-9 to the series' iconography. Sometimes an early Doctor would introduce something that would be more readily associated with their replacements, such as the Cybermen, who appeared at the end of Hartnell's run but are mostly associated with Troughton, or the sonic screwdriver and jelly babies, which were introduced by Troughton but became more associated with the 1970s Doctors. When the series was revived in the twenty-first century, it also introduced characters, monsters and elements that became iconic and returned regularly. The Weeping Angels, the Judoon, the Ood, Captain Jack and River Song, along with concepts such as psychic paper and the Time War, all returned alongside different Doctors to those who originated them.

By the twentieth anniversary, however, the law of diminishing returns was starting to kick in. In the final decade of the original run, from 1979 to 1989, this steady supply of new iconic elements came to an end. No monsters from this period have ever been reused with a later Doctor. The only new characters that returned were Sabalom Glitz and the Rani, who first appeared in Sixth Doctor stories and returned in the Seventh Doctor's era. Nothing new from this period was reused in the revived series until the classic companions Tegan, Ace and Mel were brought back for the *Power of the Doctor*, a 2022 story specially designed to celebrate the BBCs 100th anniversary. The period when the programme became aware of its own history, then, and started to reuse elements of its own past more regularly, was one when it failed to generate new iconography for the future.

None of these concerns were apparent, however, when BBC Enterprises organised a celebratory event over the Easter weekend of 3–4 April 1983. This was held at Longleat, a stately home and safari park in Wiltshire, then owned by the right-wing landowner and Conservative politician Henry Thynne, the 6th Marquess of Bath. Although large parts of the house and estate were open to the public, this did not include the house's 'Hitler Room', where Thynne kept the world's largest collection of Hitler's artworks. At the time of the *Doctor Who* celebration, this amounted to a grand total of sixty of Hitler's paintings. As Robert Harris recorded in his book *Selling Hitler*, 'Lord Bath acquired the pictures for posterity and confessed to a certain "admiration" for the Nazi leader: "Hitler did a hell of a lot for his country," he explained.' Had a signage mix-up brought the visiting *Doctor Who* fans to Thynne's Hitler Room by mistake, the Longleat exhibition would be remembered very differently.

For the *Doctor Who*-loving public, however, there were far more interesting things to look at than one aristocrat's Nazi collection. There were costumes, sets and models, including the TARDIS interior and UNIT HQ. There were opportunities to watch old episodes and bid on screen-used props in an auction. Visual effects and make-up teams demonstrated their work, and merchandise stalls sold countless T-shirts, hats and Target novels. There were talks and signing sessions from the stars, including Jon Pertwee, Peter Davison, Patrick Troughton, Elisabeth Sladen, Nicholas Courtney, Janet Fielding and Heather Hartnell, William's widow. To the surprise and delight of many, there was even Tom Baker himself, although he was uncomfortable appearing alongside the other Doctors.

Although some 13,000 tickets had been pre-sold by post from

BBC Enterprises, no one had been quite sure how many people would turn up. Appearing on the children's magazine programme *Saturday Superstore* a week before the event, cast member Mark Strickson told viewers that, 'If you want to go to Longleat now, just turn up on the day because the box office is now closed. Don't bother writing in to get a ticket. Just turn up.' After the exhibition opened, however, the message quickly became very different. Radio 2's Ed Stewart afternoon programme began issuing warnings that people without tickets should not attempt to attend. By this time the roads of Wiltshire were gridlocked with immense traffic jams as over 50,000 people descended on the celebration.

For those who turned up, most of their time was spent queuing as tents, talks and demonstrations struggled to deal with the overwhelming numbers. Peter Davison took to walking up and down the queues in costume, talking to fans and shaking hands, not unlike royalty. To many in the queues, of course, he was far more than that. Despite the long wait, those who attended often talk of the two days as a deeply magical time. For a lot of fans, it was the first time they realised just how many other people shared their enthusiasm for this strange show. It was the first time they met their tribe.

A number of the cast members present had just finished filming the feature-length anniversary special, *The Five Doctors*, which would be screened later that year on 25 November, two days after the programme's twentieth anniversary. Intended as a celebration of the programme's past, the story crammed in ten old companions, including a cameo from K-9, and as many monsters and villains as possible, including Cybermen, Yeti, a Dalek and the Master. The story promised all the previous Doctors, which it technically delivered. Hartnell had died eight years earlier, but he was represented by archive footage at the start, while the part of the 'First Doctor' was recast and played by Richard Hurndall. Tom Baker initially said he would consider returning if he liked the script, but he subsequently had a change of heart. He was represented instead by footage from an uncompleted story of his that was scrapped following strike action. The audience was then informed that Baker's Doctor was trapped for the rest of the story in an unstable portion of the time vortex. Pertwee, Troughton and Davison were all present and as charismatic as expected, however, so even without Tom Baker fans had much to be excited about.

The Five Doctors was the sort of brief that would terrify most writers. To include that many old elements into a story that still made sense, and which had to be satisfying on its own terms, would require a rare skill. Even Robert Holmes, the original choice of writer, failed to crack it. Fortunately, Terrance Dicks rose to the occasion – he was always a man able to make writing an adventure romp seem effortless. To explain why all the characters requested by the brief came together, Dicks put the blame on a rogue Time Lord in the heart of Gallifrey. The wishes of the BBC, in the form of the anniversary special brief, once again appear as the desires of Time Lords inside the fiction.

The Five Doctors was the programme turning inwards and talking about itself, rather than reaching out and surprising us. The result may have been tonally different from the cerebral stories of the Davison era, but it was full of the spirit of the previous two decades and it quickly became a fan favourite. It was, by design, focused on the past. Now that the show was understood as something with a past that could be explored in this way, a tension grew between the temptation to refer back to earlier glories, which would excite the fanbase, and the need to change and evolve into something as yet unseen.

When the critic Elizabeth Sandifer wrote about the story, she described it in terms of the Longleat exhibition, with every different character and element listed as if they were a museum exhibit, encased in glass, along with a factual description. All those elements were present to be examined and catalogued, but items displayed in a museum are no longer living, vital, evolving things.

4. The Keeper of the *Doctor Who* Flame

Nathan-Turner's relationship with the fan community was complex. He could be incredibly scathing, as shown by his nickname for them: 'barkers'. Matthew Waterhouse, who played Adric, has described how Nathan-Turner reacted when he realised that Waterhouse was a fan of the programme. The room initially fell silent, before Nathan-Turner asked him if he was a member of the Doctor Who Appreciation Society. The group's name was spoken, Waterhouse said, 'as if it was a terrorist organisation'. According to Waterhouse, Nathan-Turner told him to, 'Think of the most vicious, bitchy queen you've ever met. The worst of the fans are much, much worse.' His approach, he announced, was that, 'Until they turn on me, I'll be polite to them.' And yet, for Nathan-Turner, something about the fan community was incredibly attractive.

Nathan-Turner actively courted the fan audience. He became a regular and enthusiastic guest on the American convention circuit, where he was initially treated as much a star as his actors were. The adoration and sense of importance he found there was appealing, and the lucrative financial rewards certainly didn't hurt. 'Hugely important to him, that adulation,' said Janet Fielding. 'Absolutely key. He could walk into one of those conventions and he was a big man. No other show was going to give him that.' A common complaint about Nathan-Turner, from actors and production staff alike, was that he dedicated so much time to attending conventions and drumming up publicity that making the actual programme suffered. The more that Nathan-Turner engaged with the fandom, the more he seemed to find the immediate applause of a small but vocal fan community to be more appealing than focusing on the needs of the casual, mainstream audience. Increasingly, the show was shaped in a way that he thought the fans would like, particularly through the addition of references to its past.

When the series started, the character was called 'Doctor Who' by writers, actors and viewers alike. The name was occasionally used on screen, for example by the evil computer WOTAN who summoned the character by announcing that 'Doctor Who is required'. Yet for fans for whom the series was part of their identity, the silly, childish nature of the name began to bristle. Their solution was to argue that, while the name of the programme was *Doctor Who*, the character was actually just called 'The Doctor'. To please this small section of fandom, Nathan-Turner dutifully changed the name of the character in the credits from 'Doctor Who' to 'The Doctor'. It was a small change, but it suggested that fan perspectives could shape the programme.

High-profile fans gained increasing access to the production team and received permission to enter Broadcasting House and watch filming on studio days. On occasions they would sneak pictures of the sets and publish them in fanzines before the story had been aired. One fan who prized his access was the independently wealthy collector and DJ Ian Levine. 'A crucial, sometimes controversial force within Northern Soul,' as the DJ and dance music historian Greg Wilson describes him, 'Ian Levine probably unearthed more rare records than any other DJ during the scene's heyday.' He applied his collector's instincts to *Doctor Who* and was responsible for finding and preserving many old episodes that would otherwise have been lost. Levine became close to Nathan-Turner and began to act in the capacity of an unofficial continuity advisor. This may seem an unusual situation, but when fans knew far more about the history of the programme than the production team did, it made a strange sort of sense.

Nathan-Turner was a showman with a great love of variety, pantomime and light entertainment – qualities that sat awkwardly with the nihilistic, bleak worldview favoured by his script editor Eric Saward. These were not influences which were appreciated by a teenage male fanbase wishing that the programme they loved was more serious and less embarrassing. Nathan-Turner found that while American fans were usually respectful and adoring, British fans could be prickly. Signs that they were preparing to turn against him were apparent in an argument that erupted at a party after the first day of Longleat. This was, ultimately, an argument about exactly who was the keeper of the *Doctor Who* flame – the fans or the producer. As one fan shouted at Nathan-Turner as he walked out, 'Just remember – we'll still be here long after you've gone!'

In 1983, the bitterness of Nathan-Turner's coming clash with fandom was still largely in the future. On the surface, the crowds of Longleat and the fun of *The Five Doctors* gave the impression that *Doctor Who* was in rude health. The anniversary celebration was broadcast during the BBC's *Children in Need* charity night, a high-profile slot which delighted Nathan-Turner. The episode received a positive critical reaction, if only a small bump in viewing figures. Very few people would have then predicted that, less than two years later, the BBC would attempt to cancel the series.

Peter Davison would not be around at that point, however. He first had doubts about continuing in the role during the filming of the final story in his first series – *Time-Flight*, a story in which Concorde went back in time and landed in prehistoric Earth. By the time this was shot, Davison wrote, 'the budget was all but gone, and no amount of decent writing can make up for polystyrene monsters and a foot-long model of Concorde at the back of a perspective set in Studio 8 of Television Centre.' He made the decision to leave shortly after the Longleat convention while he was in Yorkshire filming an *All Creatures Great and Small* Christmas special. 'I was never very happy with my second series. I think it just got a little bit dull, and the stories a bit over-complex. I didn't feel that I had a lot of room to embellish the character and for me, that presented too limited a challenge.' Davison did not see a way for the programme to improve, given the restrictions of the budget and what he referred to as Nathan-Turner's 'megalomaniac tendencies'. 'John and I have always got on well, but we did have a creative difference over the direction that he wanted *Doctor Who* to go, and the direction I thought it should take,' he has said.

In his autobiography, Davison wrote that, 'I burnt my bridges and tried to imagine a life after *Doctor Who*, never imagining that there wouldn't really be one.' This remark is not a reflection on his later work, for of all the classic Doctors it was probably Troughton and Davison who worked the most consistently for the rest of their careers. But at the time, Davison had thought that being *Doctor Who* was just one job among many. Unhappy with his series creatively, he would not have imagined that this job would overshadow the rest of his life's work, including seemingly more popular and successful roles such as Tristan in *All Creatures*. Davison had thought that leaving the role of the Doctor behind was possible. But just as the programme now had a past, it also had a future. He did not then realise that being the Doctor was a lifetime commitment.

8

The Target (1984–86)

1. Unfair Attacks

When Colin Baker was a baby, in the final years of the Second World War, the house opposite his family home took a direct hit from a German bomb. The explosion sent a piece of the bomb casing smashing through his window, which embedded in the head of his cot. His family 'all rushed up to my bedroom and found the back of the cot demolished by a bit of shrapnel', Baker recalled. They found 'a bit of bomb that, had I been sitting up, would have obliterated my infant barnet'. Baby Colin, fortunately, survived this near miss. Indeed, he slept through the whole thing. But the incident established a pattern that would recur throughout his life – Baker would find himself a target, in ways that were unprovoked and quite unfair. But he would ultimately survive all these attacks.

When Baker was three years old, for example, his family moved from London to Rochdale where, after he started school, he was bullied for his posh southern accent. Called 'Waterworks' after the other children found how easy it was to make him cry, he was a target once again, despite being quite blameless. 'I was just a tosser who wore glasses. I acquired more bloody noses in those early years than I like to remember,' he recalled. His response to this abuse was to 'play the fool' and amuse others, in order to curry favour with his classmates. 'That's where the acting started, changing the accent', he said. The bullying, ultimately, 'made me the man I am now'.

His initial career was spent working in a solicitor's office where he learnt first-hand the extent to which the law was a tool to protect the wealthy, rather than a means for achieving justice. It was an experience that left him determined to tell the truth as he saw it, regardless of the consequences. Leaving the profession at the age of twenty-three, he enrolled at the London Academy of Music and Dramatic Art. He rose to fame in the hugely successful mid-1970s drama series *The Brothers*, playing the loathsome merchant banker and proto-yuppie Paul Merroney. Baker's performance was so compelling, and his character so despicable, that he was voted the Most Hated Man in Britain by readers of the *Sun* in 1976. He often received abuse from members of the public in the street, who saw little distinction between the actor and the character that he played. On one occasion Baker was on the way to an awards ceremony to collect an award with the rest of the cast of *The Brothers*, when he was punched in the face by a member of the public. Baker collected the award with a tooth missing. Once again, he had become a target, despite doing nothing more wicked than performing his job to the best of his abilities.

John Nathan-Turner gave Baker the role of the Sixth Doctor in 1984, deliberately moving away from Davison's pleasant characterisation to lean into Baker's on-screen nasty persona. About a year after he got the part, the BBC attempted to end *Doctor Who*. As might be expected, Colin Baker was blamed for this, in the eyes of the public at least. He was the obvious target and, wearing the Sixth Doctor's bright, tasteless, multicolour coat, he certainly attracted attention.

Once again, Baker's role as the target was unfair. The programme was at the mercy of executive-level BBC politics, the most significant of which being the arrival of Michael Grade as Controller of BBC One in September 1984. Grade had previously worked at LWT, where he competed for audiences with the BBC and often criticised them publicly. In an interview given before he joined the corporation, he singled out *Come Dancing* and *Doctor Who* as evidence of 'the BBC's senility', the type of deadwood cluttering up the BBC's schedules which he said they needed to get rid of. Relaunched versions of *Doctor Who* and *Come Dancing* – now retitled as *Strictly Come Dancing* – are now regarded as the crown jewels of the 21st-century BBC. Now they are properly financed, reinvented by talented people and fully supported by the corporation, they have become the two programmes most commonly held up to support arguments for the continuing existence of the corporation. Grade's opinions, then, suggest that he was more attuned to seeing flaws than he was at recognising potential. It is, after all, much easier to destroy things than it is to nurture or build something of worth. Within six months of joining the BBC he tried to cancel *Doctor Who*. *Come Dancing* was cancelled a few years later.

Grade was the nephew of the great media proprietor and impresario Lew Grade. Nowadays he would be seen as a nepo baby – someone who owed his career in media to family connections rather than talent – though that would neglect his many achievements, including championing the work of Dennis Potter and his period as the second chief executive of Channel 4. He now sits in the House of Lords as Baron Grade of Yarmouth and is the chairman of Ofcom. Yet he is fully aware that, long after he has gone, the thing he will be remembered for is his attempt to kill *Doctor Who*. It is a role that Grade now appears to embrace, for example by sitting down for an hour-long interview for the

Blu-Ray release of Colin Baker-era *Doctor Who*. 'Everywhere I went,' he said in 2022, 'I wasn't Michael Grade who put *Live Aid* on TV, or *The Singing Detective* or *Bread*, [I was] the man who cancelled *Doctor Who*.' Talking to Matthew Sweet for a Radio 4 documentary in 2023, Grade admitted that 'My involvement in Doctor Who's attempted assassination will overshadow what I regard as my real achievements in broadcasting, but there you go.' When he was asked if there was anything that he enjoyed about being immortalised for his role in the *Doctor Who* story, he replied with just one word: 'No.'

As Controller of BBC One, Michael Grade would naturally have felt that he was above all the programmes on his schedules, able to cancel or continue them with a word like a Roman emperor. He had not realised, at that point, that *Doctor Who* was already bigger than he was.

2. 'We Wanted It to Die'

Michael Grade arrived at the BBC the year after Jonathan Powell replaced David Reid as Head of Series and Serials. Reid had been the last person in BBC management who was supportive of the show. He valued both John Nathan-Turner's passion for the programme and his ability to get it made on such a small budget. 'John was immediately someone you liked,' Reid recalled. 'Just one of those characters, lovely, flamboyant, sparkling eyes – with enormous enthusiasm. He lived and breathed *Doctor Who* and that meant it was a little bit of the department that was running itself.'

Powell, in stark contrast, took an immediate dislike to Nathan-Turner. 'My memory is that whenever [Nathan-Turner] came into the office, what I really wanted was for him to leave. We didn't fight but we didn't get on. I don't think he understood quality work. There was just something about him. I wanted him to go – *and* his bloody programme actually.'

When Grade joined the BBC as Powell's boss, he was greeted by a memo from Powell that read, 'Here are the programmes we are making for you next year. I'd really like to see you as soon as possible because, despite the planning system, I'd like you to know that we will change whatever you want because we have other ideas and if you don't like the stuff we are doing, I'm very happy to cancel them.' Clearly Grade was not going to face internal executive opposition in his desire to cancel *Doctor Who*.

It is not unusual for incoming executives to cancel legacy programmes. Even if they are continually successful, they will not get any credit or praise for making them. It is also the case that, when a new boss arrives in a hierarchical organisation, their underlings quickly adopt their tastes and prejudices, often to a more extreme extent. Grade was certainly not shy sharing his feelings about *Doctor Who*, or the type of people that watched it. As he said in a 2014 interview, 'I thought it was horrible, awful. I thought it was so out-dated. It was just a little show for a few pointy-headed *Doctor Who* fans. It was also very violent and it had lost its magic.' Very quickly, Nathan-Turner found that no one in BBC management supported the programme. Powell described how the show was then seen by the BBC management, 'It was terrible [. . .] What it needed was triple the budget. It was made, as far as I can tell, for nothing. But it wasn't worth investing in. It was a problem child, it really was. It was an embarrassment. It had become a laughing stock. Nobody wanted it to succeed – we wanted it to die.'

Grade's arrival came after Nathan-Turner had cast Colin Baker as the Sixth Doctor. There is, it can be argued, a recurring pattern in the casting of Doctors. When a showrunner or producer casts their first Doctor, they pick a person who is exactly what the show needs at that point in time in order to be fresh and relevant. When they come to cast their second Doctor, however, they essentially just cast themselves. For example, Steven Moffat's first Doctor was the youthful, awkwardly handsome Matt Smith, who was perfect for building a more international audience following the success of the David Tennant years. When he came to cast his second Doctor, he chose a slightly scary older Scotsman who was perhaps a little too clever by half. The showrunner and character, in other words, had much in common. When John Nathan-Turner cast Peter Davison as a young, polite, handsome and vulnerable Doctor, this was exactly what was needed at a time when many thought that *Doctor Who* could only be the Tom Baker show. After Davison regenerated, he turned into a round-faced, curly-haired, slightly messianic, arrogant figure in outrageously colourful bad-taste clothing. It was not hard to see similarities between the character and their creator. 'Oh, I think absolutely, *absolutely* he was casting himself,' Peter Davison has said. Or in the words of Jonathan Powell, 'Colin Baker did seem to be him. I think that *Doctor Who* was his fantasy and he was Doctor Who. He got sort of trapped into this thing, which became his ego and he became synonymous with it. I remember absolutely thinking, "He's just creating something in his own image."'

When Davison left, Nathan-Turner wanted a Doctor entirely different to the likeable but mild Fifth Doctor. He decided that the Sixth Doctor should be arrogant, pompous and vain, and Colin Baker was a strong enough actor to give him exactly what he wanted. The Sixth Doctor was intentionally created to be dislikeable – exactly like Nathan-Turner appeared to Jonathan Powell. The broader intention, however, was to make him a figure like Mr Darcy in *Pride and Prejudice*. 'In the first few chapters, you think he's a prig, and a pig, and unpleasant, and arrogant and supercilious,' Baker has said. 'By the end of the book, you realise he's the only truly decent, caring person in the whole of the story. And that's the plan I had for my Doctor.' This was, perhaps, how Nathan-Turner hoped his relationship with Powell would develop over time.

The plan, of course, assumed that the series would continue long enough for this character arc to play out. It also assumed that people who initially disliked the character would stick around long enough to see them change. This was not something that Michael Grade had any intention of letting happen. In his opinion, Baker's portrayal was 'absolutely God-awful'.

Baker's initial story, when his Doctor was at his most dislikeable, is seen by many fans as the low point of the entire canon. In a 2009 *Doctor Who Magazine* poll, the final Peter Davison story *The Caves of Androzani* was voted the greatest story in the history of the programme. *The Twin Dilemma*, the story that immediately followed and Colin Baker's first, came bottom of the poll, the worst story in the history of *Doctor Who*. Baker found this poll difficult. 'I can only say that it wounds me,' he admitted. 'I should be able to rise above it and pretend I don't care. But I actually do care.' Baker was always scrupulously honest.

After being informed that his show was cancelled, Nathan-Turner immediately began to fight the decision. He worked against the corporation that employed him, with the initial intention of getting public opinion on his side. He may not have been able to speak to the press himself, but he did have Ian Levine and an army of fans ready to do as he instructed, and he used them to leak the news. He gave Levine the official password – 'snowball' – which informed Fleet Street journalists that his information was coming from a BBC insider.

The news first reached the public on 26 February 1985, in an article in the *Evening Standard.* Two days later, the *Sun* ran with the headline, Dr. Who Axed In Plot By The BBC. The *Daily Star* launched a 'Save Doctor Who' campaign, complete with Colin Baker stickers, and Ian Levine was photographed breaking the screen of his television with a hammer. 'Britain's top *Who* fan Ian Levine declared war on the BBC decision yesterday – by smashing his TV set!' the *Sun* reported. 'Irate Ian, a 32-year-old record producer, ripped down his aerial and sent his licence to Mr Grade in protest.'

Grade held an emergency meeting with Jonathan Powell, Managing Director of Television Bill Cotton and Chief Press Officer Keith Samuel. Initially they joked about fans threatening to attack the Houses of Parliament with Daleks. Samuel, Powell recalled, then said, 'If they take the Daleks to the House of Commons, that photograph will be on the front page of every single newspaper in the entire world.' It was the thought of this that caused Grade and the BBC to back down. 'At that point we said, "OK, maybe we haven't cancelled it – maybe it will come back in a year's time." If that hadn't happened, it would have gone. But the judgement was that it simply wasn't worth it. There was too much else going on and it was not worth the aggro.'

It was officially announced that the series wasn't cancelled. Instead, it was going to take an eighteen-month break before returning, for financial reasons. After his attempt to cancel *Doctor Who* had failed, Grade went on a skiing holiday in the French Alps, fully intending to forget all about the programme. He was not expecting a heavily pregnant *Daily Mail* journalist to follow him up the mountain to ask him to explain himself. He did not know then that those questions would follow him around for the rest of his life.

It was, on one level, a victory. *Doctor Who* had proved able to defend itself in a way that it couldn't when the BBC had first tried to cancel it, in 1963, before the first episode had even been broadcast. Then, it had been saved only by Verity Lambert's determination. Now, it was protected by the loyalty and passion of its fanbase. Grade was thwarted in his attempt to cancel the series outright, yet he was not personally impacted by these events and his stellar career continued as before. *Doctor Who* fandom, however, had been damaged. Its most dedicated and extreme fans had been brought to public attention, and this did not do them any favours. The casual newspaper reader was not impressed by the sight of a man in his thirties smashing his telly because something they saw as a children's programme had been cancelled. The idea that there was something wrong with adult *Doctor Who* fans was reinforced.

Many people who had grown up with the show, and who were drawn to it and felt a connection with it, were in a state we might call fan-curious. They had not come out to either themselves or their families as full-blown fans, yet they could very easily have taken their interest further if they had connected with the wider fan community. The appearance of this particular strain of fandom in the media, however, gave them reason to pause. There was a striking disconnect between the qualities of the programme that attracted them, and the tone and atmosphere of the fans they were seeing in the media. The imagination, wonder, absurdity and mischief that they were drawn to seemed notably absent. Fandom looked cringingly embarrassing, so they kept their distance and retreated deeper into the fan closet. As a result, a great untapped and unformed reservoir of enthusiasm for the programme remained invisible. It would not reveal itself until the twenty-first century.

The most cringeworthy moment for the perception of fandom was a song called 'Doctor in Distress', a celebrity charity record organised by Levine and Nathan-Turner, in the hope of keeping pressure on BBC management. This was released under the unfortunate band name of 'Who Cares?' The record came three months after its main inspiration, the Band Aid single 'Do They Know It's Christmas?', had raised millions of pounds for famine relief. The Ethiopian famine and an eighteen-month wait for more episodes of *Doctor Who* did not strike many as comparable causes, and in that context the *Doctor Who* record appeared incredibly tasteless. Early press reports spoke of the hope that artists including Elton John and Holly Johnson would be part of the record, but alas the final line-up of stars was not quite so bright. Besides Colin Baker and Nicola Bryant, who had been press-ganged into singing against their better instincts and to their eternal regret, the record also featured Bobby Gee from Bucks Fizz, comedian and impersonator Faith Brown, members of the Moody Blues and Matt Bianco. The finished Hi-NRG dance record was, by common consent among everyone involved, unforgivably awful. 'I cringe because I hate it so much,' said the record's producer Ian Levine. '"Doctor in Distress" is inexcusable. I've never lived it down.'

The battering that the public image of fandom suffered from stunts like 'Doctor in Distress' came at a time when BBC management was speaking publicly about the creative failure of the programme and its production team. Michael Grade was a guest on *The Jimmy Young Show* in September that year, where he said that 'the people who make *Doctor Who* have got rather complacent. The show got rather violent and lost a lot of its imagination, a lot of its wit, and had failed to capture a new audience.' That the BBC would publicly criticise its own programmes and staff like this seems barely believable now. Public perception of the show understandably became increasingly negative. It became common knowledge, among those who didn't watch it, that it was nowhere near as good as it used to be. Adults who did watch it were believed to be emotionally stunted 'anoraks'. The fans may have won the battle, but at some cost. In the long run Michael Grade was going to win his war.

3. Peri

If the BBC's own audience research is anything to go by, the Colin Baker years were less appealing to the general audience than previous eras. 'While the character of Doctor Who is generally considered likeable, the portrayal by Colin Baker is not so highly regarded,' the Television Audience Reaction Report stated in its summary. The report noted that responses were mixed, and that some enthusiastic voices were highly supportive of the current series. Others, however, were tuning out. 'One in five of the sample audience decided to stop watching the series at some point,' it reported. 'The reasons they gave for ceasing to watch the series were varied, but tended to concentrate on what respondents regarded as its stupidity, boringness, repetitiveness and unoriginality.'

Many different criticisms have been levelled at the Colin Baker years, to rationalise why this varied and inventive run of stories was received so badly. The most common argument is simply that Baker's wild multicoloured coat was to blame. 'I seriously think that the costume was the greatest mistake in the history of television,' Russell T Davies has said. It is quite a fabulous coat, in its way, and Baker was a skilful enough actor to give the impression that he was comfortable wearing it. Yet given the choice, he would have chosen something dark and simple for this interpretation of the character, such as the leather jacket that Christopher Eccleston's Doctor would wear in 2005. The multicoloured coat, Baker believed, made it difficult for viewers to take the show seriously. The coat 'said the wrong thing about the Doctor,' Baker believed, 'and it said the wrong thing about the programme.'

The second most frequent accusation was the return of that serious complaint from the 1970s – the programme had once again become too violent. In the 1970s, the two scenes which received the most hostile press attention were a sequence in *Terror of the Autons*, where police officers were revealed to be murderous aliens, and the final shot of the third episode of *The Deadly Assassin* in which the Doctor apparently drowned. The 1984 season, curiously, also included scenes in which police officers are revealed to be murderous aliens, and an end-of-episode shot of the Doctor underwater, once again apparently drowned. This may be nothing more than an odd coincidence, but it is tempting to see this as the programme testing its old boundaries and seeing if they still held. In the 1970s such scenes were considered unsuitable for small children, but the series now saw itself as more mature and serious, with an older audience who were unafraid of darker stories.

Finding that it could now get away with scenes like these, the programme proceeded to push further. In the following season – Baker's first – the level of violence became noticeably elevated. *Doctor Who* now offered blood, torture, hangings, crushed hands and syringes being stabbed into necks. This violence was presented with a striking lack of compassion or empathy. Baker's Doctor showed zero concern after a pair of guards had fallen to their deaths in a bath of acid, for example, callously saying, 'You'll forgive me if I don't join you,' as he collected his coat and left. It was perhaps not just the violence but the overall context of script editor Eric Saward's bleak, nihilistic universe that left people disturbed. This was a brutal universe that lacked any sense of redemption. Michael Grade and Jonathan Powell both referred to this level of violence to justify their belief that the series should end.

Looking back at those years with contemporary eyes, however, it is not the coat or the violence that are the most disturbing aspects of Baker's era. It is the treatment of his assistant Peri, an American botany student played by Nicola Bryant.

Peri arrived in the series in Peter Davison's penultimate story. When we first meet her, on a boat off the island of Lanzarote, she is attempting to persuade her stepfather Howard to allow her to go travelling with 'a couple of really nice English guys'. Howard doesn't argue, but instead he tricks her. He traps her on the boat, prevents her from leaving, and when she attempts to escape she nearly drowns. Fortunately, she is rescued by Turlough, who carries her back to the TARDIS where she is left to recover and sleep. In the TARDIS bedroom she has a nightmare, calling out, 'I'm sorry, Howard. I didn't mean it. No, Howard. Please don't leave me alone. Don't . . . don't turn out the light.' The 2003 *Doctor Who* novella *Shell Shock* by Simon A. Forward, clearly influenced by those words, added further background to her relationship with Howard. The book claimed that Peri had been sexually abused by her stepfather while her mother was in the next room. Even for those who feel that this book went too far, Peri's nightmare at the very least established Peri as a young woman with a fear of abandonment and a troubled relationship with father figures.

When she was cast, Bryant developed a background for the character herself, to help her play the role. She decided that Peri goes off with the Doctor because he reminds her of her late father. It is Peri's misfortune, then, that almost as soon as she meets the charming Peter Davison, he regenerates into an older man – Colin Baker's unstable Sixth Doctor, whose post-regeneration trauma causes him to experience violent mood swings. In his first full episode, in the sanctity of the TARDIS control room, the new Doctor puts his hands around Peri's throat and attempts to strangle her. Even after these violent episodes start to recede, the Doctor remains cavalier with her life. He sends Peri through a transportation machine without knowing if it will kill her, and at one point uses her as a human shield.

After his first attempt on her life, Peri doesn't try to escape from either the Doctor or the TARDIS. Instead, she continues to follow him around, attempting to pacify his moods. The Doctor announces that he will atone for his violent attack by becoming a hermit in some 'hellish wilderness', but he also decides that Peri will accompany him as his disciple. In doing so, he insists that she will continue to suffer for his actions. The meek way that Peri accepts this role suggests that she can't imagine any other way of relating to an older man. With this exchange, their relationship is established as an abusive co-dependent one.

Peri remains with the Doctor and undergoes perhaps the most traumatic time of any companion. He belittles her constantly, for example in *The Two Doctors* when he says, 'Do try and use your brain, my girl. Small though it is, the human brain can be quite effective when used properly.' She is repeatedly tied up, tortured and experimented on. In her final episode she is killed by a Josef Mengele-type doctor, who shaves her head and transplants an alien mind into her body. We later learn that she escapes this fate and marries King Yrcanos, a battle-hungry warlord played by Brian Blessed. Peri again finds herself in a relationship with a loud, controlling, violent and abusive older male, as that pattern plays itself out once more in her life.

Throughout her time with the Doctor, Peri's role in the plot is to be an object, appraised and studied by friends and foes alike. In *The Caves of Androzani* she is kidnapped by the leather-suited, masked figure of Sharaz Jek, who falls in love with her at first sight. 'How could I ever let you go?' he tells her. 'The sight of beauty is so important to me.' Peri had the same effect on the villain in the 1985 radio story *Slipback* and on Mestor, the slug monster from *The Twin Dilemma*, who refuses to kill her because he finds her appearance 'pleasing'. This was toned down from the original script, in which the giant slug man explained that he found her attractive because, despite his current appearance, he has 'human ancestry'. The sexual implication in the giant slug's words caused Peri to 'shrink in horror'. Interest in Peri's body is not always sexual. In *The Two Doctors*, the alien chef Shockeye has high hopes for her as a meal. 'Oh, what a fine, fleshy beast,' he says as he knocks her out. 'Just in your prime, and ripe for the knife!'

That Peri was intended to be sexualised was evident from her costume. Her first story was filmed in Lanzarote, so the bikini and the shorts she wears made sense. This was followed by filming in a quarry near Poole in Dorset in November, where she was expected to wear the same outfit. 'It's like [Peri] never got to put proper clothes on for what felt like the rest of that season,' Bryant has said. 'I was really stuck in some terribly 80s sexist crap, really, most of the time.' The outfit was in no way suitable for the cold weather, and at one point the cameraman said to the production assistant, 'Can you slap her? She's gone blue.' By the end of the week her lungs were wheezing. She went to a doctor who diagnosed pneumonia and prescribed antibiotics, along with two weeks' rest. Bryant recalls that she then 'took a bath, and lumps of my flesh fell off my feet. At which point I went back to my doctor, and I went, "What's happening to my feet?" And he went, "You've got frostbite." There's not a lot you can do with that, you just kind of wrap it up. Nowadays, you would sue, wouldn't you?'

For the next season, the outfit got worse. Nathan-Turner

dressed Bryant in a series of Day-Glo leotards, coupled with a pair of matching shorts. 'Being stuck in a leotard and shorts – that's not normal clothes,' Bryant has said. According to Colin Baker, 'It was a gay man's idea of what heterosexual men want.' 'The reason they bothered me,' Bryant explained, 'is that, like most women, you know what your assets are. I've got a nice smile and an hourglass figure [. . .] If he wanted sexy, I could do sexy – it just wouldn't have looked like his idea [for the costume].' Arguing against the costume, however, was not an option. 'I did not answer back,' she explained. Nathan-Turner 'was kind to me, generally, but only if I did as I was told'.

Nathan-Turner typically had good relationships with female friends, who invariably described him as kind and thoughtful, as well as fun and gossipy, but his relationship with *Doctor Who* female companions was more complicated. Speaking in 2022, Bryant said that, 'I think, at [that] stage in my life, I did seem to attract people who want to control me. And I think there was a huge element of control in [how Nathan-Turner treated me]. He wasn't unloving. He adored me. He cared for me. I think he wanted to "discover me" and make me something. And I think he wanted to go beyond even what we were doing in *Who*, in some strange way. I was always *his* girl. He was always, "I found her". But there was a lot of "you will not do this" and "you will not do that".'

Once Bryant did say no to Nathan-Turner, when he wanted to cast her in a pantomime in Southampton while they were also making *Doctor Who.* Studio days for *Doctor Who* could be an exhausting eighteen hours long, and Bryant didn't see how she could commit to the pantomime at the same time. 'I got my agent to say "no", because I thought that's what you do. It was made very clear to me that "no" was not an option – very clear. I was, shall we say punished? I was in trouble. On set, from the moment my agent called, I was not spoken to for the rest of that day.'

As an example of how she was 'punished', Bryant cites the mini-episode *A Fix with Sontarans*, which was produced for Jimmy Savile's now notorious Saturday evening programme *Jim'll Fix It*, and which brought eight-year-old fan Gareth Jenkins into the TARDIS. *Doctor Who* viewers were surprised that, instead of including Peri alongside Colin Baker, the earlier character of Janet Fielding's Tegan was used instead. 'Everybody wonders why I didn't do the Jimmy Savile, and everyone wonders if I suspected Jimmy Savile,' Bryant told interviewer Matthew Sweet. 'No, this was a demonstration of how I could be punished. So Janet was asked to do it, instead of me.'

Bryant's relationship with Nathan-Turner broke down at a convention in the 1990s, ahead of a memorabilia auction. Nathan-Turner had convinced himself that Bryant had slept with a man that his partner Gary Downie was interested in. As they were backstage preparing for the auction, Bryant has said, 'JN-T came up to me, spat in my face and said, "How dare you?" I was shaking. I can't believe that he would think that I would do that. I was shocked and I'm still shattered at the thought of it now. I adored John and from that point on, I never spoke to him again.'

In Peri's final story, there is a scene where she is shackled to a rock under the green sky of an alien beach as the tide rises higher and will eventually drown her. The Nathan-Turneresque Doctor stands above Peri, criticising and abusing her. 'You are expendable! You have no value,' he shouts. Viewers were largely confused about what was happening in this scene, as indeed were the actors and the director. Had the Doctor been turned evil by his earlier exposure to a brain-transference pulse? Was he just pretending to be evil, as part of a larger scheme? Or was the whole scene faked by sinister forces meddling in the Time Lord trial? Speaking in the 1990s, Colin Baker said that, 'There was a point when I said to Eric Saward, the script editor, "When I'm tying Peri to this rock and threatening to torture her, am I doing it for some subtle reason of my own, because I think I'm being watched or whatever, or because I've been affected by the mind probe, or is the Matrix lying?" Those were the three alternatives as I saw it. He said, "I don't know, you'd better ask [the writer] Philip Martin." So I got in touch and gave him those three alternatives. He said, "I don't know, Eric wrote the trial stuff, all the Matrix stuff was added after, by Eric, you'd better ask him." So I went to John Nathan-Turner, he said, "Oh, whichever you like." I felt it was the Matrix lying, so I really was torturing Peri. But it was very difficult. You expect the writers to know what's happening, but that's not always the case.'

Whatever the intention, the scene feels even more unsettling when you remember that Nicola Bryant had a particular dislike of the sea, and realise that it was filmed on the beach at Telscombe Cliffs in Sussex, just over the road from Nathan-Turner's house. It is a scene that sums up how the character of Peri was treated during her years on the show – continually abused, for reasons that are never made entirely clear. It suggests that, whatever was going wrong with the show in the mid-1980s, it was a bit more serious than Colin Baker's multicoloured coat.

4. 'Doable Barkers'

The pattern that repeated throughout Baker's life – that of becoming a target for attack through no fault of his own – happened again after the publication of the 25 March 2013 edition of the *Daily Mirror*. The front-page headline DOCTOR WHO SEX SCANDAL was accompanied by a smiling photo of Baker in full costume, standing next to producer John Nathan-Turner. Although the article made clear that it was Nathan-Turner who was the subject of allegations, that wasn't the immediate impression that anyone who glanced at the front page would have got. The subsequent abuse that Baker received from people in the street suggested that many did indeed come to this erroneous conclusion. Once again, the innocent Baker had become a target for reasons that were entirely unfair.

The scandal followed the publication of Richard Marson's 2013 biography *JN-T: The Life and Scandalous Times of John Nathan-Turner*. As well as covering Nathan-Turner's life and career, the book also included a chapter entitled 'Hanky Panky', which detailed sexual relations during the 1980s between Nathan-Turner, his partner Gary Downie and a number of young, often teenage, gay *Doctor Who* fans. Marson states clearly in his book that 'Although I did meet some people who felt that their treatment at the hands of John and Gary was inappropriate, it would not be true to say that I've found anyone willing to testify to coercion or abuse.' That said, there are questions of power and control involved in Nathan-Turner's and Downie's behaviour which few would be comfortable with now.

Marson, a teenage *Doctor Who* fan who went on to become the editor-in-chief of *Blue Peter*, included his own personal recollections of meetings with Nathan-Turner and Downie during this time. After a set visit to the filming of *Resurrection of the Daleks*, Marson was invited to join the cast and crew for a drink in the BBC club on the fourth floor of Television Centre. Being only seventeen, Marson ordered an orange and lemonade. He was quite unprepared for the moment when, after Nathan-Turner had introduced him to Downie, the question, 'Have you ever had two up you?' was whispered in his ear. A more serious incident occurred about a year later, when Marson visited a largely empty

BBC Union House one evening to pick up some photographs. He was collected from reception by Downie, who proceeded to grope and kiss him against his will in the lift. Marson fled as soon as the lift doors opened and hid under the desk in a nearby empty office. Searching for a weapon to help him fight off Downie if he was found, he grabbed a script off the desk and rolled it up tight, like a baton. It was only when he had made it to the safety of the London Underground that he realised he was carrying the script for *Timelash* episode two.

Nathan-Turner was always resolutely 'out' and never hid his sexuality, which took courage in the 1980s. The drama department of the BBC was welcoming in this respect, as it was a place where an openly gay lifestyle was accepted. 'When I left the BBC in the 60s and came back in the early 80s, I couldn't believe how everybody seemed to be gay,' the assistant floor manager Val McCrimmon recalled. 'The BBC had got ever so camp. There were men who, when I'd left, were married. When I came back, they were gay. I was just amazed.' Accusations of a 'gay mafia' were common. As Peter Davison said in a 2016 interview, 'Grade didn't like what he saw as the "Gay Mafia" at the BBC, and he didn't like John. He wanted to get rid of him.' While the phrase is unfortunate, there was evidence of favouritism at the time in the hiring of gay associates. Nathan-Turner, for example, was able to arrange for his partner Gary Downie to be hired as an assistant floor manager. 'John got Gary into the BBC and then kept him there,' the director Andrew Morgan told Marson. 'They had a very loving and caring relationship and that was great, but actually Gary wasn't good at his job and John was. Gary was difficult to place. I always dreaded working with him because he was unreliable.'

Like the drama department, early organised *Doctor Who* fandom was also strikingly gay. In the view of actor Matthew

Waterhouse, *Who* fandom 'was wholly dominated by queer men of a bitchy nature'. In his autobiography, Waterhouse explained that he 'did not assume that absolutely every *Doctor Who* fan was gay, but that heterosexuals were a peculiar minority, as in certain corners of New York after dark. In a reversal of the usual assumption, it could be taken that any particular fan was gay until it was revealed that he wasn't.'

Many theories have been given as to why this fantastical series about a largely asexual alien resonated so strongly with the gay community. For the later showrunner Russell T Davies, 'It's easy to draw a link between gayness and fandom. So easy, maybe it's true. Because as those teenage years advanced, two things synced up. I was gay and went silent, watching all the parties and fancying boys at a remove instead of getting drunk on cider, scared of giving myself away. At exactly the same time, I watched TV fiercely. Both things became closeted. *Doctor Who* became the other love that dares not speak its name.'

The gay community's interest in *Doctor Who* was evident as early as 1975. The London Lesbian and Gay Switchboard used a pair of Daleks to promote a fundraiser, a promotional gimmick that made the front page of *Gay News*. 'Gays who failed to attend the Gay Switchboard Benefit at Hammersmith Town Hall last Saturday will be exterminated,' the report began, alongside a photograph of the Daleks attracting attention in Portobello Road. The article also speculated about Dalek sexuality, claiming that '1 in 20 Daleks are!' This interest led to the founding of LGBTQ+ fan groups such as The Sisterhood of Karn, and was reinforced when Davies included *Doctor Who* fandom in his groundbreaking 1990s drama series *Queer as Folk*. *Doctor Who*'s ongoing importance to the LGBTQ+ community is such that, when the 2007 London Pride march clashed with the series finale, the organisers arranged for the episode to be screened in Trafalgar Square in case too many people stayed at home to watch it.

That so many young boys and men in early *Doctor Who* fandom were gay provided Nathan-Turner with plenty of opportunity to abuse his position. Nathan-Turner courted the fan community and could provide privileged access to the making of *Doctor Who*. Being in favour with John gave a devoted fan like Ian Levine access to scripts, studio days, tapes and crew – along with an elevated status in fandom and, at times, input into the development of future stories. But all this came at a cost. Ian Levine told Marson about his visit to Nathan-Turner's flat in early 1980. 'That's the one time I had to get fucked by him – he wouldn't take no for an answer. I had no choice. It was, "You want a favour, I want a favour back."' Levine said that Nathan-Turner later told him to arrange an orgy for them. The command was given, Levine recalls, in the style of 'a Roman emperor. I had to have eight people in my house. In the end, I went upstairs and watched TV. It was just horrible. It made me feel sleazy and unclean.'

Nathan-Turner was a man with many friends, who still talk about him with warmth and affection. The same cannot be said for his partner. 'Gary held John back because there were so many people who couldn't abide Gary,' Colin Baker has said. 'I adored John but I was very wary [of] and occasionally rather disliked Gary. Gary was not nice.' In Ian Levine's view, 'Away from Gary, he was a wonderful person who would do anything for you – larger than life, the life and soul of the party. But Gary was like a black widow spider, spouting venom in his ear.' At conventions, it was usually Gary's role to arrange sexual partners for him and John. They referred to suitable young male fans as 'doable barkers'. Nathan-Turner's decision to target the programme towards an older audience of teenage boys, rather than children, and his desire to engage with the fan community, may have been a creative decision unrelated to his sexual life, but not everyone sees it that way.

Nathan-Turner's behaviour would, of course, be a sackable offence now. In the aftermath of the scandals surrounding predatory paedophiles like Jimmy Savile and others, the BBC would not tolerate a producer abusing his position to gain sexual favours from teenage fans. While the heterosexual age of consent was sixteen, the homosexual legal age at that time was twenty-one. This was widely seen as discriminatory and few in the gay community respected the law, but the fact remains that legally, underage people are unable to give consent to sexual acts.

Nathan-Turner had hoped that *Doctor Who* would be a springboard to a great career in broadcasting, but the longer he stayed with the programme, the more it seemed that no one else in the industry wanted to work with him. In the gossip-hungry world of the BBC, it seems unlikely that Downie's and Nathan-Turner's behaviour would have been much of a secret. Nathan-Turner's on-screen achievements were considerable, but it was his behaviour that would ultimately shape his reputation.

5. On Trial

When the series eventually returned to the air after its eighteen-month 'hiatus', the line between the on-screen fiction and the behind-the-scenes drama had become even more blurred and slippery. The new series took the shape of a long, fourteen-episode story called *The Trial of a Time Lord*. It felt almost like a cry for help from the production team, as their real-life struggles pushed their way into the broadcast stories.

In this series, the Doctor was put on trial by the Time Lords and informed that, if found guilty, he would be executed. The Time Lords, as we have seen, represented the BBC inside the fiction of the stories. BBC management wanted to kill off *Doctor Who*, and that drama was now repeating itself on screen.

Inside the corporation, and perhaps to some extent inside John Nathan-Turner's mind, Nathan-Turner was *Doctor Who*. It is striking that, when Colin Baker returned to the role after eighteen months away, he had physically changed to increasingly resemble Nathan-Turner. Baker had put on weight and grown his hair, which had then been curled in a way that resembled his producer. When the Doctor was stood in the dock in his brightly coloured bad-taste clothes, it did not take too much imagination to see a double layer of meaning in this on-screen psychodrama.

The idea that production staff bleed into on-screen characters is not unusual for *Doctor Who*. As Elisabeth Sladen has admitted, 'I think I may have based Sarah a little bit on Barry Letts.' In 2004, when Christopher Eccleston was looking for a character for the Ninth Doctor, he decided to play him as his showrunner Russell T Davies. 'Right in front of me was a man who wore a leather jacket and whose brain was genius level, a tinder box of ideas,' he later wrote. 'Russell had energy, he had humour. And there was no one who wanted to be the Doctor more than he did.'

But if the Doctor being judged by the Time Lords was an on-screen representation of Nathan-Turner being judged by the BBC, then who was the prosecutor? In the story, this was a character called the Valeyard, who was revealed to be an evil future version of the Doctor formed from the darker sides of his nature. The Doctor's future, in other words, was trying to destroy the Nathan-Turner Doctor.

Here we are reminded of that threat Nathan-Turner received from a fan during the Longleat celebrations: 'Just remember – we'll still be here long after you've gone!' The fans saw themselves as the programme's future, and they were then trying to bring about the end of Nathan-Turner's reign. The glossy fan magazine *Doctor Who Bulletin* – or 'Doctor Who Bullshit', as Nathan-Turner used to call it – was especially relentless, featuring banner headlines such as JN-T MUST GO NOW or 89% OF FANS WANT A NEW PRODUCER. The BBC, in its wisdom, brought these sentiments to a wider audience by broadcasting programmes in which the state of *Doctor Who* was debated and discussed for the benefit of viewers unaware of these squabbles. In 1987, BBC Two's *Did You See . . . ?* programme, for example, featured interviews with disgruntled fans, including Nathan-Turner's one-time friend Ian Levine, who had fallen out with the producer and begun publicly attacking him. 'The last eight or nine years have seen a very steep decline in the quality of the show,' Levine told the programme. 'It's become a sort of mockery pantomime version of its former self.' From this fan perspective, destroying Nathan-Turner was necessary to protect *Doctor Who*'s long-term future.

In America in the 1980s, organised fandom was marked by dressing up, coming together and celebrating the programme. American fans had typically stumbled upon repeats of Jon Pertwee and Tom Baker episodes on an obscure PBS channel, fallen for the programme's unique, wonderful and faintly ridiculous stories, and felt the need to celebrate this unexpected treat in their lives. In their eyes, the joyless way that UK fandom spent their time intellectually debating and crucifying the programme was baffling. British fans, in contrast, had grown up with the series and it had taken root in their maturing psyches. It was part of them. They felt the accusations that it was bad and stupid keenly and desperately wanted the programme to grow and mature in the same way that they themselves were changing. What happened to *Doctor Who*, in this context, impacted them on a deep level that made little sense to outsiders.

The dark side to British fandom is well documented. It attacked members of the cast and crew in ways that were extremely cruel. The most notorious instance of this came in issue 9 of the *MLG Megazine*, a publication produced by the Merseyside Local Group of the Doctor Who Appreciation Society, which joked about the death of Colin Baker's son Jack, who died as a baby from sudden infant death syndrome.

The idea that fans were the programme's future seemed delusional at the time. Programme makers and the viewing audience were typically seen as two segregated demographics. Few people without Oxbridge backgrounds believed that working in the creative side of the BBC was a realistic aspiration. Yet fans did prove to be the future, thanks to a combination of dogged determination and the changing media landscape of the past few decades. All the showrunners of 21st-century *Doctor Who* are lifelong fans, as are actors like David Tennant and Peter Capaldi. Outside the television series, *Doctor Who* novels and audio adventures are usually created by fans who have found a way to utilise their fandom professionally. That fans were the future of *Doctor Who* is illustrated perfectly by the inclusion of teenage fan Chris Chibnall in the 8 December 1986 edition of BBC One's afternoon discussion programme *Open Air*. 'It hasn't improved that much since it went off the air. It could have been a lot better, it could have been slightly better written,' Chibnall told presenter Pattie Coldwell. 'It was very cliched. It was very routine, running up and down corridors and silly monsters.' Chibnall would become the showrunner of *Doctor Who* from 2017 to 2022.

The battle between the darker side of organised fandom and John Nathan-Turner, then, can be seen as a fight over the question of who actually owns *Doctor Who*. Just as the longer-haired, fuller-figured Colin Baker brought to mind Nathan-Turner, so too can the future essence of the Doctor, the Valeyard, be seen as the representation of the darker side of British fandom. The battle was fought between two sides who both saw themselves as the rightful voice of the programme. It was painful and personal, because both sides identified with the show to the extent that their sense of identity had merged with it. It was hard, in this context, to watch *The Trial of a Time Lord* and not see the battle between the Valeyard and the Doctor in a Time Lord court as a parable for the BBC wanting to kill the series, and using the fans' attempts to destroy Nathan-Turner as their excuse to do so.

The Valeyard's stated desire – the death of the Sixth Doctor – made little sense in the story, for it was never explained how the future Doctor would still exist after they had killed themselves in the past. It makes perfect sense, however, on this higher, metaphorical level. As organised fandom saw it, Nathan-Turner's love of light entertainment, pantomime and showbiz, along with his lack of understanding of character and story, would be the death of *Doctor Who*. For the sake of the programme's future, he had to be removed.

One casualty of all this bad blood was script editor Eric Saward, whose relationship with Nathan-Turner began to deteriorate. He was, instinctively, more in tune with the darker, older, less showbiz version of the programme that fandom was calling for, and he increasingly found himself in disagreement with his boss's decisions. He was also burning out after several stressful, difficult years in the job.

The Trial of a Time Lord was Saward's suggestion. As he recalled, 'I was talking to my partner Jane Judge, who used to be the production secretary on the show. She said, "Well, you're on trial, aren't you, really?" I said, "Yeah, we are, aren't we?" She said, "Why don't you take that as your theme?"'

'I remember my first reaction to that was, "Ooh, risky . . .",' Colin Baker later said. 'To try and mirror reality with art and all that was a dangerous strategy.'

Saward's plan was to base the structure of the season on Dickens's *A Christmas Carol*. Three stories would be presented as evidence at the trial, one from the Doctor's past, one from his present and one from the future. These would then be wrapped up by a further two episodes to be written by Robert Holmes, which would culminate in the Doctor and the Master fighting above a 'time vent', which they would fall into at the end. This idea was inspired by Arthur Conan Doyle's 1893 short story 'The Final Problem', in which Sherlock Holmes and Professor Moriarty fight atop the Reichenbach Falls and seemingly fall to their deaths. Conan Doyle had intended this story to be the end of Holmes, before public pressure persuaded him to resurrect the character eight years later. The character of the Master had originally been created as a Moriarty to the Doctor's Sherlock, so the drama of the fall could have been a fitting end to the series. 'There may have been,' Colin Baker has speculated, 'a certain amount of wanting to aid the downfall of the programme whether conscious or subconscious in Eric's mind when he wrote that.'

Saward became close to Robert Holmes after he approached him to write the script for *The Five Doctors*. He soon came to see him as a mentor figure. Nathan-Turner had been against reusing any writers from before his time, dismissing them as 'old toots', but Saward had fought for Holmes. He believed that he was the greatest classic series writer of all. He managed to persuade Nathan-Turner to ask him back and the result, 1984's *The Caves of Androzani*, more than justified his return. Saward then made a point of using him every year. As a result, Holmes was commissioned to write the first story, plus the concluding episodes, of *The Trial of a Time Lord*.

In theory, when the series returned to our screens after eighteen months away, it could have come back strongly – at least in terms of scripts. Saward had an extended period of time to commission and develop them, and because the new series was just over half the length of previous ones his workload was considerably smaller. In actuality, scripts were rejected as unworkable, and replacements were once again commissioned at the last minute. The replacement scripts which became the story *Terror of the Vervoids* were written by the husband-and-wife team of Pip and Jane Baker. The Bakers could be relied on for turning in usable scripts quickly, but Saward actively disliked the more traditional tone of their work.

Saward decided to resign, explaining his reasons in a 2 April 1986 letter to Jonathan Powell. He admitted that he had 'somehow lost credibility with myself'. He went on to say that he had 'put the best writer (Robert Holmes) the series ever had in hospital and, out of sheer desperation, I am now working with two of the most talentless people (Pip and Jane Baker) who have ever had the nerve to set pen to paper [. . .] Saddens me to leave in such a silly melodramatic way, but I am sick to death of *Doctor Who* and the way it is run.'

Saward's reference to putting Holmes in hospital referred to his guilt about pushing him for scripts as his health was deteriorating. Holmes turned in scripts for the opening story of the season and, while not his strongest work, it was still solid enough to go into production. He also wrote the season's penultimate script, but died before completing the final episode.

Saward was deeply affected by his death. Out of necessity, he returned to the job he had just quit to write the final episode himself, based on his conversations with Holmes about how the series should end. When he turned in this final script, however, Nathan-Turner would not accept the 'time vent' ending. 'I wanted an ending that clearly implied the show was back in business, with no question marks looming over its future,' he said. As Nathan-Turner saw it, the time vent ending would allow the BBC to end the series. He fought against it like the Doctor fighting the Valeyard, because as producer it was his job to keep the show running. Symbolically, he was also fighting to save himself.

For Saward, however, to change the ending was to vandalise Robert Holmes's final work. 'It was the one time in his life when [Nathan-Turner] should have kept his mouth shut and let it go through,' he said later. 'But he couldn't do it, he just couldn't do it.' He saw Nathan-Turner's requests as a command to add a 'walk-down, happy pantomime ending', so he refused to allow his script to be changed.

In the circumstances, Nathan-Turner turned to the only people he knew who were competent enough to write a whole new, different script, containing no elements from Saward's draft, within the brief period of time remaining, with which to somehow end the series. These writers were the eternal professionals Pip and Jane Baker, who arrived like the cavalry to ensure that the Valeyard failed in his evil scheme. Thanks to Pip and Jane, the BBC had no excuse to end the series, the Doctor defeated his twisted future self and Nathan-Turner kept control of *Doctor Who*.

In the aftermath of these events, the aggrieved script editor responded by giving a bitter, angry interview to the cult film and television magazine *Starburst*. Entitled 'Revelations of a Script Editor', Saward relentlessly attacked Nathan-Turner. He called him a 'very paranoid individual' and 'the biggest Prima Donna on the show', whose drinking and obsession with lucrative American conventions actively damaged the production of the programme. He also said that both Colin Baker and Bonnie Langford, who had been hired as the new companion Mel, were 'not very good' and should not have been cast. The interview exposed the toxic working atmosphere of the programme, as Saward viewed it, to the wider world. Colin Baker, in particular, has never forgiven Saward, and has threatened to hit him if they ever met again. Nathan-Turner's reaction, as he later wrote, was that he 'shook with rage [. . .] How could someone I'd worked with for so long say such things? If I was that awful, why had he stayed on the show for five years?' Saward's score-settling interview was widely seen as unprofessional. It may have been one of the reasons that he never worked in mainstream television again.

All these clashes have come to define the Sixth Doctor's era. The drama backstage leaked into, and ultimately overwhelmed, the drama on screen. Yet the characters of the Sixth Doctor and Peri would eventually be redeemed by a series of audio stories that would begin fifteen years later, in which their potential was allowed space to flourish and shine. The character of the Sixth Doctor has been allowed to develop in the way originally intended, and 'Ol' Sixie' has become a firm fan favourite. Colin Baker may always be fated to be a target for unfair setbacks, but he is dogged and determined, and he will get there in the end.

9
The Mystery (1987–95)

1. The Human Bomb

When he was around eight years old, Kent Smith's mother had a nervous breakdown and was taken away to an asylum. As a child Kent would visit her, but he often referred to himself as an orphan because that was what he effectively was. During the Second World War, his English submariner father had been killed in action while Kent was still in the womb. Raised by his maternal grandmother in Dunoon on the Firth of Clyde, he was a Scottish boy raised by an Irish family with a very English name – Percy James Patrick Kent-Smith, or just Kent to his friends and family.

Very little about Kent Smith's upbringing was typical, secure or stable. Like Tom Baker, he underwent religious training, and between the ages of twelve and sixteen he studied to be a priest at Blairs College seminary in Aberdeen. Unlike Baker, Kent was not 'randy for martyrdom' and had no great desire to lead a spiritual life. The discovery of girls when he left the seminary was enough to tempt him along a different path.

Kent left Scotland and moved to London following a failed romance and a broken heart. To his surprise he was quickly offered a good job at an insurance firm because he had an English double-barrelled surname and had been a boarder in a Scottish seminary. That he had no aptitude or interest in the work wasn't important. 'That's when I realised that the English class system was really bananas,' he has said, 'because they believed that the Scots were hard working. Well, I proved them wrong.' He quit after five boring years to become a hippy. Living in a bedsit in Belsize Park, a friend told him that there was a job he would be perfect for in the box office of the Roundhouse theatre. They were looking for a hippy who could add up.

It was while working at the Roundhouse that he met the experimental theatre director Ken Campbell, who was looking for an actor to join his stable. This was not normal theatre work. The Ken Campbell Roadshow was an anarchic comedy troupe who took performances out of the respectable world of the theatre and brought them to the people, performing in shopping centres, old people's homes, working men's clubs and a lot of pubs. Campbell wanted someone to set fireworks off in his coat, wrestle in his underpants, bang nails up his nose and lie on a bed of nails while bricks were broken on his chest. Kent was in his late twenties at the time and had taken to saying 'yes' to everything in the hope that it would cause something interesting to happen in his life. Despite his lack of experience, he was hired on the spot.

Very quickly, Kent learnt clowning and circus skills. His attempts to break an (imaginary) world record for having a ferret down his trousers brought the Roadshow a modicum of tabloid infamy. 'We got involved with the audience, directly and physically,' he recalled. 'We left the stage and broke all the walls, and we got down amongst them'. All the other actors who became the Doctor studied at prestigious drama schools, but they did not learn half the things that Kent did.

With Campbell, Kent developed a show called *An Evening with Sylveste McCoy, the Human Bomb*. He played the title character, a fictional stuntman who, at the climax of the show, detonated a bomb on his chest. The show was a great success and Kent performed it around the world, from Jerusalem to Umeå in Sweden, near the Arctic Circle. The name 'Sylveste' came from the American folk song 'My Brudda Sylvest'', which the Wolfe Tones had popularised under the name 'Big Strong Man'. It was a song about a giant of a man who could perform miraculous acts of strength. The joke was that Kent was a skinny, weedy little guy playing the big strong stuntman. The name stuck, although McCoy would add an extra 'r' to the name when he realised that 'Sylveste McCoy' had an unlucky thirteen letters.

In 1986, John Nathan-Turner was informed by his bosses that *Doctor Who* would continue after the messy *Trial of a Time Lord* season, but only if he replaced Colin Baker. BBC management did not specify what kind of replacement they wanted, but it seems unlikely they expected such an unconventional force of slapstick and anarchy as McCoy. Indeed, they favoured his mentor, the RADA-trained Ken Campbell, as their preferred candidate for the role. In his multicoloured coat, Baker had been repeatedly criticised for looking like a clown. It says something of Nathan-Turner's stubbornness that his response to these criticisms was to hire an actual clown.

McCoy had done television by this point, but mainly children's series such as *Jigsaw*, *Tiswas* and *Vision On*. If he was known to the public, it was as the man who put ferrets down his trousers. He was not, on the face of it, an obvious choice to play a 900-year-old Lord of Time. But after Nathan-Turner had seen him playing the title role of the Pied Piper at the Olivier Theatre, he knew immediately he had his man. McCoy had qualities that he would find nowhere else. He had the clowning and variety experience that Nathan-Turner loved and the anarchic radicalism that new script editor Andrew Cartmel hoped for. He would be the first Doctor to speak with a natural, regional accent. He did not possess the acting credentials and the gravitas that marked earlier Doctors, but he had that certain spark of magic that *Doctor Who* needed.

McCoy had memories of the Patrick Troughton era of the series, but he had seen little of it during the 1970s and '80s because he was usually working in theatre while it was on. He did not know, at that point, what other actors had done with the role. 'I discovered I'd been handed one of the great television acting roles, where you could do anything with it,' he said. 'The canvas was enormous, and you could do all sorts of things. That was a blessing.'

It would take him a while, however, to realise what he wanted to do. His first story had been written for Colin Baker. The script contained nothing that would guide him to his portrayal, and his first director didn't give him a steer. As a result, he arrived on set and did what he had learnt from his days as a pre-punk performance artist. He performed pratfalls and played the spoons, as if he had a room of rowdy punters to win over, rather than the single eye of a television camera. The Doctor is always unpredictable after a regeneration, but rarely are they that desperate for attention.

Working with script editor Andrew Cartmel, however, McCoy began to refine the Seventh Doctor and steer him into a more unexpected arena. There was great mystery at the heart of the character, they recognised. It was time to embrace it.

2. Mystery

Mystery is, of course, central to the format of the series. It is present in its very name – *Doctor Who?* It is a subject whose appeal should not be underestimated.

The desire to discover what it is that we do not know is perpetually irresistible. The hunger to know what lies over the horizon spurred the great age of exploration in the fifteenth and sixteenth centuries. The urge to know what happened before our time led to generations of archaeologists digging the dirt beneath our feet and painstakingly unearthing the story of lost cities and the deep past of our ancestors. The entire edifice of science is built on the desire to discover how the world around us works. Religions are similar, although they focus more on immaterial mysteries than material ones. Novelists and playwrights, meanwhile, are driven to explore the mysteries of the human heart, while occultists search for knowledge outside of establishment approval. The word 'occult' derives from the Latin for 'hidden', which stirs in us a desire to know.

Our craving for mystery is one of the reasons that the best-selling novelist in history is Agatha Christie. Her work illustrates an important part of the human psyche. Logically, it should not matter to the reader exactly which one of Christie's characters is the murderer. They are all, ultimately, just invented fictions. They don't exist and the solution to the mystery is, therefore, of no importance. If anything, it is a distraction from more important, real-world matters, and the idea that evolution would shape our brains to care about things like this is quite illogical. Yet we do care. Given that over two billion of Christie's books have been sold, it seems that we care more about the solution to mysteries than pretty much any other literary concern.

Our close animal cousins do not care about what it is that they do not know. They notably never practise archaeology, literature or chemistry, and if you settle down to watch a Poirot movie with cats or dogs, they will be uninterested in the outcome. Finding mystery seductive is a uniquely human trait and it is no exaggeration to say that all the great accomplishments of civilisation rest upon it. Given the extent to which whole edifices of human knowledge and culture are the by-products of the irresistible appeal of mystery, it is surprising how little this constant driving behavioural force is studied. Rather aptly, the reason why we are so drawn to mystery remains a seductive mystery.

As stories such as Doctor Faustus or the myth of Pandora's box warn us, the desire for knowledge can be a dangerous thing. In Mary Shelley's novel *Frankenstein*, the crazed doctor admits that, 'One man's life or death were but a small price to pay for the acquirement of the knowledge which I sought.' Here Shelley was warning us that the urge to understand mystery can be so seductive that it can negate our regular moral behaviour. Yet for all that we can be warned against it, our need to know what it is that we do not know never leaves us.

There are two distinct types of mystery. The first is puzzles that we are able to solve. A specific piece of information is missing, but it can be deduced from everything else we know. This is the Agatha Christie type of mystery, which underpins the cosy crime drama phenomenon. The world is initially an ordered, tidy, comprehensible place, until a mystery arises – usually, a murder – that highlights what is unknown about that world. When this mystery is ultimately solved, the world is returned to its rightful order. Our current mental model of the world is sufficiently advanced that it can absorb this new information without suffering too much of an impact. Mysteries like this, as crime publishers know, are incredibly popular.

The second type of mystery is when we are presented with something that is unfathomable. This is the type of mystery that you would find in the work of the film-maker David Lynch, not Agatha Christie. The known world butts up against something so strange and incomprehensible that we don't even have adequate metaphors to describe it. There is nothing in the known world that can explain this mystery, and we lack the tools or the clues to make sense of it. If we were to understand it, our previous concept of the ordered world would never be the same again. The theory of relativity is one example of a mystery like this, and so is quantum mechanics, in that they both overthrew deeply held beliefs about how the world worked. They leave our world more complex and inexplicable, in contrast to the neat and tidy explanations of Christie-style puzzles. Mysteries like this in books and films are considerably less successful financially, and yet they linger with people over time in the way that neat, solvable mysteries don't. Over thirty years after David Lynch's TV series *Twin Peaks* was broadcast, those who watched it still remember that 'the owls are not what they seem', long after all memories of TV mysteries from the early 1990s have gone.

The *Doctor Who* format, rather brilliantly, absorbed both types of mystery – the solvable in this world and those whose answer is beyond our current one. Each individual story contains mysteries that are resolved satisfactorily at the end, such as the true identity of the villain or what their evil scheme is. There are also the cliffhangers at the end of an episode – the viewer was left wondering how the Doctor would survive such imminent danger, and would need to tune in the following week to find out. Mysteries like these drive the narrative of each individual story and have helped make the series so popular.

Behind those comprehensible mysteries, however, was an unsolvable one, in the form of the character of the Doctor. When we first met them, they were an enigma who we knew nothing about, not even their name. They were a being from a higher realm who descended into the mundane world of man in order to meddle with the lives of us mortals, and as such they behaved more like a character from myth than a normal television character. Such a tantalising mystery intrigued us for far longer than the four to six weeks which most stories took to tell.

But over time, we started to discover things about this character. This was, perhaps, inevitable. If a mystery is to obsess us, there needs to be hints, theories and moments of revelation. These are most effective when they are used as key plot moments in the ongoing story, such as the reveal that the Meddling Monk also had a TARDIS in *The Time Meddler* (1965), showing us that the Doctor's TARDIS was not unique. In *The War Games* (1969), the Doctor was unable to save the day by himself and had to call on his own people for help. In this way we discovered, for the first time, the existence of the Time Lords. Sometimes writers could not resist casually dropping information about who the Doctor was into their scripts, regardless of whether it was needed to advance the story. The planet that the Doctor came from was a mystery throughout the first decade of the series, but we learnt of Gallifrey in 1974's *The Time Warrior*, when the Doctor casually mentioned it in conversation with a Sontaran.

By the end of the 1970s, so much had been revealed about the Doctor's background that they were no longer a mystery. By then we knew where they had come from, how they learnt to travel in time, and even details such as how well they had done in school. One of the most appealing and powerful driving forces of the format had slowly atrophied. In 1980, incoming producer John Nathan-Turner recognised this problem, and knew that he had to inject mystery back into the programme. His only solution to this difficult problem, however, was to add a question mark motif to the collars of Tom Baker's costume.

This was the response of a marketeer rather than a writer. The question marks were a brand, something Nathan-Turner continued with the costumes of the Fifth and Sixth Doctors. When the Fifth Doctor took off his cricket jumper, we saw he also sported a pair of question mark braces. They were apt in a way, as the programme was by then filmed at Television Centre in White City, a building shaped like a question mark when seen from above. The curved corridors, it was said, were needed because BBC staff were usually too drunk to walk in a straight line.

By the time Sylvester McCoy became the Doctor the problem was so acute that his costume, and specifically his pullover, was smothered in question marks. From his third story onwards, the handle of his umbrella also became a question mark, a design choice notably more popular in fandom than the clothing. Although abandoned after the 1980s, this styling has lingered in the collective memory of the series. In the 2015 story *The Zygon Invasion*, for example, the Doctor announced that he wears question mark underpants. All these question marks, needless to say, did not solve the problem of diminishing mystery. Stamping something with a sign which declares that it is supposed to be a mystery does not really make it one.

For these reasons, Sylvester McCoy, Andrew Cartmel and his team of writers decided to actively tackle this problem and intentionally add mystery to the character. Episodes began to hint that there was more to the Doctor's history than we knew. In *Silver Nemesis* (1988), for example, the seventeenth-century alchemist Lady Peinforte learns the secret of the Doctor's past. 'There'll be a reckoning with the nameless Doctor whose power is so secret,' she says, 'for I have found his secret out. In good time, I will speak it. I shall be his downfall.' The secret, she hints, involves Gallifrey and the old time, the time of chaos. Other hints linked the Doctor to the legendary Time Lord figures Rassilon and Omega, and also, in the novelisations of these stories, to a previously unknown figure called the Other.

The production team remained cautious about dropping hints

like these. In *Remembrance of the Daleks* (1988), the Doctor originally told Davros that he was 'far more than just another Time Lord', but the line was cut for fear that it was going too far. These crumbs and clues, however, were perhaps less significant than the effect that these ideas had on the character. The Seventh Doctor behaved very differently to his predecessors. Whereas past Doctors would arrive in an adventure by accident, the Seventh Doctor acted purposefully. He arrived at a location already knowing what was going on, with his own plans already playing out. He was now a Machiavellian character, who kept his cards close to his chest and laid elaborate traps for his enemies that played out over centuries. His new teenage companion, an archetypal eighties Londoner named Ace, never really knew what he was up to, or why they travelled to the places that they did. Whereas previous companions could clearly see that the Doctor was a hero and a force for good, Ace could only cling to this belief as a matter of faith.

On the surface, the Fifth and Sixth Doctors seemed different to previous Doctors and to each other. Their personalities, clothing and attitudes certainly varied wildly. On a deeper level, however, nothing had changed about the character's behaviour and backstory since Tom Baker took over the role in 1974. The question of why the Doctor travelled, and behaved as he did, had been at the heart of the original incarnations. Hartnell was a wanderer because he had been exiled from his own people. Troughton, unable to steer the TARDIS, was buffeted around the universe by the forces of chance and chaos, while Pertwee was stuck on Earth as a punishment. Tom Baker was the first to wander the universe because he chose to, delighting in what he found. Such was Baker's impact on the programme that this has become our default idea of how the Doctor acts.

This motivation wasn't examined or questioned over his next

two incarnations, even though it didn't always feel in keeping with their characters. Davison's Doctor seemed as if he might be happier if he settled down somewhere, rather than wandering the universe aimlessly, while Colin Baker's Doctor might have enjoyed taking up a grand position, such as Lord President of Gallifrey. It was only with the arrival of McCoy's Doctor that the question of why they acted as they did was investigated once again, and used to illuminate the character.

McCoy's Doctor could see the grand dramas playing out across time and space from a level far above us mere mortals. He actively strove to shape events for the greater good, even if that meant innocent people getting hurt along the way, or companions being put in danger without their consent. He seemed, at times, to be the agent of an unseen higher power. Later novels gave him the title Time's Champion. As McCoy described the process of evolving the Doctor, 'It was like peeling an onion, stripping away the previous interpretations to reveal a new and more interesting layer to the character.'

Andrew Cartmel's attempts to reinject mystery into the Doctor became known, in fan circles, as the Cartmel Masterplan. This name suggested that he knew what he was doing, and that he had a final version of the character worked out from the beginning. This was far from the case, but he was inching forward, taking risks and reframing the audience's assumptions about the character. Altering mythology like this is a tricky business. Every new question raised creates the demand for an answer, yet giving answers removes mystery and defeats the purpose of the whole enterprise. It is not always easy to give answers that simultaneously raise new questions, while also not contradicting established continuity. Nor is it easy to do so in a way that doesn't become bogged down inside the fiction of *Doctor Who* and confuse, alienate and lose casual viewers.

Ultimately, McCoy and Cartmel were able to inject just enough of that most vital and seductive of qualities, mystery, back into the character, so that a sizeable cohort of fans and writers once again became captivated and intrigued by the character of the Doctor. Doing so would be more important than they then realised. This renewed interest and enthusiasm for the Seventh Doctor would keep the character alive when, in 1989, the inevitable finally happened, and the BBC stopped making *Doctor Who*.

3. The Greatest Show in the Galaxy

The title of the story was Nathan-Turner's idea. Both the script editor Andrew Cartmel and the writer Stephen Wyatt disliked it, but they appreciated that Nathan-Turner was not otherwise meddling in the scripting process, so they begrudgingly accepted his choice. Like *The Trial of a Time Lord*, Wyatt's story was one where the line dividing the events on and off screen was at its thinnest. The final story in McCoy's second season is set in the Psychic Circus on the planet Segonax, and it is difficult not to see this circus as a metaphor for *Doctor Who* itself. At a time when press and public opinion were routinely dismissive of the programme, when ratings were dwindling and the BBC seemed ashamed of it, Nathan-Turner's inner showman fought back. He believed in *Doctor Who*. He knew that it was wonderful. This story, he proudly declared, would be called *The Greatest Show in the Galaxy*.

The production of this story showcases two of Nathan-Turner's great strengths. Its title illustrates his tireless championing of the show, while the process of getting it made highlights his professional determination and his understanding of practical details. It began well, and a period of location filming led to high morale within the cast and crew, who were conscious that they were producing unique and visually striking work. The team were then expecting to go into the studio to finish filming when the BBC's studios were discovered to be contaminated with asbestos. Those studio sessions, which were needed to complete the episodes, were abruptly cancelled. In the BBC-wide production chaos that followed, all other available studio spaces were booked up.

It looked like the story would have to be abandoned, much like a Douglas Adams-scripted story called *Shada* was abandoned after location filming had finished in 1979, due to strike action. Nathan-Turner, however, refused to be beaten. *The Greatest Show in the Galaxy* was an allegory for the whole series. The idea that such a symbolically important *Doctor Who* would not be broadcast on his watch was not something he could accept. The problem was that, legally, the story had to be filmed on BBC premises, and there were no BBC studios available. Most producers would have given up, but not Nathan-Turner. He ultimately solved the problem by erecting a large tent in the car park at BBC Studios Elstree, and filming the rest of the material inside it.

A circus is a thrilling, traditional and brash entertainment aimed at the whole family, much loved by that great admirer of popular variety John Nathan-Turner, which survives due to a strange, difficult to define magic – just like *Doctor Who*. It is also scary, especially for those who find clowns frightening. In this story the clowns take the place of the monsters, and the performance of Ian Reddington's Chief Clown in particular has haunted many a nightmare. The Doctor's companion Ace is frightened of clowns and so is Sophie Aldred, the actor who plays her – just to further blur the line between on and off screen. That the setting was called a 'Psychic Circus' is also appropriate – where else does *Doctor Who* exist, if not in our minds?

That the circus in the story represented *Doctor Who* itself is not hard to deduce. The story includes a nerdy teenage fan character called Whizz Kid who was played by the eighteen-year-old Gian Sammarco, then best known for playing the title role in *The Secret Diary of Adrian Mole*. Whizz Kid is obsessed with the Psychic Circus and is a clear parody of the obsessive 'barkers' that plagued the production team. As the character says, 'Although I never got to see the early days, I know it's not as good as it used to be, but I'm still terribly interested.' It is a sharp, witty portrayal of fandom, if noticeably unaffectionate. Whizz Kid is killed off screen by unknown forces, and all that is broadcast of his fate is his screams. Just in case viewers fail to pick up on the story's real meaning, it is spelt out clearly at the end. 'Enjoying the show, Ace?' the Doctor asks his companion. 'Yeah,' she replies. 'It was your show all along, wasn't it?'

Despite how the uberfan Whizz Kid was treated, neither he nor the clowns are the ultimate enemy of *The Greatest Show in the Galaxy*. These are a representation of the general, non-fan audience. Those viewers are initially presented as a family group of mother, father and daughter, who are watching the circus. They are dressed in mid-twentieth-century clothes and are middle class, much like how the BBC imagined the audience for the programme when it began in 1963. It is this family who sit and joylessly judge the circus acts, eating crisps and popcorn as they discuss their hope that something better will come along soon. The circus attracts a steady stream of creative, imaginative and unusual performers, all desperate to entertain. They dream of stepping into the circus ring and winning the approval of this family audience. They do not realise that if the family is unimpressed, their life will be over.

In the final episode, the Doctor penetrates the veil of the Psychic Circus and discovers the truth of the situation. Hidden by the traditional circus ring is a place described as the Dark Circus, a mythological realm in which the circus ring is, on an archetypal level, a gladiatorial arena. Here the family are revealed to be a trio of beings called the Gods of Ragnarok. In Norse mythology Ragnarök is the destruction of the world, an impending apocalypse that is impossible to avoid. In *Doctor Who* terms, it is the coming cancellation of the series.

'I have fought the Gods of Ragnarok all through time!' the Doctor exclaims when he discovers their identity. This came as a surprise to fans, as these gods had never been mentioned before, yet it makes sense given what they symbolise. It is only keeping these gods entertained that prevents them from initiating the apocalypse, because *Doctor Who* will come to an end when the viewers lose interest and switch off. In response, a steady stream of entertainments was presented in the ring of the Psychic Circus, in the hope that they would sustain the interest of the unimpressed family audience sufficiently for the show to continue. This stream of acts represents the run of stories placed before the audience since 1963.

In the ring of the Dark Circus, where the real, deeper identity of the family audience is revealed, the true identity of the Seventh Doctor is also uncovered. Here he performs escapology hanging upside down by his feet, as well as conjuring tricks and clowning. The person we see performing for us is Sylveste McCoy, the Human Bomb, using the circus tricks and stunts he learnt during his days in the Ken Campbell Roadshow to keep his audience's attention. He also juggles at the start of this story, a skill he had to learn for this story. The writer had just assumed that McCoy could juggle. He seemed the type.

Ragnarök, by definition, can't be postponed forever. Despite Sylveste's performance, the apocalypse comes to the Dark Circus and the Psychic Circus is destroyed in an enormous explosion. McCoy was, after all, the Human Bomb, set to explode at the end of the show. This results in one of the most iconic shots in the Sylvester McCoy era, as he strolls casually away from the circus while it explodes behind him. The explosion turned out to be much larger than expected and McCoy was much closer to the blast than planned, but he barely flinches. He continues casually strolling, swinging his umbrella, consciously aware that there can only be one take of this particular shot and he has to get it right.

In that shot we see the coming future of *Doctor Who*. The Gods of Ragnarok will ultimately lose interest in the entertainment provided, and bring about the apocalypse. On screen the Psychic Circus is destroyed, and off screen *Doctor Who* will be cancelled when the ratings fall away. And yet, the Seventh Doctor casually strolls away from those exploding worlds and into his future, able to survive in the world by walking away from the dying programme that created him. In doing so, his trickster nature was once again on display – particularly in his disregard for boundaries and his status as an agent for change.

For script editor Andrew Cartmel, when the Doctor penetrates the veil and sees the Dark Circus underneath the layer of circus imagery, he completes his transformation into 'a formidable, mysterious entity'. When the story starts, the Doctor still seems whimsical. 'He seems a victim, and a none too astute one at that,' Cartmel wrote. 'But by the end of the story he has been retrofitted with mysterious attitudes and abilities and an all-knowing air. The implication is that he got them into this scrape because he was planning to do so, as a way to engage the enemy.' The Doctor had taken a journey into the underworld, discovered the true nature of his show, and was reborn through this knowledge.

For the Doctor, the apocalypse was necessary because it brought an end to the terrible cruelty inflicted on entertainers by the Gods of Ragnarok, who would routinely destroy any acts that did not keep them fully entertained. 'How many people have you destroyed, I wonder?' the furious Doctor asked them. 'That's what you like, isn't it? Taking someone with a touch of individuality and imagination, and wearing them down to nothingness in your service!'

Over the years, many people working for *Doctor Who* gave their all to keep the Gods of Ragnarok amused. Some, undoubtedly, gave too much. John Nathan-Turner was one such person. His career never recovered from the cancellation of *Doctor Who* in 1989. After delivering the final episodes of the twenty-sixth series, he spent the next year sitting in his office hoping that the BBC would assign him to something new. Nathan-Turner was the last of the drama department's staff producers, and their current policy was aimed at cutting permanent staff jobs in favour of temporary contracts. They had no interest in keeping him in the BBC and did not want him working on other programmes. Offered a healthy settlement to resign, he eventually did so. When he left the BBC for the last time on 31 August 1990, the *Doctor Who* office ceased to exist.

Nathan-Turner was still only forty-three years old. He knew the world of television production inside out, had extensive contacts in entertainment, was passionate and committed and he always worked hard. In theory, he should have had a great career ahead of him. In actuality, the freelance world was brutal. He got bits of work in local radio and he kept himself busy with charity shows, corporate work and pantomimes, but he would never again produce another television series. He continued to pitch a variety of different programmes to the BBC and other broadcasters, but no one wanted to know. His friend Anita Graham recalled him saying, 'I've sent them so many things. *Everything* I've sent can't be rubbish, can it?' In her view, 'I don't think he ever got over the rejection and I don't think anybody would.'

Nathan-Turner's career had been dominated by *Doctor Who*,

which was seen as a show that went off the rails and failed badly. His science fiction experience did not fit well with his light-entertainment instincts. As much as he needed to distance himself from *Doctor Who*, the programme could still help pay the bills when nothing else would. He was hired as a presenter for the new satellite channel BSB for *Doctor Who Weekend*, in which he helped promote repeats of old episodes. He continued to attend conventions and worked on the VHS and DVD releases of old *Doctor Who* stories for BBC Enterprises. In 1993 he produced *Dimensions in Time*, a 13-minute-long charity story for *Children in Need*, in which the last five Doctors and over a dozen companions crossed paths with the cast of *EastEnders*. It was intended as a celebration of *Doctor Who*'s thirtieth anniversary and it utilised a new 3D filming technique, but it also displayed Nathan-Turner's inability to handle story and character. It made little sense to fan or casual viewer alike. As Peter Davison has said, 'I suppose you could question whether you can have an anniversary special for a show that had been cancelled four years previously.' Such was Nathan-Turner's energy and determination, however, no one at the BBC really questioned this. 'I don't think he was necessarily the best producer for *Doctor Who*,' Davison has said, 'but he could get publicity for a passing cloud.'

So it was that Nathan-Turner never really escaped the shadow of *Doctor Who*. He became, his friends say, something of a broken man. Always a heavy drinker, his alcohol intake increased and his health deteriorated. He died on 1 May 2002 at the age of fifty-four from multi-organ failure and alcoholic liver disease. His death at such a young age came as a great shock to those who had worked with him. He may have been hated by fans and his reputation was stained by his inappropriate sexual behaviour, but he was well loved by most who knew him. 'The last time I spoke to him,' Janet Fielding has said, 'I'd been out partying with Peter

Davison and [production secretary] Sarah Lee. We'd been to Soho House, and then we went back to Sarah's at around 3:30 in the morning. We decided to give John a call and he was awake when we rang. We told him that we missed him and we loved him, and he was clearly moved. He died soon after.'

Nathan-Turner's ashes were scattered at St Margaret's church in Rottingdean, where he is remembered by a plaque on a wall which gives his dates and describes him simply as 'Producer of Doctor Who'. It may seem odd to describe a man by the job he had been removed from thirteen years earlier, but this is how he will always be remembered. St Margaret's faces a small green with houses once lived in by the writer Rudyard Kipling and the painter Sir Edward Burne-Jones. Nathan-Turner's plaque does not face these Victorian luminaries, however. It is turned ninety degrees away from the front of the church, and instead faces what was the Tudor Close Hotel, the building that inspired the murder-mystery board game Cluedo. It was not Nathan-Turner's fate to face the respectable creative world. He was at right angles to this, facing the source of popular mystery itself.

4. Going Underground

After all the press campaigns and charity singles, and the noise and struggles of Michael Grade's attempt at cancellation, the actual end of the series was a quiet affair. The Doctor walked off television screens with Ace at the end of 1989's aptly named *Survival*, telling Ace about worlds where the sky is burning, the sea's asleep and the rivers dream, and walked straight into a series of original novels released by Virgin Publishing, who had just acquired W.H. Allen, the publisher of the Target imprint.

Nigel Robinson, the editor at Target, had first spoken to John

Nathan-Turner about publishing a range of original *Doctor Who* stories in the mid-1980s. Target were running out of television stories to novelise, especially as the later series only contained four new stories a year. They had experimented with original stories about the companions Harry Sullivan and Turlough, but these found a noticeably smaller audience than books that featured the Doctor. The BBC turned down their initial request to do original novels, however. Nathan-Turner controlled the future of the character, and he wasn't prepared to let others use him to tell their own stories.

The situation changed in 1989, when it became clear that the series was not going to continue. It was agreed that the novels would follow on from *Survival*, the last story of the classic era, making them an unbroken continuation of the Doctor's adventures. Granting Virgin the licence meant that the character continued to live on and earn the BBC money. What remained was to work out what type of stories these books would tell – and who was going to write them.

The editor of the range, Peter Darvill-Evans, took the bold step of inviting unpublished authors to submit pitches. This was, he admits, 'considered insane at the time. It was partly because I was new to book publishing, so I didn't know how it was done. I didn't have any literary agents I could lunch with. Most editors have a slush pile where unsolicited manuscripts go, and they just moulder in a corner. My slush pile was the main pile.' He could do this, however, because he knew how much talent there was in the *Doctor Who* fan fiction world. One such unpublished author was Paul Cornell, who would later adapt his novel *Human Nature* for David Tennant's Doctor. 'Fan fiction trained me for [writing the New Adventures],' he has said. 'I'd sort of been training all my life for that moment – or at least since I was nine.'

The strapline for the series was 'Stories too broad and deep for the small screen' and, unlike the Target novelisations, they were aimed at the fan market rather than children. Swearing, sex and drugs entered the world of *Doctor Who*, much to the horror or perhaps amusement of the tabloids. SEXTERMINATE HIM! DR WHO'S TOO BLUE: FANS ZAP PORNO TIMELORD ran the headline of an August 1991 *News of the World* report. The book that caused the reaction, *Timewyrm: Genesys* by John Peel, opened with a description of the character of Ace sleeping naked, and the New Adventures novels in general had rather a prurient interest in the character. *Cat's Cradle: Warhead* by the ex-script editor Andrew Cartmel, for example, included a lengthy description of her having a shower. Later books swapped her 1980s bomber jacket for a skintight rubber catsuit. Sophie Aldred, who had played Ace on screen, gamely accepted this new characterisation, posing for photographs in this new costume. As the actor and New Adventures writer Mark Gatiss described it, 'In a way it was the apotheosis of the fan mentality of "I'm actually too old for this show but I don't want to admit it." So there was an attempt to make it sort of grown up. And I think in the process, probably most of us involved were slightly guilty of producing things that, in a way, were actually more juvenile than the show was.'

Since the very beginning of *Doctor Who*, fans had taken the character and used him in their own stories. Fan fiction such as this was common in the fanzine world, while some fans went further and wrote and recorded unofficial *Doctor Who* audio plays. Between 1985 and 1991 twenty-eight stories were released by a company called Audio Visuals, which featured a young actor called Nicholas Briggs as the Doctor. Briggs would go on to voice the Daleks, Cybermen and other monsters in the television series when it returned in 2005. These stories were clearly in violation of copyright laws, and the *Doctor Who* production office were aware of them, but the BBC turned a blind eye, having no desire to unnecessarily antagonise the fan community.

Audio stories on cassette tape were one thing, but what fans really dreamt of was making their own *Doctor Who* films. Today, enthusiasts can make videos on their phones, but back in the 1980s and 1990s gaining access to cameras, editing suites and other equipment was expensive and difficult. Nevertheless, it was only a matter of time before unofficial *Doctor Who* films arrived, given the dedication of fans like Bill Baggs and Keith Barnfather. The Doctor Who Appreciation Society had its own drama department, which encouraged early attempts to make *Doctor Who* fan films on 8mm film.

In 1987, before the original series had ended, a company called Reeltime raised the £5,000 required to make and distribute the first independent *Doctor Who* spin-off film. *Wartime* was thirty-five minutes long and featured the actor John Levene reprising his role of the much-loved UNIT soldier Sergeant Benton – now promoted to Warrant Officer. It was a steep learning curve for the inexperienced production crew. They found themselves wildly underestimating how many scenes they could shoot in a day, or how much chaos inevitably arises with a production of this kind. The crew were leaving Watford Gap service station on their way to the location, for example, when two police cars cut in front and forced them to stop. Armed police ordered them to keep their hands visible while they took their keys. At the time, anti-terrorism squads believed that the IRA were running guns along the M1, and this patrol had received word that a member of the public had spotted rifles in the back of their van. The crew had to convince the officers that these were just props for their *Doctor Who* fan film.

One of the quirks of the original run of *Doctor Who* is that the copyright to many monsters and characters remained with their creators, if they were not BBC staff. As a result, it was possible to make films involving *Doctor Who* monsters such as Sontarans or Autons by reaching an agreement with their original writer, and many independent spin-off videos took advantage of this. What those film-makers really wanted to do, however, was make their own *Doctor Who*, and to do that they needed the character of the Doctor himself. The BBC was relaxed about fan-made media when it was not made commercially available, but sales of videos were necessary to recoup the high production costs. Different film-makers, it turned out, had different ideas about how far they would push copyright law.

For these reasons, Bill Baggs's BBV Productions produced a series of videos called *The Stranger*, starring Colin Baker and Nicola Bryant, who had played the Sixth Doctor and his companion Peri Brown. In these videos they played The Stranger and Miss Brown. Legally these were two entirely unrelated characters, even if it was very easy to imagine that you were watching the Sixth Doctor and Peri, and that their TARDIS was just out of shot. The pair arrived in each story without any explanation or backstory, just as the Doctor and their companion always had. The Stranger described himself as a universe-travelling 'wanderer, an explorer', which allowed for a few winks to camera. In the second *Stranger* story *More Than a Messiah*, Miss Brown tells someone nursing an injured man that 'I've got a friend out there. He might be able to help.' 'Is he a doctor?' is the reply. 'Well . . .' says Bryant, with a cheeky pause.

Not everyone was comfortable with this copyright-skirting approach. 'I thought [Baggs] was bonkers to do it and risk being sued by the BBC,' said Nicholas Briggs, who wrote the third *Stranger* film, 'but I was hungry for the experience and keen to be involved.' *More Than a Messiah* opens with Baker and Bryant's characters on a strange alien beach under a brightly coloured sky.

It was not very different to Peri's torture scenes in *Trial of a Time Lord*, not least because it was filmed on the same stretch of beach. Other scenes were filmed in the Wookey Hole cave system in Somerset. It was here that Colin Baker met a form of planetary nature goddess played by Sophie Aldred. In keeping with the portrayal of Ace in the Virgin New Adventures books, Aldred's character, together with Colin Baker, have no clothes on in one scene, for reasons that are not clearly explained.

The atmosphere on this shoot was tense, even in comparison to other micro-budgeted semi-professional film shoots. The actor and writer Nigel Fairs believed that this was due, in part, to the cave system itself. 'It has quite an oppressive atmosphere, especially if you're working,' he has said. 'It's underground, so I suppose it's going to. It was quite weird and tempers were really getting frayed.'

Doctor Who had filmed in Wookey Hole for the 1975 story *Revenge of the Cybermen*, where the crew also reported a disturbing atmosphere and strange events. An electrician broke his leg, another crew member suffered an attack of claustrophobia and Elisabeth Sladen was nearly killed in an incident with an out-of-control boat on an underground river. Fortunately, stuntman Terry Walsh realised in time what was happening, and jumped into the river to save her. The director Michael E. Briant, who saw a strange figure in the caves late one night when they were believed to be empty, has described the caves as 'cursed'. Sladen and fellow actor Ian Marter struggled with a strange scene in their scripts while they were down in the caves. 'It was just dialogue between him and me but, stare as hard as I might, I couldn't make head nor tail of it,' she recalled. 'Without doubt it was the most unfathomable text I'd ever been asked to learn.' After Sladen and Marter failed to understand this short scene, Sladen marked it on her copy of the script with an asterisk. When the scene wasn't recorded that day, they asked the director Briant about it. He didn't know which scene they meant, so Sladen showed him her script. Although the asterisk she had made by it was easily found, the mysterious incomprehensible *Doctor Who* scene had vanished, both from her copy of the script and from Marter's. 'The bottom of the page was blank. I swear to you, it had been covered in text. Now, though, it was completely white. Ian was shaking his script upside down, as if he was trying to tip the missing words out. We both stood there, dumbstruck. Where was the passage? We'd both seen it. Hell, we'd both learned it!'

It's fitting that, seventeen years later, The Stranger would also appear in those same caves, as if *Doctor Who* stories were a form of emergent property of the underworld, something that ultimately came from somewhere deeper than the BBC drama department. The BBC may have stopped telling those stories, but the stories didn't stop. They came forth in any way possible, and in whatever media they could, be that comics, books, plays, audios, video games or fan films. The fans were, as they had promised Nathan-Turner, the guardians of *Doctor Who*'s future. The BBC would not have been able to stop them, even if they'd tried.

10

The Romantic (1996–2003)

1. Daleks vs Time Lords

The original run of *Doctor Who* ended quietly. There was no official announcement and little press or public interest in its quiet disappearance, let alone enthusiasm for a campaign to save it. On 13 October 1989 a short memo was sent from the Head of Drama Mark Shivas to Jonathan Powell, who had now become the Controller of BBC One. 'You asked me to drop you a note to confirm that the drama group has not offered a series of DR WHO for 1990/91. This is that note.' The series had come to an end.

For the last three years of its life, *Doctor Who* had been scheduled against ITV's *Coronation Street*, one of the most reliably high-rating programmes of the day. At a time when multiple television screens in a household were a luxury, few children were able to watch what they wanted when *Corrie* was on. Fortunately, video cassette recorders were starting to become common so people could record the show and watch it later, but time-shifted viewing like this was not then included in the ratings. The programme had found a new, distinctive voice and it felt reinvigorated, as stories in its final season like *Ghost Light* and *The Curse of Fenric* demonstrate. Yet this was not enough to save it. The dwindling rating reports declared that the Gods of Ragnarok had switched off. *Doctor Who* was essentially ignored to death.

It is not the case, though, that the BBC saw this as the final end. Viewers expected television science fiction at that time to have production values like *Star Trek: The Next Generation*, which had launched in 1987. *Doctor Who* had always been a largely studio-bound multi-camera production. Even as early as 1967, it had begun to look old-fashioned when compared to lavish single-camera location-based productions shot on colour film, like ITV's *The Prisoner*. By the time *Star Wars* burst onto cinema screens a decade later, the dated nature of *Doctor Who*'s production was hard to ignore. A further decade later, in the late 1980s, its production values were a joke. If *Doctor Who* was to continue, it would need to be properly financed and fit into the contemporary television environment. This was not something that the BBC was prepared to do themselves, but they began to explore the possibility of developing the series as a co-production with an independent producer.

When the 1990 Broadcasting Act came into law, the BBC was compelled to source 25 per cent of its drama from independent companies – a huge shake-up for an organisation built to create and produce the majority of its drama in-house. The Act was the work of Margaret Thatcher's Conservative government, who wanted to deregulate, liberalise and bring competition to British broadcasting. A full privatisation of the BBC was politically unacceptable so the intention was to slowly hollow it out and privatise parts of it internally. In this way, the corporation would gradually merge with the private sector, without the general public noticing or complaining. A similar approach would later be applied to the NHS. Given these circumstances, *Doctor Who* seemed to be an ideal candidate for outside production – assuming that the right independent partner could be found.

Inside the BBC, these changes were seen as vandalism. The corporation had spent decades building up the skills and personnel needed to create high-quality popular drama. From their perspective, these teams were about to be destroyed for ideological reasons. Yet the sense that the BBC had to change was unavoidable. The corporation was widely recognised as something of a closed shop, and the cultural attitudes of its staff failed to represent large parts of the country. The BBC is supposed to service the needs of viewers in England, Wales, Scotland and Northern Ireland, for example, yet not once in the sixty-year history of *Doctor Who* has the TARDIS ever landed in Northern Ireland. Whether privatising parts of the BBC would improve this situation, however, was far from clear.

The process of 'modernising' the BBC, by getting other people to make its programmes, was spearheaded by John Birt after he was appointed Director General of the BBC in 1992. His system of reform, known disingenuously as 'Producer's Choice', was widely hated in the drama department. In a lecture at the Edinburgh International Television Festival in 1993, the playwright Dennis Potter famously described Birt as a 'croak-voiced Dalek'. Birt's slightly inhuman methods of communication – his heavy use of business jargon became known as 'Birtspeak' – did have something of the Dalek about it. The comparison stuck, and the satirical magazine *Private Eye* started depicting Birt as a Dalek in cartoons.

The line between events on and off screen can get very blurred around *Doctor Who*. As we've noted, the original production-focused BBC drama department seeped into the *Doctor Who* universe in the form of the all-powerful Time Lords. In the 1990s, these people came under attack by ideological forces represented as Daleks. This struggle led to *Doctor Who*'s 'wilderness years', the sixteen-year period when private-sector companies and the

BBC argued over the future of *Doctor Who*, while no series was made. When the show finally returned, in 2005, it had its own in-universe explanation for the struggles that had been fought during the time it was off air. It told us that a great Time War had taken place in a period between the classic and the new series, and that this Time War was a battle between the Daleks and the Time Lords. As fictional narratives go there was, on one level, some truth to this.

2. 'Segal Couldn't Tell Us Apart'

Whenever the BBC was approached about the status of *Doctor Who* during this period, they did not say that it had been cancelled. They were, they insisted, exploring co-production options in order to bring it back reinvigorated and fit for the media landscape of the 1990s. All this was technically true. The corporation held conversations with numerous producers about the programme's future, including Verity Lambert's production company Cinema Verity.

The most important of these approaches came from the British-born production executive Philip Segal, who was initially the director of drama development at Columbia Pictures. Segal had loved *Doctor Who* as a child. He first approached the BBC about the property in 1989, three weeks before the final studio session for *Ghost Light*, the last recorded Sylvester McCoy story. He continued his attempts to make an international series for years, during which he moved from Columbia to ABC Television, and then Amblin Entertainment. Throughout this time, he did not find the BBC enthusiastic or easy to deal with. On 27 April 1992, for example, the BBC's Head of Series Peter Cregeen wrote to Segal and told him that, 'I am afraid I think a new series is premature. When the time is right – and I think it needs a while off the air – we may yet make another series in-house.'

'It was, at the time, hated,' Segal said about the BBC's attitude to *Doctor Who*. 'I mean they *hated* it. It wasn't like, "Ah no, it's yesterday's news." It was rubbish to them. It was something that wasn't really worth discussing.' Segal, however, was tenacious and not inclined to take no for an answer. He kept pushing, and he had some moments of luck along the way. While giving the BBC's Alan Yentob a tour of the impressive sets for Amblin's *seaQuest DSV*, for example, Steven Spielberg happened to wander onto set. This meant that Segal was able to engineer a conversation about *Doctor Who* with Spielberg and Yentob, something that made Yentob view the series in a different light.

It took him seven years, but Segal eventually reached a deal to bring *Doctor Who* back in the form of a one-off TV movie, to be produced by Universal Studios. It would be part-funded by BBC Worldwide and broadcast on the Fox network in the US, along with the BBC in the UK. The film was intended as a 'back door' pilot, in that Fox had an option to pick up a *Doctor Who* series afterwards if reaction to the film was sufficiently favourable. It was not the series that Segal had been hoping to make, but it could have been the first step to one.

Auditions began for a British male actor to play the new Doctor. Liam Cunningham, Robert Lindsay and Anthony Head were among those considered, but the BBC was particularly keen on the Liverpudlian actor Paul McGann. His profile was higher in the UK than the USA, due to his roles in *Withnail and I* and *The Monocled Mutineer*. Segal dutifully watched McGann's 1995 series *The Hanging Gale*, to see what the actor was like. This was a BBC and RTÉ co-production about the Irish Great Famine of the mid-nineteenth century, which focused on the lives of four brothers. McGann played Liam Phelan, the brother who had joined the priesthood and who was therefore usually dressed in a long dark frock coat. With his matching long dark hair, McGann's character looked undeniably, strikingly Doctorish. As Segal later told the actor, when the Liam Phelan character turned up on screen his immediate reaction was, 'Who's he? He's my Doctor! I want him!'

The problem was that Segal wasn't entirely sure which actor was which. Paul was one of four McGann brothers who had all become actors, much to the surprise of their parents. They were a normal Liverpudlian Catholic family, from a similar background to Tom Baker, with no connections to the entertainment industry. The closest thing that the family had to theatrical roots was performing in their church choir, yet despite this all four of the boys went on to have successful and respected acting careers. The brothers were close, with only five years in age separating the four of them, and they were also musicians who played together in a band called The McGanns. This led to their breakthrough, when they appeared together in a musical based on the songs of Leiber and Stoller called *Yakety Yak!* The play transferred to the Astoria Theatre in 1983 and made the McGanns a legitimate West End success. *The Hanging Gale* was the first and only time the McGanns appeared together on television, as the four real-life brothers played four fictional brothers. Segal responded to the tape by calling in Paul McGann for a screen test, but unbeknown to Paul, Segal also screen-tested his brother Mark. 'I think that was because Segal couldn't tell us apart,' Paul said. 'He wasn't sure which one it had been.'

McGann was initially unsure about accepting the role. Had it become an ongoing series, he and his wife would have had to move to Canada where production would be based. They had two young boys at the time and had to weigh up whether they wanted them to grow up in Canada or the UK. Eventually, however, Segal wore him down. Paul McGann signed on to become the Eighth

Doctor – assuming, of course, that the series happened. The hoped-for series relied on Segal and his team creatively reworking the show in a way that would make sense in the broadcasting world of the 1990s, a challenge which was far from easy.

3. The Hero's Journey

By 1994, Segal had produced an elaborate series bible to outline his vision for the rebooted show, which he used to raise financing for his proposed series. It was known in fan circles as the Leekley Bible, because it was largely written by the American writer and producer John Leekley. It was bound in brown leather with an image of a planet and alien language embossed in black on the front. Mixing dark gothic fantasy with universe-spanning science fiction, the document used medieval-style fonts and was illustrated throughout like an ancient illuminated manuscript. It was a self-consciously ponderous and epic vision of what *Doctor Who* could be, a version of the show devoid of playful silliness.

The Leekley Bible was written in the first person by a character called 'Barusa' – Cardinal Borusa from *The Deadly Assassin*, who had now somehow become part of the TARDIS. Stylistically, it leant towards the gothic Philip Hinchcliffe-produced early Tom Baker era, which was then commonly viewed as the gold standard for the series. But while it was inspired by *The Deadly Assassin*'s depiction of Time Lord history, it did not seem to realise that Robert Holmes had been mocking that overly reverential, solemn depiction of Gallifrey, not embracing it.

The new series bible described a programme being rebooted from the ground up for a new audience, and as such it took many liberties with established lore. Barusa was now the Doctor's grandfather, and the Master was the Doctor's brother. It was this new Eighth Doctor who stole a TARDIS and ran away from Gallifrey, negating at a stroke the previous twenty-six seasons of the show. The original series was not entirely forgotten, however, for it could be mined for stories and monsters. Adventures like *The Talons of Weng-Chiang*, *Earthshock* and *Horror of Fang Rock* would be retold in the planned new series, and we would meet such horrors as 'Spider Daleks' and the robotic 'Cybs'.

The character of the Doctor was given a new purpose. After his evil brother the Master claimed the presidency of Gallifrey, the Doctor left his home planet on a quest to find their father, a legendary Time Lord called Ulysses, who was lost somewhere in time and space. The Doctor's mother, we learnt, was a 'peasant girl' on Earth called Annalisse. After many adventures, the Doctor was going to find his father, bring him home to Gallifrey and claim the presidency of Gallifrey from the Master.

The format of *Doctor Who*, in other words, was to be forced into the well-worn 'hero's journey' story structure popularised by Joseph Campbell in his book *The Hero with a Thousand Faces*. Our hero would begin by facing a moment of crisis, when the evil Master seized power. He would then embark on a quest into unknown lands aided by a wise old mentor, in the form of his grandfather Barusa's spirit. Finally facing and confronting his father, he would return home with his new knowledge and be celebrated as the saviour of his people. This story structure had been used to great effect by George Lucas in his original *Star Wars* film, but the unprecedented success of that movie had caused Hollywood to fixate on this overused narrative at the expense of more original and imaginative story forms. The Leekley Bible, ultimately, was the sort of tried and tested creative development that a committee would agree to, and that an executive would sign off. It was safe, it was sane and it was logical. It was not, in other words, the spirit of *Doctor Who*.

Fortunately, Segal's vision of the series continued to evolve during the pre-production period. By the time he had secured funding and production was able to start, the finished script contained only hints of this 'hero's journey' backstory. This was written by the British-born screenwriter Matthew Jacobs, who is now best known for his work on *The Young Indiana Jones Chronicles* and Disney's *The Emperor's New Groove*. Jacobs had visited the set of *Doctor Who* in 1966 at the age of ten, when his father played Doc Holliday opposite William Hartnell in *The Gunfighters*. His pitch was set in San Francisco on New Year's Eve 1999, and involved the regenerated amnesiac Doctor attempting to remember who they were before the Master stole their remaining regenerations. To write his story he had to balance often contradictory notes from Universal, Fox, BBC Worldwide and Segal, all of whom had different visions for the film.

Sylvester McCoy was hired to briefly return to the role and regenerate into Paul McGann. The BBC was against this, but it was important to Segal that his film was a continuation of the original series, and not a reboot. Near the start of the story, McCoy steps out of the TARDIS in San Francisco in the middle of gang violence and is immediately gunned down. For such a Machiavellian, game-playing Doctor, it felt strangely apt that he was brought down in this random, unforeseen way. Rushed to hospital, we learn he has two bullets in his leg and that a third went through his shoulder – injuries from which he should easily survive. The surgeons, however, are disturbed by his double heartbeat and rush him into surgery to 'repair' his heart abnormalities. It is this well-intentioned heart surgery that ends the life of McCoy's Doctor. Seeing him struggling to avoid being anaesthetised and then killed in an expensive, state-of-the-art American medical centre, it was hard not to see the cheap and cheerful British version of the show being held down and put to sleep by the glossy new production team, who didn't fully understand what they had or why they were about to unintentionally kill it.

Of course, McCoy's corpse in a San Francisco morgue is not the end of the Doctor, who once again regenerates. McGann steps into the role and immediately embodies the spirit of the Doctor. His Doctor is intensely curious, sincere and playful, with a slight undertone of melancholy. His performance in the TV movie has greater weight, perhaps, because the film was not successful enough to lead to a series. We have so little of his performance on screen that it makes what we do have seem more precious. The production values and budget were far in advance of anything *Doctor Who* had attempted before. Huge sets and extensive location filming were shot on 35mm film, and imaginative editing and directorial flourishes finally replaced the antiquated multi-camera studio shoots. McGann's Doctor immediately proves that this most mercurial of characters can happily step into an all-new media landscape.

Although little of the backstory contained in the Leekley Bible made it to the screen, Segal's new interpretation did contain elements that contradicted the original series. Most of these could be explained away with a bit of imagination. In *The Deadly Assassin*, we learnt that an engineered star called the Eye of Harmony was hidden underneath the Panopticon on Gallifrey. Also known as Rassilon's Star, this wondrous object was a colossal form of cosmic energy that somehow gave the Time Lords the mastery of time travel. In the TV movie, the Eye of Harmony is now located inside the Doctor's TARDIS. This was the type of continuity problem that Whovians take in their stride. Clearly, they reasoned, at some earlier point in time the Eye of Harmony had been moved into the Doctor's care, for reasons unknown. The revelation that the Eye of Harmony was now inside the

Doctor's TARDIS may have contradicted what we had already been told, but it didn't fundamentally change the series in any way. It just gave fans another thing to argue about, which was always welcome.

A more serious change was that, in a moment of excitement, the Eighth Doctor kissed his new companion Grace Holloway, much to her delight. This new Doctor, to the horror of much of fandom, was no longer asexual. He had regenerated into an attractive romantic lead. His long, curling hair and nineteenth-century clothes were a direct steal from McGann's character in *The Hanging Gale*, as if he had just stepped from one series into the other. This outfit gave him a soulful, Byronic aesthetic, so the fact that Grace was attracted to him surprised no one. The issue was, however, that he also seemed to be attracted to her.

The notion that the Doctor was asexual largely stems from Tom Baker's portrayal. He was aware of human attraction, but he didn't seem to fully understand it. 'You're a beautiful woman, probably,' he told the Countess Scarlioni, played by the ex-Bond Girl Catherine Schell in *City of Death*. He would introduce Sarah Jane Smith with the innocent, delighted line, 'She's my best friend!' This asexual portrayal continued throughout the era of John Nathan-Turner, who had a strict edict of 'No Hanky-Panky in the TARDIS!' The relationship between the Seventh Doctor and Ace may have been very close and emotionally complex, but it was clearly a father–daughter relationship and nothing more.

Prior to Tom Baker, however, the picture was a little different. Jon Pertwee appeared hurt when Jo Grant effectively left him for a younger man, and when we first met the Doctor he was travelling with his granddaughter. As we noted earlier, Sydney Newman had not approved the script changes that made Susan the Doctor's granddaughter, and he was furious when he realised that this idea would make it to screen. Newman saw the Doctor as an otherworldly figure from the heavens who came down to Earth and upturned the world of humans. As Hartnell described his character, he was really a wizard, not a scientist. Neither of these character types would be expected to have a domestic side. For Newman, the idea that the Doctor was a sexual being diminished him. A great many fans saw the character this way as well, and this may even be a factor in why the programme developed such a following in the gay community. Because the vast majority of relationships on twentieth-century television were presented as heterosexual by default, something a little different was, if nothing else, a break from the norm.

The idea of a newly romantic Doctor generated a great backlash from fandom. 'I was at a convention in Chicago right after it first came out,' Philip Segal has said, 'and I got physically assaulted by someone who was so angry at the idea that the Doctor would kiss anyone. Physically, I thought he was going to hurt me, I was very scared. It was a very bizarre moment.' Segal later rationalised why this upset fans so much: 'Once he kisses somebody, he no longer belongs to everybody. He belongs to someone else.'

This strong, very vocal reaction did not help improve the public impression of *Doctor Who* fans. The general audience could not see a problem with a character on television being romantically attracted to someone. They found it easy to stereotype *Who* fans as people who were angry about the Doctor having a love life because they didn't have one themselves. In time, however, this fan backlash subsided. When the show finally returned in 2005, the Doctor continued to be romantically attracted to people – particularly Rose, Yaz and River Song. It took a few years, but fandom came to accept this change. In this, it was no different to any of the other changes that occurred to the series over the years.

There was one change that the TV movie made, however, which is unique in *Doctor Who* history. It remains the only major change to the lore of the televised programme that was so unacceptable to fandom that it has been ignored ever since. Yet this unmentionable idea doesn't, at first glance, appear to be particularly objectionable. It was that the Doctor was half-human.

4. Half-human

The key that opens the Eye of Harmony, the TV movie tells us, is a human eye. This immense source of power only opens when a human being looks directly into a light at its edge. The idea is appropriate for a film attempting to resurrect the franchise, because it reverses the symbolic message given in *The Greatest Show in the Galaxy*. In that story, the show was destroyed when the Gods of Ragnarok – the human audience – stopped watching. Without an audience who cared enough to look at it, *Doctor Who* was cancelled. To resurrect it, the TV movie demanded that a human look once again at the source of the Time Lords' power.

Yet given what we had previously been told about early Time Lord history, the idea that only a human eye could open the Eye of Harmony does not make sense. How was Gallifreyan society founded on this great source of power which no Gallifreyan could open? The inclusion of the idea shows that elements of the Leekley Bible were still intended to be made explicit – particularly the idea that the Doctor was born on Earth to a human mother. Being half-human would therefore make him the only Time Lord who could access this great power. Presumably his enigmatic missing father Ulysses designed the Eye like this to ensure that no other Gallifreyan – and in particular, the Master – could use it.

In keeping with the Leekley Bible, McGann's Doctor told a scientist at a New Year's Eve party that he was 'half-human on my mother's side'. Some fans would later try to dismiss this as a joke, but the Doctor's half-human eyes were integral to the story. 'See that?' the Master asked his assistant Chang Lee when he learns why he has been unable to unlock the Eye. 'That's the retinal structure of the human eye. The Doctor is half-human! No wonder!'

Why is the idea that the Doctor is half-human so unacceptable to Whovians? Defining the Doctor as half-human, half-Gallifreyan would explain why he spends so much of his time attempting to save the planet Earth. It would also make him easier to identify with. From a script editor's point of view, it makes perfect sense. But *Doctor Who* operates on a level far removed from standard Hollywood character motivation. It requires mystery, and it starts to founder when mystery is lost. Definitively defining the character's backstory is exactly the sort of thing that a professional script editor would advise you to do. For normal programmes, they would be right to do so. *Doctor Who*, however, is not a normal programme.

There have been many changes made to *Doctor Who* over the years which were unpopular and potentially unwise, but which become accepted in time. That this idea was established so clearly on screen but has since been so roundly rejected is unique. When the series returned in 2005, it made a point of defining the Doctor as resolutely non-human. Christopher Eccleston's Ninth Doctor, for example, refers dismissively to humans as 'stupid apes'.

The only other item of the Doctor's backstory that has been so routinely ignored over the decades is the fact that he had, and abandoned, a granddaughter. The programme even managed to ignore the implications of this in the twentieth-anniversary special *The Five Doctors*, which was quite an achievement given that Carole Ann Ford made a cameo appearance. When the Doctor's feelings about abandoning Susan were finally addressed in the 2024 series, the Doctor told the Head of UNIT Kate

Lethbridge-Stewart that he had a granddaughter but that he wasn't a father yet – such are the complex twisted lives of time travellers. This contradicted numerous earlier references the Doctor had made to being a father, but it was the necessary price of acknowledging Susan while keeping the Doctor a non-domestic mystery. Newman may have been on to something when he thought that a domestic side to the Doctor lessened him.

While the existence of Susan is firmly accepted, the half-human idea remains taboo. When the 2017–22 showrunner Chris Chibnall dramatically rewrote the Doctor's backstory during the Jodie Whittaker years, he ensured that he didn't contradict even minor references throughout the long history of the series. The only exception was the idea that the Doctor was half-human, which he happily ignored. Perhaps one reason why the Whovian world felt able to ignore this lore change was because the story had been made by Universal, rather than the BBC. If a story is produced outside the BBC, fan convention unconsciously seems to recognise, then the continuity involved can be ignored in a way that BBC-produced continuity can't – even when, as in this case, it was part of a story broadcast on BBC One to 9.08 million viewers. In these circumstances, it is possible to relegate it to the status of other official tie-in media, such as novels like Marc Platt's *Lungbarrow*, which offered a version of the Doctor's history that the TV series paid no attention to.

Until the existence of McGann's Eighth Doctor was acknowledged in the 2007 story *Human Nature*, a faction of fandom was unwilling to accept the TV movie as part of the *Doctor Who* canon, despite the inclusion of McCoy. Here is another example of the unusual presence that the BBC has in *Doctor Who*'s on-screen adventures. It is not just that they appear inside the narrative as Time Lords. Their absence affects the stories also.

5. Jackie Tyler and River Song Meet the Krotons

The TV movie was a noticeable hit in the UK. It showed that there was still a domestic audience for *Doctor Who*, if the BBC ever got its act together and made it. Before the film was broadcast in the UK, however, it was already clear that a Paul McGann series was not going to happen. The film had been broadcast in the USA thirteen days earlier. It had been scheduled against an emotional episode of the hit sitcom *Roseanne*, which dealt with the aftermath of John Goodman's character's heart attack, and received a disappointing 5.6 million viewers. Because of these low ratings, Fox declined to exercise its option to commission a series. Even before UK viewers were introduced to the Eighth Doctor, his further television adventures were not going to happen.

Between the UK and USA broadcasts, on 20 May 1996, Jon Pertwee died. A dedication was immediately added to the UK screening. Pertwee had loved being the Doctor. He returned to the part whenever he was asked, and enjoyed wearing the costume for conventions, public appearances and even interviews. At the start of the 1990s, he approached the BBC with the idea of returning to the role on radio. He may have looked older than he did in the early seventies, but his voice was still unmistakably that of the Third Doctor. The BBC being what it is, the idea took some time to enter production, but eventually two new *Doctor Who* adventures were broadcast on BBC Radio, *The Paradise of Death* (1993) and *The Ghosts of N-Space* (1996). These starred the 1974 cast of Jon Pertwee, Elisabeth Sladen as Sarah Jane Smith and Nicholas Courtney as the Brigadier, and were written by Barry Letts. *Doctor Who*, always a time traveller, had slipped back in time.

The failure of the McGann movie to lead to a new series was

a hard blow for fandom. Whether that America-focused series would have been accepted as a valid continuation of *Doctor Who*, or whether it would share the fate of the Doctor's half-human status, is something we will never know, but the anguished reaction to the lack of a series suggests that fandom was heavily invested in its fate. Ever since the cancellation, the one hope on the horizon had always been an international co-production. Once Fox walked away, that hope faded. By that point, a lot of talented and well-connected people had attempted to revive *Doctor Who* on television, and they had all failed. The chances that others would try shrank desperately. There was no longer any belief that a new series would return to our screens. Yet as the Pertwee radio stories had shown, that didn't necessarily mean that earlier eras could not spring back into life.

In 1999 it was announced that an audio company founded by fans, Big Finish, had secured the rights to make new *Doctor Who* stories. They had signed up three previous Doctors to star in them – Peter Davison, Colin Baker and Sylvester McCoy. Paul McGann would join in 2001, giving his Eighth Doctor the series of adventures that television denied him. According to Stephen Cole, the consultant to the *Doctor Who* book and video ranges at BBC Worldwide, 'As far as the BBC is concerned, these new stories are seen as part of the official *Doctor Who* canon. A great deal of responsibility comes with that status, and Worldwide did not assign this licence without careful thought.' To write these new adventures, the company turned to fans who had already proven themselves in official and unofficial *Doctor Who* stories, including Nicholas Briggs, Mark Gatiss, Paul Cornell, Robert Shearman and Andrew Cartmel. Although Steven Moffat ultimately decided against writing for the range, he was involved in initial meetings. The company was named after 'The Big Finish?', a 1990 episode of Moffat's ITV children's drama *Press Gang*.

The range began with regular monthly releases, each containing a complete new story. Over time it expanded, and at the time of writing there are a half-dozen new stories released every month in multiple different ranges. The range has now been running for a quarter of a century, and in that time well over a thousand full-cast *Doctor Who* audio adventures have been commercially released. This high output can seem overwhelming, but it does mean that every fan's whims and wishes are being catered for. Initially the company focused on faithfully recreating specific eras of the television series, but as time went by they increasingly mixed up different characters and monsters from different eras of the programme. The lore and continuity of the series was a playbox that offered endless possibilities, although the endless permutations could offer scenarios that verged on the ludicrous. The question of whether the world needs stories in which Jackie Tyler and River Song meet the Krotons, a race of robots from Patrick Troughton's era, is up for debate.

Like the convention circuit, Big Finish became a regular source of work for actors who had appeared in the series. It was not just Jon Pertwee who found that his character in *Doctor Who* was with him for life. Tom Baker eventually joined the team, finding a great deal of joy in playing his Doctor again, and the 21st-century Doctors Christopher Eccleston, David Tennant and Jodie Whittaker also signed on.

At first, Big Finish was a way for the fan community to keep the series alive when all hope that it would return to television had faded. In time, full-cast audio adventures ultimately changed *Doctor Who* in a profound way, even if their significance was not immediately apparent when Pertwee first suggested the idea in the early 1990s. Previously, eras of *Doctor Who* had come to a natural end. The characters of different Doctors and their companions had existed only for a finite number of stories. Thanks to Big

Finish, that is no longer the case. *Doctor Who* had been a linear progression of adventures, but now every moment along that timeline was fizzing with potential and capable of generating new stories. The past was never over. *Doctor Who* had become fractal.

11

The Survivor (2004–05)

1. 'God Help Anyone in Charge of Bringing It Back'

Although senior BBC management disliked *Doctor Who* in the 1980s, there were many junior members of staff who still loved the programme, even if they kept that fact quiet in professional circles. One such person was Oxford's Jane Tranter, who joined the BBC in 1985 as a 22-year-old secretary in the radio drama department. She transferred to the trainee floor manager scheme a couple of years later. 'The only thing I could really, really get excited about [in television drama],' she said, 'was the fact that I was working in the same building that *Doctor Who* was being made in. *Doctor Who* wasn't regarded by everybody in the same way that I saw it, which was really the most glamorous show that the BBC could be making.' She recalled how John Nathan-Turner 'would whirl through the BBC, followed by an entourage, and the rest of us all looked a bit dowdy or a bit earnest.'

Tranter managed to get herself assigned to the role of marking up the floor of the *Doctor Who* rehearsal room, a task which required her to come in on the weekend when the rest of the production crew was at home. 'It was a great privilege. I loved it. I just couldn't believe it . . . there I was, all on my own – *bloody* dusty floor, I remember – marking up the TARDIS for this show that I had just loved and loved and loved growing up.' Here was the start of Tranter's career in drama in which she would, among her many other achievements, become the executive producer of HBO's *Succession*.

Another young industry figure was the Welsh screenwriter Russell T Davies. In 1987 Davies had a brief career in front of the cameras, when he presented a single episode of the BBC preschool series *Play School*, many years after Tom Baker had walked off with Humpty. The rehearsal rooms were in North Acton, in the building which was, he knew, historically used by *Doctor Who*. He went to the canteen during his lunch break and, as he wrote thirty-six years later, 'I was in the same room as *Doctor Who*. Oh my God. I could see them. Over there. Sylvester McCoy and Bonnie Langford – all smiles and energy – and a lot of young actors, all laughing and hooting and chatting. A bright bunch of fun. Even from a distance, I could tell; that's fun over there.' But even though they were in the same room, Davies still felt a world away. He remained by himself, finishing his lunch, thinking, 'That's actual, real, genuine *Doctor Who* being made over there, and I'm over here. I'm in the wrong place. Oh, how I wished. How I wished with all my heart that I could be on that side of the canteen.'

Davies's love of the series was evident throughout the early years of his career, not least in *Damaged Goods*, the Virgin New Adventures *Doctor Who* book he wrote in 1996. Like the rest of that series, the book was considerably more adult than the television show. Writing in the *Guardian* in 2003, Davies recalled how he 'wrote a *Doctor Who* novel in which the six-foot blond, blue-eyed companion interrupts the hunt for an interdimensional Gallifreyan War Machine to get a blowjob in the back of a taxi. Like you do.'

The series that made Davies's name was a drama centred

around three gay men in Manchester. Originally titled *Queer as Fuck*, the series was fresh, brave and a critical sensation when it eventually hit screens under the toned-down name of *Queer as Folk*. One of the lead characters, Vince Tyler, was written as a massive *Doctor Who* fan. The romantic climax of his storyline saw him attempting to choose between different partners, before realising that the guy who could list all the actors who played the Doctor must be the one. The success of that series gave Davies credibility, and with credibility came power. Executives wanted to meet with him, because working with the writer of *Queer as Folk* was something they could brag about. At over six foot four, Davies was physically a big man with a big personality and, after *Queer as Folk*, his reputation became as big as the rest of him. Whenever there was talk of writing for the BBC, he let it be known that the only BBC programme he wanted to work on was *Doctor Who*.

Davies was aware that bringing the series back would be a challenge. The franchise might not survive another perceived misfire after the Philip Segal movie. In a 1999 *Doctor Who Magazine* article Davies, alongside writers Steven Moffat, Paul Cornell, Lance Parkin, Gareth Roberts and Mark Gatiss, gave his views on how the series could creatively work in the contemporary broadcasting environment. 'Oh I'd love to do it, absolutely,' he said. 'Although it would depend on what they were doing. If the producer was a fool, and I thought the way they were doing it was wrong, then no, I'd rather die.' The article ended with a prophetic quote from Davies: 'God help anyone in charge of bringing it back – what a responsibility!' In similar comments in a *Gay Times* interview the following year, he revealed that his concern wasn't just about whoever produced the programme, but about the BBC itself. 'I wouldn't produce it,' he explained. 'I would never produce for the BBC. I would rather die.'

Davies wasn't the only person concerned about working with BBC drama. Following the introduction of 'Producer's Choice' and John Birt's internal reorganisation, morale in the department had plummeted. The original job of making drama had been replaced by an endless struggle with a vast, dysfunctional bureaucracy – or at least, that was the view among programme makers. The extent of the problem was illustrated when the Head of Drama Charles Denton resigned in 1996, on the grounds that the BBC had become an 'Orwellian nightmare'. Despite approaching virtually every significant figure in British television drama to replace him, the BBC was unable to find a single person willing to take on the job. The position remained vacant for a year.

After the millennium, however, things started to change. Throughout the 1990s Jane Tranter's career and her reputation had been growing, just as Russell's had. In 2000, she became the BBC's Controller of Drama Commissioning at the same time that Lorraine Heggessey became the new Controller of BBC One. BBC One's Saturday evening schedule was then widely considered to be lacklustre and in dire need of a shake-up. It had become too reliant on a run of barely distinguishable entertainment and game shows. It needed something different which would appeal to a wide family audience as counter-programming and, being a *Doctor Who* fan, Tranter knew exactly how the BBC had solved this problem in the past. She was also in a position to interest the new Controller of BBC One in the idea. 'I was the mad, passionate fan, and you can be a real bore if you are a fan,' she told historian Paul Hayes. 'So you have to be careful. But I thought this was an opportunity here. Because Lorraine would always listen to ideas. I'd drop it into the future planning meetings – little gentle hints, not all the time.'

During the Wilderness Years, the subject of reviving *Doctor Who* in some form never went away. Many different professionals had attempted to engage with the BBC in the hope of bringing it back. None of them had been able to sufficiently enthuse BBC management to the point where they could break through the apathy, corporate dysfunction and questions over rights issues that had kept the series off TV screens for so long. Clayton Hickman, who was then editor of *Doctor Who Magazine*, was involved in one bid with writers Gareth Roberts and Mark Gatiss. With hindsight, he acknowledges that the bid was timid and unambitious, both embarrassed about and dismissive of the programme's history. 'We all suffer from fan shame,' he said. 'It's ingrained into us, in that other people thought it was silly, and you'd cringe into yourself, even though you love it [. . .] That is taken on even when you're talking to the people who own *Doctor Who*, and who actually might like to be making money from *Doctor Who*. You still feel like they're just going to look at you like you're crazy.' Or as Gareth Roberts concluded, 'Russell's version is so bold – ours was apologetic.'

After Russell T Davies was introduced to Jane Tranter by their mutual friend Nicola Shindler at a press launch for the series *Linda Green*, everything changed. Tranter recognised that Davies, with his ability to ground huge ideas in emotional, character-driven drama, was exactly what *Doctor Who* needed. With Russell, there was no embarrassment about the series or its past. He was unapologetic about his love for the show, and he wanted everyone else to see it like he did. While others had argued that a low-budget version could work in BBC Two's cult-TV slot, Davies wanted it to be the biggest, most celebrated show on BBC One. This was typical of his approach to his scripts. *Queer as Folk* worked because Davies was unapologetic about the male gay lifestyle – he was proud of the part of his life he had spent in the clubs of Manchester's Canal Street, and he was determined to celebrate it. If he had watered it down to meet the straight world halfway, it wouldn't have worked. He now took a similar attitude with *Doctor Who*.

But Davies did have doubts. Bringing back *Doctor Who* was a high-risk move. If he was not able to make the country love the show the way that he did, then he would have a high-profile failure that could wipe out his credibility and damage his ability to get his own shows made. He also worried about going to work for the BBC, but here the changes in the corporation worked in his favour. The BBC needed to increase the amount of programming made outside of London, and the intention was for *Doctor Who* to be produced in Cardiff by BBC Wales. In 2003, the Head of Drama at BBC Wales just happened to be Davies's friend Julie Gardner. Her remit was to invest in local training and production, and to build a centre of drama skills and excellence around the Welsh capital. This meant that Davies would be working 150 miles away from the upper levels of BBC management. Rather like the Doctor, his adventures would be free from Time Lord interference – or at least, largely free.

Lorraine Heggessey made the announcement that Davies was going to bring back *Doctor Who* in an interview for the *Daily Telegraph*. By announcing these plans in such an establishment newspaper, Heggessey was showing her faith in her showrunner and demonstrating that the BBC, like Davies, saw nothing to be embarrassed about with *Doctor Who*. The level of seemingly casual homophobia in the resulting article is an awkward reminder of the attitudes commonly expressed in newspapers at the time. The interview was headed, *Doctor Who* Ready to Come Out of the TARDIS for Saturday TV Series. 'In a development that may alarm purists,' the article stated, 'the new series is being written by Russell T Davies, the creator of *Queer as Folk*, the controversial Channel 4 drama about gay life in Manchester.' This development seemed to alarm *Daily Telegraph* journalists far more than it did *Doctor Who* fandom, who were overwhelmingly overjoyed by news of Davies's involvement. 'Lorraine Heggessey, the Controller of BBC One, insisted yesterday that she did not expect a gay Doctor Who,' the article reassured its readers.

Not everyone was as enthusiastic about the return of *Doctor Who* as Tranter and Davies. Focus groups commissioned by the BBC were ominous. *Doctor Who* still had name recognition, they reported, but it was widely seen as shoddy, silly and embarrassing. As Tranter sums up the situation, 'I think it's fair to say that absolutely nobody else within the BBC thought that it was a good idea.'

There were powerful voices within the BBC who did not want troublesome *Doctor Who* back. After Mark Thompson took over as Director General from Greg Dyke, he asked Tranter if the proposed series could be stopped. Given the money already spent and the very public announcement, there was no way that this could be done without causing the BBC a huge amount of embarrassment. On the face of it, a commissioning issue like this was an odd thing for a new Director General to involve themselves with, and Tranter has speculated that Thompson's desire to spike the relaunch may ultimately have come from above. A new Chairman, supposedly a non-executive role with no power over programming, had been appointed at the same time as Thompson. That new Chairman was Michael Grade.

The news that *Doctor Who* was coming back generated a huge amount of press coverage. Clearly, the show's name recognition was still strong after its long absence, and a level of untapped interest was discernible. The tone of the newspaper articles, however, was troubling. Many journalists viewed the show as silly and embarrassing, and assumed that their readers did too. This was brought into focus by a tabloid article which claimed that the magician Paul Daniels had been cast as the Doctor. Daniels was a light entertainer who had never acted, worlds away from talented serious actors like William Hartnell or Patrick Troughton. The suggestion revealed the extent to which the show was viewed as light entertainment, rather than good drama – a perception that desperately needed correcting.

2. 'I Changed It'

Christopher Eccleston was out for a run when he found that his mind kept returning to a news story he had just read. The story had been the announcement of Russell T Davies bringing back *Doctor Who*. There was something about this that confused him.

During his Salford childhood, Eccleston had never been a fan of the series. 'When I was a kid, *Doctor Who* had never really meant anything to me,' he later wrote. '*Doctor Who* seemed to me like your typical white middle-class authority figure. He was an upper-crust eccentric, very male, posh.' What, then, was a writer of Davies's calibre doing bringing back a kids' show like that?

But the more he thought about it, the more sense it made. This wasn't Davies wasting his talent on a daft kids' show, he realised, but a kids' show receiving the attention of a major writer. It was exactly what children deserved, he thought, because if you give them good stuff at the start of their lives they will expect and demand it for ever more. 'I knew how much I'd invested in TV as a child, how it had sparked my imagination, my sense of me,' he wrote. '*Doctor Who* had to be the same. I felt Russell was exactly the man to do that.'

As he continued his run, Eccleston realised that what Russell was now doing – working for children – was the last thing that anyone would expect of Eccleston himself. He knew how he was perceived in the industry – intense, brilliant, difficult. He was above all seen as incredibly serious. Best known for TV series such as *Hillsborough* and *Our Friends in the North*, he was attracted to stories of social justice and truthful depictions of troubled working-class men, rather than roles that would lead to wealth and celebrity. He did not do adverts or voiceovers and he had a cast-iron reputation for integrity. At a time when the tabloid press viewed the show as something that might cast Paul Daniels, he was about the last name anyone would expect to take the role. He was also, for the same reasons, exactly what the programme needed.

Eccleston then thought about the character of the Doctor, a Time Lord. 'That means he's travelling through time,' Eccleston realised. 'He's never at home. He's lonely. I had a thought – "I can do lonely."' Eccleston finished his run, returned home and emailed Davies his thoughts on the role. 'I put a PS – just on instinct, really, saying, "if you're ever auditioning for *Doctor Who*, can you put me on the list?"'

Davies had worked with Eccleston before, on his 2003 ITV series *The Second Coming*, and knew immediately that he would make a superb Doctor. He would also have known, however, that Eccleston wasn't driven by the same career-minded motives as other actors. He had recently taken the film company Working Title to court, for example. Eccleston had worked for Working Title on the 1998 historical movie *Elizabeth*, and they had published a tie-in book which included an untrue anecdote about Eccleston violently threatening a writer. He won a public apology and substantial damages, which he donated to Sport Relief. Working Title was almost the only British film company that regularly got films made at the time, so suing them could be an unwise career move for an actor. For Eccleston, however, there was a principle at stake, and that trumped everything else. Eccleston was never afraid of rocking the boat.

As a child, he was always disappearing into a world of make-believe. He would spend hours playing at being a different person, such as his hero James Bond. 'I would lose myself so thoroughly in my own imagination that I experienced what I can only describe as a series of petit mal seizures,' he later wrote. 'It happened a few times, like I'd hypnotised myself, convinced myself I was that character.' Being an unusually imaginative child may have been why he was bullied in infant school, by an older girl. In response, he too became a bully when he moved up to junior school, forcing a kid to give him his crisps. 'I'll carry the absolute shame of that to the grave,' he later wrote. 'I picked on the weakest, most vulnerable kid, and I bullied him. There's no excuse for it.' The shame he felt from his brief period as a bully taught him that actions mattered because they could not be undone. Doing what was right rather than what benefited you would become the guiding principle of his career. He always saw his work as having a strong moral component.

Eccleston went on to attend the Central School of Speech and Drama in London, where he struggled with its middle-class culture as well as his own issues of body dysmorphia and anorexia. He describes himself as 'a lifelong body hater'. Given the extent to which your physicality is judged when you are an actor, it is a particularly challenging career for people with these problems. After graduation, but before he started to work regularly, Eccleston supported himself through shoplifting and nude modelling. 'I was extremely body-conscious, and so what did I do? Went and took all my clothes off and had it spoken about as if it was a lump of meat. There's obviously some bottle in there.'

It was not easy for Eccleston to become an actor, despite his natural talent. He had to force himself to overcome his own psychological demons, especially in the early years when he was unknown and devoid of connections. Self-medicating was a part of this process. 'I loved getting drunk,' he has admitted. 'Alcohol, sex and performing all offered a release from the torment of the rest of the day.' He kept going through a sense of inner conviction and determination, which gives him an aura of intensity both on screen and off. His on-screen intensity would allow him to portray someone alien, while his off-screen intensity made a sceptical industry take the relaunched show seriously. With Christopher Eccleston as the face of the show, all the baggage and credibility issues that the series suffered from fell away.

Eccleston played the role in a beat-up leather jacket with a crew cut, using his normal Salford accent – a very different portrayal to the frock-coated folk memory of the Doctor. After he was interviewed on set in costume for a news programme, many fans assumed that the actor was just wearing his normal clothes, and continued to speculate as to what his *Doctor Who* outfit would be. At a stroke the issues that Eccleston had with the character when he was growing up were fixed. As he said, 'I did something positive. The role – posh, received pronunciation – needed changing. And I changed it.'

In a similar way, Davies elegantly fixed the other problem with the programme's history. Its decades of backstory could be off-putting to a brand-new audience. For all that fan writers would lean into stories of Gallifrey and Time Lord politics, that was a very different story to that of Ian and Barbara discovering a strange police box in a junkyard in 1963. As the journalist and ex-*Doctor Who Magazine* editor Gary Gillatt has noted, *Doctor Who* was always in danger of descending into 'men in Time Lord collars shouting at each other about the imminent collapse of the tachyon barrier, or some such'.

Davies wiped away all that Time Lord lore. In the period when the show had been off the air, he decided, there had been a Time War. The two time-travelling species the Time Lords and the Daleks had fought each other across time, and both had been wiped out. The Doctor had fought in the war, and he was the last man standing. He was, therefore, a survivor, traumatised by survivor's guilt. This was the character who Billie Piper's teenage shopgirl character Rose met at the department store where she works, and who took her on a journey across the universe. His mythology was simple and uncluttered – he was the Last of the Time Lords. His gradually revealed past was seductively intriguing, like all the best mysteries. Davies had simplified and reimagined the series' lore so that it drew people in rather than pushed them away.

Davies's focus was on humanity, not the alien. As he described the Doctor in an early series proposal document, 'considering he's an alien, he's more human than the best human you could imagine'. This approach was to apply to the stories, as well as the characters. 'If the Zogs on the planet Zog are having trouble with the Zog-monster . . . who gives a toss? But if a human colony on the planet Zog is in trouble, a last outpost of humanity fighting to survive . . . then I'm interested.' His approach to the rest of the backstory was pragmatic. The Doctor remained an alien with two hearts who travelled in a time machine that appeared as a 1950s police box – an image more absurd in the twenty-first century than it had been in 1963. 'Of THE MYTHOLOGY,' he wrote, 'the fiction of the Doctor has got 40 years of back-story . . . Which we'll ignore. Except for the good bits.'

Davies believed that, contrary to popular opinion, the iconography of the show was strong. He resisted the urge to redesign the Daleks, which many fans assumed would be inevitable. He knew that the original design could not be beaten. They needed to build better-quality props than before, not fret about the silliness of the sink plunger.

Much of his approach involved not mentioning what had happened in twentieth-century *Doctor Who* – but not contradicting it either. Davies slowly and gradually introduced references to the past as he went along, when he was confident that the new, stripped-down version of the show had an audience that wouldn't be scared away by them. There was no mention of Gallifrey, for example, during the first two Billie Piper series. The relaunched show may have begun by assuring viewers that they did not need to know anything about the original series, but it would gradually become something of a gateway drug into classic *Doctor Who* fandom.

3. 'Images of Johnny B'

How accurate, exactly, is our understanding of *Doctor Who*'s history? Stories about behind-the-scenes events and attitudes are endlessly retold in fan circles, but do they closely resemble the truth of what really happened? Those involved in the production of the series often remark on the gulf between fan myths and actuality. 'I've learnt, over the years, that when the *Official History of Doctor Who* says that in 1973 Barry Letts said X, Y and Z, it was probably no such thing,' Russell T Davies has written. 'That event was just chiselled into anecdote 25 years later [. . .] is anything ever true?' 'Wikipedia is truly sometimes [highly inaccurate about *Doctor Who*],' Janet Fielding has said. 'I look at some of the stuff on me and I go, "Really? Wrong!"' Or as the 2017–22 showrunner Chris Chibnall has said, 'Having been in the hot seat, I'm really sceptical of all the interviews and the overviews.' The reality of most production decisions, he says, are not really recorded. 'Nobody knows. It's not on emails, it isn't anywhere, because a lot of it happens in the room. People say, "You liked this, you didn't like that, you had trouble with this, this went really well," and you think, "Oh God, none of that's true."'

From a historian's perspective, however, the history of twentieth-century *Doctor Who* is on more solid ground than many subjects. Pretty much every living contributor has been interviewed multiple times. Contradictory recollections have been highlighted and interrogated. The BBC archived production paperwork from the entire classic era, and this is made available to researchers at the BBC Archive building at Caversham. The availability of all this paperwork seems even more miraculous when you consider the way that the actual episodes themselves were junked. Dedicated and talented historians such as Richard Bignell, Paul Hayes and many others have researched the subject in minute detail, separating myths from facts and increasing the amount of information we can trust. We can now say with some confidence which early journalists should not be trusted, which actor anecdotes are false memories and which crew members have recollections that tend towards the fanciful. This large quantity of primary and secondary sources, the availability of historical records and detailed, meticulous cross-referencing have left the historical study of classic *Doctor Who* in a situation that historians of other subjects would envy.

With 21st-century *Doctor Who*, however, the situation is different. We still have many interviews and primary sources, but they are not quite as unvarnished. Regarded as promotion, they tend towards the 'company line' and exhibit a greater level of bias than before. The tendency is to play up the positive and minimise the negative, and deliver an uncontroversial take about how wonderful everything was. There is a greater sense that, as Chibnall said, if you weren't in the room then you don't really know.

We feel confident, for example, that we understand the reasons why the 1976 Tom Baker story *The Brain of Morbius* was broadcast with a script credited to the pseudonym Robin Bland. The original writer Terrance Dicks was unhappy with rewrites on his work performed by Robert Holmes. He requested that his name was taken off and replaced with 'some bland pseudonym'. Dicks, Holmes and the producer Philip Hinchcliffe have answered questions about this incident, and their recollections tally well. It was, ultimately, just a professional disagreement that didn't damage the relationship between Holmes and Dicks, or harm their careers in any way. As they saw it, there was no reason not to honestly answer questions about incidents like this. As a result, the 'making of' documentary on the *Brain of Morbius* DVD can tell the whole story, to the benefit of those interested in *Doctor Who* history and the detriment of no one.

The twenty-first century, however, is a very different world. The rise of social media has generated a great deal more caution among broadcasting professionals. A reasonable comment can be portrayed as shocking when taken out of context, and it is considered unprofessional to talk too openly about working relationships with colleagues. A thoughtless comment casually given may come to define a person's legacy. With *Doctor Who*, the residual memory of Eric Saward's infamous *Starburst* interview, and its effect on his future career, may also be a factor. As a result, behind-the-scenes documentaries on modern *Doctor Who* releases are considerably thinner than those on classic ones, despite their on-set access.

There are, however, a lot of rumours. *Who* fans are a gossipy lot. They happily share unsourced accounts of dangerous health-and-safety failures involving burning sofas, chatter about which cast members have blocked each other on Instagram or arguments involving high-level staff being 'erased' from *Doctor Who*. In the absence of any reliable confirmation or repudiation, these stories tend to grow and become more extreme. Accounts of disagreements first become blazing arguments, then become physical fist fights. Productive working relationships become nasty, spite-filled feuds and seemingly amiable members of the production team are turned into cocaine-fuelled monsters.

This official silence is most noticeable regarding the reasons for Christopher Eccleston leaving the series after one season. The news broke a matter of days after his first episode aired. This was watched by an impressive 10.81 million viewers, making it the seventh most watched programme of the week. The relaunch of the series was, to the surprise of many at the BBC, an unprecedented success, and Eccleston's performance was widely seen as a major part of this. The announcement that he was leaving so quickly was therefore a huge shock.

The BBC put out a press release which stated that his reason for leaving was a fear of typecasting. It quoted Eccleston saying that 'he hoped viewers continued to enjoy the series'. When a further statement was issued five days later, it fuelled the sense that what had really happened was being covered up. In this statement, Jane Tranter said, 'The BBC regrets not speaking to Christopher before it responded to the press questions on Wednesday 30 March. The BBC further regrets that it falsely attributed a statement to Christopher and apologises to him.'

Eccleston remained quiet about what happened for many years. After walking away from the series, he started appearing in American genre films and television series, including *Heroes*, *GI Joe: The Rise of Cobra* and *Thor: The Dark World*, in which his talents were severely underused. This was more out of necessity than choice. As he told the *Guardian* in 2018, 'I was told by my agent at the time: "The BBC regime is against you. You're going to have to get out of the country and wait for regime change." So I went away to America and I kept on working because that's what my parents instilled in me.' This was well-paid work, but it was not a happy period for the actor. 'Working on something like *GI Joe* was horrendous,' he said. 'I just wanted to cut my throat every day. And *Thor*? Just a gun in your mouth. . . . I really paid for being a whore those times.'

Gradually, Eccleston started talking about his reasons for leaving, but only in the broadest of terms. 'My relationship with my three immediate superiors – the showrunner, the producer and co-producer – broke down irreparably during the first block of filming and it never recovered,' he said in 2018. At a convention in 2023 he was a little more specific. When asked what it would take for him to return to the role, he replied, 'Sack Russell T Davies. Sack Jane Tranter. Sack Phil Collinson. Sack Julie Gardner, and I'll come back. Can you arrange that?'

While Eccleston did not specify exactly why he wouldn't work with these people, other comments he made suggested his unease at the way he felt crew members were treated, both by upper management and by a director he describes as 'atrocious'. During an acting masterclass at the Theatre Royal Haymarket in 2010, he told students that 'I didn't agree with the way things were being run. [. . .] It's easy to find a job when you've got no morals, you've got nothing to be compromised, you can go, "Yeah, yeah. That doesn't matter. That director can bully that prop man and I won't say anything about it." But then when that director comes to you and says, "I think you should play it like this," you've surely got to go, "How can I respect you, when you behave like that?" So, that's why I left. My face didn't fit and I'm sure they were glad to see the back of me.'

Eccleston's relationship with the programme is complicated. He displays a great deal of affection for the character and the fan community. Paul McGann has spoken about meeting Eccleston at his first convention, and the look of delight on his face when

McGann asked how he was getting on. 'It's amazing!' Eccleston told his predecessor. Despite declining to appear in the fiftieth-anniversary special on television, he has returned to the role for Big Finish and has now played the Ninth Doctor in more stories on audio than he did on television. At the same time, however, he minimalises references to *Doctor Who* when he is promoting his current roles. In the programme for the Old Vic's 2023 production of *A Christmas Carol*, in which Eccleston was a superlative Scrooge, there was a detailed list of his previous film, stage and television roles. The role that he is most famous for was notably absent. Promoting the play on the Channel 4 magazine programme *Sunday Brunch*, Eccleston was talking to the actor Jason Isaacs when Isaacs made a light-hearted reference to the TARDIS. Eccleston momentarily forgot that the pair were on live television. He reacted by turning to Isaacs and spitting the word 'Twat' in his face.

Speaking to the *Radio Times* in 2020, he said he thought that, 'If I stay in this job, I'm going to have to blind myself to certain things that I thought were wrong.' Because we don't know the specifics of these 'certain things', we don't know how valid Eccleston's criticisms are. Without knowing the other side of the story, we're unable to judge whether Eccleston's decision to leave the show was an admirable moral stance, or an overreaction. Other members of cast and crew, it should be noted, have spoken positively about working with Collinson, Davies and Gardner. The highly respected director Graeme Harper, who has directed eighteen *Doctor Who* episodes from the 1980s to the late 2000s, was impressed by them. 'I found them extraordinary,' he said. 'It was a very, very happy team.'

From the accounts that we have, it's clear that the production of that first series of *Doctor Who* was incredibly chaotic. Genre television on that scale, with prosthetics, CGI, stunts and action sequences, wasn't being made in the UK at the time. There wasn't the skilled, experienced workforce needed to get it right from the beginning. As producer Phil Collinson admitted, 'I did spend the whole pre-production period, and the whole first couple of months in the job, being absolutely, abjectly terrified.' The first block of filming, directed by Keith Boak, was particularly difficult and overran by a week, throwing the rest of the production into chaos. Uncertainty about whether an alien family called the Slitheen should be rendered in CG or as practical costumes, to give one example, led to heated arguments, wasted time and reshoots. Part of the problem was that BBC Wales did not have the experienced staff and established infrastructure to make a programme like this. As Mal Young, the BBC Controller of Continuing Drama Series, has explained, 'To be quite frank, there were no [national] dramas coming out of Wales. I don't think that's a big secret – there was nothing.' The skills needed to produce a series like *Doctor Who* had to be built from scratch.

Over the following years, this is exactly what happened. South Wales is now recognised as an attractive base for television production, thanks to its skilled technical staff and a thriving media ecosystem. As the BBC Director General Tim Davie said in 2023, 'In 2004 we decided to reboot *Doctor Who* in Wales. That decision has a tremendous legacy we can be proud of. It has delivered over £134 million to the Welsh economy – and over a quarter of a billion to the UK as a whole.' Davie's comments were included in a press release which stated that 'the regeneration of the show in Wales is widely acknowledged as the catalyst for investment in the South Wales creative cluster and its specialism in high-end television and drama production. Analysis by Cardiff University's Centre for the Creative Economy for the report pinpoints *Doctor Who* as the moment 'the South Wales creative cluster shifted from strength to recognised excellence'. In an April 2006 *Doctor Who*

Magazine column, Russell T Davies wrote, 'I still find plenty of moaners complaining that the much-longed-for BBC Wales Drama Department isn't what they wanted, simply because it's making huge primetime dramas with worldwide sales, instead of small intense shows called *I Was Born in Wales and I'm Cross*. Episode One: "Daffodil". Well, sod your small-nation thinking. Camelot is here; we built it while you were whingeing.'

That 'recognised excellence' was still a dream in 2004, however. In badly run television productions, more-junior team members often absorb the impact of the disorder, finding themselves working longer hours in more stressful conditions. For Eccleston, the way that junior members of the team were allegedly treated during filming was sufficient to cause him to walk away from *Doctor Who*.

The culture of television production was notoriously toxic during the early noughties. Eccleston has spoken about how he felt he had to protect his young and then relatively inexperienced co-star Billie Piper, because this was in the days before the Me Too movement drew attention to abusive workplace culture. Eccleston aside, many of the male cast of that series have been accused of differing levels of inappropriate behaviour. Bruno Langley, who played the short-lived companion Adam in two episodes, pleaded guilty to sexual assault charges in 2017. Noel Clarke, who played the secondary companion Mickey for two series, has been accused of verbal abuse and sexual harassment by dozens of women. He denies these claims, and the Metropolitan Police have declined to investigate further, saying that the allegations do not meet the threshold for a criminal investigation. John Barrowman, meanwhile, who played Captain Jack Harkness, quickly became notorious for exposing his genitals to members of the cast and crew, a practice he believed to be incredibly funny.

Barrowman's behaviour was not a secret. Many members of

the cast have talked about it in interviews and at conventions, with varying degrees of tolerance towards his behaviour. When Elisabeth Sladen returned to play Sarah Jane Smith once again, she remarked in an interview that Barrowman exposed himself 'to everyone else, but not to me'. Barrowman responded by saying, 'No way am I going to whop it out for Sarah Jane Smith. It'd be like whopping it out for the Virgin Mary! Actually, I did try, but she was looking the other way.'

Barrowman has behaved the same when working on other programmes. It did not, initially, affect the producer's desire to work with him. He was subsequently made the lead on the spin-off series *Torchwood*, which ran for four seasons. When behaviour like this is tolerated by upper management, junior staff know better than to complain about it, should it make them uncomfortable. Barrowman believed that his fellow workers found his behaviour funny at the time, and that the backlash was the result of changing attitudes. 'I think if it was now, it would be crossing the line. Fifteen years ago, it was bawdy behaviour,' he said on the daytime talk show *Lorraine* in 2021. 'They've tried to turn it into sexual harassment which it absolutely is not.'

When Davies and Gardner left the production, the cast made them a tribute video, called *The Ballad of Russell and Julie*, in which David Tennant, playing Russell, sings about his inability to block out 'images of Johnny B getting his cock out'. The video then cuts to Barrowman winking at the camera. The video contains many in-jokes that would have made sense to the cast and crew, but which are hard for outsiders to decipher. References to fires being started by Barclay menthol cigarettes, Phil Collinson letting 'his raging temper loose' and Russell's dirty thoughts about the actor who played Midshipman Frame sound like they would have become well-worn anecdotes on the convention circuit during the classic years. Yet these aspects of the production of 21st-century *Doctor Who* remain discreetly veiled.

Given the state of social media and the tone of fandom over the last decade, it is hard to see this more cautious approach changing any time soon. It may now be impossible to know the history of the production of a major modern-day franchise in anything like the detail that is known about classic *Who*. We are left, instead, with increasingly extreme rumours.

12

The Lonely God (2006–09)

1. Niche Construction

After Christopher Eccleston walked away from the role, there was never any doubt as to who would succeed him. A BBC press release from 31 March 2005, five days after the new series began, confirmed that 'Christopher Eccleston will not be returning as the Doctor' and ended by casually stating that 'The BBC is currently in discussion with David Tennant for the role of Doctor Who.'

A confirmation of sorts appeared on screen a couple of days later. David Tennant was offered the job while he was rehearsing for a new version of *The Quatermass Experiment*. This was due to be broadcast on BBC Four on 2 April 2005 and, in a nod to the original production fifty-two years earlier, it was performed live. Tennant played Dr Gordon Briscoe and Jason Flemyng starred as Professor Bernard Quatermass. As scripted, Quatermass's first line to Briscoe was supposed to be 'Good to have you back, Gordon.' For the live broadcast, Flemyng changed it to 'Good to have you back, Doctor.'

Tennant was a lifelong fan of *Doctor Who*, as was his *Quatermass Experiment* co-star, the actor and writer Mark Gatiss. Ever since they met, the pair had held long conversations about how they would play the Doctor, should they ever be cast in their dream role. When Tennant was offered the part, he waited until both he and Gatiss were off mic before taking him to one side to tell him the news. 'It was extremely sweet,' Gatiss recalls. 'I think he was quite nervous about telling me in case I tried to kill him and take his TARDIS.'

Tennant discovered the series at the age of three. 'I saw Jon Pertwee turning into Tom Baker,' he recalled. 'I remember that experience prompting a conversation with my parents about what actors are and what they do that very much was the beginning of my decision to do that as a career.' His gran knitted him a Tom Baker scarf and a Peter Davison cricket jumper, and at school he wrote an essay declaring that he would one day play the Doctor. He acted in school plays before training at the Royal Conservatoire of Scotland. In 1992 he received his first major review, for his performance in the play *Merlin* at the Royal Lyceum Theatre in Edinburgh. According to the theatre critic of *The Scotsman*, 'The cast of eighteen are uniformly excellent with the exception of David Tennant, who lacks any charm or ability whatsoever.' It was the sort of nasty, dumb criticism that could cause a promising young actor to quit the profession, but Tennant was single-minded enough to keep going.

During *Doctor Who*'s Wilderness Years, Tennant's love of the series led to him taking small roles in Big Finish audios, such as the Nazi soldier Feldwebel Kurtz in the 2001 story *Colditz*. After he was cast as the lead in the Russell T Davies scripted miniseries *Casanova*, he finally met Davies and immediately let him know he was willing to take any part in the new show. 'One of the first things I said to him was, "If there's any little walk-ons in *Doctor Who*, I'm very happy to come and wave a tentacle in a suit for a day",' Tennant recalls. When Davies and Julie Gardner told him that Eccleston was leaving and asked if he would take over the role, it wasn't even necessary for him to say yes. 'Frankly, I would say we got him at "hello",' Gardner recalled. 'There was a pause, which was quite dramatic, because Russell and I were hanging on his every word, and then his next question was, "What would I wear? I think I'd need a big, long coat." '

Like Tennant, Russell T Davies's love of *Doctor Who* also went back to his early childhood. His first clear memory is watching William Hartnell fall to the floor and turn into Patrick Troughton. 'I didn't realise he was regenerating,' Davies recalled. 'What I do remember is that all the controls of the TARDIS were clicking up and down on their own. I thought that was terrifying, and that burnt itself into my brain.' Not only was this his first memory of television, it was his first ever memory – the moment when his identity and his sense of himself began. The series immediately became a focus for his creativity, and at the age of four he entered the *Blue Peter* 'Design a Monster' competition. Children were invited to invent a potential *Doctor Who* monster which was capable of defeating the Daleks, and Patrick Troughton himself helped judge the entries. The competition sparked the imagination of a generation of British schoolchildren, and the programme claimed to have received a quarter of a million entries. Russell didn't win, but his entry certainly sounded as imaginative as his later *Doctor Who* work. The creature he submitted, he has said, was a 'tap monster'.

Tennant's casting proved that the relaunched show could be successful without Eccleston and that it had a long-term future. His energetic, wide-eyed, enthused portrayal of the Doctor soon made him the definitive version of the character in the mind of the public, claiming Tom Baker's title as the archetypal Doctor. It is tempting to speculate about the extent his experience of being a young fan played in this. Tennant knew what *Doctor Who* at its best could feel like to a child. He understood how thrilling and exciting it should be, and that youthful reaction seemed to fuel his portrayal of the Doctor. He was able to pass on what *Doctor Who* meant to him to a new generation.

Here was something curious about the successful return of the show. It wasn't simply the case that the programme's future was secured when writers like Russell T Davies and actors like David Tennant brought it back. *Doctor Who* made Davies and Tennant become writers and actors in the first place. It inflamed their imaginations and inspired them to be artists, even before they attended school. '*Doctor Who* made me a writer, it really did,' Davies said in a 2005 interview. 'I used to make up *Doctor Who* stories. I used to walk home from school burning with them!' In this, Davies was not alone. *Doctor Who* left its audience dreaming up future scenarios and adventures. The cliffhanger endings to episodes in the classic series, in particular, caused children to imagine what was going to happen next in the story and, in doing so, it made them think like writers.

In turn, the series that Tennant and Davies created led to a new generation of children being inspired to work in the creative industries. An important factor in this was the sister series *Doctor Who Confidential*, which was broadcast on BBC Three immediately after each episode between 2005 and 2011. This behind-the-scenes look at how the programme was made was unusual for the time, and it introduced a whole generation of children to the idea that making programmes like *Doctor Who* was a job that people could do. The 1972 book *The Making of Doctor Who* had a similar impact on children in the 1970s.

'You go into edit suites and TV studios up and down the land,' Davies said in 2023, 'and you'll meet editors and runners and boom operators who work in the industry because they used to watch *Doctor Who Confidential*.' Many young professionals brought things full circle and gravitated to working on *Doctor Who* itself. The assistant location manager Alex Moore, for example, has been a dedicated fan since he watched *Rose*, the first episode of the relaunched series, at the age of eight. VFX editor Matt Nathan was also hooked by that first episode. It was his love of *Doctor Who* that pushed him towards studying film at Nottingham University and set him on the path to his current career. Floor runner Devante Fleming also fell in love with that series, and used to spend hours studying the 2005 reference book *Doctor Who: Monsters and Villains*. There are also older fans involved in the current show, such as the storyboard artist John Erasmus, who was obsessed with Jon Pertwee and inspired to become an artist by the covers of Target books.

Doctor Who may just be an immaterial idea, yet it does something that biologists call niche construction – the process of an entity actively altering its environment for the benefit of its long-term evolutionary survival. Niche construction recognises that life is rarely lucky enough to find an unexploited landscape rich in everything it needs to flourish. Instead, by existing in and engaging with that landscape, it alters it in a way that is hopefully beneficial. *Doctor Who* was no longer a set of stories reliant on the prior existence of writers and other creative professionals to keep going. It was a set of stories that created the writers and other professionals who would keep it alive. From an evolutionary point of view, this is high-level stuff.

When biologists talk about niche construction, they assume that it is something which only living things do. While an exact definition of life is a difficult thing to pin down, it generally involves moving, changing, reacting and consuming, which are all things that *Doctor Who* does. There is a presumption, however, that to be classed as a living thing it is necessary to physically exist. For this reason, the claim that *Doctor Who* is alive strikes many as absurd. It is far less controversial to say that it behaves *like* a living thing, not that it is one. That position seems far more reasonable. It only becomes troubling should you attempt to work out what the difference is between something that is a living thing, and something that just acts like one.

2. The Lonely God

At the beginning of March 2007, before the third new series had started to air, Davies was dreaming up stories for what he intended to be his, and most likely David Tennant's, final full series. He wanted to find a scenario which the series had never dared do before, something that would really stretch Tennant as an actor. When inspiration struck, he emailed the journalist Benjamin Cook and outlined the idea. 'A child. Give the Doctor a child!' he wrote. 'A daughter. Pre-titles sequence: the Doctor and [his companion] are trapped underground. Door explodes open. Smoke clears. Great big sexy Amazon of a woman standing there, loaded with guns, and says . . . "Hello, dad!"'

This image evolved into the 2008 episode *The Doctor's Daughter*, written by Stephen Greenhorn. The actor Georgia Moffett, who had previously auditioned unsuccessfully for a role in another episode of the same series, *The Unicorn and the Wasp*, was cast in the title role. In another example of the line between on- and off-screen *Doctor Who* being permeable, Moffett was the Doctor's daughter in real life – her father was Peter Davison. The production team insisted this was not the reason why she was hired, but it was certainly a pleasing coincidence.

A couple of months after they had filmed the episode, Tennant rang Moffett and asked her to go with him to a play. Peter Davison recalls her saying, 'I don't really like plays very much,' but she went along regardless. 'He took her to several plays, and she couldn't really figure what was going on,' Davison recalled. 'It was a good, I would say, two months before he even summoned up the courage to make it a date. After about three months, maybe more, she told me, "We were having dinner, and I suddenly felt his hand on mine!" That was the first time he'd done anything at all that would indicate he was in any way interested.' The couple married four years later.

For Davison, Tennant's interest in his daughter makes sense. 'He became Doctor Who, he became this huge, iconic figure, and I think he found that girls found it difficult to cope with that. He was the Doctor, and girls found it hard to talk to him.' Georgia, however, wasn't remotely bothered by the fact that Tennant was the Doctor. Her dad was also the Doctor, and few things are less impressive to girls than the things that their dads do. Because her background had convinced her that being the Doctor was normal and mundane, she was one of the few women who acted normally around David Tennant.

That *Doctor Who* had brought David Tennant a level of fame that made relationships with women awkward was something new. Historically, the show was something that few women were interested in. In the first episode of Russell T Davies's relaunch, the character of Rose, played by Billie Piper, attempted to find out more information about the mysterious Doctor. Finding a website that collated previous sightings, she went to meet Clive, the researcher who set up the site. When Clive's wife asked who knocked at the door, he told her that, 'It's something to do with the Doctor. She's been reading the website.' Surprised by this news, his wife responded with 'She? She's read a website about the Doctor – and she's a she?'

Back in 2005, this would have been a reasonable reaction. Although originally intended as a programme that would appeal to all the family, its audience had skewed male from the 1970s on. Fandom, in particular, was overwhelmingly male, to the point where many *Who*-curious women found it oppressive and off-putting and kept their distance. The general tone of fandom at the time is perhaps neatly illustrated by the hugely influential 1995 book *Doctor Who – The Discontinuity Guide*, by Paul Cornell, Martin Day and Keith Topping. This made a point of detailing the episodes in which it was possible to see a flash of the companion's knickers.

In response, Davies's first episode placed the young everywoman shop assistant Rose at the heart of the series. Unlike companions from the classic era, Rose was given a family, home and job, along with a boyfriend and unfulfilled dreams. By anchoring the wild imagination of the series to a relatable female character, people who had little interest in science fantasy found themselves becoming hooked. Among the celebrations in the BBC that followed the relaunched programme's superb ratings was an awareness that the show was being watched by two demographics that BBC One found particularly hard to reach – teenage girls and under-tens of both sexes.

When David Tennant replaced Christopher Eccleston in series two of the reboot, female interest in the series continued to increase, as did the emphasis on the emotional side of the Doctor's character. Davies was drawn to writing romantic relationships, and to writing about unrequited love in particular. Even when he wrote about the world's greatest lover in *Casanova*, the script focused on Casanova's unrequited love for the character of Henrietta. 'I just love writing about it,' he has said, 'because I spend my life in a state of unrequited love. It's a healthy state to be in, I think – bitter, but good.'

A romantic side of the Doctor had been introduced in the Paul McGann movie. It was perhaps inevitable that Davies was going to build on this, rather than back away from it. 'The truth is, old *Doctor Who* was an entirely sexless series,' Steven Moffat has said. 'The Doctor wasn't the only sexless character among a whole lot of sexually motivated ones. The Brigadier never got a date either, and no one bothered to mention it – neither did Sarah Jane Smith. It was that kind of show, as a lot of shows were in those days. When *Doctor Who* came back, it had to fit into modern television.' The Generation Z audience wanted to watch people they connected with and cared about, and for this they had to be fully formed, believable characters.

Although the bond between the Doctor and Rose had quickly developed into something strong and powerful, the fact that Eccleston was nearly twice Piper's age prevented their relationship from initially appearing romantic. When David Tennant took over the pair looked like a couple, even though he was over a decade older than Billie Piper. The mainstream audience became hooked on the giddy nature of their early-days relationship, in which Rose fell deeply in love with the Doctor. So too did many people watching at home, as Tennant's charm and open-hearted delight in life made him an easy, unthreatening crush for many. 'I resisted jumping his bones,' Piper said of Tennant, 'but women really fancy him. He's got a gorgeous face, and an energy that's contagious – the spirit of a child. My girlfriends were all in love with him.' Piper's nickname for her co-star was 'David Ten-Inch'.

By getting the audience invested in the Doctor and Rose's relationship, Davies was setting people up to be heartbroken. The end of their relationship formed the devastating climax to series two. At the end of the episode, they were granted a brief conversation on a Norwegian beach before they were separated into different universes, physically unable to ever meet again. 'I love you,' Rose told the Doctor. 'Quite right, too,' he replied. 'And I suppose, if it's one last chance to say it, Rose Tyler . . .' But at that moment the walls between the universes closed, the Doctor vanished and the sobbing Rose never got to hear the rest of his sentence. The scene may have traumatised the young generation, but *Doctor Who* was now unmissable. The programme had never been this emotionally engaging before. Sections of fandom complained about the writing becoming 'soapy' and longed for the relatively emotionally stunted scripts of the classic era, but the mainstream audience was hooked.

The programme had entered its third Golden Age of mainstream popularity. *Doctor Who* usually thrived when it mixed the mundane and everyday with the cosmic and fantastical. Each of its previous Golden Ages – the Dalekmania period of the mid-1960s and the mid-1970s Jon Pertwee–Tom Baker era – featured a Doctor who travelled with contemporary human companions, allowing us to see those stories through relatable eyes. Sections of fandom often complain that the programme is too Earthbound and hope to see the Doctor travelling with alien companions, or with people from different periods of Earth history. A writer like Davies knows that this is not the way to reach the huge mainstream audience that he wanted. He believed that the fantastical alone was not enough. It is the context of the fantastical being encountered by the mundane that truly hooks us.

In Davies's writing, the Doctor became a 'Lonely God'. The Last of the Time Lords was a powerful eternal being fated to always be alone. The fundamental character of the Doctor had, once again, changed. Previously, for all that his skills and mastery of time travel had made him appear godlike to humans, the Doctor's own people had viewed him as little more than an outsider or a troublemaker. To them, he was a poor student and an irritant. Beyond the fact that he stole a TARDIS and ran away he was, in Gallifreyan terms, nothing special. But after the Time War, he was very special indeed. He was a man who had committed genocide and wiped his own people from the face of time itself. The fate of the whole universe had rested in his hands, and he had acted as he saw fit. Davies had changed the Doctor from an aimless troublemaker into one of the most important figures that the universe had ever known.

As Davies's biographers Mark Aldridge and Andy Murray have noted, the 'Lonely God' archetype appears frequently throughout Davies's writing. Characters as diverse as Casanova, Stephen Baxter in *The Second Coming* and Max Vivaldi in *Mine All Mine* are men who have to spend their days 'coming to terms with his own specialness, which could be seen equally as either a blessing from the gods or a dreadful curse'. Wrestling with such specialness is something that a writer as gifted as Davies must be familiar with. He has talked about the extent to which his mind is unable to switch off and stop working on stories – a rare talent that must be both maddening and wonderful. Perhaps it is not surprising that, being gifted and cursed in his own way, Davies is driven to explore and understand this particular archetype.

3. The Content Avalanche

'Oh, it's God!' exclaimed Princess Diana, as she recognised the eighteen-year-old Russell T Davies backstage in a Swansea theatre. Diana was attending a concert of youth orchestras and choirs in September 1981, as part of her inaugural tour of Wales. Davies had been a dancer in a performance of Vaughan Williams's *Job*, and he had danced the key role of God. Diana started chatting to Davies and asked him what he intended to do with his life. Davies truthfully admitted that he had no idea. She looked him in the eye and told him what his path must be. 'Dance, dance, dance!' she said.

This is the sort of incident that would only really happen to Russell T Davies. His life is funnier, more dramatic and camper than most. This is true of his personal history as well as the scripts he writes. When he was born, for example, his mother was given too much morphine and 'lost her mind'. She experienced, according to Russell, a 'complete 48-hour trip. It was like a science fiction film where she was floating in space, and giant God-like heads were talking to her. They said, "We're sending you back to a parallel Earth [. . .] in which your first-born child, your daughter, is dead. And if you speak to anyone from this parallel Earth you have to stay there forever."' Mrs Davies then attacked a nurse, which resulted in her being confined to a psychiatric ward. Russell's father came to the hospital with a bunch of flowers only to find the baby alone in a cot and the mother's bed empty and stripped. He was told that she was psychotic and had been sectioned. Fortunately, she recovered, but as births go it was considerably more melodramatic than most.

In terms of character, Davies had much in common with his predecessor John Nathan-Turner. At heart, they were both showmen with a deep love of television and soaps that was relatively unusual in an industry that tended to value more artistic or literary material. In the science fiction world, their populist, mainstream tastes were extremely rare. They both put themselves into the spotlight, appearing on television so often that they became almost as well known as their Doctors. They were brave and ambitious in their plans for the show, and launched spin-off series in the hope of expanding the brand. They had a knack for generating publicity and maintained control over every aspect of the production of *Doctor Who*. They had also both adopted 'stage names' in the style of actors. Davies added the invented middle initial T, while the plainly named John Turner first considered calling himself Jonathan Turner before settling on the more exotic John Nathan-Turner. As a result, they were both commonly referred to in fandom by three initials – JNT and RTD.

Davies, however, was a writer, and Nathan-Turner was not. Here was the main difference between the man celebrated for reviving *Doctor Who*, and the man criticised for killing it. Understanding character and story was Nathan-Turner's greatest weakness and Davies's greatest strength. Davies's success showed that Nathan-Turner had been doing a lot of things right, but without stories that resonated with large audiences it all came to nothing.

This applied to their attempts to launch spin-off series. In 1981, Nathan-Turner managed to produce a fifty-minute pilot episode of *K9 and Company*, in which Elisabeth Sladen's Sarah Jane Smith was paired with the popular robot dog for a proposed series of Earthbound adventures. Viewing figures were strong, but the BBC declined to commission further episodes. Twenty-six years later, Russell T Davies developed a similar concept called *The Sarah Jane Adventures*. The metal dog had a smaller role as a young teenage cast joined Sladen, her alien supercomputer and her sonic lipstick in a series of bright, pacey stories. The show was successful enough to run for five seasons from 2007 to 2011, until Sladen's unexpected early death from pancreatic cancer. Broadcast on the CBBC channel, it served as an introduction to the main show for a generation of children. Davies showed that, once again, what Nathan-Turner tried to do could have been made to work.

Davies's ambitions were far larger than just one spin-off series, however. As well as creating one series for younger viewers, he developed a second aimed at adults. This was *Torchwood*, in which John Barrowman returned to his role as the undying Captain Jack Harkness, who was now leading a team that protected Cardiff and the wider world from threats too alien and strange for the police to deal with. It followed the adventures of a secret-ish team who work from an underground base at Cardiff Bay, complete with alien technology, invisible lifts and a pet pterodactyl.

As television series go, *Torchwood* was something of a social climber. Its first series was broadcast on BBC Three, its second on BBC Two, its third on BBC One and its fourth was a co-production with the American network Starz. Davies said that he was 'not allowed' to call the programme '*Doctor Who* for grownups', but it was similar to *Doctor Who*-style Earthbound stories with an added layer of sex and swearing. It was reminiscent of the Virgin New Adventures books from the 1990s, in that its attempts to make it more adult could on occasions seem quite adolescent. For the generation that were not allowed to watch *Torchwood* because they were too young when it was first screened, discovering it in later life has been quite traumatic. Conversations around consent have changed radically since the late 2000s, and a main character's use of an alien pheromone spray that makes people desperate to have sex with him is particularly unacceptable. Despite changing attitudes, however, the series still has a strong fanbase of its own. When the fan favourite character Ianto Jones, Captain Jack's main love interest, was killed off in series three, fans built a memorial shrine to him near Roald Dahl Plass at Cardiff Bay. This grew into a wall of artwork, poems and messages remembering Ianto from fans around the world.

Like *Doctor Who*, *Torchwood* also had its own behind-the-scenes documentary series, *Torchwood Declassified*, as well as novels, comics and audio adventures. It could not, however, hope to compete with the impact of the main show, which by then had exploded into an unavoidable cultural colossus. By this point, the yearly series of episodes was only a small part of the content avalanche that *Doctor Who* had become.

As well as *Doctor Who Confidential*, two series of the children's magazine show *Totally Doctor Who* were broadcast in 2006 and

2007. The second series of this included an animated *Doctor Who* story called *The Infinite Quest*, and another animated Tenth Doctor adventure, *Dreamland*, would appear in 2009. Specially shot introductory scenes for each episode of the second series, called TARDISodes, were released online, along with a series of audio commentaries. The programme was also unavoidable away from the screen. Toy shops were stuffed full of Daleks, TARDISes and action figures, and a voice-changing Cyberman helmet was the must-have toy for Christmas 2006. Shoppers in the yoghurt aisles of British supermarkets took home *Doctor Who* Frubes in Sonic Strawberry flavour, and *Doctor Who* trading cards were swapped in school playgrounds. Dozens of Ninth or Tenth Doctor original novels arrived in bookshops and a new magazine, *Doctor Who Adventures*, launched in 2006 and ran for over a decade. Like *The Sarah Jane Adventures*, this was specifically aimed at a younger audience, who might find the existing official publication, *Doctor Who Magazine*, dry, wordy and bogged down in things that happened before they were born. That publication had been going since 1979, when it was initially launched as *Doctor Who Weekly*. It had played a pivotal role in keeping *Doctor Who* alive during the Wilderness Years, acting as a central hub to connect the different areas of activity, such as books, audios and conventions, which between them formed a formidable Whovian industrial complex. When the BBC relaunched the series, there was talk about bringing external licences back in-house again, such as the magazine and Big Finish audios. Davies fought against this and ensured that they continued as they were. He knew how important they were to the long-term health of the *Doctor Who* ecosystem. Despite the collapse of the magazine market over the last decade or so, *Doctor Who Magazine* is still going strong, reliably appearing on the shelves of supermarket magazine displays every month. It celebrated its 600th issue in February 2024.

Davies's approach was to keep pushing for more content, keep being noisy and keep demanding people's attention. He didn't take the ratings success for granted. He knew he had to keep building. In doing so he was turning *Doctor Who* from something that a family might watch every Saturday to something that you thought about during the week. He was taking viewers and, without them really noticing, turning them into fans.

Russell T Davies knew no show he worked on would ever be so much fun, or allow his imagination to roam so freely. 'I dread the day I leave the programme, because then I'll have to go back to writing bedrooms, offices and pubs,' he said, 'and maybe a field, if I'm lucky.' It was, however, a punishing workload. As David Tennant said ahead of filming series three, 'When filming begins in earnest next week, it will feel like we've started running and can't slow down for nine months. Each day blasts into the next, the scripts keep coming, the lines keep needing to be learnt; it is a relentless and unstoppable beast of a schedule. Friends and family get used to not hearing from you for months on end as the machine of production lurches back into life and steals the rest of your life away. Nothing can quite prepare you for the peculiar, delightful torture of working on this show.'

After four series, Davies had achieved everything that he had set out to do. He had taken a series that was seen as an embarrassment and turned it into what was then the best-loved drama on British television – in the eyes of both the public and the BBC itself. *Doctor Who* radically changed British drama, opening the doors to family-focused genre storytelling in the years before the Marvel Cinematic Universe normalised fantastical storytelling at the cinema. Many of the television series that followed, such as the BBC's *Robin Hood* and *Merlin*, or ITV's *Primeval*, would not have been commissioned if it had not been for the success of *Doctor Who*. 'The show's success is so mad that I don't think any of us will get our heads round it till it's all over and we look back on it in ten years' time and say, "Blimey, that was weird!"' Davies said.

Where previously Russell T Davies had been seen as a visionary writer with a unique radical voice, he was now seen as a visionary writer with a unique radical voice and popular, mainstream sensibilities. Along the way he had positively changed the portrayal of LGBTQ+ people on British television, helping to normalise their representation in places where they had previously been invisible. He was awarded an OBE in the Queen's honours list in 2008, the first *Doctor Who* writer or producer to be recognised in this way. He topped the *Independent*'s Pink List in 2007, making him, as he put it, Britain's 'Number One Gay'.

Davies had had an exit strategy since the end of 2005. During the filming of the episode *Doomsday*, Davies, Collinson, Tranter and Gardner made a pact. 'We decided that we'd have a fourth series (David's third), with a big ending, after which we'd take the show off the air, just for a short while, apart from the odd special, so that we could have a breather, and a new production team could settle in, find its feet, and prepare for Series Five [. . .] Julie, Phil, Jane and I committed to that initial promise, and we're sticking to our word.' BBC management made an official request for him to do a fifth series, but he declined. Getting the succession right was as important a part of the job as making the show. The future of *Doctor Who* was as important as the present.

And so, after five exhausting but unimaginably successful years, Russell T Davies walked away from his childhood love, intending to make more adult programmes. For the entirety of his life, there had been a part of his brain that was forever thinking up *Doctor Who* stories. Having given the show everything he could, that part of his mind gave one last satisfied flare, then switched itself off.

13
The Time Traveller (2010–13)

1. Timey-wimey

Given that *Doctor Who* was a show about a time traveller, it's surprising how rarely time travel was the focus of stories. Typically, the TARDIS would take our heroes somewhere in time and space and wait patiently while an adventure played out, before taking them to their next story afterwards like a glorified temporal taxi. Stories in which the Doctor intentionally used his time machine during the drama – like *The Ark* (1966) or *City of Death* (1979) – were surprising and rare. Using the TARDIS intentionally mid-story often clashed with the Doctor's established difficulty in steering it to where he wanted to go. When the TARDIS did feature in the plot, it was much more likely to be lost or stolen than it was to be used as an actual time machine.

In 2010, the Scottish writer Steven Moffat succeeded Russell T Davies as *Doctor Who* showrunner. His vision for the programme embraced the idea of time travel and its implications. 'I think time travel is fascinating. I think the timeline of a story is fascinating,' he has said. 'Largely, even in my era, the TARDIS is like a bus, and it delivers you to the next adventure. But sometimes the Doctor's unique relationship with time can be at the centre of a story. Because it's not just that he's got a time machine – he lives in one. The whole universe is alive and well outside his blue doors. It's not that he knows he was at Churchill's funeral, it's that he's having dinner with Churchill next Tuesday. That's a very, very different view of the universe.'

In this context, it is fitting that the time-bending nature of Moffat's era began in the past, before he took over as showrunner, when he contributed scripts to each of the Russell T Davies series. In Moffat's classic 2007 story *Blink*, for example, David Tennant's Doctor tells us that, 'People assume that time is a strict progression of cause to effect, but actually from a non-linear, non-subjective viewpoint, it's more like a big ball of wibbly-wobbly, timey-wimey stuff.' Here was Moffat's vision statement for his forthcoming era of the programme. His scripts and story arcs would prove to be very wibbly-wobbly timey-wimey indeed.

In the 2008 two-part story *Silence in the Library* – another story Moffat wrote before he got the job of showrunner – the Doctor travelled to a planet-sized library in the fifty-first century. Here he met an archaeologist called Professor River Song, played by Alex Kingston, who seemed to be his wife. It transpired that the Doctor and River Song were fated to meet each other in reverse order, where his first meeting was her last, and vice versa. 'Look at you. Oh, you're young,' River tells the Doctor, to his amusement. 'I'm really not, you know,' he replies, every inch the thousand-year-old Time Lord. But from River's perspective, he was young – the youngest she'd ever seen him. While the Doctor felt old and weary after his endless adventures, River knew that he was just getting started. The programme had been on the air for forty-five years at this point. It was susceptible to being dismissed as old or on its way out. But as Moffat recognised, there were far more adventures in front of the Doctor than behind.

'You know when you see a photograph of someone you know, but it's from years before you knew them,' River tells the Doctor, 'and it's like they're not quite finished. They're not done yet. Well, yes, the Doctor's here. He came when I called, just like he always does. But not my Doctor. Now my Doctor, I've seen whole armies turn and run away. And he'd just swagger off back to his TARDIS and open the doors with a snap of his fingers.' The Doctor didn't recognise this warrior-like description of himself. He didn't immediately believe that you can open a TARDIS with the click of your fingers. But River wasn't talking about the man we were then watching. She was describing the man he was going to be, after Moffat took over the show.

Once he had gained the top job, the new showrunner spent the best part of the next decade telling the story of the Doctor and River Song and filling in details of events briefly mentioned during their first meeting. *Silence in the Library* was highly rated when it first aired, yet it became increasingly emotionally powerful as the years went on and we learnt about River's history, and the Doctor's future. This level of narrative ambition, however, was not present at the birth of this significant character. 'Russell and I went through a phase of trying to work out *Doctor Who* titles with rude acronyms to wind up people on internet message boards,' Moffat admitted after he left the show. It was common for fans to refer to an episode like *Genesis of the Daleks* as GOTD, for example, or an episode like *Wild Blue Yonder* as WBY, confident that they were talking to others who were sufficiently invested in the series to understand. 'I just went with *A River Song Ending*. [Russell] said, "What's a river song?" And I said I'll just call someone River Song, and she'd better die, and that way we've got the acronym. Then we didn't use the title.'

From River's perspective, our first meeting with her saw the end of her life. At the end of the episode, she was electrocuted linking her mind to the library's computer, saving everybody in a courageous act of self-sacrifice. *Silence in the Library* may have been broadcast before Moffat's era had begun, but its full impact was only evident when it was watched after it had ended. For the audience, meeting a new character and watching them die is one thing. Seeing the death of someone you've followed for eight years is quite another. Unlike the classic series, the relaunched era was written with the understanding that episodes were not just broadcast once and never seen again. Writers now knew that stories were fated to still be watched decades in the future, in random orders. Moffat was writing episodes designed to work best years after they were first broadcast.

It was while Moffat was writing *A River Song Ending*, the story which would ultimately be titled *Silence in the Library*, that he received the email asking him to take over the series. The job offer would then allow him to finish the story he was already writing. Such is the mixed-up timey-wimey mind of a writer raised on *Doctor Who*.

2. 'Oh, That's Him'

Moffat is always wrestling with time. He intended to hire someone older as David Tennant's replacement, most likely a man in his forties with presence and gravitas. As he described his views on the character in 1999, 'I don't think young, dashing Doctors are right at all. The Doctor should always be a bit more Picard and a bit less Kirk. He should be 40-plus and weird looking.'

Moffat was not prepared for the young man who casting director Andy Pryor brought in on the first day of auditions, the 26-year-old Matt Smith. Smith was only born during Peter Davison's era of *Doctor Who*. Many questioned how someone could play the Doctor when they didn't look old enough to have earned a doctorate. And yet, much to Moffat's surprise, the audition showed that Smith was, without doubt, clearly the Doctor. 'He was just spot-on, right from the beginning. The way he said the lines, the way he looked, his hair . . . we just thought, "Oh, that's him!"' Whatever that strange star quality was, in which someone could appear human and alien at the same time, Smith had it. As broadcaster Matthew Sweet summed him up, 'Matt Smith has got a fascinating face. It's long and bony, with a commanding jaw. He looks like someone who could have been in Duran Duran. He has a quality of the old man trapped in the young man's body.'

Because he was so young when he was cast, Smith did not have a lot of history to bring to the role. As his biographer Emily Herbert admitted, 'His childhood was by and large uneventful [. . .] Matt sometimes seemed almost too normal to be an actor. He loved footie and going to music festivals. There was no inner darkness. The close relationship with his parents was one element of that; they kept him grounded.' The biggest personal drama in his early years had been the end of his dream to become a professional footballer, although this was hardly an unusual event in a young boy's life. In Smith's case, he developed spondylolysis, a stress fracture in his lower back. 'Yes, I was in a mess. Football was everything. You think it's the one thing you do in your life, your whole focus,' he said. 'But it's like anything . . . it's not the disappointment, it's how you react to it. I went to do my A-levels and started doing drama.' That he was able to bounce back from the disappointment and divert his energies into a new interest illustrates his determination. 'There are great disciplines from being a sportsman that you can transfer into being an artist,' he has said. 'The preparation, the sacrifice, the constant desire to improve.'

Playing football had shown Smith the importance of a work ethic. He understood from an early age that you needed to put in the effort in order to succeed, a lesson he credits his father with teaching him. 'I think my dad instilled hard work in me: you know, the idea that you should always work harder than the person next to you in a team. He was from the north, and hugely loving, but there was a toughness in his love, which I feel really grateful for. I am hard-working, but I'm also better with structure in my life.' This was an attitude that fitted well with his ambition and desire for status. As he later described the reason why he ran, successfully, for the position of head boy at Northampton School for Boys, 'I just wanted the mantle. I wanted to run things. I wanted control. It was the highest position, and I wanted the highest position. Why not?'

During his early career as an actor, Smith repeatedly crossed paths with actors linked to *Doctor Who*. His breakthrough role was in the emotionally harrowing play *That Face*, which starred Lindsay Duncan as his mother and Felicity Jones as his sister. Both actors would appear in David Tennant episodes of *Doctor Who*. In Smith's early TV work, he was often on screen with Billie Piper. The pair appeared together in *Secret Diary of a Call Girl*, *The Ruby in the Smoke* and *The Shadow in the North*. Tabloid journalists claimed they were a couple after they were photographed walking hand in hand in 2006, but both insisted that they were just friends. Having repeatedly worked with actors like this, the idea of entering the world of *Doctor Who* must have seemed to him perfectly plausible.

A combination of aspiration, hard work and talent had served Smith well throughout his life. He went along to the audition determined to impress, and the young, ambitious man tore up Steven Moffat's plans for *Doctor Who* as he did so.

3. 'We're All Stories in the End'

Just before Matt Smith took over the series, the Doctor was implicitly identified as a story. 'This song is ending,' an Ood told the Tenth Doctor just before his regeneration, 'but the story never ends.' Smith's Eleventh Doctor agreed. At the finale of his first series, he admitted that 'We're all stories in the end'.

Earlier in that adventure, the Doctor recalled a fairy tale about 'A goblin, or a trickster, or a warrior [. . .] The most feared being in all the cosmos. And nothing could stop it, or hold it, or reason with it. One day it would just drop out of the sky and tear down your world.' In this fairy tale, this trickster was defeated by a good wizard. 'I hate good wizards in fairy tales,' River Song says. 'They always turn out to be him.' This dialogue was a deliberate ploy to mislead the viewer. The nameless, terrible thing that dropped out of the sky and tore down your world was the Doctor himself, when seen from the perspective of the monsters. His enemies are astute enough to recognise that the Doctor is still a trickster wearing the mask of a hero.

'For me, *Doctor Who* is a fairy tale,' Moffat has said, explaining his approach to the show. 'It's not really science fiction. It's not set in space; it's set under your bed [. . .] Although it is watched by far more adults than children, there's something fundamental in its DNA that makes it a children's programme and it makes children of everyone who watches it. If you're still a grown up by the end of that opening music, you've not been paying attention.'

We tend to think that stories are trivial entertainments that don't really affect us, but if we look at our lives, we see that this is not the case. Most of us spend more of our spare time consuming story than any other pastime. When we have rare and precious leisure time, we usually spend it in front of the television, at the cinema or in the pages of a book. We might spend hours scrolling through social media, playing video games or gossiping with friends – activities that provide us with our storytelling fix, because they involve following the fate of different characters as they react to a series of events. Our ideologies and religions are stories. So are national identities, sports teams and the monarchy. Sometimes a ninety-minute game of football can be a better story than a prize-winning novel.

As we noted earlier, our identities are ultimately nothing more than a story. We instinctively distil our rich, complex and contradictory lives down into a single tale, in which we might see ourselves as the hero in a rags-to-riches narrative, or perhaps the victim in a tragedy. As Chris Chibnall has said, 'Human beings are story addicts. We are born as story addicts in a way that no other creatures that we know of are.' To us, story is a drug. We seek more and more of it. This is, perhaps, why we need mystery so badly.

A story is a simple and efficient way of making sense of the world, which defines certain incidents and details as more important than others. They are not the complete picture and rarely entirely true, but they are useful and can be powerfully seductive. The world we live in is, essentially, a complex construction of interlocking stories, because this is the way our minds filter reality. Our innate inclination is to turn the chaotic mess of the world into a comprehensible story because this will help us predict what comes next.

The importance and power of stories are frequently highlighted in areas outside of fiction and traditional storytelling. Politicians, businesspeople and marketing agencies all acknowledge the extent to which people understand the world not through facts or data, but through stories. The business sections of bookshops are full of books that celebrate and even glorify storytelling and, in particular, its power to manipulate others. This unintentionally points to the dark side of our addiction to story. Story, ultimately, is a controlling master. It is a tool that can be used against us. Plenty of people want to manipulate us, for their benefit and not ours. Not all stories have our best outcomes at heart.

The natural shape of stories requires an antagonist as much as a protagonist, so we habitually seek out a bad guy to differentiate ourselves from – a 'them' to blame for all that is wrong. Yet no villain sees themselves as evil. They too are following a story in which someone else is the bad guy, and this justifies their terrible actions. When a terrorist enters a crowded marketplace and detonates a suicide bomb, they do so because of a story. They believe in that story so fully that they place themselves into its narrative as a character, and give their lives to it. In that story, they believe they are a hero. For all the talk of the magic or wonder of storytelling, it can crush us as easily as it elevates us. It is hard to defend yourself from the lure of a strong story, especially one that confirms your prejudices and clearly identifies a villain you can feel morally superior too.

Good stories are always convincing, but that does not necessarily make them true. Our culture is underpinned by unquestioned stories, such as the notion that technological progress is always positive or that wealth is achieved through hard work. An absurd conspiracy theory can be every bit as compelling as a peer-reviewed academic narrative, if the story is strong enough. We might think that we're not gullible enough to fall for such nonsense, and that this only happens to other, stupid people, but this too is a story we tell ourselves.

When Plato outlined his vision of Utopia in *Republic*, he declared that an ideal society would need to banish storytellers. Plato believed that society should be ordered according to the wisdom of philosophers, and that 'the poet with his words and phrases' would seduce the people away from that wise order. He recognised that we are at the mercy of the stories we are exposed to, which can build a civilisation or lead us to war. Yet despite this, we still need them. In Steve Lyons's 2005 *Doctor Who* novel *The Stealers of Dreams*, the Doctor, Rose and Captain Jack visit a planet where fiction is outlawed. The result is a society in decline, unable to imagine what it needs to do to progress and flourish. As Ursula K. Le Guin noted, 'There have been great societies that did not use the wheel, but there have been no societies that did not tell stories.' Stories, ultimately, are like food. We need the nourishment they provide, yet we are drawn to unhealthy junk. In extreme examples, they can be a way for malign others to poison us.

The religious scholar Alan Watts used the word 'people' as a verb when he claimed that the universe 'peoples'. Here he was referring to the fact that life is an emergent property of the natural world, and that people do not come into this world, they come out of it. Consciousness is an emergent property of life and, where it is sufficiently advanced to imagine the future and remember the past, this consciousness develops to the point where it creates stories. This is what the theatre director Daisy Campbell means when she says that nature 'stories'. On a cosmological scale, stories are rare, unlikely things, absent from the great majority of planets but, from this perspective, they are also the highest flowering of the natural world.

Doctor Who is perhaps the most perfectly evolved story-creating entity that there has ever been. It is a single idea that keeps itself alive by endlessly generating new stories. It should not be surprising that it is so addictive, or so able to convert casual viewers into committed Whovians. Being a product of random evolution, it has no end game or idealised perfect state. It is just doing what it needs to do to survive. It feeds on our attention and our imagination and, in return, it offers pleasure, enthusiasm and an escape from the pressures of the material world. It is possible, however, to fall too deeply into the world of *Doctor Who* stories.

There can come a point when the number of hours that we give to the show impacts on the quality of our lives. When your interest goes beyond simply watching the television episodes, you find yourself in a seemingly infinite sea of further stories, in books, comics and audio, all of which demand your attention. Then there is the endlessly fascinating history of the show to explore, as well as the convention scene and discussion forums. All are capable of absorbing a considerable amount of your life. If you are prepared to give hours of your attention to the show every single day, *Doctor Who* will take that attention and continue to reward you for it. You will never reach the point where you know all there is to know. Yet should a *Who* fan of many years' standing add up the amount of time spent engaged with the show in one form of media or another, along with the amount of time spent thinking about it during their daily life, they might start to question whether the show has demanded too much of them.

Doctor Who can be greedy. Just as story can have an unhealthy control over us, so too can *Doctor Who* demand more than it is wise to give. There is a point where a pleasurable, entertaining escape can block out the full richness of life. When we watch it as a child it is often claiming us for life. As Chris Chibnall has said, *Doctor Who* is 'the show that is on in the corner of the room, and it gets its hooks into the children who are watching it. It's like story heroin. And our parents have been dealing it to us for sixty years.'

4. 'Home. The Long Way Round'

When *Doctor Who* returned to screens in 2005, the idea that adults enjoyed fantastical stories was still heretical, in the eyes of television programmers at least. This was despite the success of Peter Jackson's *Lord of the Rings* adaptation (2001–03), the *Star Wars* prequels (1999–2005) and the Harry Potter novels (1997–2007). Because it was believed that an adult audience would be reluctant to watch a series as silly and child-friendly as *Doctor Who*, many professionals saw the relaunch as a career-ending folly. Its immediate success therefore came as a bit of a shock, highlighting the extent to which television producers had been failing to give the audience what they wanted.

By 2013, as *Doctor Who* reached its fiftieth birthday, the media landscape had radically changed. The first *Avengers* film had just taken over $1.5 billion at the box office, and the Marvel Cinematic Universe was entering its imperial phase. Film and television audiences were showing a seemingly unquenchable thirst for superheroes, science fiction and fantasy, and television executives and film moguls were doing all they could to satisfy them. Many old sci-fi franchises, such as *Star Trek* or *Battlestar Galactica*, were rebooted. In a few short years, the notion of adults enjoying shows that had previously been labelled 'cult' had become normalised. Journalists now wrote about these shows without including insults aimed at the adults who watched them, which for older *Doctor Who* fans was quite a novel experience.

In this new landscape, *Doctor Who* was now seen as one of the BBC's 'crown jewels'. Along with *Top Gear* and the *Strictly Come Dancing* format, it was financially one of the corporation's greatest money-spinners. The fear that only Davies's and Tennant's version of *Doctor Who* could connect with mainstream audiences had been silenced by the success of Moffat's version and the fizzing chemistry between Matt Smith and his co-stars Karen Gillan, Arthur Darvill and Alex Kingston. As executive producer Brian Minchin said, 'The weirdest thing about *Doctor Who* now is, everyone takes for granted that it's huge.' As well as international programme sales, toys, DVDs, video games and other merchandise, there was a semi-permanent *Doctor Who* exhibition in Cardiff and a show called *Doctor Who Live: The Monsters Are Coming!* which toured the arenas of England, Scotland, Wales and Northern Ireland. In these circumstances, the fiftieth anniversary of the show in 2013 was clearly something that the BBC was going to celebrate.

A focal point for this anniversary was the Official 50th Celebration, which took place over 22, 23 and 24 November 2013 at the ExCel Centre in London. 'Here you can meet the people who make the show possible, avoid the strange, strange creatures roaming the hallways, have your photo taken in the TARDIS, learn to walk like a monster, find out how these incredible stunts really happen and so much more,' the programme promised, alongside a packed schedule of talks and rooms full of props and merchandise. Among all the television coverage were three particular highlights. The main focus was the feature-length anniversary episode *The Day of the Doctor*, which earned a Guinness World Record for the largest ever simulcast of a TV drama, being broadcast at the same time in ninety-four countries. It was also released in cinemas in 3D on the day of broadcast, taking over $10 million at the box office. In the UK, it was the highest-rated programme of the week and the most watched drama of 2013, as well as one of the most profitable shows that the BBC had ever made.

As well as *The Day of the Doctor*, there was *An Adventure in Space and Time*, a feature-length drama written by Mark Gatiss about William Hartnell, Verity Lambert and the programme's creation, and Peter Davison made a half-hour comedy for BBC iPlayer called *The Five(ish) Doctors Reboot* which followed Davison, Colin Baker and Sylvester McCoy as they attempted to sneak their way into the fiftieth-anniversary special. The anniversary was therefore celebrated by a new blockbuster special episode, a biographical deep dive into the programme's history and a fun real-world caper set in the world of conventions and fandom. *Doctor Who* was now more than just the show itself. When the BBC celebrated it, they celebrated every aspect of it.

Moffat originally planned to write an episode in which Matt Smith's Doctor met his two predecessors. Tennant agreed to return but Eccleston ultimately declined, a difficult position which Moffat solved by creating a previously unknown incarnation of the Doctor. This was the version of the character who had fought in the Time War and was played by screen legend John Hurt. This surprise 'War Doctor', it was explained, came after Paul McGann's Eighth Doctor and before Christopher Eccleston's Ninth.

The addition of this new Doctor prevented the story from simply being a backwards-looking nostalgia exercise. The programme's history was celebrated by the inclusion of David Tennant and Billie Piper, along with Daleks, Zygons and a surprise appearance by Tom Baker. Or at least, it would have been a surprise if Baker had not gleefully spoilt it days before. Hurt's new incarnation, in contrast, was something new. He allowed the series to bring closure to the overriding narrative that had framed the show since its return. Hurt's Doctor believed that he had destroyed Gallifrey to end the Time War, and the later Doctors carried the guilt of this act. This story revealed that, with the aid of his future selves, Gallifrey had in fact been saved and transported to a 'parallel pocket universe' somewhere. With this plot, the character of the Doctor was reinvented once more. He was no longer the Last of the Time Lords, a traumatised survivor burdened by the guilt of genocide. He was now the saviour of his people. The only problem was that he didn't know where the pocket universe that contained them was. He didn't know how to reach them.

By this point Moffat was finishing his planned three years and was intending to leave the show, along with Matt Smith. His intended final act was to reinvent the show one more time. For the first fifty years, the show had been the story of a man who wandered the universe after running away from, or being exiled from, his home planet. The next fifty, it seemed, were going to be the opposite. The Doctor spelt this out in the dialogue that ended the episode, where he recalled a conversation with his companion Clara. 'You're not going anywhere, you're just wandering about,' Clara told him. 'That's not true,' the Doctor replied. 'Not any more. I have a new destination. My journey is the same as yours, the same as anyone's. It's taken me so many years, so many lifetimes, but at last I know where I'm going. Where I've always been going. Home. The long way round.'

'Periodically, *Doctor Who* must change a lot because that's what *Doctor Who* does best,' Moffat has said. 'It doesn't survive change, it survives because of change.' *Doctor Who* was going to become a story about someone searching for their lost home, and Moffat was going to leave the programme behind and get on with the rest of his career.

Or at least, that was the theory.

5. Made of Some Sort of Steel

The Day of the Doctor was a huge success, regardless of whether you measure that by ratings, cinema takings, audience appreciation figures, social media hype or the fact that a 2014 *Doctor Who*

Magazine poll voted it the best story of the programme's first fifty years. There were, of course, dissenting voices. For all of Moffat's talents and achievements, it was hard for anyone on social media to miss the fact that a vocal section of fandom actively hated him. A community on Tumblr ran accounts with names like *i-hate-moffat*, *whohatesmoffat*, *stfu-moffat* and *anti-moffat*, which used a picture of him with his eyes painted a diabolical red as its avatar.

The overlapping fandoms of Moffat's *Doctor Who* and *Sherlock*, along with the unrelated American show *Supernatural*, became a Tumblr phenomenon called Superwholock. In this community, Moffat was viewed as a moustache-twisting villain who would take beloved characters and torture them, traumatising their fans as he did so. For many this was just a joke, but some took it seriously. Moffat had honed his craft writing snappy dialogue in the 'battle of the sexes' sitcom *Coupling*, and that style of dialogue seemed outdated and misogynistic to many younger fans. This made him morally indefensible to some, especially when compared to the lauded fan-favourite creators of the day, such as Joss Whedon, Neil Gaiman and J.K. Rowling.

Anti-Moffat sentiment led to over four thousand people signing an online petition addressed to Danny Cohen, the Director of BBC Television. 'We sign this petition to ask that the BBC remove Moffat from creative control,' it demanded. 'Fans feel that the show's overarching plots, which are under Moffat's direction, are convoluted, poorly written, and presented in a hamfisted way. They also feel that the characters created under Moffat's watch are overly stereotyped, unrelatable, "tropey", and seriously lacking in both development and emotional depth.'

One of the most notorious anti-Moffat voices was the writer Claudia Boleyn, who became known for the intensity of her attacks. According to Boleyn, *The Day of the Doctor* 'was an utterly awful piece of television that I am honestly quite surprised the BBC allowed to air. It lacked plot, characterisation, and most importantly, lacked the essence of *Doctor Who* [. . .] I'm ashamed of it. I truly am. New viewers won't want to tune back in. Old viewers are giving up watching in disgust. *Doctor Who* has lost its heart and soul.' The qualities that so many people admired, and which made Moffat so successful, were, for Boleyn, entirely invisible. Fandom had always had histrionic voices that condemned the show in similar terms to these, but those attacks had historically remained within fandom. In the social media age, they became fodder for the outrage-attention economy and spread widely.

The single-minded nature of Boleyn's attacks on Moffat are now seen in the context of her struggles with mental health, which she writes openly about on her website. 'I have Emotional Intensity Disorder (otherwise known as Borderline Personality Disorder),' she explains. 'I experience extremes of emotions and struggle with the concept of identity [. . .] Recently, I have made peace with my disorder, and have decided to reclaim my life, on my own terms. I aim to make up for the many years lost to mental illness.' *Doctor Who* fandom had always attracted people who were neurodiverse to varying degrees, and anyone who has spent any time on *Doctor Who* forums will be familiar with posters on the autistic spectrum. Fandom in general is becoming increasingly aware of these issues and is slowly learning how to navigate them better, and *Doctor Who* fandom is a community where many neurodiverse people have been able to find a home. The rise of social media, however, meant that atypical, extreme reactions which would once only have been found in the letter pages of niche fanzines were now elevated by algorithms and broadcast to the mainstream, where all nuances of the personalities and psychologies involved were stripped away. Here these views were mixed with those of trolls, legitimate criticism, attention farmers, deep nerdery and some angry and unpleasant voices, giving the overall impression that *Doctor Who* fandom was a petty, unpleasant place. Not as bad as *Star Wars* fandom, admittedly, but still pretty horrible.

All this is not a fair reflection of Who fandom, which is overwhelmingly quirky, enthused and imaginative. For those working on the show, however, the very public abuse it generated was difficult. Moffat speaks positively about fandom as a whole, but notes that, 'An impossibly small number of incredibly rude, attention-seeking people have dominated, or it seems to me have dominated, the online discourse about it. Which means I have to say to all the writers and directors who come onto the show, you will not go on social media. You will not go there because I don't want you upset. I don't want you coming in one morning crying, I don't want you in a state of misery.' Moffat was still on Twitter when he became showrunner, and he tweeted the response he received to the 2011 mid-season finale. 'Only one death threat, two demands for my immediate resignation, and two for my suicide. IT'S A HIT!!' He closed his account the following year.

Toxicity has always been a problem in *Doctor Who* fandom. Given the ever-changing nature of the show, it almost seems baked in. When people drawn to the show want to understand what it is about the programme that is important to them, they enter fandom and attempt to navigate the vast history of the programme. Certain eras don't initially seem to have the same magic, so arguments about which periods, stories, writers or actors are better than others begin. This process can be linked to that important stage of *Who* fandom – growing out of the series during teenage years, when a new adult identity is formed and the delights of childhood are rejected. Most people simply drift away from the show during this period with little drama, but those with connections and relationships within fandom can remain, despite no longer enjoying the programme. They may then vocally decry the current version for being different to the programme they initially fell in love with. Many young fans are familiar with an older cohort confidently informing them that the thing they love is not good.

Long before social media, *Doctor Who* fandom found places online to discuss the show, most notably the newsgroup rec.arts.drwho during the 1990s, and forums such as Outpost Gallifrey that replaced it. These spaces struggled with toxicity and abusive attitudes. Russell T Davies recalled a period where he couldn't stop smoking, eating bad food or 'browsing Outpost Gallifrey to read how crap I am'. In his book *The Writer's Tale*, he recalled how the writer 'Helen Raynor went on Outpost Gallifrey last month and read the reviews of her two Dalek episodes. She said that she was, literally, shaking afterwards. Like she's been physically assaulted. I'm not exaggerating. She said it was like being in a pub when a fight breaks out next to you. I had to spend two hours on the phone to her, talking her out of it.'

Since then, the evolution of the internet has meant that the problem has only got worse. YouTube creators know that the platform's algorithms reward extreme positions over more nuanced discussion. All sides in the never-ending culture war know that a popular franchise such as *Doctor Who* can bring attention to their talking points. The comedian Sooz Kempner appeared in a 2023 multimedia *Doctor Who* spin-off called *Doom's Day* and after an announcement video appeared online, the abuse began. Describing the experience to the podcaster Richard Herring, she joked that, 'The people who like it really like it and the people who hate it, well they sure do keep their feelings hidden on the internet! [. . .] From the way it's been received as far as I'm concerned, I'm the shittest actor who has ever lived, and the ugliest.' At the time of writing, the leading forum Gallifrey Base carries a disclaimer that reads, 'If you are a person who harbours intolerance toward any of your fellow human beings, you should consider either leaving the forum voluntarily, or never post anything that exposes your intolerance. From now on, think hard about what you're about to post before you post it, and leave it out if you think it might earn you a ban. Bigots . . . go away.'

That the cast and crew have to shield themselves from fandom, Moffat has said, 'Pains me to an extraordinary extent. Because the relationship between a fandom and a show should be permeable. They should be talking to each other. Because particularly in *Doctor Who* where the creatives of *Doctor Who* grew out of the fandom of the show, the idea that we don't just hang out in the same bar, the idea that the storyteller doesn't sit around the same campfire as the audience is abominable. It is not the way it's meant to be.'

Russell T Davies has also spoken about his anger at the effect of online discourse on young writers, but unlike Moffat he thinks there *should* be a divide between the audience and the artists. He discussed an article in the *Observer* where Rachel Cooke argued that those critical online voices wrote from a deep sense of exclusion. 'She wrote about that with some anger, but also with a lot of sadness. I don't see the sadness myself. I think it's *right* that they're excluded [. . .] sometimes I think I must be made of some sort of steel. I read that stuff and it doesn't stop me, not ever. I've got quite high-flown and fancy beliefs about art that maybe put it all into perspective. Principally: it is not a democracy. Creating something is not a democracy. The people have no say. The artist does. It doesn't matter what people witter on about.'

As the algorithms behind social media evolved during the 2010s, the visible toxicity of fandom increased. The need for writers and actors to be made from the same kind of steel as Davies, it seems, is now an increasingly necessary part of being creative.

14
The Death and Resurrection Show (2014–17)

1. 'She Cares So I Don't Have To'

When Steven Moffat first took on the job of *Doctor Who* show-runner, he intended to stay for three years. By a quirk of fate, he found himself also writing another massive hit BBC series at the same time. This was *Sherlock*, starring Benedict Cumberbatch and Martin Freeman, a series he co-created with Mark Gatiss. This was a thrilling situation but also a punishing workload. 'Every single time I did a series of *Sherlock* I was running between the two shows,' he said. 'Running between the fiftieth and I think *His Last Vow* on *Sherlock*, it was just insane, no one is meant to live like that.'

Moffat ultimately remained in charge of *Doctor Who* for seven intense, exhausting years, during which time he produced six series and multiple specials. 'I always sort of assumed that I would leave with Matt,' he said, but 'I was so insanely busy, I didn't have time to leave.' Given the extraordinary demands on his time and the narratively ambitious nature of his work, Moffat found little time to work on a handover plan. 'People were saying, "Well, who's the next Doctor?" And I'm going "What? Oh yes, I'd better find one." And before I know it, I'm auditioning Peter

Capaldi. That's when I suddenly got excited.' Capaldi was an established, respected Scottish actor, then best known for his role as the abusive, scene-stealing Malcolm Tucker in the political satire *The Thick of It*, and he was also a long-term fan. The thought of Capaldi as the Twelfth Doctor was just too enticing to walk away from.

'I bumped into Steven Moffat at the Scottish BAFTAs,' Capaldi has said. 'I'd never met him before. I was asking him what was happening next. I didn't know that Matt Smith was going to leave. I was just interested to know what monsters were coming back and what was going on.' After this conversation, Moffat's mental shortlist for the Twelfth Doctor had just one name on it. 'I knew he might say yes and the moment I thought of him playing the Doctor, I couldn't bear to think of somebody else.'

Moffat also asked Mark Gatiss for his suggestions as to who to cast after Smith, and Gatiss gave him a list with 'Peter Capaldi' at the top, underlined, followed by some blank space and then other names. Gatiss knew Capaldi, and knew he was a long-term Whovian. He invited him to the set of *An Adventure in Space and Time*, knowing that Capaldi would be thrilled to see their recreation of the 1960s TARDIS. 'He was showing me the TARDIS and the Daleks and stuff like that,' Capaldi recalled. 'He said, "How would you feel about being Doctor Who?" First of all, I thought that's a bit of an odd question. I said, "Well, I think that ship's sailed, hasn't it?" Meaning that Doctor Whos were generally younger than I was. He said, "Oh, I don't know." I sort of didn't think more about it, but of course I was being scoped out. They were sort of trying to figure out where I stood. I remember I said, "Can I get a photo taken of me in the TARDIS, at the control panel?" And he said, "Yeah." So I went against the TARDIS control panel, and all these people started taking photographs. "I thought, this is odd."' He got the call a couple of weeks later. He was still trying to keep his casting secret when Brad Pitt's zombie movie *World War Z* opened, in which Capaldi had a small role as a doctor with the World Health Organization. He was credited as playing 'W.H.O. Doctor in Wales'.

For an actor who loved the show so passionately as a child, taking on the role was meaningful. He recognised that there was something important and ineffable about it no other job shared. 'Essentially there is something there that it's not good to examine too closely,' he said. Explaining why he had no intention of returning to the role after he left, Capaldi said, 'I have a very mythical and personal concept of *Doctor Who*, which is that he's not on television. He's in time and space. So, if I show up again in the show I'm only coming along to do a cameo, or to do an anniversary special or something like that, then I'm an actor in a TV show. Whereas, I'm Doctor Who, really. So I haven't got time for that.'

For all his charisma and talent as an actor, casting Peter Capaldi in 2013 was a risky move in an ageist culture. Like William Hartnell, he was fifty-five when he started in the role, considerably older than all the Doctors since the first. The audience that came to the show with David Tennant or Matt Smith understood the Doctor as a kooky space boyfriend. This was a portrayal that worked well, but Moffat knew that the programme must not keep repeating itself. 'We've had two quirky young men as the Doctor,' he said. 'A third quirky young man? It looks like a formula.'

Moffat briefed his writers that this was not going to be a Doctor with the puppy-dog charm of Matt Smith. 'Steven said that the new Doctor would be brusque and a lot more alien,' screenwriter Jamie Mathieson recalls. 'He would not relate to humanity as well as before, and Clara would be his human interface device. He would be using her as a buffer. He'd be quite unfeeling in a lot of situations, he's going to be dismissive, he's going to be sarcastic. The more he spoke about it, the more

I was reminded of the character Gregory House from the show *House*. So that was my mental shorthand – I was just writing House in the TARDIS. I had a bit [in my script *Mummy on the Orient Express*] where the Doctor bluntly says to someone, "Yes, you're going to die. But tell me what you can see, because maybe I'll be able to save the next person." Steven's reaction was, "Yes! More of that. That's the tone I want."'

This was a radical change. The Doctor's compassion for regular humans had been a consistent element since the show returned. 'An ordinary man: that's the most important thing in creation,' Eccleston's Doctor says in *Father's Day*. 'Human beings! You are amazing!' enthuses Tennant in *The Impossible Planet*, and Smith's Doctor in *A Christmas Carol* tells us that, 'In nine hundred years of time and space, I've never met anyone who wasn't important.' In this context, it was quite a shock when Capaldi arrives and announces that '[Clara's] my carer. She cares so I don't have to.'

For old-school fans, familiar with older, spikier Doctors, this was a valid and enjoyable approach, but it did cause some people to turn off, particularly younger viewers. By Capaldi's last season, the viewing figures had dropped noticeably. This has to be seen in the context of the general collapse in broadcast audiences in the 2010s, thanks to competition from streaming, but it was noticeable that new *Doctor Who* toys were no longer arriving on the shelves of toy shops. *Doctor Who Adventures*, the magazine aimed at younger viewers, went from weekly to monthly in 2013, then bi-monthly in 2016, before being cancelled shortly afterwards. A young adult spin-off series, the Patrick Ness-scripted *Class*, failed to find an audience. It was now many years after the excitement of the Eccleston series and it was easy to take the show for granted. While *Doctor Who* had typically been broadcast at a child-friendly start time of between 6 p.m. and 7:30 p.m., Capaldi's first season went out as late as 8:30 p.m. This meant that it was still being broadcast after the watershed. *Doctor Who* was no longer gaining a new generation of kids. It was instead focusing on its existing, ageing audience.

At the end of the Matt Smith era, Moffat had retooled the programme to give the Doctor a new purpose: he was now searching the universe to find his lost home, Gallifrey. 'I asked Steven about this during the writing of the fiftieth,' recalled the script editor Richard Cookson. 'I have a feeling he felt the Doctor would essentially just keep on travelling, and we'd maybe scatter the odd crumb across the upcoming series, but not make it a quest; it wouldn't define the show as a mission going forward.' Very quickly, however, Moffat came to the conclusion that a character repeatedly failing to find something is inherently undramatic. 'I recall developing series-eight episodes with different guest writers, and several of them came in with that question [about whether finding Gallifrey was the new arc], or would write into a script a clue about Gallifrey or the Time Lords, and Steven would suggest we take it out.' As Moffat later admitted, 'I don't think there's any plot at all in the Doctor looking for Gallifrey. I think it's boring.' The idea was quickly shelved and Gallifrey was located without any fanfare a couple of years later.

Instead, the arc of this new Doctor was more introspective. What drove him was not an external quest, but a desire to understand his own nature. Specifically, as he asked Clara, he wanted to know if he was a good man. It seemed an odd question, given that the audience had seen him helping others and risking his neck for the greater good countless times. Viewers had no doubt that he was a good man, so the question seemed initially undramatic. What the question did do, however, was allow the Doctor to examine themselves. In doing so, the show began to investigate the nature of *Doctor Who* itself.

Those who remembered the Colin Baker years were conscious of how risky an initially rude and unpleasant Doctor could be.

But while Baker was not given the opportunity to evolve the character over time as initially planned, Moffat and Capaldi were able to explore the full development of this introspective incarnation. Through explorations of heartache and loss, the Twelfth Doctor became increasingly open-hearted and vulnerable, seemingly getting younger as he got older. By the last episode of his final series, he finally knew who he was and what he stood for. Facing death from an attack by Cybermen, he pleads with two incarnations of the Master to work with him. 'I'm not trying to win,' he tells them. 'I'm not doing this because I want to beat someone, or because I hate someone, or because I want to blame someone. It's not because it's fun and God knows it's not because it's easy. It's not even because it works, because it hardly ever does. I do what I do, because it's right! Because it's decent! And above all, it's kind. It's just that. Just kind.'

With this speech, the Doctor understood who he was. As Capaldi summed up *Doctor Who*, 'It's a gas and a good thing in the world.' The Doctor then uses this vision of himself in an attempt to convert evil towards good. As he pleads with the Masters, 'You're going to die too, some day. How will that be? Have you thought about it? What would you die for? Who I am is where I stand. Where I stand, is where I fall. Stand with me.'

The Doctor was telling us that he was defined by his actions. The motivation for those actions was the understanding that the only goal that matters was to be kind. *Doctor Who* had questioned what it was and why it existed, and concluded that it was an invitation to live a better life. This may sound like a glib motivational speech, but it was the wisdom of age, hard won through three seasons of Capaldi's Doctor. This eventual conclusion seemed far more compelling because it came at the end of the journey from the dark, uncaring initial version of Capaldi's Twelfth Doctor. In cynical, anxious times, the programme found an ideal to aim for.

2. The Snow Globe

The TARDIS, as we noted earlier, was a television-like portal to the Otherworld that lived inside the television. Televisions had changed dramatically since the show had first appeared, becoming flat glass screens rather than solid wooden boxes, but the basic concept remained. This idea took on a deeper meaning in 2014, when Ben Wheatley directed Peter Capaldi's debut episodes as the Twelfth Doctor. At the start of production, Wheatley approached the art department with an unusual request. He wanted them to build an exact replica of the snow globe from the final episode of *St. Elsewhere*, an American medical drama from the 1980s. There was no reference to it in the script, but the art department dutifully built it anyway.

The snow globe featured in the last scene of *St. Elsewhere*'s final episode. This showed a teenage boy named Tommy Westphall sitting on the floor, staring intently into the globe and rocking slightly as his father Dr Donald Westphall entered. He was one of the main characters in the series, a senior doctor at St Eligius, a run-down Boston hospital. Somehow, however, the doctor had now become a construction worker, returning home to his family after a long day at work. Donald's father, who had previously died in the series, was sat dozing in a chair, babysitting. What we were seeing was clearly a different reality to that of the rest of the show.

Tommy did not respond when his father approached or talked to him. 'I don't understand this autism thing, Pop,' a despairing Donald said to his father. 'Here's my son, I talk to him, I don't even know if he can hear me. He sits there all day long in his own world, staring at that toy. What's he thinking about?' The series ended as the camera tracked into the snow globe, revealing that it contained a replica of the St Eligius hospital. In the final moments of the series, we discovered that *St. Elsewhere* had occurred in the mind of an autistic boy vividly imagining the events occurring inside a snow globe. It was a bold, unexpected twist, if one that was not universally popular with the audience.

The twist became even stranger after the rise of the internet, when people started discussing the deeper implications of this scene. *St. Elsewhere* had included several episodes in which its cast had crossed over into other television series. For example, in a 1985 episode called 'Cheers', Dr Donald Westphall and some of his colleagues visited the Boston bar that featured in the sitcom *Cheers*. Here they met characters including Norm, Cliff and Carla. Did this mean that in the fiction of *St. Elsewhere*, the sitcom *Cheers* was also part of Tommy Westphall's imagination? And if that was the case, then surely the *Cheers* spin-off series *Frasier* was as well?

In what became known as the Tommy Westphall Universe Hypothesis, people began to investigate just how many television shows existed within the shared universe of Tommy Westphall's imagination. Thousands of connections were discovered, and programmes as diverse as *Breaking Bad*, *The Office* (both British and American versions) and the 1960s *Batman* were all shown to be connected. Before long it seemed that pretty much any scripted television show was part of Tommy's imagination, if you hunted for connections with enough ingenuity and wit. That one simple snow globe, in other words, contained almost the entirety of television drama.

To give an example of how this works, we can include *Doctor Who* as part of Tommy Westphall's imagination in the following way. As we've just seen, both *Cheers* and *Frasier* are part of the same fictional universe. The character of John Hemingway from the *John Larroquette Show* once called into Frasier's radio show, so that show is also part of the shared universe. The Yoyodyne corporation, which would manufacture spaceships in *Star Trek: The Next Generation*, was referenced in *The John Larroquette Show*. In the *Buffy the Vampire Slayer* spin-off series *Angel*, the interdimensional law firm Wolfram and Hart did work for both Yoyodyne and Weyland-Yutani, the evil corporation from the *Alien* franchise. A Weyland-Yutani spacecraft was seen in an episode of the sci-fi sitcom *Red Dwarf*. In a different episode, alert viewers would have spotted the TARDIS in the background of the *Red Dwarf* hangar bay. *Doctor Who*, by the logic of interconnected and referential film and television programmes, therefore exists inside the formidable imagination of a child staring at a snow globe.

Or at least it did, until Ben Wheatley took that snow globe and intentionally placed it inside the Doctor's TARDIS. 'I now wish I'd put it somewhere more where you can see it,' he said. 'It just went in with all the tat in the TARDIS re-dress they did for Peter Capaldi. I don't think it's on camera anywhere. I didn't make an effort to get it in shot because I thought my work had been done at that point.'

Doctor Who had always claimed other stories. As Terrance Dicks often joked, what you needed for a *Doctor Who* adventure was a good, original idea, it just didn't need to be your own good, original idea. The programme would often lift stories from films, television shows and books, force the character of the Doctor into them and see what happened. Stories as diverse as Mary Shelley's *Frankenstein*, J.G. Ballard's *High-Rise* or Anthony Hope's *The Prisoner of Zenda* were all retold as *Doctor Who* adventures – renamed *The Brain of Morbius*, *Paradise Towers* and *The Androids of Tara*, respectively. What Wheatley had done, however, took this idea much further. He had performed an occult act. He had added something hidden and unseen by the audience, but which was still considered to have meaning and impact – in the mind of the director, at least. 'I thought I'd take the oldest television programme, more or less, and put all of television inside it. It made sense to me. The power of this show that had been around forever – it should claw back all of American television. It was a conceptual power grab.'

We often think of television as a trivial thing, but this does it a disservice. In *Light of Thy Countenance*, a comic written by Alan Moore and illustrated by Felipe Massafera, television is given a voice. It understands how much human awareness is focused on it and its power to attract our attention. 'You sit at night there on the couch beside your partner yet have only eyes for me,' it tells us. 'You listen to my voice in rapt attention yet grow bored or easily distracted when your loved one speaks.' Billions of people spend hours every day focused on television, and the stories it tells. People had worshipped at altars and idols for untold millennia, yet those objects of reverence have not received anything like the amount of attention that television absorbed in the late twentieth century. No god in history has received as much devotion.

Wheatley's 'conceptual power grab' established the idea that *Doctor Who* contains all of television – while still paradoxically remaining part of television. In a similar way, the series *Doctor Who* also exists within the fiction of *Doctor Who*. That, at least, appeared to be the implication of a scene in 1988's *Remembrance of the Daleks*, which was set in London in 1963. Ace left the room after she had switched on the black-and-white television, so she did not hear the continuity announcer telling us that, 'This is BBC Television. The time is a quarter past five and Saturday viewing continues with an adventure in the new science fiction series, Doc—' The programme then cut to the next scene, but it did appear that Ace had narrowly missed watching the first episode of *Doctor Who*. That *Doctor Who* exists within *Doctor Who* was confirmed in 2014's *In the Forest of the Night*, in which a bus can be seen with an advert for the series on its side.

The TARDIS was inside the snow globe, yet the snow globe was also inside the TARDIS. That uncanny blue box exists inside television, yet it contains the entirety of television storytelling. This is not rational thinking. It is mysticism. The within is without. As above, so below. The logic of this situation may not satisfy the materially minded, but rationality is not what powers *Doctor Who*.

3. Death and the Doctor

The writer Jamie Mathieson attended a cast read-through of one of Steven Moffat's Christmas scripts. 'It was very well received and there was a round of applause at the end,' he recalls. 'I expected Steven to be pleased, but at the end he sighed and said – I'm paraphrasing here, but it was something like, "That's great. You all love it. Now I've got to go and write another one. And it just goes on and on and on."' For Moffat, the read-through was no victory because he had to go straight back to the keyboard and write another amazing episode. 'The memory of that stuck with me because it seemed like a little view into the inside of his head. It was like, "This is a treadmill. I am on a fucking treadmill."'

Exhausted by the workload, Moffat had wanted to leave *Doctor Who* earlier, but his obvious successor was then unavailable. Chris Chibnall was the last of the old-school fans who had both written for the show and who had also, crucially, created and run a mainstream hit television series unrelated to *Doctor Who* – in Chibnall's case, the smash-hit crime drama *Broadchurch*. This gave him sufficient experience and the necessary kudos needed for the BBC to trust him with such a high-profile series. But when

Moffat wanted to leave, Chibnall was busy finishing the third series of *Broadchurch*. Moffat duly stayed on for a further series of *Doctor Who*, and then another special, until the new team was ready. He did so out of a sense of duty. As he said afterwards, 'I've done whole jobs that have taken less time than the time it's taken me to find the door on *Doctor Who*.'

His big fear was that he had run out of stories to tell. 'By the time I wrote [the end of Capaldi's last season], I was in a state of worry about whether there was anything left in the tank,' he admitted. The fear proved to be unfounded. According to a *Doctor Who Magazine* poll in 2023, Moffat wrote half of the top ten greatest stories of all time, and the top two, *Heaven Sent* and *World Enough and Time*, were Capaldi stories from the end of Moffat's era. By the time he had left, he had written forty-two stories, which was then more than any other writer in the history of *Doctor Who*. Like Russell T Davies, he was awarded an OBE for services to drama in the Queen's honours list.

Facing the choice of attracting a new generation of viewers or allowing the series to age up in the hope of keeping its existing audience, Moffat chose the latter. In doing so he leant into the age and unusual longevity of the show, and references to the programme's past increased. His final story began with the caption 'Previously on *Doctor Who*... 709 episodes ago,' and picked up on events from a lost 1966 episode. This is a type of storytelling that is only possible on *Doctor Who*, and it would be a shame not to take advantage of the unique opportunities it offers. It is not, however, an approach designed to attract a new generation of seven-year-olds.

Time passes strangely when you are exhausted and overworked. It is in keeping with the timey-wimey nature of the Moffat era that the Doctor seems to age a lifetime during that period. When we first met Moffat's original Doctor, he was the youngest we had ever seen him, boyishly peering out of a crashed TARDIS and befriending a small child. He had the energy and the freshness needed to launch a whole new era. By the time we get to Moffat's final story six seasons later, the Doctor had gone from being 907 years old to around 2,000 years old. He was now a grey-haired old man in the company of another grey-haired old man, both of whom were welcoming their approaching deaths and refusing to regenerate. The idea that the Doctor wanted to give up and die was a new and radical one.

The Matt Smith years had begun with the young new Doctor growing into the powerful being, feared across the universe, that River had described at their first meeting. The Peter Capaldi years, in contrast, were obsessed with decline and death. There were two visits to the end of the universe where everything – or nearly everything – was dead. Stories like *Death in Heaven* featured a virtual afterlife called the Nethersphere, and the aliens in Capaldi's final story snatched people from the moment of their deaths in order to honour and record their memories. All four of Jamie Mathieson's scripts involved people dying, only for their bodies to be reanimated and used against their will. So too did both of the Cybermen season finales. Both Capaldi's main companions, Clara Oswald and Bill Potts, died at the end of their travels with the Doctor, as did Clara's partner Danny Pink. They were all magically resurrected, but not as regular normal living humans. This was highly unusual for 21st-century *Doctor Who*, which as a rule didn't kill its companions. Death and dying is a regular feature of the show, of course, but it's unusual for it to be the theme.

The story which came top of the *Doctor Who Magazine* 2023 poll was Moffat's 2015 classic *Heaven Sent*. 'During the Capaldi years, I was always looking to do one [episode] per season that was experimental,' Moffat said. 'Once a year, you're supposed to do one that's completely mental [...] *Heaven Sent* was a very risky one.' The story explored the Doctor's response to the death of Clara in the previous episode. The majority of this story was a single-hander episode, with Peter Capaldi acting alone, trapped for billions of years in the purgatory of his own grief. This took the form of a gloomy, puzzle box-like castle. '[With] *Doctor Who*, you've got to talk about monsters and it's a sort of circus – kids love it, and everybody's got to be entertained, but actually underneath it all, there's a sense of melancholy and death,' Capaldi commented after that story was voted the greatest ever. 'That particular episode's just all about death and I think that's fascinating that that episode became the all-time favourite [...] [Kids are] smart in the sense they understand instinctively that there's darkness and there are things around and the monsters are manifestations of that.' The programme's director Rachel Talalay responded on social media by saying, 'I tend to describe it as a meditation on grief, not death. Feels more universal. But it is fascinating that it's so appreciated.'

These themes fitted well with the older, introspective Doctor – the one who ignored the quest to find Gallifrey and instead asked, 'Am I a good man?' On paper, it might sound odd that the Doctor tried to stop his regeneration because he hoped to die. But this was in the context of a Doctor who had finally discerned who he really was, and accepted himself. Perhaps he did not then want to change, and have that long, painful process start all over again.

If this was the case, he had not been paying full attention throughout all those explorations of death, as the programme analysed itself. All those stories were not, ultimately, about death – they were about the impossibility of death. They were all stories of transformation and resurrection. Clara, Bill, Danny Pink, Heather, even the cyber-resurrected Brigadier – in all these examples, death led to change, not annihilation. This change could be monstrous and terrifying, as with the Cybermen, or it could be a moment of grace. What it could not be was avoided.

That this idea was the heart of *Doctor Who* was made explicit in the characterisation of Missy – a female incarnation of the Master. Missy attempted to change. She wanted to become good but ultimately, she was unable to do so. Missy, and all incarnations of the Master, were the opposite of the Doctor in that they were a fixed villainous personality, unable to transform. Even when the programme killed them off, they just returned as normal a few years later, with no explanation. In the *Doctor Who* universe, the Master was what the Doctor fought against. By existing as a form of fixed anti-Doctor, Missy revealed the fundamental truth of *Doctor Who*. Stasis was death, change was life.

The Doctor had to always change, whether he wanted to or not. That was the hard-won revelation of the Capaldi era. A never-ending story cannot die.

4. They Cross Generations

The belief that *Doctor Who* will go on forever is an act of faith. None of us know what the future has in store. Many fans, especially those who lived through the trauma of the mid-1980s hiatus, live in fear that the series is about to come to an end. They are triggered by fluctuations in viewing figures, afraid that every dip and stumble indicates the certainty of cancellation. All this assumes that *Doctor Who* is a regular television show – something that is either in production or is not, which can be ended at a stroke by a visionless executive. Such an idea is comforting, in a way. The idea that *Doctor Who* has evolved into something else before our eyes can be a little unsettling.

Tradition and longevity add importance and weight to all things. Even a sort-of children's programme with a daft name can become significant, if you wait long enough. In time, a regular television character may be reclassified as something more – a heritage property, a folk hero, an archetype or, if you wait long enough, a legend. Perhaps in time the *Doctor Who* story will be thought of more as a myth. The Doctor did, after all, come down from the heavens and land on Earth to save us from evil. They show us the qualities that we need to live a good life. They champion kindness, imagination and bravery, and they reject weapons and violence. They also know we need adventure, wonder and an encounter with the beyond. Perhaps they know us better than we know ourselves, so perfectly do they give us what we need. Religions have been built on far less.

Seemingly endless stories are told about this saviour from the heavens – a vast outpouring of adventures that we share and treasure. These differ from the majority of stories in our media, because they cross generations and allow families to come together in a weekly shared ritual. In the 1960s *Doctor Who* was seen as something for children, but those children grew up and introduced their own kids to these stories and, eventually, their grandchildren too. Whovian families like this bond over that most valuable of things, a shared cross-generational cultural touchstone.

In this context, the similarities between religion and what *Doctor Who* has become are striking. For Whovians, the classic era is their Old Testament – the founding stories which are forever retold, given the weight of untouchable scripture by their age. The Wilderness Years are an important parable of suffering and faith. The modern series attracts a congregation for its stories of morality, transcendence and Weeping Angels. It is hard for an organisation like the Church of England to compete with this, given that it is unable to spice up its parables with a few Daleks or Zygons.

For most people, *Doctor Who* is just a small part of their wider lives. There are others, however, who devote themselves to the subject on a much deeper level, until it becomes part of their identity. In a similar way, most people in a religious community are content to be the congregation, turning up once a week and then going about their business, while some are compelled to enter the priesthood. Fandom can be seen as a sort of church, which rewatches the old stories and keeps them alive in a similar way to monks chanting an ancient sacred text. The history of the faith is recorded and debated. Great theological arguments tackle and defend the contradictions in the canon, like medieval scholars debating how many Weeping Angels can dance on the head of a pin. Just as one holy book can lead to tens of thousands of rival sects, so too can *Doctor Who* fandom split into different factions, all favouring different aspects of the same text. Fandom, like religion, can be a positive and rewarding part of who we are, or it can tip into fundamentalism and zealotry.

Some fans take up professional positions in the world of *Doctor Who*, perhaps working in magazines, books, audio or conventions, or restoring old episodes for modern release. They preserve and protect the programme's legacy and form a sort of priestly caste. The amount of love and care devoted to the classic series Blu-Ray releases, in particular, has no equivalent for any other television show, and treats the old episodes with unparalleled reverence. Above these priests is a closely guarded inner sanctum that demands a higher level of commitment and secrecy – those who work on the programme itself. At the top of the hierarchy is the showrunner, the Doctor's representative on Earth. This person has the power to make papal pronouncements which must then be accepted as part of the canon.

Doctor Who is not the only entertainment franchise that has evolved in ways that resemble religion. Writing in the *New Statesman*, Amelia Tait discussed the phenomenon of 'Disney adults' – people who engage deeply with Disney entertainment long after they have stopped being children. The appeal of being a Disney adult, she argues, is essentially that of belonging to a religion and forming communal bonds over shared stories. 'Over the past 100 years, the Walt Disney Company has entwined itself with our families, memories and personal histories. In many ways, Disney is a religion that one is born into, the same way a 15th-century English baby was predestined to be baptised Catholic. Choice doesn't necessarily come into it – we see Mickey Mouse around us like our ancestors saw the cross; a symbol that both 18-month-olds and 80-year-olds recognise.'

For Tait, the phenomenon of Disney adults was deliberately created by the Walt Disney Company, who methodically marketed merchandise, holiday cruises and even entire towns at adults. 'If we accept that Disney adults were created, rather than spontaneously generated, then why are we scrutinising the congregation instead of the church?' she asked. This is a situation very different to *Doctor Who*. There were decades when the BBC actively did not encourage adults to engage with the show. They did what they could to prevent this, not least by keeping it off the air. Yet during those times, the programme connected to adults regardless.

Doctor Who is a show that acts in ways that no external person or company can steer, even in ways at odds with its owner. Given that it behaves like a living thing with its own sense of agency, it might have a greater claim to be viewed as a religion than most. If nothing else, it sheds a great deal of light on the way that religions form.

15
The Foundling (2018–22)

1. Her Own Cupboard

There is often one specific moment that defines a new Doctor in the popular imagination. It may come at the start of their era, like Matt Smith's newly regenerated Doctor craving fish fingers and custard. It may come later in the run, such as Sylvester McCoy mocking Davros's megalomania as demands for unlimited rice pudding. Or it may be a little quirk, repeated across an era, like Tom Baker asking people if they would like a jelly baby. For some reason many of these character-defining moments are pudding- or sweet-based.

It's not the case, however, that the defining moment for Jodie Whittaker's Thirteenth Doctor was her delight at discovering the TARDIS's new custard-cream dispenser. In March 2020, in an attempt to slow the spread of the Covid-19 virus, the UK entered lockdown. Children were taken out of school, separated from their friends and grandparents, and had to come to terms with the danger that so frightened their families. Like the rest of the country, Jodie Whittaker was also forced to stay at home. But she had her *Doctor Who* outfit with her, so she climbed into her own cupboard and filmed herself, in character as the Doctor, in a message aimed at children, which the BBC then uploaded to

YouTube. It may have been outside of the series, but the empathy she displayed captured her version of the character perfectly.

In the video, Whittaker never mentioned lockdown, or the virus. She was, she claimed, self-isolating by hiding in a cupboard to keep herself safe from an army of Sontarans. But the TARDIS had detected an upsurge in psychological signals that meant 'someone, somewhere might be a little bit worried', so she was sending a message of support and advice. 'Remember, you will get through this and things will be all right, even if they look uncertain, even if you're worried – darkness never prevails,' she promised. She recommended telling bad jokes and practising kindness. 'Look out for each other. You won't be the only one worried. Talking will help, sharing will help. Look out for your friends, your neighbours, people you hardly know, and family – because in the end, we're all family.' She ended by advising children to 'Listen to doctors – they've got your back.' The Doctor had not spoken reassuringly to children on their level like this since Patrick Troughton had warned them about the Yeti becoming scarier. While the Twelfth Doctor resonated more with older viewers, the Thirteenth was once again speaking to kids.

'The thing that you have to make a call on,' the new showrunner Chris Chibnall said, 'is yes, you are dealing with a figure that is a very intrinsic part of adults' identities. But the job of the show is not to serve that. The job of the show is to create new versions of that for kids who are five and up [. . .] I hope that enough adults will go with us. But my job coming in with Jodie is to go, "If you were a ten-year-old girl – or a ten-year-old boy for that matter, because I don't think ten-year-old boys have any problem with female role models – then are you going to remember these stories? Are you going to rewatch your favourite episodes? Are you going to love these characters?"'

Jodie Whittaker's excitable and child-friendly portrayal might have surprised those only familiar with her pre-*Doctor Who* work, in which she was often cast in emotionally harrowing or tragic roles. She played the mother of a murdered child in Chris Chibnall's *Broadchurch*, a woman unable to engage with the world following the death of her twin in *Adult Life Skills*, and a woman who has an illegal wartime abortion in the television adaption of Sarah Waters's *The Night Watch*. As Whittaker described her career, she was usually cast as 'the girl that's got bloody mascara running down her face because she's got some trauma in the corner'.

Whittaker grew up in the village of Skelmanthorpe, near Huddersfield in Yorkshire. Like Christopher Eccleston, she was a child with an exceptionally vivid imagination. As she later recalled, 'I played on my own for hours. I didn't need anyone. All my dolls and teddy bears had a voice. My bed was a boat, my window was a magic mirror.' She was, she admits, 'crap at school [. . .] I always found it difficult to sit there and have someone talking at me.' Characteristically, she saw the positive side of this. 'If I'd have been good at everything at school, I might not have known I was good at acting.' Whittaker attended the Guildhall School of Music and Drama, graduating with an acting gold medal and the reputation as the funniest performer in her year. Her graduation piece involved her cycling across the stage dressed as a clown.

'The line between Jodie and Sylvester McCoy and Patrick Troughton always felt very strong to me,' Chibnall said, 'right from her first audition. But she had not seen [those Doctors], at that point. That was just her. When Jodie walked in and read for the Doctor, we knew it was the Doctor, and when other people read, you know it's not.' Many Doctors have spoken about the extent that their personal identity has merged with the character, but only Whittaker went fully method and, being pregnant when she filmed her final episode, actually played the role with two hearts.

2. 'It's about Time'

It had taken fifty-four years, but Jodie Whittaker had become the first woman cast as the incumbent Doctor. The ground for this change had been prepared during the Steven Moffat era. He established in story that Time Lords can change gender. This was most notable with Missy, the female version of the Master, but a Gallifreyan general and the mysterious Corsair were also established as having changed sex. Moffat knew that although parts of fandom were resistant to change, those changes would be more readily accepted if they had precedent in earlier episodes. It was as if the history of *Doctor Who* was a sacred text, and anything that was in accordance with it could avoid accusations of heresy. Of course, given that Gallifrey was originally entirely male and there was no such thing as a female Time Lord during the first fifteen years of the programme, it is a very mutable sacred text.

Talk about the Doctor becoming female had been around since 1980, when Tom Baker suggested that we shouldn't assume his successor would be male. John Nathan-Turner also raised the idea in the 1980s, although he never intended to cast a woman. He just knew that the idea would get the programme more press coverage. At the time, there was considerable resistance to the idea, from both men and women. 'I know there's this big debate about whether the Doctor should be a woman. I'm not too sure about it,' said Sarah Sutton, who played Nyssa, in a 1984 BBC radio interview. 'I don't know whether it would work.'

The world had changed radically by 2017, when Chibnall was developing his version of the series. His starting assumption was that, 'If it's going to be a new Doctor, then it has to be a woman. There was no pushback or no questioning about that from the

BBC.' Pre-launch promotion leant into the social significance of this move, with one trailer showing Whittaker's Doctor underneath a glass ceiling, which then shatters, followed by the phrase 'It's about time'. The audience was clearly ready for this change, and they tuned in in huge numbers for Whittaker's debut. The average 28-day audience for Capaldi's last season had been 5.88 million. The debut of the first female Doctor the following year doubled this, with 11.46 million watching the episode in the first twenty-eight days. Change had once again led to rejuvenation.

There were very few voices who outwardly stated a belief that the Doctor should not be a woman. There were, however, a notable number of older male *Doctor Who* fans who spoke loudly and angrily about the Jodie Whittaker era being the lowest point in the show's history. Criticism was rarely aimed at Whittaker directly, but instead focused on the quality of the dialogue, character behaviour, plot holes or the question of whether the four-member TARDIS team had enough to do. Weak scripts and redundant companions were not new in the history of *Doctor Who*, of course, but now they were deemed unforgivable. Those making the attacks saw them as valid critical appraisals and denied they were expressing internal misogyny. That their reactions matched the pattern of abuse aimed at high-profile female protagonists in the *Star Wars*, *Star Trek* and Marvel franchises was, they insisted, just a coincidence.

Those who took a dislike to this era did not have to look hard for online voices that shared their views. The rise of 'HateTubers' on YouTube and 'anti-fans' across social media, in which people build a following by hating a popular individual or cultural phenomenon, has grown to the point where it attracts academic attention. In March 2023, the journal *Nature* published a study entitled 'Negativity drives online news consumption', which analysed over 100,000 online news stories to see what aspects of headlines people were psychologically drawn to. As the authors explain, 'We found that negative words in news headlines increased consumption rates (and positive words decreased consumption rates). For a headline of average length, each additional negative word increased the click-through rate by 2.3%.' Those YouTubers who wanted to attract an audience, in other words, could find more success being abusive than by being positive.

Although this helps to explain why such channels were popular, that still leaves the question of why people can feel so much negativity towards media properties in the first place. Looking at the anti-fans of influencers in particular, researchers at Cardiff University claim that these intense negative reactions come from a position of exclusion. When an object of interest becomes a significant part of our lives, we psychologically relate to it as if this was a normal human relationship. Yet a relationship with a TV show or an online personality can never be reciprocal, and this realisation can leave people feeling bitter. The resulting behaviour is the fandom equivalent of obsessively stalking an ex, rather than letting a relationship end naturally. Other studies claim that we often form parasocial relationships unconsciously and rarely recognise the extent to which they affect us. Parasocial relationships are the relationships we have with people that we don't know in real life, such as actors or characters in books. A show like *Doctor Who* can get its hooks into us on a deeper level than we admit, but this can never be the mutual, equal relationship that we psychologically crave.

In these circumstances it is not uncommon for feelings of love, even unrecognised ones, to tip over into hate. A show like *Doctor Who* that regularly changes radically, without consulting the audience or gaining their approval, is particularly vulnerable to this effect. The picture is further complicated by far-right groups and other extremists who use criticism of popular media as wedge issues to separate young boys, in particular, from mainstream thought. Extremists like this rarely start backlashes against women or people of colour in film and television, but they are quick to amplify them when they emerge.

The anger and abuse was not all one-sided. Peter Davison spoke positively about the change during an interview at San Diego Comic Con. 'I think it's a fantastic opportunity for her and I think it will be hard for some fans to adjust to it [. . .] but I think the important thing is that those who are uncertain should be encouraged to watch it with an open mind. I think the time for discussion about that is past. They've made the announcement that Jodie Whittaker is the next Doctor and that's great.' He did, however, add a caveat. 'If I feel any doubts about it, it's the loss of a role model for boys, who I think *Doctor Who* is vitally important for. I feel a bit sad about that, but I understand the argument that you've got to open it up. She has my best wishes and full confidence. I'm sure she'll do a wonderful job.' The idea that the Doctor was an important role model for boys – because he relied on his brain rather than guns or his fists – may seem a valid point, but such nuances were lost on social media, as was the context within which Davison's positive comments were framed. Davison was angrily condemned for raising it, and the abuse that followed caused him to close down his Twitter account. His last posting read, 'All this toxicity about a sci-fi show has been sobering, so I'm calling it a day. [Twitter] used to be fun. Now it's not.'

The anti-Thirteenth Doctor critical movement was often referred to online by the hashtag #NMD, which stood for 'Not My Doctor'. This was, in truth, a fair description. The Thirteenth Doctor was not the Doctor of these older viewers. She was the Doctor of a new generation of fans, one that was young and female-skewing. They were in general an upbeat, creative bunch, fond of cosplay, fan art and emotional positivity, who fell in love with the idea of the cute, dorky Whittaker Doctor travelling the universe with her unlikely friends. When this new young generation felt drawn to exploring the larger world of *Doctor Who*, they found established online Whovian communities to be unbearable hives of negativity, and fled in horror. Instead, they built their own online communities, safely away from the rest of *Doctor Who* fandom. Many would describe themselves as fans of Jodie Whittaker and the Thirteenth Doctor, rather than fans of *Doctor Who* as a whole.

It may be that this split will naturally heal. There are already signs that many older fans who condemned this era have come to think more positively about it, after giving it a rewatch away from negative online discourse. Fans of the Thirteenth Doctor, meanwhile, may well find that there is more to *Doctor Who* as a whole, if they get drawn into the Ncuti Gatwa era. But if *Doctor Who* fandom is some form of proto-religion, then it is one that is highly susceptible to schisms and sects.

3. 'The Absence of a Set Destiny'

The beginning of the Chris Chibnall and Jodie Whittaker era was a forward-looking fresh start intended to welcome new viewers rather than comfort older ones. The initial Thirteenth Doctor series in 2018 included no references to old characters or monsters, beyond the Doctor herself and the TARDIS. This was highly unusual. The last series to do this was season sixteen, Tom Baker's 'Key to Time' series, back in 1978. The only reference to established backstory was the admission that Whittaker had recently been an older Scotsman.

The programme also looked and sounded new. The series was filmed, for the first time, with anamorphic lenses, and location filming in South Africa and Andalusia in Spain took full advantage of this modern cinematic aesthetic. A new composer, Segun Akinola, dialled down the previously bombastic music. The show's production values now fitted into the international era of high-budget streaming box sets. It would not have looked out of place on Netflix or Amazon Prime. It no longer appeared to be a quirky British oddity that played by its own rules.

Whittaker was not the stern, sometimes frightening figure that had come before. With her yellow braces, rainbow T-shirt and big work boots, she had the air of a friendly children's television presenter. And yet there were hints that something a little more troubled was going on under the skin. The interior of her TARDIS was far more alien, disorientating and frightening than before, and so was the new title sequence. For all that Whittaker's Doctor valued and needed her companions, she was not always entirely honest with them. She was struggling with issues surrounding her past, which she kept from her friends.

Doctor Who showrunners have always imprinted parts of themselves on the series, and Chibnall was no exception. 'I had a cancer diagnosis when I was 22,' Chibnall told *Doctor Who Magazine*. 'That was quite scary, when I had that, and I had to tell my mum and dad.' This experience was written into Bradley Walsh's character Graham, and it was reflected in the Doctor's awkwardness when Graham was talking about his fear that his cancer would return. 'The Doctor's reaction in that scene, I've had that numerous times,' he said. 'People do behave with you like that in that situation.' According to Chibnall, it is inevitable that *Doctor Who* writers put parts of themselves into the stories. 'You have to pour yourself into it, because it demands so many of your ideas,' he said. 'You're churning out scripts and your preoccupations come through, as much as you would wish to try and hide them. You would think it would be the show in which it's easiest to hide, but it's not.' One particular aspect of Chibnall's lived experience came to shape the backstory of the Doctor herself. This was his experience of being adopted.

The self-examination of the Capaldi years had exposed the soul of the character, but revealing so much about them had once again eroded their sense of mystery. This made it necessary to once again attempt that most difficult of tasks – changing and reinvigorating the character to give them a new sense of mystery, without breaking existing continuity. Chibnall's approach was to rewrite all that we thought we knew about their past. Hartnell's Doctor, he decided, was not their first incarnation. The Doctor's memory of their early days had been wiped by a mysterious and morally suspect organisation called the Division, and she discovered that she had had countless earlier incarnations. The Doctor, it turned out, wasn't a child of Gallifrey, as they had always believed. The Doctor had been found as a young girl underneath a portal to another universe from which she may or may not have come. The Doctor, then, was no longer the Last of the Time Lords. She wasn't even a native Time Lord. She was a foundling. Her origin and parents were unknown.

The world of myth and folk heroes has a special interest in characters who are orphaned as children or whose parents are otherwise absent. A list of such characters includes Batman, Luke Skywalker, Harry Potter, James Bond, Snow White, Superman, Cinderella, Spider-Man and Simba from *The Lion King*. It is as if a disturbed relationship with the memory of parents is a central part of being a hero. Children live controlled lives where parents make the rules and tell them what to do. Although they fear losing their mum or dad, that idea does contain an aspect which they can find liberating, and maybe even exciting. 'I have a thing on my desk which somebody gave me years and years ago,' Chibnall said, 'which is a list of all the fictional figures who are foundlings and adoptees. It's just a frame and a print. I think about that a lot. It's something to do with the absence of a set destiny, isn't it? It's possibility and mystery, and not being defined by your parents.'

Performing surgery on the mythology of the Doctor at this scale is a delicate business, especially if you do not wish to contradict decades of backstory. With the exception of that one damned, taboo fact – that the Doctor is half-human – the Whittaker era managed to create a new mythology that fitted neatly with what we had already seen, assuming that we were prepared to rethink a few long-standing assumptions. Certain fan debates were settled by this new history, not least of which was the identity of a group of mysterious faces called the Morbius Doctors. In the 1976 story *The Brain of Morbius*, the Doctor took part in a battle of minds with Morbius, a renegade Time Lord. Morbius's mind pushed the Doctor back down his timeline, as illustrated by the appearance of images of Pertwee, Troughton and Hartnell in the centre of a brain-wrestling machine. Eight other faces then appeared, implying that there were many earlier incarnations that we had never seen before. 'It is true to say that I attempted to imply that William Hartnell was not the first Doctor,' producer Philip Hinchcliffe later clarified. These earlier Doctors were played by members of the crew, including Hinchcliffe, writer Robert Holmes and the production assistant Graeme Harper, who went on to direct stories in both the classic and relaunched eras. The idea of these earlier incarnations did not sit well with some fans, however, especially after they were seemingly contradicted by later stories. Elaborate theories were concocted to explain them away, such as claiming they were earlier incarnations of Morbius or the Other.

It meant little to the great majority of viewers when those faces once again flashed onto the screen in Whittaker's 2020 episode *The Timeless Children*. In fandom, however, it was profoundly significant. As we've noted, the line between the character of the Doctor and producers and writers can be a blurred one. Many saw the Sixth Doctor as a manifestation of Nathan-Turner, and Eccleston based the Ninth Doctor on Russell T Davies. Sometimes it is only aspects of the behind-the-scenes staff that became part of the character, such as Barry Letts's Buddhism or Chris Chibnall's experience of being adopted. The inclusion of the Morbius Doctors in *The Timeless Children* pushed this idea further. Now the likes of Philip Hinchcliffe, Robert Holmes and Graeme Harper are officially accepted as being the Doctor.

Chris Chibnall was attempting something similar to what Andrew Cartmel did back in the late 1980s, when he tried to bring mystery back to McCoy's Doctor. 'I loved what [the Cartmel-era writers] did in that era,' Chibnall said. 'I think the scripts in that era are really fantastic. It's one of my favourites. It felt like they were all talking about each other's scripts. It felt like it had a cohesive sense of where they were going in the whole era.' In a similar way, Chibnall introduced a system similar to an American-style writers' room, in which his writers would meet and discuss their scripts together. 'I wanted Jodie's era to feel mythic,' Chibnall said. 'I wanted it to feel a bit epic and unknowable. And it's really hard for a show that's been going for sixty years to feel mythic. You've got to generate new stuff. You have to build the edifice up again.'

Having ambitious plans, and carrying them through, are two very different things. The pandemic was an extremely challenging time for film and television production, which requires large numbers of people to work closely together without falling ill. A programme like *Doctor Who*, with complicated action sequences along with different sets and actors each week, was particularly challenging to produce under lockdown.

When the pandemic hit, the original ideas for the third series were thrown out. There was simply no way it could be made in the world as it was then. But Chibnall demonstrated a level of determination similar to that which allowed John Nathan-Turner to complete *The Greatest Show in the Galaxy* when he had no studio. A new series was invented from the ground up, based on what was practically possible, which was called *Flux*. This was a series designed as one six-part story in which characters and sets were reused in multiple episodes and the story structured to keep actors apart. The plot concerned a deadly and previously unimagined wave of death and destruction rippling through the universe, something in keeping with the mood of the post-pandemic world. It set the Doctor against eternal beings from the dawn of time, making it perhaps the closest that the new series has got to the Wilderness Years adventures of the Seventh Doctor. With *Flux*, Chibnall was able to finish reworking the Doctor's new mythology. The character he would hand over after three seasons was a very different one to the one he inherited.

This new storyline involved a complicated mix of lost memories and corruption in the early days of Gallifrey, but at its heart the new mythology was powerful and simple. The Doctor didn't know where they came from, just as they didn't know where they were going. When the Thirteenth Doctor had the chance to reclaim her lost memories, she chose not to. Impossibly old but constantly reborn as new, the Doctor was now a character defined by their current actions. With an uncertain past and an unknown future, this Doctor decided it was the present that mattered.

4. 'To Disrupt from a Place of Love'

The classic era of Doctor Who was a product of the twentieth century, and the values which were then widespread are evident. In 1961, two years before the programme began, the population of the UK was 99.2 per cent white, and the 0.8 per cent of the population who were non-white ethnic minorities were rarely visible on screen, or behind the scenes. That a BBC employee with Waris Hussein's ethnicity was given the job of directing the first episodes of the series was a highly unusual situation, and not one that was often repeated.

This was a time in which there were precious few decent roles written for non-white actors, who naturally found it difficult to gain experience and learn their craft. As Cleo Sylvestre, the first Black actor to appear in *Doctor Who*, recalled, 'You felt that anything you did would be judged against your race. So if you failed, they'd say "Black people can't act", or whatever. It was quite a responsibility.' Sylvestre was hired as an extra to play a concubine in a now lost episode of the 1965 William Hartnell story, *The Crusade*. This was the same year that Laurence Olivier was critically applauded for his performance of *Othello* in blackface. At the time, television worked under an assumption that cast and crew would be white. 'Nowadays, make-up artists know all about Black skin,' Sylvestre said. 'But the first time I did a show at the BBC, the make-up room was in a panic because they didn't have any Black make-up. They only had white make-up.'

The Crusade was a historical adventure set in Palestine in the twelfth century, and as such the story had numerous non-European roles. These were played by white actors in dark make-up. The practice of blackface was common on British television at the time, as can be seen in many episodes of 1960s *Doctor Who*. As late as 1977, the villain Li H'sen Chang in *The Talons of Weng-Chiang* was played by the English actor John Bennett in yellowface.

Blackface aside, depictions of race in early *Doctor Who* were mixed and, in many aspects, complicated. There were 1960s *Doctor Who* stories that can be seen as progressive for the era. These tended to be set in the future, where non-white characters were depicted in positions of authority and multi-ethnic casts were depicted as normal, in a similar way to *Star Trek*. The powerful politician Mavic Chen, the Guardian of the Solar System in the forty-first century, was dark-skinned and seemingly of South East Asian ancestry, for example. This may initially seem like a progressive statement for 1965, but the fact that he was played by the white actor Kevin Stoney in dark make-up, and that he ultimately betrayed humanity to the Daleks, complicates this. Not all members of the cast and crew supported these visions of a multi-ethnic future. When the Bermudian actor Earl Cameron was cast as an astronaut in Hartnell's final story, *The Tenth Planet*, he was the first Black actor to portray an astronaut on television. William Hartnell was unhappy with this casting, because he did not believe that Black people were capable of becoming astronauts. Hartnell did not live long enough to see Guion Bluford, the first real-life Black astronaut, enter space in 1983.

By the Sylvester McCoy era at the end of the 1980s, the programme saw itself as intentionally anti-racist, for example by highlighting Ace's disgust when she finds a sign in the window of a 1960s boarding house that reads 'No Coloureds'. These attitudes were mainly reflected on the level of script, however, and the cast and crew remained overly white. When the programme returned in the twenty-first century, its on-screen representation of Black people was noticeably improved, even if Asian people initially remained few and far between. In 2005 Noel Clarke's Mickey Smith became the first recurring Black character, and Freema Agyeman's

Martha Jones became the first Black primary companion in 2007. But behind the cameras, key creative roles such as writers and directors remained overwhelmingly white and male. This was a reflection of the demographics of *Doctor Who* fandom during the Wilderness Years, where many of these creatives came from.

It was not until the Chris Chibnall era that a concerted effort was made to better reflect the diversity of the country both in front of and, crucially, behind the cameras. For the first time episodes were made with non-white creatives in the key positions of writer, director and composer. That some people would be angry about this was something that Chibnall accepted from the start. 'What [the success of] *Broadchurch* gave me was a little bit of a shield to go, "I can take the shit for this," because I have a career, I have a thing outside of this,' he said. 'All the shit can attach itself to me, and these new people can get to do the work that they want to do.'

The results of these changes were visible on screen, and the influx of new voices offered the programme what it always craved – new stories to tell. The first series included episodes about Rosa Parks and the partition of India, which the series would never have attempted before. It would go on to introduce viewers to historical figures like Mary Seacole and the Second World War spy Noor Inayat Khan. This influx of women and people of colour quickly demonstrated their value. As the director Rachel Talalay has calculated, '24 per cent of the highest-rated modern *Doctor Who* episodes were directed by women [. . .] Given that only 15 per cent of all modern *Who* episodes are helmed by women, that's punching above its weight, or more technically, highly statistically significant.' To make these calculations, Talalay included any episode of 21st-century *Doctor Who* that had a rating of 9.0 or above on the website IMDB. The first episode of modern *Doctor Who* to have a female director, 2007's *Blink*, is IMDB's highest rated, with a score of 9.8 out of 10. Talalay's own *Heaven Sent* took second place.

Perhaps the most important act of diversity was the casting of the Black London actor Jo Martin as a previously unknown incarnation of the Doctor. Known as the Fugitive Doctor, she came from a period of the Doctor's life – seemingly, before the William Hartnell incarnation – which the character had no memory of. Martin's portrayal of the Fugitive Doctor was one of the best-loved aspects of the Chibnall years, and probably the aspect of that era which fans are most keen to see return in the future. From the moment she introduced herself – 'Let me take it from the top. Hello, I'm the Doctor. I'm a traveller in space and time, and that thing buried down there is called a TARDIS' – the question of when a non-white actor would be cast as the incumbent Doctor, as opposed to a mysterious figure from the past in a guest-starring role, became a matter of when, not if.

Martin's inclusion rewrote the story of the Doctor in a significant way. It was now not the case that the character of the Doctor had been a white male for their first dozen regenerations, before female and non-white incarnations appeared. By placing the Black Fugitive Doctor before Hartnell, the character of the Doctor was rewritten as diverse from the start. Diversity was not just added late to the story of the Doctor. It was now baked in. We 'came in to disrupt in a positive way,' Chibnall said, 'to disrupt from a place of love.'

5. Bad Wolf

Throughout the first series of relaunched *Doctor Who*, Christopher Eccleston and Billie Piper kept encountering the words 'Bad Wolf', regardless of where they were in space and time. In the final two-part story of the series, it was revealed that Bad Wolf was a television company in the future. At the end of the series Piper's character Rose – now a sort of goddess, having accidentally absorbed the time vortex – took the words from the Bad Wolf Corporation logo and spread them throughout time. In doing so she left a trail that paradoxically brought her to the present moment where she was able to save the Doctor.

In 2015 Jane Tranter and Julie Gardner left BBC Worldwide to set up their own television production company in Cardiff. In a nod to their role in bringing back *Doctor Who*, and the impact it had on their careers and reputations, they named this company Bad Wolf. It is possible that Jane Tranter's deeply ingrained Whovian fandom may have also played a part in this decision. The company signed a first-look deal with HBO and began producing a string of ambitious, expensive, internationally focused TV series, including *His Dark Materials*, *A Discovery of Witches* and the Billie Piper-starring *I Hate Suzie*. While many British television companies are boutique operations content to operate in their national market, Bad Wolf was a media company that operated in the world of global streaming and box-set-bingeing consumers. The television company Bad Wolf had originally been nothing more than part of a *Doctor Who* story about the future, but it had left the world of fiction and manifested in the real world.

The last years of the Jodie Whittaker era were a time of constant anxiety regarding the future of the BBC. The Secretary of State for Digital, Culture, Media and Sport, Nadine Dorries, had a particular dislike of the corporation, which she claimed was based on its socially unrepresentative hiring. Her concern, she said, was about 'how the BBC can become more representative of the people who pay the licence fee, and how it can be more accessible to people from all backgrounds, not just people whose mum and dad worked there.' She was also aware that changing viewer behaviour in the digital world was undermining the argument for the BBC's universal remit. 'Only one in 20 people under the age of 30 watches BBC TV live – a demographic timebomb for the Corporation,' she noted.

In response, Dorries announced a two-year freeze on the licence fee and spoke of the corporation's funding model as something which would end when the BBC's charter was next renewed, in 2027. 'This licence fee announcement will be the last. The days of the elderly being threatened with prison sentences and bailiffs knocking on doors are over. Time now to discuss and debate new ways of funding, supporting and selling great British content. It's over for the BBC as they know it.' The licence fee, she believed, was just 'an anachronistic poll tax enforced by the criminal justice system', and she intended to do away with it, even if this meant the end of the BBC in its current form. Russell T Davies was forthright in his reaction to her comments. 'The woman's an idiot, a big fucking idiot,' he said.

Many people, both within and outside the BBC, believed that Dorries was deliberately intending to destroy the corporation for ideological reasons. There were certainly many voices in the Conservative Party who wanted to see the end of it. Boris Johnson's advisor Dominic Cummings, for example, worked at a think tank that called the BBC his party's 'mortal enemy'. Thanks to the short-lived nature of Dorries's ministerial career, the immediate danger that she presented to the BBC passed quickly, but concerns about its long-term survival remained. In 2023, the licence fee was called a 'regressive tax' that needed to be re-examined by the head of Ofcom, Michael Grade. In the *Doctor Who* story, Grade is forever doomed to play a man who destroys because he is unable to recognise things of value.

Doctor Who was no longer the defenceless thing that it had been when the BBC considered scrapping it before the first episode had aired. It now had a fanbase who were able to protect the series when, as with Michael Grade in 1985, the BBC tried to cancel it. But how would it survive if the BBC itself ceased to be? In order to live, *Doctor Who* not only required an audience, writers and other creatives to make it, it also needed a television company that would fund and distribute it. As we have seen, it had a steady supply of viewers and writers because the programme itself created them. Now it had also created Bad Wolf, a television company ideally suited to the early 21st-century streaming television ecosystem. Bad Wolf was the perfect candidate to take on the show if the BBC could no longer do so.

Under the terms of the BBC's previous charter the corporation now had to offer its existing shows out to private companies for external tender, to further the process of gradually privatising the corporation from within. This meant that in-house, BBC-created series like *Holby City* and *Songs of Praise* could no longer be made by the BBC, but would instead be made by external production companies. During the Chibnall years, this 'external company' was BBC Studios, a commercial subsidiary of the BBC set up in 2018. This technically satisfied the new rules, but there was political pressure to get genuinely independent companies making the BBC's 'crown jewels', in order to demonstrate the BBC's willingness to change. As a result, the days of *Doctor Who* as a programme that was made by the BBC itself – or by BBC Studios in the Whittaker years – were numbered.

Yet there now existed an external company perfectly suited for making this most tricky of shows in the modern era. It was the company run by the same women who had successfully brought the show back in 2005, and who clearly understood and loved it. Even better, this company was based in Cardiff, allowing them to rehire crew members who had worked on the BBC version of the show. So it was that in 2023, as it was celebrating its sixtieth anniversary, *Doctor Who* left the BBC behind, and established itself in a company that the programme itself had created.

During Chris Chibnall's rewriting of the *Doctor Who* myth, he unpicked the bonds that connected the Doctor to the Time Lords. The Doctor was now no longer a member of that fearsome race. True, they had lived with them for some time believing, inaccurately, that they were one of them. Now that they knew the truth, however, they were free to wander without them. To ram the point home, Chibnall removed the Time Lords from current *Doctor Who* lore by destroying Gallifrey and converting them into Cybermen. The Time Lords, in the fiction of the programme, had become automatons who were dead men walking, dark shadows of their former selves. As always, the echoes between the BBC and the Time Lords are striking – just like *Doctor Who's* uncanny ability to create the conditions it needs to survive.

16
The Bridge (2023)

1. 'A Divine Right'

In 2019, Russell T Davies and Steven Moffat were interviewed by the *Radio Times*. They were asked if they still thought up *Doctor Who* stories, now that they were no longer working on the show. 'I kind of do,' Moffat admitted. In particular, he never stopped thinking up *Doctor Who* monsters. Davies, in contrast, was adamant that he didn't. 'It stopped with me like that,' he said, snapping his fingers.

A year later, Davies took part in *Doctor Who* 'tweetalongs' during the pandemic lockdown. These were mass viewings of old episodes on iPlayer or DVD, organised by Emily Cook of *Doctor Who Magazine*, during which fans came together virtually and key members of the cast and crew shared their memories and thoughts on Twitter. Texting Davies after one such tweetalong, Catherine Tate confessed how much she had enjoyed the experience, and how much she and Tennant would love to work on the programme again. Davies felt duty bound to inform the BBC that Tennant and Tate, one of the most popular TARDIS teams ever, were interested in returning to the show.

He knew that an odd time for the programme was coming up. Chibnall and Whittaker were leaving in a 2022 special extended episode called *The Power of the Doctor*, intended as a celebration of 100 years of the BBC. It featured old companions and references to the classic series, including a brief cameo from William Russell as original companion Ian Chesterton, fifty-seven years after he had last appeared in the show. The following year would then be the programme's sixtieth anniversary. This again lent itself to nostalgia, and as such it was not the ideal time to launch the next Doctor. A Tennant and Tate special for the sixtieth anniversary might be a way to form a 'bridge' between the Whittaker Doctor and the fresh new post-BBC era that must undoubtedly follow.

The idea of bringing this beloved cast back at that point had a lot going for it. Many of those who had watched the show as children in the golden era of the late 2000s, during the days of David Tennant, Cyberman voice-changing helmets and *The Sarah Jane Adventures*, had since grown up and drifted away. They were also starting to become parents. If they could be reminded why they loved the show, then they might start watching it with their own children.

Davies informed the BBC about Tennant and Tate's interest in December 2020. The response was silence for four months, before he was eventually called in for a meeting. Here he discovered that the BBC had bigger plans than just getting the old team back for one special. They wanted Davies to make a series of three specials with Tennant and Tate for the sixtieth anniversary, which would be produced out of house by his friends at Bad Wolf, then cast a new Doctor and continue in the role as showrunner for the foreseeable future. Their aim was to attract a big, international streaming company as a co-production partner, which would give the show a mainstream global showcase for the first time and massively increase the budget.

On hearing this, the part of Davies's mind that had stopped thinking up *Doctor Who* stories back in 2010 sprung back to life and compelled him to agree. But the Russell T Davies who was surprised in this meeting was a different man to the one who had originally left the show. He had become, if anything, a more ambitious writer. The critical acclaim for the emotionally devastating Channel 4 series *It's a Sin* (2021), which may well be his masterpiece, had made his reputation bulletproof. He had also become increasingly political and angry. Accepting a Best Drama award for *It's a Sin* at the 2021 South Bank Sky Arts Awards, Russell warned Conservative voters that they were voting for 'murderers, bastards, abusers and liars'. Collecting an 'Inspiration' award from *Attitude* magazine in 2021, he first called the Tory government 'bastards' before turning his attention to the controversial Tufton Street-based campaigning group the LGB Alliance – an organisation which is pointedly not an LGBT Alliance. 'To cut out the "T",' Davies told his audience, 'is to kill.' On a personal level, in his time away from the series, he had nursed his late husband through a terminal illness. He had gone through one of the worst things that anyone could go through, in other words, and as a result he feared nothing.

Davies knew that he was good. He saw no reason to affect false modesty and pretend otherwise. He also seemed to think that he was the only person who should be running *Doctor Who*. Explaining why he returned to the job in his *Doctor Who Magazine* column, he wrote that, 'As I considered this show's future in a brand-new TV environment with a mighty quest ahead, I thought . . . I'm needed. Yup. There are times in life when you have to put modesty, insecurity and doubt aside, and know what you are capable of.' Interviewed by Alan Yentob, he claimed that 'I have a divine right' to control *Doctor Who*. When a podcast interviewer, talking about his return to *Doctor Who*, said, 'It's like you're Charlie in *Charlie and the Chocolate Factory* and you've inherited the chocolate factory,' Davies was quick to correct her. 'I built the chocolate factory,' he insisted. He believed that the new version of *Doctor Who* that he was writing was pure brilliance, describing the forthcoming season finale *Empire of Death* as 'the most magnificent finale ever shot on planet Earth. No hype! I swear that's true.' At times the returning showrunner appeared almost messianic. As he tellingly said in 2024, 'I shouldn't say that we're confident, because that is asking for a fall, but we are very confident.' It was Davies's job to hype the series, of course, but it was hard to deny that a faint whiff of hubris now accompanied him.

Davies had seen how society had changed in the years after *Queer as Folk*, and how accurate representation of gay people on television had been a necessary step on the path to greater acceptance in wider society. He knew, therefore, that a big, mainstream show like *Doctor Who* could be a powerful tool for social change. The programme had become more overtly feminist during the Chibnall era, and the mix of ethnicities in the crew and on screen now echoed the country to a greater degree than before. But there were still parts of society, he knew, who did not get to see themselves reflected on television. As he told *The Times* in 2023, 'There's six-year-olds watching this show, and I'm not trying to educate them or change their minds – they simply need to see things, a bigger world. I genuinely think that's one way to unknot bigotry. Show them the whole world. Race, colour, sexuality, religion. Wheelchairs. That's their world. That's our world. We need to show all of it.'

With Davies attached, the BBC and Bad Wolf secured a deal with Disney+ to stream the programme globally, outside of the UK and Ireland. This agreement was held up by the BBC as proof that they were modernising and adapting. In a March 2024 speech entitled 'The Future of the BBC', Director General Tim Davie said that, 'We will utilise commercial partners much more actively in areas like programming and technology to increase our horsepower. Our recent deal with Disney on *Doctor Who* is a good example of how we can work to deliver more value through third-party funding.' The idea that *Doctor Who* was key to the future of the BBC had become so common that it was even expressed by Steve Coogan's BBC-hating comic character Alan Partridge. 'If the BBC ever had a heart it went into cardiac arrest when they cancelled *Tomorrow's World* and *Goodnight Sweetheart*,' he said. 'It's only kept alive by the intravenous drip of licence-fee money and the ventilator of *Doctor Who*.'

On the same day as Tim Davie's speech, however, Russell T Davies was a guest on the *They Like to Watch* podcast, where he revealed that he saw the relationship between *Doctor Who* and the BBC very differently. 'You've got to look in the long term at the end of the BBC, which is somehow, surely, undoubtedly on its way out in some shape or form,' he said. 'Is *Doctor Who* going to die then? No! You've got to prepare for that kind of stuff.' For Davies, it wasn't the case that *Doctor Who* was saving the BBC. As he saw it, the move to Bad Wolf and the deal with Disney were steps to safeguard the future of *Doctor Who* when the BBC inevitably came to an end. As much as he had previously supported and fought for the BBC, he now saw it as a lost cause. His priority was to save *Doctor Who*.

For the section of fans who had railed against the perceived political progressiveness of the Jodie Whittaker years, news that Russell T Davies was returning to take over the programme was initially a cause for celebration. They had, after all, spent the previous years arguing that it wasn't as good as it used to be, back when Davies was at the helm. The return of the old team from a previous golden era was, in this context, everything they had been hoping for. That Davies's era had been criticised by conservative fans at the time for its 'gay agenda', or the fact that Davies was clearly determined to be far more radical than Chibnall had been, did not initially seem to register.

It only took five minutes for this delusion to fall away. This was the length of a special scene broadcast ahead of the sixtieth specials as part of the *Children in Need* fundraiser. After the Thirteenth Doctor had unexpectedly regenerated back into the form of David Tennant, he landed in Skaro at the point when Davros was inventing the Daleks. Davros was once again played by Julian Bleach, but he was now portrayed as able-bodied, rather than using a mobility chair shaped like the bottom half of a Dalek. Most fans assumed that this was Davros at an earlier point in his timeline, before his accident, but Davies made it clear in the scene's commentary that this was how he was going to portray Davros from now on.

Throughout the first sixty years of *Doctor Who*, almost every character who had used a wheelchair or the Space Age equivalent of a wheeled mobility seat had been portrayed as evil. For wheelchair users in the UK, the experience of hearing the word 'Davros!' shouted at them in the street was far too common. In recognition of this, Davies took Davros out of his chair, added a positive wheelchair-using character to the returning cast and arranged for the step underneath the TARDIS door to transform into a ramp, making the TARDIS wheelchair-accessible for the first time. A number of old-school fans were furious about these changes. As they saw it, the original design of Davros was iconic and Davies was contradicting established continuity for ideological reasons. Long-term fan Ian Levine was one who had, before this five-minute scene had been broadcast, looked to the return of Davies as saving the show from progressive values. He then wrote on Twitter, 'Russell T. Davies has now caused the most massive backlash against him. All his former supporters, like me, have now turned against him. He went one step too far.'

Davies, naturally, was unrepentant. When angry fans complained to him personally on his Instagram page he took the time to reply to many of them personally, but he had no sympathy whatsoever for their complaints. Replying to one lengthy argument about the nature of Davros, Davies simply replied 'Tough'. After a question about whether he would change the Cybermen 'so it doesn't upset our friends with robotic limbs', he replied, 'oh poor baby 😢'.

The furore about Davros's mobility obscured a more significant change that Davies made to the Doctor. Although in most of their stories they had been largely asexual, when they were attracted to someone it was always a woman – from the fifteenth-century Aztec woman Cameca to the 21st-century Sheffield lass Yaz. After Davies returned, however, the Doctor's sexuality changed. Following a brief meeting with Isaac Newton, the Doctor realised he was now attracted to men. Fandom accepted this change with very little complaint – a change of sexuality was not entirely unexpected for this most fluid of characters and the change did not contradict the past in the way that Davros's new legs did.

The first episode of the sixtieth-anniversary specials, *The Star Beast*, introduced a teenage trans character, Rose Noble. Right-wing and culture-war voices in the media were furious, and the BBC received 144 complaints, claiming that the character was 'inappropriate'. Davies, naturally, was unconcerned. He had spoken at the press launch about how transgender people were vilified in certain parts of the media, and condemned 'newspapers of absolute hate, and venom, and destruction, and violence [. . .] Shame on you, and good luck to you in your lonely lives.'

If anything, Davies seemed to welcome these attacks. He knew how significant it was to show a trans teenager with a loving and supportive family on a mainstream BBC One programme in 2023. The long-term impact of this on the 8.36 million viewers who saw it was far more significant than 144 complaints. If anything, he seemed to be goading the transphobic population, aware of how unpleasant they looked to others, and knowing that their bitterness was ultimately making the case for a more accepting society. The thumbnail images made by furious 'HateTubers' to promote their angry responses also appeared equally ridiculous, such as an image of David Tennant leaning out of the TARDIS with an added speech bubble saying, 'I hate men'.

Davies had talked about how the show needed to be 'noisy' if it was to survive in the global television market. There is nothing like controversy to get people talking. The intentionally inclusive nature of the sixtieth-anniversary specials certainly didn't put off the mainstream viewing public, who tuned in in huge numbers. When Tennant had drawn audiences of around 8 million in the late 2000s, the show was seen as a huge hit. He now drew identical figures when he returned fifteen years later, even after the collapse in terrestrial viewing figures caused by streaming. The BBC, naturally, was ecstatic.

When Disney had signed on to be international distributors for the new era, Davies's stellar reputation had been part of the package that convinced them to invest heavily. Quite whether they realised what he was intending to do with the show, however, was not clear. In the new behind-the-scenes series *Doctor Who Unleashed*, Davies talked about the changes he was making to established *Doctor Who* lore, such as regeneration. 'It's a new thing, it's the sixtieth – imagine how much fans love new things and will really rejoice when this happens,' he said. Then his head tipped back, and a rich Welsh belly laugh erupted from deep within.

17
The Doctor (2024–)

1. 'In Case Either of You Have a Magic Wand'

Ncuti Gatwa is an actor with genuine star quality. After his breakout role playing Eric Effiong in Netflix's teen drama *Sex Education*, he quickly became a cover star on magazines including *Rolling Stone, Elle, Gay Times, Teen Vogue, GQ, Attitude* and *Time*. One of the Kens in the movie *Barbie*, he appeared with Ryan Gosling on stage at the 2024 Oscars during the performance of 'I'm Just Ken'. He played Romeo in the Shakespearean section of King Charles's Coronation Concert and placed first in the *Radio Times* TV 100 Power List. Handsome and extraordinarily charming, he loves fashion and dresses with flair. His signature scent is a closely guarded secret, but he is generally accepted to be the best-smelling Doctor yet. All this displays a level of showbiz dazzle far above any of the previous Doctors.

Gatwa's personal story was also very different. He was born in Kigali, Rwanda, in 1992, during the civil war. In 1994 his family fled the genocide against the Tutsi, during which somewhere between half a million and a million Tutsi were slaughtered by Hutu militias, typically with machetes. Young Ncuti grew up in Edinburgh, before moving to Dunfermline when he was fifteen. He and his family became aware of the third Golden

Age of *Doctor Who* around this time. It was, he said, 'something I remember as almost over our heads, something we knew was important culturally, like the royals'.

Gatwa studied acting at the Royal Conservatoire of Scotland, supporting himself by working as a go-go dancer in an LGBTQ+ night club. He moved down to London to become an actor but, following the painful break-up of a relationship, he became homeless for five months, couch-surfing at the homes of friends. 'The only thing stopping me from being on the streets was the fact I had friends,' he recalled. 'Being a 25-year-old man with no money or job affected my sense of self-worth. Rejection became unbearable. Auditions weren't just acting jobs, they were lifelines.' His poverty meant that he lost weight due to 'eating only one meal a day'. At this point fate changed his script, and the role of Eric in *Sex Education* turned his life around.

Fate is central to Gatwa's worldview. He is a student of astrology, the belief that our fates are controlled by the stars. Astrology, he says, 'probably filled a gap that religion left in me. I couldn't put my faith in an old book that had been used for so much evil. I found astrology so accepting. It helped me accept my own darkness, and other people's darkness, too.' If fate is a matter for the stars, then even the hardest of lives can be transformed, if the stars so wish. 'I'd love to play either Willy Wonka or Doctor Who,' Gatwa messaged his agents on 24 September 2021, 'just in case either of you have a magic wand.' 'This is good to know,' came the response, 'especially for Doctor Who.' The audition came soon afterwards.

Gatwa prepared for the audition by watching old episodes. Whereas most previous Doctors had felt their identity merge with the character in costume and on set, this was the moment when Gatwa looked at the Doctor and saw himself. As he said,

'This person survived a genocide. This person fits in everywhere and nowhere. I am the Doctor. The Doctor is me.'

Davies was looking for an actor with great emotional intelligence. 'I want a young audience watching, and they talk about their emotions, express their emotions in a healthy way,' he said. He auditioned many male, female and non-binary actors, but then, 'Along came Ncuti, who is one of those actors who pour with feeling,' he recalled. 'When he is sad, tears pour from his eyes; when he is happy, that smile lights up the universe.' Davies knew immediately that he had found his Doctor. Although he would never have hired a Doctor for his real-life backstory, Gatwa's history was a perfect fit for Davies's progressive vision of the series. The political right were obsessed with immigration, and the collapsing government obsessed over an ultimately doomed attempt to ship immigrants to Rwanda. Against this background, placing a Rwandan immigrant at the heart of this British cultural institution and allowing the country to see how talented he was, and how much people like him could offer our culture, was exactly the sort of thing that Davies wanted to use the series for.

Gatwa is open about his struggles with his mental health. The pressure of living up to expectations impacted on his anxiety to the extent that, in the run-up to his *Doctor Who* debut, 'I almost didn't even leave my house.' He is also troubled by the state of the world, and he shared his fears with his showrunner. 'We were talking about the world. I was like, "I just think it's just not in a good place is it, and I don't think it is going to get better, Russell. It seems like the human race is kind of useless!" All of us. White, Black, whoever.' Russell replied, 'Ncuti, you can't not have hope. You have to have hope in life. And you have to have hope in the fact that we are useless, but we're also full of amazingness and wonder. Hope is what saves us.' Davies's words encapsulated the essence of *Doctor Who*, but they also reminded Gatwa that he had been given the same advice by his mother. Gatwa's full name is Mizero Ncuti Gatwa, and in his mother's native Kinyarwanda language *mizero* means hope or faith.

Gatwa shot his first scene of his first series during a night shoot at Cardiff Bay Barrage, on 17 December 2022. Filming had begun weeks earlier, but overruns on the final series of *Sex Education* had forced production to start without him. By practical necessity, he was not given an opportunity to ease into the character. Gatwa's first scene after he arrived on set was one of the most emotionally devastating in the programme's history.

The episode was called *Dot and Bubble*. It was set in a future colony called Finetime, where a wealthy settlement of young rich adults was being preyed on by giant slug creatures. The Doctor and his companion Ruby Sunday help a resident of Finetime called Lindy to escape, only for her to reject his offer to save her life at the end of the episode. Instead, she heads off into a jungle with other Finetime residents, to their almost certain deaths. To Lindy, the Doctor was not one of her all-white peers, and she did not possess sufficient empathy to trust him. The episode was not just about racism, but about how racism arises naturally in enclaves of privilege – a profound theme for a space slug story.

This scene was very different to anything the series had done before – especially given the extent to which all-white casts had been common in the programme's past. Its message was somewhat diluted by the following story, which took place in a morally identical society, the English Regency period. Here the young, wealthy and privileged were entertained in great luxury, just as in Finetime, and regarded those outside their elite social group as less than human. This story did not condemn this society, however. It portrayed it as aspirational and exciting, and a fun excuse for historical cosplay. Still, it was clear from *Dot and Bubble* that the Doctor was going to be placed into emotional spaces that had never been explored before. For the newly arrived Gatwa, it would be a demanding scene to act.

In costume and on set, with the lights and cameras on him, Ncuti Gatwa summoned the character. 'It became clear to me that there isn't a mould you need to step into to portray the Doctor,' Gatwa said. 'It can come out of you naturally.' It was a role that came with far more history, baggage and expectation than anything else a young actor might face. It was a character twice as old as Gatwa, and one that was so much bigger than any of the countless actors, writers and directors who had brought it to life over the past decades. It embodied the necessity of hope that his mother had named him after. It was a central touchstone of British culture, yet it was also a radical, anti-establishment spirit. The Doctor was camp and silly and inspired and a survivor of genocide and quite beautiful, and so was Gatwa.

To step into that character was not like taking on any normal acting role. It was an identity that he would never be able to step out of and leave behind. Gatwa understood the importance of this fiction. He believed that taking it on was his fate. The director called 'action' and he entered the role.

Gatwa's performance in that scene was one of the great moments in *Doctor Who* history. He embodied the hope and the hurt of that most human of heavenly beings as he was rejected by the smallest of souls. He wept and was wounded, as he pleaded with the woman rejecting him to allow him to save her life. Russell T Davies's faith in the young actor had been justified. It was a superb performance. Ncuti Gatwa, as fate had long known, was the Doctor.

Dot and Bubble, with its bravado climactic scene, was broadcast on 1 June 2024, to huge critical acclaim. It also received the lowest ratings of the twenty-first century series.

2. Roughly Half

The average seven-day ratings for Gatwa's first eight-episode series was 3.7 million. This was roughly half the 7.2 million that the David Tennant and Catherine Tate starring sixtieth-anniversary specials received six months earlier, and a large decline on Jodie Whittaker's 6.13 million and Peter Capaldi's 6.41 million. But although *Dot and Bubble*'s audience after seven days was a series low of 3.38 million, this was still enough to make it the most watched programme on British television the day it was broadcast.

The digital world has hit linear broadcast television hard – not just through the rise in streaming, but also through the addictive nature of phones. Ratings have plummeted across the board. When people slumped down on the sofa after a hard day at work, it used to be normal to flick on the telly and see what was on. Nowadays, people are more likely to pull out their phones and flick through that instead. All this is ominous for the long-term future of television in general and the BBC in particular.

Those who grew up before the internet understood meaningful culture to be something they had to go out and hunt down. They spent hours flicking through the racks in second-hand record shops, tracking down music they had read about in magazines but which they had no other way of hearing. They went through the television-listings magazine every week, searching for the few programmes that genuinely enthused them, and memorising at what time was their only chance of watching them. Programmes, films, books and music came and went, and there was no expectation that media would remain easily available long after its initial release. In this context, the good stuff was extremely precious. If you found it, it meant a lot. You certainly would not have described it with a word like 'content'.

This is hard for those raised in the twenty-first century to imagine. All they have known is a tsunami of content. Almost the entirety of recorded music is readily available with just a click or two, and new music struggles to compete with the biggest artists in history. Television programmes are watched at a time that suits you, with past episodes queued up and waiting for your attention. Old films and books can be found instantly on Amazon or eBay, and obtained even more quickly by those comfortable with illegal means. *Doctor Who* is now just one title in a seemingly never-ending sea of science fiction, fantasy and superhero entertainment. The question of which aspects of culture you are going to give your limited attention to can be overwhelming, especially when your phones eat up so much of your spare time. Where once we hunted culture, we now spend our energies filtering it out, desperately trying to narrow down our options. We look for reasons not to watch things. We can be grateful when a particular artist is 'cancelled' because that permits us to immediately dismiss all their work.

It was originally the case that social media showed you the updates of people that you had chosen to follow. Those people have since become increasingly marginalised in our feeds, as the platforms are now optimised to show us what they think will keep us engaged instead. Our curated online worlds have shifted from a social graph to an interests graph. It used to be the case that our online world was understood in terms of what platforms we used. Now it's increasingly defined by our interests – or, in the broadest sense, our fandoms. This has led to a rich but highly splintered culture. We now no longer assume that when we meet someone new, we will have at least some passing familiarity with their favourite bands or programmes. It is normal for passionate music fans to have never heard of some of the most-streamed artists on the planet. We all manage to find things that we love, but our cultural touchstones are far broader and more niche than ever before.

Doctor Who was launched at a time before culture splintered, when there was only one national television channel. Even by the time the classic series ended in 1989, most British households still only had four channels. Entertainment was scarce, so lovers of science fiction, fantasy or cult genre shows gravitated towards *Doctor Who* in part because there was very little else to choose from. In the twentieth century, you could expect any child in a playground to know about Daleks, Cybermen and the Master, because *Doctor Who* was broadcast on Saturday evenings on BBC One. The privilege of that mainstream positioning has long gone. There is now no central culture to highlight and no central place to display it. The odds of achieving immense success and broad cultural recognition among all the churn and noise of the cultural maelstrom are vanishingly small.

Doctor Who's position in our culture has naturally been affected by all this. For those who the algorithms deemed to be enthusiastic to the series, their feeds during the 2024 Ncuti Gatwa series were a joy, full of jokes, artwork, far-fetched theories and uncountable Sutekh and Susan Twist memes. Those whom the algorithms considered to be unhappy about inclusive social change found their feeds full of criticism, despair and reports of the death of *Doctor Who*, a once great franchise killed by political ideology. Those who had no interest in the series frequently saw nothing at all. It might as well not have been on, for all that they knew.

In this environment, the question of what size of audience would make *Doctor Who* a success is a tricky one to answer. Given the increasing importance of the 'long tail' of viewing, in which programmes continue to be watched months or years after first broadcast, it is certainly not something that can be settled by looking at the overnight ratings. Russell T Davies was given a specific brief when he was brought back, which was to bring in the under-16s and the 16–34 audience that the BBC otherwise struggle to reach. As a 2022 study reported, fewer than one in twenty in the 18–30 demographic watched live BBC programmes on a daily basis, and more than a third never watched the BBC live. The BBC recognised that losing this demographic put their long-term future at risk. 'I was brought back to bring in a younger audience. That's been massively successful,' Davies said. 'The audience no one ever gets are the under-30s. They just don't watch television any more. But those figures are astronomic for *Doctor Who*, it's their top programme in that bracket [. . .] according to the people who juggle the numbers, all targets have been reached and exceeded. The BBC are running around like mad things.' A spokeswoman told *The Times* that *Doctor Who* was the BBC's top drama for under-35s that year, and one of the biggest programmes for the demographic across all streamers and broadcasters.

Whether the BBC considered the loss of so many viewers an acceptable price to pay for that slice of the younger demographic is another question. The programme had foregrounded progressive political attitudes since the 2017 story *Thin Ice*, in which Capaldi's Doctor punched a racist because of the way he spoke to the Doctor's Black, lesbian companion. It is rare for the Doctor to punch someone, but this lapse of character was well received by the programme's core audience. Speaking on *The Rest Is Entertainment* podcast in April 2024, writer Richard Osman revealed data about the political leanings of the audiences of different television programmes. For those classed as progressive activists, he announced, *Doctor Who* was one of their favourite programmes, along with *Blue Planet* and *Question Time*.

The sense that *Doctor Who* had become a programme for progressives only was evident when the right-wing politician Nigel Farage declared that *Doctor Who* was a programme that 'I used to love, but they've completely ruined!'

In September 2024, the politician Kemi Badenoch launched her campaign to become leader of the Conservative Party with a video focused on criticism she had received from David Tennant over her stance on trans issues. Badenoch's pitch for becoming leader was to declare that she was 'not afraid of Doctor Who'. This statement was much mocked by those who watched the show, not least for the extent to which it made her sound like a supervillain. But Badenoch was not trying to appeal to people who watch *Doctor Who*. The video led to her becoming the leader of the Conservative Party.

Davies's new version of the show was happy to alienate viewers with Farage's or Badenoch's views, and the showrunner made no attempt to court that part of the audience. The problem was that it was also losing viewers with more centrist views. Even in its Golden Age periods of mass popularity, the programme had always been political and always been righteous. What turned the general audience off was the perception that it could be self-righteous.

Davies's focus on the young was also intended to help solve a similar problem with its international distributer, Disney+. Given the size of the Disney organisation, the strength of its marketing and the amount of press that it generates, it is easy to assume that the streamer is a bigger part of the television landscape than it is. According to the Nielsen ratings, in the year to May 2024, Disney+ averaged just 1.9 per cent of American television viewing. It is also easy to assume that the streamer has a young audience, given their strength in pre-school and animation, but its largest brands such as Marvel and *Star Wars* appeal more to Millennial and Generation X viewers than to Gen Z. According to the television analytics firm Samba TV, at the start of 2024, 59 per cent of Gen Z's streaming viewing was on Netflix, where shows like *Bridgerton* and *Stranger Things* are hugely successful. Only 5 per cent of that viewing was with Disney+.

In the eyes of Disney+, *Doctor Who* is a mid-range show considerably cheaper than their major shows, but which could help them with a demographic they have been failing to reach. Disney+, like all streamers, are secretive about their ratings so it is difficult to assess how well it has performed for them, but it is unlikely that the total number of viewers is their main concern. What they are interested in is the demographic breakdown of the audience, whether the show prompts new subscribers, and whether its availability affects the 'churn' of subscription cancellations.

When Russell T Davies brought *Doctor Who* back in 2005, he was chasing a 'three generational' audience, consisting of children, parents and grandparents. In this, he was more successful than the industry believed possible. The programme remained a ratings hit in the years that followed, but the show's audience gradually started to skew older. After his return, the under-16s and the 16–34 demographics are now the priority – even at the expense of long-established viewers. The story that opened Gatwa's first season featured a space station staffed with talking babies, a snot monster and a farting spaceship. The 'three generational' audience was clearly no longer the target.

It is difficult for any television drama to survive in the current broadcasting environment, in which programmes have become vastly more expensive to produce at a time when they will be viewed by a fraction of historic audiences. The programme Davies developed may appear to be designed to build a new young audience, but it may be more accurate to say that it is designed to attract an audience that broadcasters and distributors will pay for. *Doctor Who* always finds a way to adapt to the changing world. Delivering a demographic that other shows can't reach is one way that the show can survive in the chaotic and splintered world of streaming.

3. 'There's Always a Twist at the End'

'We're in a very busy science-fiction/fantasy world now,' Davies has said, referring to the television landscape of the 2020s. 'We've got to do what other shows don't. It's *Doctor Who*'s unique territory.' His solution to finding a niche where the show can survive is to offer this audience a programme unlike anything else they are currently being given. Programmes that become major global phenomena tend to be polished, sane and have all the rough edges removed, to make sure there is nothing preventing large audiences from embracing them. This is clearly not a good fit for *Doctor Who*. By playing up how different the show is to everything else, however, the programme might just be distinct enough to grow a new young audience, and survive.

Davies took a maximalist approach to his new version of *Doctor Who*. Everything that it could do, it would do. Tonally, there was no way of predicting where the show would go next. Episodes in Gatwa's first season lurched from historical *Bridgerton*-style romances to tense Hitchcockian suspense, disturbing unresolved Welsh folk horror, an outrageous overblown musical and a *Black Mirror*-style monster movie about social media bubbles. Fans were initially surprised to learn that Gatwa would be wearing very different outfits in each episode, rather than having a set Doctor costume as his predecessors all had. When they saw how eclectic the series was, however, that decision made sense. Clashing together wildly contrasting styles like this might seem a bold move, but it is in tune with the splintered online zeitgeist. The approach is called metamodernism. It is perhaps best illustrated by the public's embrace of the 'Barbenheimer' phenomenon of 2023, in which the two very different films *Barbie* and *Oppenheimer* were somehow enhanced by being embraced together.

This embrace of everything is visible in the new series' approach to its past. In an effort to welcome a new demographic of viewers, the series was billed as 'season one'. This naming system worked well for Disney+, who wanted to portray the show as something fresh and new, which anyone could jump on board. Part of the reason why the audience for their *Star Wars* and Marvel content skews older, even though these shows seem ideal for a younger demographic, is because the sheer size of their narrative universe can seem overwhelming and off-putting to newcomers.

When Davies initially brought back *Doctor Who* in 2005 he kept references to classic Who to an absolute minimum in his original 'series one'. For this 2024 'season one', in contrast, he loaded it with references to the past, including villains from the 1970s, companions from the 1980s, and deep-cut characters from comics and lost 1960s episodes. The series even included a 'memory TARDIS', which was built entirely out of references to the past. This was spun off into an iPlayer repeat season called *Tales of the TARDIS*, in which newly filmed sequences with classic cast members topped and tailed old stories. A repeat of the William Hartnell story *The Time Meddler*, for example, brought back the actors Peter Purves and Maureen O'Brien, who were both in their eighties at the time, in character as Steven and Vicki. This new 'season one' of *Doctor Who*, therefore, was a jumping-on point of a fresh, new series, and the culmination of decades of lore at the same time. A metamodern approach allows you to have your cake and eat it too.

That Davies had no interest in being constrained by the established rules of the show was apparent from the start. When Jodie Whittaker's Thirteenth Doctor regenerated back into David Tennant, the Doctor's clothes regenerated too. There was precedent for this, if you went back far enough, because William Hartnell's clothes changed when he became Patrick Troughton.

But it was still unusual enough to concern traditionalist fans, who hoped in vain for an in-story explanation.

A bigger change came when it was time for Tennant to bow out once again. Instead of regenerating into Gatwa in the normal way, he bi-generated – he split in two, meaning that two versions of the Doctor existed at the same time. Speaking on the programme's commentary, Davies stated his belief that when this happened, it rippled back down the Doctor's timeline and happened to all the previous Doctors as well. He was changing the on-screen story of *Doctor Who* to match the extended world of books, audios and comics, where all old Doctors still exist and continue to have new adventures. Ultimately, he was denying any established idea or tradition that limited the imagination. As he saw it, every *Doctor Who* story you could imagine should be real. The series was no longer operating under the principle of logic, or world-building, or tradition. It was operating under the principle of play.

Another change was the nature of the monsters the Doctor must face. Previously, these had typically been aliens from other planets, requiring the programme to adhere to science fiction tropes, however loosely. Now, the monsters became supernatural. A pantheon of gods had been mentioned in the programme's past, but appearances by such elemental antagonists as the Toymaker, the Trickster and the Guardians had been rare. Now, they became the focus of the show. Instead of being pitted against Sontarans, Cybermen and Daleks, Gatwa's Doctor was confronted by goblins, the bogeyman, fairy-circle magic, the god of music and the god of death. This change was the result of Tennant's Doctor trying to trick an adversary with a line of salt at the edge of the universe, the programme claimed, an explanation that makes little sense using the logic of science fiction, but works well enough in the dreamlike logic of myth.

The show was also prepared to break some of the most fundamental rules of television drama. *Doctor Who* started to appear self-aware. It knew that it was a television show, and so did certain characters within it. It was not the first time that the Doctor had broken the fourth wall and looked directly into the camera and at the viewer, of course. Doctors including Hartnell, Tom Baker, Sylvester McCoy and Peter Capaldi had all done this in the past. There had also been a story in the Troughton era which took the TARDIS crew into the Land of Fiction, which played with the Doctor's fear about not being real. Following Russell T Davies's return, however, the programme became far more up front about its fictional nature.

In *The Devil's Chord*, Gatwa's Doctor says that he thought some music he heard was non-diegetic, referring to sound that is not heard by characters in a story, but which is heard by the audience, such as a film score. After we met the newly mobile reimagined Davros, Tennant's Fourteenth Doctor referred to the canon rupturing, where 'canon' refers to the established facts of a fictional world. This awareness of the fictional nature of the show was not shared by regular human characters, such as Millie Gibson's Ruby Sunday. In *Space Babies*, she recognises that the situation was like 'a children's story come to life', but she did not follow that thought through and realise that she was part of that fiction. That awareness is reserved for higher beings like the Doctor, the enigmatic Mrs Flood or Maestro, the god of music. Maestro even went as far as to look into the camera and start playing the *Doctor Who* theme, in order to get the title sequence started. At moments like this it is clear that we are watching a story that knows it is being watched.

The Devil's Chord ended when the Doctor stopped Ruby and warned her that there was something serious that she had to know. 'With all of my adventures throughout Time and Space,' he said, 'I have to tell you there is always a twist at the end.' Then he turned to the camera, winked and launched into an epic twist-based musical number, complete with large-scale choreographed crowds. It included cameo appearances from *Strictly Come Dancing*'s Shirley Ballas and Johannes Radebe, and even an appearance from the series' composer Murray Gold, who was credited in the titles as 'Himself'.

The title of the song – 'There's Always a Twist at the End' – played into another stream of discourse surrounding the series. The same actor had, for some strange reason, started popping up in minor roles in different episodes. This mystery built until the end of the final story, when the Doctor wondered if the woman could be his long-neglected granddaughter, Susan. What made this speculation seem plausible to many viewers was that the mysterious woman was played by an actor named Susan Twist. Russell T Davies had been aware of Susan Twist ever since she appeared in a short play he wrote for a Manchester theatre company in 2016. 'I was already saying to the production team, "You must cast Susan," because she is a brilliant actress,' he said. 'But also . . . that name is fascinating, isn't it? Susan Twist. I'd tucked that away in a corner of my mind, thinking "Imagine if we did a twist around Susan." So it just came together. It's so mad.'

The narrative of this season, then, was not confined to the on-screen drama. It enveloped real-world production matters, which contributed to a lot of the surrounding online discourse. With self-aware fictions on screen and real-world people in the overall story of the season, the boundary between *Doctor Who*'s on- and off-screen aspects was now impossible to define. *Doctor Who* had been larger than the story on screen for many years, but now it was confidently revelling in that fact. Tricksters have no respect for boundaries.

In the first story of Russell T Davies's 2005 relaunch, the

character of Clive defines the Doctor as a legend woven through history who appears at times of disaster and who has one constant companion – death. Clive was killed by invading Autons shortly afterwards. That he may have been right was the Doctor's great fear – after all, wherever he went, death did follow. This was the reason he gave Kate Lethbridge-Stewart for never going back and seeing his granddaughter. 'You've seen my life. I bring disaster, Kate. Disaster. What if I go back and ruin her?'

In Gatwa's first run of stories, this fear was personified into the season's big monster – Sutekh, the god of death, who had attached himself to the TARDIS during a 1975 Tom Baker story and had been accompanying the Doctor ever since. Ever since then, as the Doctor blindly continued his travels, he had unwittingly been bringing Death to the entire universe. Clive, it seems, had been right.

But the Doctor, of course, defeats the monster. He collides death with itself and in doing so – perhaps more symbolically than logically – he brings life. It is life, after all, that keeps the universe from being more than the dust and ash that Sutekh craves. When the Doctor realises this at the end of the series, it allows him to redefine himself. 'I pride myself that I am better than you,' he tells the defeated Sutekh. 'Because if you're death . . . then I must represent life! Surely, that's what I am. Life!' The Doctor, like his monsters, had left science fiction behind and become archetypal. He was life, and for the first time he knew it.

When Russell T Davies returned to the show, he purposely wrote the Doctor as being aware that they were a character in a story, winking at the camera and performing song-and-dance routines for the audience. As it was *Doctor Who* that made Davies a writer in the first place, however, the ultimate credit for that act is up for debate. Certainly, there were less explicit hints that the Doctor had known their true nature long before Davies's time.

Perhaps they had known when Troughton's Doctor warned children that the Yeti may scare their parents, or when Hartnell raised a glass to the viewers at home on Christmas Day 1965. Perhaps they had been aware since *Planet of the Spiders*, the final Jon Pertwee story, in which the Doctor confronted the illusion of the self and understood the true nature of identity. Perhaps they knew during *The Greatest Show in the Galaxy*, when McCoy pierced the veil of the Psychic Circus and came face to face with his true audience. Could they have been self-aware when the character first climbed out of BBC production paperwork, unbidden and without a creator, back in 1963? That's a preposterous, implausible idea, of course, but physical life emerged in a very similar way. Would immaterial life be any different?

'That's what I am, life!' Ncuti Gatwa shouted into the time vortex as he defeated the god of death. Very few fictional characters could get away with making such an extraordinary claim. *Doctor Who* had long behaved like a living story, but now it knew that it was one and it was telling us so plainly.

Such was the extraordinary act of imagination that we call *Doctor Who* season one, or *Doctor Who* series fourteen, or *Doctor Who* season forty, depending on your preference. It was a series, after all, about including everything, so you are free to define it as you wish. You can understand why Nigel Farage switched off in horror. It was fizzing potential, big-hearted and borderline insane. It was always going to be messy and there was never any hope that it would all make sense to the seriously minded. Yet if that is what it takes to capture the hearts of enough eight-year-olds, and stand out in a sea of sane, professional content, then it has once again evolved in exactly the way that it needed to. Such is the nature of life.

COMING NEXT . . .

It is the practice of the Brighton and Hove bus company to name each of their buses after a notable, usually deceased, local resident. As a result, you can now see a double-decker bus running along the Sussex coast road with the name John Nathan-Turner written proudly across the front. The John Nathan-Turner bus can often be spotted running the 12X route, which is an express service that doesn't stop as it rushes towards its destination. It seems an appropriate choice.

This bus runs along the road that separates the house where Nathan-Turner used to live from the beach where Colin Baker's Doctor was filmed torturing his companion Peri in 1986. If we ride this bus west into Brighton, it passes the end of Wilson Avenue, near which scenes set in a First World War battlefield were filmed for Patrick Troughton's last story, *The War Games*, in 1969. The Nathan-Turner bus then turns north towards Brighton station, but if we continue west along the coast road, we find the beach location used in the opening scene of *The Leisure Hive*, Nathan-Turner's first story as producer in 1980. Here Tom Baker dozed in a deckchair while K-9 chased a ball into the English Channel and, a little unexpectedly, exploded.

The more we follow the coast, the more filming locations for *Doctor Who* we find. Climping Beach in Littlehampton doubled for Australia in 1967's *The Enemy of the World*, while Lulworth Cove in Dorset stood in for Maiden's Point in 1989's *The Curse of Fenric*.

Just past this cove is the arch-shaped limestone rocks of Durdle Door, upon which Jodie Whittaker surprisingly regenerated back to David Tennant in 2022. Away from the coast, the south of England is littered with *Doctor Who* filming locations like these. In central London, there is barely a significant location which hasn't had Cybermen, Daleks or other monsters lumbering past. The 21st-century relaunch has stamped itself into the country more widely, with Cardiff, South Wales, Bristol, Sheffield, Gloucester and Liverpool all now having multiple recognisable locations from *Doctor Who* stories. The show is increasingly making its mark on the wider world, and parts of Paris, Amsterdam, Lanzarote, Croatia, New York and parts of Spain and South Africa are all recognisable to Whovians. These are all places now where you can experience a moment of time travel and be reminded of a *Doctor Who* story. The series has soaked itself into the landscape like the perfume of an absent relative.

This is not normal behaviour, for a fiction. Long-running characters are typically constrained to set locations, like Sherwood Forest, or fictional places like Gotham City or *Star Trek*'s United Federation of Planets. They don't immortalise your everyday world – another example of the way *Doctor Who* doesn't seem to follow the normal rules of stories. Since the very beginning, it has behaved in ways for which there are no precedents.

How things behave, of course, is not just related to what they are. Scale and complexity can change something's attributes, often radically. Hydrogen may be a colourless, odourless gas, but gather enough of it together and it becomes a blazing star. A few neurons in a Petri dish are of little use and frankly unimpressive, but put 86 billion of them into a skull and they might start composing symphonies. This rule applies to immaterial things as well as material ones. The nature of 'big data' can be difficult to grasp for the generation born into the pre-digital world, but large data sets have value that can't be predicted from studying small amounts of information – in a similar way to how climate is different to weather.

For these reasons, it may be limiting to think of a story as vast and intricate as *Doctor Who* as just a fiction. Its unique behaviour may be a sign that it has crossed some unseen limit of scale and turned into something different, which we could call a megafiction. Quite what is normal behaviour for megafictions is something we are yet to discover. Many thousands of talented, creative people have worked to construct the *Doctor Who* megafiction in the decades since the character emerged, unbidden, from a collection of BBC memos. None of those people imagined what the programme has now become, even as they were building it – let alone what it will do in the future. Is it possible, in this context, to even attempt to imagine the future of *Doctor Who*?

We can say that *Doctor Who* is a cloak that Ncuti Gatwa now wears. It is a cloak woven by many hands, intricate and loaded with significance, the property of no one and everyone. It is not an easy garment to handle, so it is fortunate that Gatwa can wear pretty much anything. Eventually the day will come for him to hand this costume on – not preserved immaculately, but changed and improved, with a part of himself woven into it. That aspect of Gatwa will have a form of immortality. It will outlive us all.

And on the character will go, we can predict, through the rest of the 2020s. Perhaps there will be a wobble in the 2030s, when it will require a remarkable imagination to reinvent the character for the 2040s. By the 2050s there is unlikely to be anyone who worked on the classic era still with us, yet their names will still be remembered, and their work still studied and enjoyed. Towards the end of the twenty-first century there will be no one left from the third Golden Age of *Doctor Who*, yet perhaps an octogenarian Gatwa will still be interviewed about his memories of David

Tennant. Perhaps his anecdotes will match those of Tom Baker for charisma, causing the newly cast Fiftieth Doctor to cite Gatwa as their favourite. Academics in the twenty-second century, assuming we all make it that far, may analyse and study those interviews, and perhaps drain them of charm and fun. Yet that will not prevent a young child in the twenty-third century encountering the Doctor through whatever technology is then used for telling stories, and feeling their world expand and their imagination soar. And in the ultimate lifespan of *Doctor Who*, the character will still be young, for their stories will be destined to be told on distant planets far across the galaxy, long after their origins as a television show designed to fix a scheduling conundrum have been forgotten. Their domain, after all, is all of time and space.

Well, perhaps. That is one potential timeline, but the future is tricky and it dislikes predictions. In the immediate future, we don't know what numbers hidden deep within a Disney+ spreadsheet will cause the entertainment giant to withdraw funding and walk away. In the longer term, no one can say how long stories about characters such as the Doctor – or Robin Hood, or Sherlock Holmes, or James Bond – will be told. Fictional characters, like human ones, don't know how long they have. The past is littered with gods now unworshipped, legends long forgotten and myths without resonance. It takes a lot of skill for an immaterial idea to surf history's changes indefinitely. The Doctor in the TARDIS, perhaps, seems more adaptable than most, but only time will tell how long their stories are told.

So what will happen next? How will the Doctor survive this time? It had to end like this, didn't it? It had to end on a cliffhanger. Our love of mystery compels us to tune in next week because that's the only way we can know what happens next.

We can never resist a good story.

Cue the theme tune.

BIBLIOGRAPHY

Aaronovitch, Ben, *Doctor Who: Remembrance of the Daleks* (Ebury, 2013)

Aldred, Sophie, and Tucker, Mike, *Ace! The Inside Story of the End of an Era* (Virgin, 1996)

Aldridge, Mark, and Murray, Andy, *T Is for Television: The Small Screen Adventures of Russell T Davies* (Reynolds & Hearn, 2008)

Baker, Tom, *Who on Earth is Tom Baker? An Autobiography* (HarperCollins, 1997)

The Boy Who Kicked Pigs (Faber and Faber, 1999)

Bond, Michael, *Fans: A Journey into the Psychology of Belonging* (Picador, 2024)

Cabell, Craig, *Operation Big Ben* (Spellmount, 2006)

Carney, Jessica, *Who's There? The Life and Career of William Hartnell* (Fantom, 2013)

Cartmel, Andrew, *Cat's Cradle: Warhead* (Virgin, 1992)

Script Doctor: The Inside Story of Doctor Who 1986–89 (Reynolds & Hearn, 2005)

Cornell, Paul, Day, Martin, and Topping, Keith, *The Doctor Who Discontinuity Guide* (Virgin, 1995)

Courtney, Nicholas, and McManus, Michael, *Still Getting Away with It: The Life and Times of Nicholas Courtney* (SciFiCollector, 2005)

Davies, Russell T, and Cook, Benjamin, *Doctor Who The*

Writer's Tale: The Untold Story of the BBC Series (BBC Books, 2008)
Davison, Peter, *Is There Life Outside the Box? An Actor Despairs* (John Blake, 2017)
Dickens, Charles, *The Old Curiosity Shop* (Penguin Classics, 2000)
Dicks, Terrance, *Doctor Who and the Web of Fear* (Target, 1976)
Eccleston, Christopher, *I Love the Bones of You: My Father and the Making of Me* (Simon and Schuster, 2019)
Forward, Simon A., Doctor Who Novellas: *Shell Shock* (Telos, 2003)
Gibbons, Dave, et al., *Doctor Who: The Fourth Doctor Anthology* (Panini, 2023)
Goodall, Nigel, *A Life in Time and Space: The Biography of David Tennant* (John Blake, 2010)
Harris, Robert, *Selling Hitler: Story of the Hitler Diaries* (Arrow, 1986)
Hayes, Paul, *Pull to Open – 1962–1963: The Inside Story of how the BBC Created and Launched Doctor Who* (Ten Acre, 2023)
The Long Game – 1996–2003: The Inside Story of how the BBC Brought Back Doctor Who (Ten Acre, 2021)
Hendy, David, *The BBC: A People's History* (Profile, 2022)
Herbert, Emily, *Matt Smith: The Biography* (John Blake, 2010)
Howe, David J., *The Who Adventures: The Art and History of Virgin Publishing's Doctor Who Fiction* (Telos, 2021)
Hyde, Lewis, *Trickster Makes the World: How Disruptive Imagination Creates Culture* (Canongate, 2008)
Le Guin, Ursula K., *The Language of the Night* (Scribner, 1979)
Letts, Barry, *Who and Me: The Memoir of Doctor Who Producer Barry Letts* (Fantom, 2009)
McGown, Alistair, *The Fanzine Book: The Golden Age of Doctor Who Underground Press* (Telos, 2023)

Marson, Richard, *JN-T: The Life and Scandalous Times of John Nathan-Turner* (Miwk, 2013)

Drama and Delight: The Life of Verity Lambert (Miwk, 2015)

Marter, Ian, *Doctor Who and the Ark in Space* (BBC Books, 2012)

Moffat, Steven, *Doctor Who: The Day of the Doctor* (BBC Books, 2018)

Molesworth, Richard, *Robert Holmes: A Life in Words* (Telos, 2013)

Newman, Sydney, *Head of Drama: The Memoir of Sydney Newman* (ECW, 2017)

Parkin, Lance, *A History of the Universe: From Before the Dawn of Time and Beyond the End of Eternity* (Virgin, 1996)

Penswick, Neil, *The Pit* (Virgin, 1993)

Pertwee, Jon, *Moon Boots and Dinner Suits: An Autobiography* (Elm Tree Books, 1984)

Platt, Marc, *Lungbarrow* (Virgin, 1997)

Rees, Dylan, *Downtime: The Lost Years of Doctor Who* (Obverse Books, 2017)

Roberts, Jem, *The Frood: The Authorised and Very Official History of Douglas Adams & The Hitchhiker's Guide to the Galaxy* (Arrow, 2015)

Robson, Eddie, *Do Time Lords Get Drunk? And Other Important Questions About Doctor Who* (Short Books, 2023)

Russell, Gary, *Doctor Who: The Inside Story* (BBC Books, 2006)

Shearman, Rob, and Hadoke, Toby, *Running Through Corridors: Rob and Toby's Marathon Watch of Doctor Who, Volume 1: The 60s* (Mad Norwegian Press, 2010)

Shelley, Mary, *Frankenstein, or, The Modern Prometheus* (Penguin Classics, 1818)

Sladen, Elisabeth, *The Autobiography* (Aurum, 2011)

Smith, Paul, *The Classic Doctor Who DVD Compendium* (Wonderful Books, 2014)

Thornbury, Gregory A., and Bustard, Ned (eds), *Bigger on the Inside: Christianity and Doctor Who* (Square Halo Books, 2015)

Troughton, Michael, *Patrick Troughton: The Biography of the Second Doctor Who* (Hirst, 2011)

Tulloch, John, and Alvarado, Manuel, *Doctor Who: The Unfolding Text* (Macmillan, 1983)

Walker, John R., *Stories from a Doctor Who TV Extra* (John R. Walker, 2013)

Waterhouse, Matthew, *Blue Box Boy: A Memoir of Doctor Who in Four Episodes* (Hirst, 2010)

Whitaker, David, *Doctor Who in an Exciting Adventure with the Daleks* (Armada, 1964)

Wilkinson, Joy, *Doctor Who: The Witchfinders* (BBC Books, 2021)

Wilson, Greg, *Discotheque Archives* (SWS, 2022)

NOTES AND SOURCES

In the sources that follow, 'DWM' refers to that great font of *Who* information, *Doctor Who Magazine*. Scripts to most 21st-century episodes can be found online on the 'Whoniverse' page of the 'Writers' section of the BBC website, www.bbc.uk/writers/scripts/whoniverse. Transcripts of all episodes are found at Chrissie's Transcripts Site, www.chakoteya.net.

Introduction

'Because it's nuts. Because it's strange. It is eccentric . . .' – Russell T Davies interviewed in *Doctor Who @ 60: A Musical Celebration*, BBC Radio 2, 15 October 2023.

'I think being Doctor Who has done me a bit of good after all these years . . .' – Tom Baker interviewed for the behind-the-scenes feature of the Big Finish production *Doctor Who: Once and Future: Past Lives.*

Pre-titles: The Conception (1962–63)

1. Verity Underground

For a detailed account of the *Underground* tragedy, see www.britishtelevisiondrama.org.uk/?p=4313 [accessed 08/01/2025]

'A very exciting actor' – *Drama and Delight*, Richard Marson, p. 41.

'I was in this little group . . .' – ibid.

'It was one of these things where nobody knew what to do . . .' – ibid., p. 42.

'How are you going to lead us?' – *Head of Drama*, Sydney Newman, p. 366.

'Every time someone went to a door . . .' – *Drama and Delight*, Richard Marson, p. 42.

2. What It Thought Was Good for Them

'Righteousness in every department of human activity . . .' – *The BBC*, David Hendy, p. 18.

'Enjoyed doing it' – ibid., p. 14.

'Paternalistic and often stuffily pompous' – Dennis Potter, James MacTaggart Lecture, 1993.

'When commercial television started, it absolutely knocked the BBC for six . . .' – *Pull to Open*, Paul Hayes, p. 58.

'One must get away from the middle-class "Who's for tennis?" type of . . .' – ibid., p. 83.

'I'll be perfectly frank, when I got to the BBC . . .' – Newman quoted at www.doctorwhonews.net/the_story_of_doctor_who/6 [accessed 08/01/2025]

'We required a new programme that would . . .' – Newman quoted at www.doctorwhonews.net/the_story_of_doctor_who/7 [accessed 08/01/2025]

3. 'Mad Scientists and All that Jazz'

'Up to the age of forty, I don't think there was a science fiction book . . .' – *Pull to Open*, Paul Hayes, p. 112.

'Not itself a widely popular branch of fiction . . .' – April 1962 *Survey Group Report on Science Fiction* by Donald Bull and Alice Frick is in the BBC Archive, and can be found online at www.doctorwhonews.net/the_story_of_doctor_who/2 [accessed 08/01/2025]

'Our news was "doped" only by suppressions, not by fabrications' – *The BBC*, David Hendy, p. 118.

'Bug-Eyed Monsters . . . The central characters . . .' – July 1962 *Science Fiction Report* by John Braybon and Alice Frick is in the BBC Archive, and can be found online at www.doctorwhonews.net/the_story_of_doctor_who/4 [accessed 08/01/2025]

4. 'Somewhat Pathetic'

'A fine opportunity to write fast moving . . .' – March 1963 memo *Science Fiction Report* from C.E. Webber to Donald Wilson is in the BBC Archive, and can be found online at www.doctorwhonews.net/the_story_of_doctor_who/8 [accessed 08/01/2025]

'A name given to him by his three earthly friends . . .' – May 1963 programme format document *DR WHO General Notes on Background and Approach for an Exciting Adventure-Science Fiction Drama Series for Children's Saturday Viewing* by Wilson, Webber and Newman is in the BBC Archive, and can be found online at www.doctorwhonews.net/the_story_of_doctor_who/11 [accessed 08/01/2025]

5. A Certain Lack of Enthusiasm

'Work to a very moderate budget' – *Pull to Open*, Paul Hayes, p. 141.

'Virtually the worst possible studio for such a project' – Drama Group Administrator Ayton Whitaker's notes on a meeting with Donald Wilson and Controller of Programme Services for Television Ian Atkins, www.doctorwhonews.net/the_story_of_doctor_who/11 [accessed 08/01/2025]

'Think twice before proceeding . . .' – *Pull to Open*, Paul Hayes, pp. 241–2.

'Is the kind of crazy enterprise which both Departments . . .' – ibid., p. 240.

'I did not particularly want to work on it . . .' – ibid., pp. 161–2.

'I didn't feel that I had anyone on staff who seemed right for the kind of idiocy and fun . . .' – Sydney Newman interviewed by Frank Gillard for the *Oral History of the BBC* collection, 29 September 1984, archived at connectedhistoriesofthebbc.org/play/?id=154

'Never had the slightest interest in science fiction . . .' – *Pull to Open*, Paul Hayes, p. 165.

'Full of piss and vinegar' – *Drama and Delight*, Richard Marson, p. 52.

'There were no means of really complaining in 1962 . . .' – ibid., p. 50.

'I don't know any children, I don't want children . . .' – ibid., p. 52.

6. The Three Musketeers

'I nearly died, I fell over laughing' – *Pull to Open*, Paul Hayes p. 179.

'I was a frightful snob and said . . .' – *Drama and Delight*, Richard Marson, p. 63.

'It was way beneath me; it was a kids' series' – ibid., p. 63.

'I remember feeling vaguely insulted . . .' – ibid., p. 68.

'Nobody wanted to touch *Doctor Who*. . . ' – ibid., p. 61.

'The more I think of "Dr Who", the more it depresses me . . .' – Waris Hussein's diary entry for 30 May 1963, online at www.radiotimes.com/tv/sci-fi/the-1963-doctor-who-diaries-of-waris-hussein-part-one/ [accessed 08/01/2025]

'We were like the Three Musketeers . . .' – *Drama and Delight*, Richard Marson, p. 66.

'I was very conscious of my ethnic background . . .' – ibid., p. 62.

'Sometimes dangerous or unpleasant, sometimes kind . . .' – ibid., p. 63.

'I went to the Cambridge Appointments Board and I said . . .' – *Pull to Open*, Paul Hayes, p. 173.

Opening Titles

'Abstract things on like "wind clouds" . . .' – *Pull to Open*, Paul Hayes, pp. 257–8.

'Ron came to hear it and said, "Jeez, Delia . . ."' – ibid., p. 255.

'Well, I just think you're completely wrong, Sydney!' – ibid., p. 288.

Chapter 1: The Exiled Wanderer (1963–64)

1. Out of the Shadows

'The Doctor is full of optimism and hope . . .' – 'Ncuti Gatwa's Guide to Doctor Who', 25 October 2022, on the official *Doctor Who* YouTube channel at www.youtube.com/watch?v=0016_t55uwI [accessed 08/01/2025]

'Used his dangerous nasty qualities as much as his . . .' – 'Maureen O'Brien in Conversation', *Doctor Who The Collection Season 2*, Blu-Ray set, disk 3.

'Doctor who? Who's he talking about?' – *Doctor Who, The Cave of Skulls*, 30 November 1963.

'I'm not a doctor of medicine' – *Doctor Who, The Forest of Fear*, 7 December 1963.

'He was a mystery. That's why he was Doctor Who . . .' – *SFX* issue 150, December 2006.

'Have you ever thought what it's like to be wanderers . . .' – *Doctor Who, An Unearthly Child*, 23 November 1963.

2. A London Urchin

'No one seemed to love me only my policeman father . . .' – *Who's There?*, Jessica Carney, p. 30.

'He never used his own difficult childhood to get sympathy . . .' – ibid., pp. 27–8.

'His nerves were certainly never the same after his breakdown' – ibid., p. 101.
'Combine being lovable and touching . . .' – *Pull to Open*, Paul Hayes, p. 231.
'He read the script and just loved it . . .' – ibid., p. 231.

3. The Portal

'A safe fairyland is untrue to all worlds' – J.R.R. Tolkien, letter to Stanley Unwin, 15 October 1937.
'You say you can't fit an enormous building . . .' – *Doctor Who, An Unearthly Child*, 23 November 1963.

4. 'A Mild Curiosity'

'They pulled that thing on me and I was livid with anger' – *Pull to Open*, Paul Hayes, pp. 287–8.
'Nearly fourteen' – *The Old Curiosity Shop*, Charles Dickens, p. 63.
'It all started out as a mild curiosity in a junkyard' – *Doctor Who, The Sensorites*, episode one – *Strangers in Space*, 20 June 1964.
'Two poor adventurers, wandering they knew not wither' – *The Old Curiosity Shop*, Charles Dickens, p. 105.
'To hypnotise' – *Who's There?*, Jessica Carney, p. 156.
'He absolutely loved the part . . .' – ibid., p. 155.
'Was going to be the definitive Quilp of our time' – *Who and Me*, Barry Letts, ebook, loc 216.

Chapter 2: The Unlikely Hero (1965–66)

1. Enter the Daleks

'No bug-eyed monsters' – *Head of Drama*, Sydney Newman, p. 445.

2. The Ultimate Evil

'There is a reason. An explanation might be better . . .' – *Doctor Who, The Daleks*, episode four – *The Ambush*, 11 January 1964.
'That is about as near to a definition as this much-abused word . . .' – 'What is Fascism?', George Orwell, *Tribune*, 24 March 1944.
'We assumed he was going to say it was terrific . . .' – *Pull to Open*, Paul Hayes, p. 289.
'If you knew what real fascists do, you would never say that' – ibid., p. 51.

'I suppose [the Daleks] were born in a flash of inspiration . . .' – ibid., pp. 207–8.

3. The Wandering Exile Was Reimagined

'It's funny, but as soon as he walked in, I felt . . .' – *Doctor Who, The Rescue*, episode two – *Desperate Measures*, 9 January 1965.

'That's sheer murder!' – *Doctor Who, The Daleks*, episode six – *The Ordeal*, 25 January 1964.

'Our fate doesn't rest with the Thals, surely . . .' – *Doctor Who, The Daleks*, episode four – *The Ambush*, 11 January 1964.

'I think we'd better pit our wits against them . . .' – *Doctor Who, The Dalek Invasion of Earth*, episode two – *The Daleks*, 28 November 1964.

'You can't rewrite history . . .' – *Doctor Who, The Aztecs*, episode one – *The Temple of Evil*, 23 May 1964.

4. Dalekmania

'I don't know to this day what the enormous appeal of the Daleks was . . .' – Terry Nation interviewed by Joe Nazarro, DWM145, February 1989, p. 17.

5. Season Three

'Bill was feeling very insecure . . .' – DWM Special Edition: 'Showrunners', March 2023, p. 15.

'Wanted to develop the programme and get it out of the somewhat childish rut . . .' – John Wiles interviewed by Jeremy Bentham, DWM Winter Special 1983/4, p. 8.

'As I recollect it, when I came back [from holiday] there was just . . .' – 'Maureen O'Brien In Conversation', *Doctor Who The Collection Series 2*, Blu-Ray set, disk 3.

'One of the things I wanted to do was redefine our attitudes to death . . .' – DWM Special Edition: 'Showrunners', March 2023, p. 13.

'Gone into the country' – *Doctor Who, The War Machines*, episode two, 2 July 1966.

'You do it the way it is . . .' – DWM Special Edition: 'Showrunners', March 2023, p. 17.

'He'd go off into these terrible rages several . . .' – 'Maureen O'Brien In Conversation', *Doctor Who The Collection Series 2*, Blu-Ray set, disk 3.

'Bill often came out with xenophobic comments . . .' – *Who's There?*, Jessica Carney, p. 171.

'Could be unnerving, when his bigotry was allowed to surface . . .' – *Still Getting Away with It*, Nicholas Courtney and Michael McManus, p. 51.

'I'm one of the few producers ever to resign from the BBC . . .' – John Wiles interviewed by Jeremy Bentham, DWM Winter Special 1983/4, p. 7.

'He could be quite intimidating if you didn't know . . .' – *Who's There?*, Jessica Carney, p. 158.

'Wearing a bit thin' – *Doctor Who, The Tenth Planet*, episode four, 29 October 1966.

'Don't you know who I am? I'm Doctor Who, Doctor BLOODY WHO!' – *Who's There?*, Jessica Carney, p. 161.

Chapter 3: The Trickster (1966–69)

1. 'I Need Change'

'Astonished at his family arrangements and I was . . .' – *Patrick Troughton*, Michael Troughton, ebook, loc 2048.

'Ever since Pat's return from America . . .' – ibid., loc 1523.

'The Artist and the Family Man' – ibid., loc 1312.

'Trip has changed me I think . . .' – ibid., loc 1394.

'Many mature actresses whom I have worked with . . .' – ibid., loc 1527.

'I need change. Things have to change all the time for me I'm afraid . . .' – ibid., loc 2159.

2. 'They Must Be Mad'

'I'd like to see a butterfly fit into a chrysalis case after it's spread its wings . . .' – *Doctor Who, The Power of the Daleks*, episode one, 5 November 1966.

'The producer and I were absolutely determined to have Patrick Troughton . . . – *Patrick Troughton*, Michael Troughton, ebook, loc 2168.

'Quite preposterous . . .' – ibid., loc 2226.

'Couldn't have done an imitation of Hartnell because . . .' – Christopher Barry interviewed by Richard Marson, DWM99, April 1985 pp. 36–7.

'I'd had a lovely wig fitted which had . . .' – *Patrick Troughton*, Michael Troughton, ebook, loc 2534.

'Be like the upper-class Steptoe' – Waris Hussein's diary entry, 29 September

1963, published on radiotimes.com on 1 May 2023 as 'The 1963 Doctor Who diaries of Waris Hussein – part one'.

'I still don't see it, but if you and Innes say it's okay, okay, go ahead' – *Patrick Troughton*, Michael Troughton, ebook, loc 2317.

3. The Trickster

'He's all right, but he's not that good' – *Doctor Who, The Romans*, episode three – *Conspiracy*, 30 January 1965.

'There are some corners of the universe which have bred . . .' – *Doctor Who, The Moonbase*, episode two, 18 February 1967.

4. Monsters

'If it wasn't for Patrick, the rest of us wouldn't have got the part' – *Patrick Troughton*, Michael Troughton, ebook, loc 3102.

'For me, he was the "guvnor" among Doctors' – ibid., loc 4954.

'I think Patrick Troughton created the Doctor as he is now . . .' – *The Doctors Revisited*, BBC America, 2013.

'Humour and wit . . .' – 'The New "Dr. Who"' (BBC Paperwork), included as a PDF file on the *Power of the Daleks* Blu-Ray.

'A very long-winded and complicated autocratic Sherlock Holmes type . . .' – *Patrick Troughton*, Michael Troughton, ebook, loc 2333.

'Over seven hundred and fifty years since I left my own planet' – Andrew Pixley, *Power of the Daleks* expanded viewing notes, p. 4.

'I don't know. Perhaps I'll never know . . .'– ibid., p. 7.

'He is the eternal fugitive with a horrifying fear of the past horrors . . .' – 'The New "Dr. Who"' (BBC Paperwork), included as a PDF file on the *Power of the Daleks* Blu-Ray.

'I was fairly confident that if I, as an adult, accepted . . .' – *Pull to Open*, Paul Hayes, p. 172.

'Nobody in the corporation is quite sure . . .' – Waris Hussein's diary entry, 21 December 1963, published on radiotimes.com on 1 July 2023 as 'The 1960s Doctor Who diaries of Waris Hussein – part three'.

'Children today are very sophisticated . . .' – *Drama and Delight*, Richard Marson, p. 55.

5. 'You Will Become like Us'

'It isn't all over. It's far from being all over' – *Doctor Who, The Tenth Planet*, episode four, 29 October 1966.

6. Prison in Space

'We need something new . . . something creative to happen . . .' – *Patrick Troughton*, Michael Troughton, ebook, loc 3297.

'Natural protective instincts towards women' – *The Prison in Space Scriptbook* (PDF edition), Dick Sharples, p. 126.

'The gentle sex' – ibid., p. 124.

'Those dear dead days beyond recall . . .' – ibid., p. 81.

'The inevitable result of giving women the vote . . .' – ibid., p. 92.

'The rot really set in when . . .' – ibid., p. 135.

'On re-reading the story, it's amusing to see what was . . .' – ibid., p. 6.

'Could be much more obviously (blatantly) feminine . . .' – ibid., p. 74.

'A real man. The first real man I've ever met' – ibid., p. 221.

'Where they belong . . .' – ibid., p. 222.

Chapter 4: The Action Hero (1970–74)

1. A 'Boy's Own' Feel

'His heart is big enough to respect . . .' – *The Dr Who Annual* (1966), 'Who Is Dr Who?' pp. 22–3.

'Jon Pertwee was definitely a more straightforward establishment figure . . .' – *The Story of Doctor Who* (BBC documentary), BBC One, 30 December 2003.

2. Pertwee, Jon Pertwee

'Created a flamboyantly dressed character, a dashing, fearless man . . .' – *Moon Boots and Dinner Suits*, Jon Pertwee, ebook, loc 65.

'Was a terrible, shocking thing . . .' – ibid., loc 3630.

'I did all sorts, [such as] teaching commandos how to . . .' – *Operation Big Ben*, Craig Cabell, p. 47.

'I mean . . . drip UNPARALLELED!' – Instagram.com/ncutigatwa, 7 July 2023.

'I love Jon Pertwee, the Third Doctor's, outfits . . .' – 'Ncuti Gatwa on

Doctor Who: "The Doctor is me"', Alison Rumfitt, *Rolling Stone UK*, July 2023.

'All right, I'll have a whirl . . .' – *Myth Makers #15: Jon Pertwee.*

'That's a frightening thing to hear' – *I Love the Bones of You*, Christopher Eccleston, p. 126.

'You have a grand scheme about how your Doctor is going . . .' – Peter Davison interviewed on *The Stranger: More Than a Messiah* DVD, BBV Productions, 1992.

'Surprisingly, it was his own personality . . .' – *Who and Me*, Barry Letts, ebook, loc 1313.

'I hadn't really found myself before *Dr. Who*. . . ' – *Radio Times Doctor Who 10th Anniversary Special*, 11 December 1973, p. 7.

'It's become part of me and I've become part of it . . .' – Tom Baker interviewed for the behind-the-scenes feature of the Big Finish production *Doctor Who: Once and Future: Past Lives.*

3. The Sea Devil

'Sucked me off the ladder and dropped me in the actual shell hole . . .' – Jon Pertwee interviewed by BBC Radio Solent, 21 October 1971.

'An angel flew down out of the sky . . .' – ibid.

'Two rather ordinary looking blokes from Naval Intelligence . . .' – Michael E. Briant interviewed in *The Sea Devils* 'making of' documentary, *Doctor Who The Collection Season 9*, Blu-Ray set, disk 4.

4. 'Something for the Dads'

'One of the reasons we were in such a state . . .' – DWM Special Edition: 'Showrunners', March 2023, p. 25.

'Obviously, she had to be attractive . . .' – *Who and Me*, Barry Letts, ebook, loc 2323.

'What Verity did was launch a brand-new series . . .' – *Drama and Delight*, Richard Marson, p. 64.

'Verity arrived with a great deal of sniggering' – ibid., p. 56.

'She had enormous boobs and once, by mistake . . .' – ibid., p. 72.

'As a woman I did have to work twice as hard . . .' – ibid., p. 83.

'What's a girl like you doing in a job like this? . . .' – *Doctor Who, The Web of Fear*, episode one, 3 February 1968.

'Here we go . . .' – *Doctor Who, The Time Monster*, episode one, 20 May 1972.

'The irony of male writers getting a male character to . . .' – *Elisabeth Sladen*, Elisabeth Sladen, p. 82.

'As the new girl on the *Doctor Who* set in 1973 I have to admit . . .' – ibid., p. 5.

'Doctor Who in those days could be a bit of a boys' club . . .' – ibid., p. 100.

'One day I made the mistake of referring to one of his tall tales . . .' – ibid., p. 123.

'I suppose it's basically true . . .' – *Robert Holmes*, Richard Molesworth, ebook, loc 7222.

'Melanie is one of those annoying young ladies who . . .' – *JN-T*, Richard Marson, p. 242.

'Nobody gave a shit about whether girls were watching it or not' – ibid., p. 274.

'One in three times that I went through a door . . .' – Nicola Bryant interviewed on *Doctor Who: 60 Years of Secrets and Scandals*, Channel 5, 25 November 2023.

'It's the biggest thing to hit white goods in years . . .' – This Zanussi advert can be found online at www.youtube.com/watch?v=R8r6HA2muMo [accessed 08/01/2025]

5. 'The Old Man Must Die'

'An early eco-warrior ' – *Who and Me*, Barry Letts, ebook, loc 3517.

'No matter what the theme, it would never be . . .' – ibid., loc 2894.

'Was explicitly planned to call attention . . .' – ibid., loc 2887.

'The sort of "religion" that I can find acceptable . . .' – ibid., loc 3315.

'Wearing a bit thin' – *Doctor Who, The Tenth Planet*, episode four, 29 October 1966.

'The old man must die and the new man will discover . . .' – *Doctor Who, The Planet of the Spiders*, episode one, 4 May 1974.

Chapter 5: The Bohemian Traveller (1975–77)

1. The Monk

'Sort of Buddhist' – Tom Baker interviewed by Mark Gatiss at the BFI, 2001.

'Incomplete personality' – *Who on Earth is Tom Baker?*, Tom Baker, ebook, loc 4289.

'Even at the age of eight I was an embarrassment . . .' – ibid., loc 391.

'All my life I have had learning difficulties . . .' – ibid., loc 2012.

'My first ambition was to be an orphan' – ibid., loc 208.

'Randy for martyrdom' – ibid., loc 1345.

'Does He really not want us to have a pal?' – ibid., loc 1423.

'He'd been sitting there for at least six months . . .' – ibid., loc 1228.

'Everybody get his dick out!' – ibid., loc 1225.

'I think, looking back, I tried too hard . . .' – ibid., loc 1490.

'Actors don't have friends . . .' – Tom Baker in conversation with the author.

'I think that to be a good actor you have to prefer strangers' – *Who on Earth is Tom Baker?*, Tom Baker, ebook, loc 3057.

'I'm afraid I have no gift for friendship . . .' – ibid., loc 3579.

'I was hit by terrible waves of anxiety . . .' – 'A Life in the Day of Tom Baker', *Sunday Times*, 19 March 1978.

'All my life I have felt myself to be on the edge of things . . .' – *Who on Earth is Tom Baker?*, Tom Baker, ebook, loc 2010.

'I kept bursting into tears and once I deliberately cut myself . . .' – ibid., loc 3272.

2. 'I Was the Doctor and the Doctor Was Me'

'I don't work for anybody. I'm just having fun' – *Doctor Who, The Nightmare of Eden*, part two, 1 December 1979.

'I didn't consciously try to be different from Jon . . .' – 'Tom Baker: How I Made Doctor Who', *Guardian*, 2 November 2013.

'Have you met Miss Smith? She's my best friend!' – *Doctor Who, The Seeds of Doom*, part three, 14 February 1976.

'Tom has such an energy, a genuine impish delight in the absurd . . .' – *Elisabeth Sladen*, Elisabeth Sladen, p. 150.

'We were so unused to seeing each other outside of the BBC's walls . . .' – ibid., p. 173.

'They watched with terrific intensity as . . .' – *Who on Earth is Tom Baker?*, Tom Baker, ebook, loc 3856.

'I began to get into the part and then the part got into me . . .' – ibid., loc 3735.

3. 'He Liked Doing What He Did'

'It's the best dialogue ever written. It's up there with Dennis Potter . . .' – 'Master of the Universe', Richard Johnson, *Telegraph*, 11 March 2007.

'Bob suffered, as they say – this terrible cant expression . . .' – *Robert Holmes*, Richard Molesworth, ebook, loc 3305.

'I think the thing about Bob was that . . .' – ibid., loc 3159.

'Some old General on the Board said . . .' – ibid., loc 289.

'I don't think there is a much better class of television . . .' – ibid., loc 3167.

'Were a snooty, too-good-to-be-true lot' – ibid., loc 5704.

'People have often asked whether I based the Time Lord society . . .' – ibid., loc 5800.

'The story is that it was about the tax man . . .' – *The Sun Makers* 'making of' documentary, *Doctor Who The Collection Season 15*, Blu-Ray box, disk 4.

'Our purpose is to amuse, simply to amuse. Nothing serious, nothing political' – *Doctor Who, The Carnival of Monsters*, episode one, 27 January 1973.

'I wonder what has happened to *Doctor Who* recently . . .' – *Robert Holmes*, Richard Molesworth, ebook, loc 9892.

'It seems that by being hidden in plain sight in his script . . .' – ibid., loc 3641.

'If heroes don't exist, it is necessary to invent them' – *Doctor Who, The Deadly Assassin*, part four, 20 November 1976.

4. 'Teatime Brutality for Tots'

'The programme was already being watched by, probably, the maximum . . .' – *Robert Holmes*, Richard Molesworth, ebook, loc 4550.

'I had decided, and Bob agreed, that we would try to make *Doctor Who* . . .' – ibid., loc 4746.

'Propaganda of disbelief, doubt and dirt . . .' – 'Doctor Who: A BBC Production' (DWM583 Supplement, October 2022), p. 7.

'The devil incarnate' – Mary Whitehouse obituary, 'Crusader was dubbed Britain's "Queen of Clean" ', Paul Lewis, *Pittsburgh Post-Gazette*, 20 December 2001.

'Teatime brutality for tots' – David Maloney obituary, 'Director of *Doctor Who* "Chillers" ', Anthony Hayward, *Independent*, 10 August 2006.

'It has to be said, both Bob and Hinchcliffe were starting to give critics . . .' – *Robert Holmes*, Richard Molesworth, ebook, loc 5477.

'I write, in anger and despair, following last Saturday's episode . . .' – Letter from Mary Whitehouse to 'The Producer, "Doctor Who"', 15 November 1976, included in *The Deadly Assassin* Production Paperwork PDF, *Doctor Who The Collection Season 14*, Blu-Ray box set, p. 276.

'I think it's extraordinary that people with the brilliance . . .' – Mary Whitehouse interviewed for the *Deadly Assassin* 'making of' documentary, *Doctor Who The Collection Season 14*, Blu-Ray box, disk 3.

'I felt that the drowning sequence, the cliffhanger . . .' – Philip Hinchcliffe interviewed for the *Deadly Assassin* 'making of' documentary, *Doctor Who The Collection Season 14*, Blu-Ray box, disk 3.

'In *The Deadly Assassin* there was a scene where I was being held under water . . .' – *Who on Earth is Tom Baker?*, Tom Baker, ebook, loc 3836.

'I am indeed aware of the previous letters that you and your association . . .' – Letter from Charles Curran to Mary Whitehouse, 6 December 1976, included in *The Deadly Assassin* Production Paperwork PDF, *Doctor Who The Collection Season 14*, Blu-Ray box set, pp. 279–80.

'There was a slightly febrile atmosphere within the BBC as a whole . . .' – Philip Hinchcliffe interviewed for the *Deadly Assassin* 'making of' documentary, *Doctor Who The Collection Season 14*, Blu-Ray box, disk 3.

Chapter 6: The Tom Baker Show (1978–81)

1. 'What Has Happened to the Magic of *Doctor Who*?'

'Once, Time Lords were all-powerful, awe-inspiring . . .' – *TARDIS 77* Number 1, January 1977.

'Irrecoverable as dead pets' – *Blue Box Boy*, Matthew Waterhouse, ebook, loc 1420.

'Maturity is not an outgrowing, but a growing up . . .' – *The Language of the Night*, Ursula K. Le Guin, p. 29.

2. 'I Wish the Daleks or Someone Would Exterminate Him'

'No, no, no, you're not by any means worse than Peter C . . .' – Letter from Sarah Newman to Keith Miller, as reproduced in *The Official Doctor Who Fan Club Volume 1: The Jon Pertwee Years* by Keith Miller and read out by Graham Norton to a mortified Peter Capaldi on *The Graham Norton Show* (series 16, episode 1, BBC One, 2014).

'These aren't the Time Lords we've seen before . . .' – Jan Vincent-Rudzki interviewed for *The Deadly Assassin* 'making of' documentary, *Doctor Who The Collection Season 14*, Blu-Ray box, disk 3.

3. 'I Thought I Could Do Anything I Liked'

'You stole my Humpty!' – author present at conversation.

'The atmosphere [surrounding the programme] had got quite heavy' – Sarah Sutton interview, *Doctor Who The Collection Season 20*, Blu-Ray box, disk 2.

'It was fun more than it wasn't, but it was a situation where the leading actor . . .' – Matthew Waterhouse interview, *Doctor Who The Collection Season 20*, Blu-Ray box, disk 2.

'Why don't you just piss off?' – *Blue Box Boy*, Matthew Waterhouse, ebook, loc 3042.

'I thought we were supposed to have a director in the gallery . . .' – *Nightmare of Eden* 'making of' documentary, *Doctor Who The Collection Season 17*, Blu-Ray box, disk 4.

'Flippant and unmanageable' – DWM Special Edition: 'Showrunners', March 2023, p. 48.

'It was a horrendous experience as far as I was concerned . . .' – *Robert Holmes*, Richard Molesworth, ebook, loc 6879.

'Halfway through, a little boy came up to him and said . . .' – *Blue Box Boy*, Matthew Waterhouse, ebook, loc 2792.

'In a way, he was too gentle to be a producer' – DWM Special Edition: 'Showrunners', March 2023, p. 47.

'He wasn't the sort of person that you'd expect to be a producer . . .' – 'Darkness & Light', *Doctor Who The Collection Season 15*, Blu-Ray box, disk 7.

'I think Graham's strength was in keeping the peace . . .' – DWM Special Edition: 'Showrunners', March 2023, p. 53.

'Argh! My arms! My legs! My everything!' – *Doctor Who, Nightmare of Eden*, part four, 15 December 1979.

'I regret that I made Graham unhappy . . .' – 'Darkness & Light', *Doctor Who The Collection Season 15*, Blu-Ray box, disk 7.

'*Doctor Who* drove me crackers – it nearly killed me . . .' – *JN-T*, Richard Marson, p. 83.

'He was very young to be a producer at the BBC, so there was a lot riding on it . . .' – DWM Special Edition: 'Showrunners', March 2023, p. 58.

'Celebrity always trumped acting ability in John's book' – *Is There Life Outside the Box?*, Peter Davison, p. 171.

'Threw up for me lots of pleasures that changed my whole life . . .' – *Nationwide*, BBC One, 24 October 1980.

Chapter 7: The Reckless Innocent (1982–84)

1. 'It's Stopped Being Fun, Doctor'

'Lower-middle-class, walk-in-the-park life' – *Is There Life Outside the Box?*, Peter Davison, p. xiv.

'I felt like I was in a scene from *A Hard Day's Night* . . .' – ibid., p. 149.

'I don't know who that person is at all . . .' – DWM503, p. 18.

'The problem was, in my everyday life, in the face I presented . . .' – *Is There Life Outside the Box?*, Peter Davison, pp. xix–xx.

'Reckless innocent' – Peter Davison interviewed on *The Stranger: More Than a Messiah* DVD, BBV Productions, 1992.

'Deeply flawed notion [that] traumatised millions of children' – *Is There Life Outside the Box?*, Peter Davison, p. 174.

'Wouldn't want us to mourn unnecessarily' – *Doctor Who, Arc of Infinity*, part one, 3 January 1983.

'There should have been another way' – *Doctor Who, Warriors of the Deep*, part four, 13 January 1984.

'It's stopped being fun, Doctor, goodbye' – *Doctor Who, Resurrection of the Daleks*, part two, 15 February 1984.

'I was always battling to put more jokes in . . .' – *Doctor Who The Collection Season 20*, Limited Edition booklet, p. 2.

'It's the first time this has happened to me . . .' – *Is There Life Outside the Box?*, Peter Davison, p. 7.

2. 'The Platonic Ideal of the Doctor'

'What's interesting about the Platonic ideal of the Doctor . . .' – Jamie Mathieson in conversation with the author, 15 February 2024.

3. Longleat

'Lord Bath acquired the pictures for posterity and confessed to . . .' – *Selling Hitler*, Robert Harris, p. 113.

'If you want to go to Longleat now, just turn up on the day . . .' – Mark Strickson, *Saturday Superstore*, BBC One, 26 March 1983.

4. The Keeper of the *Doctor Who* Flame

'As if it was a terrorist organisation' – *Blue Box Boy*, Matthew Waterhouse, ebook, loc 2050.

'Think of the most vicious, bitchy queen you've ever met . . .' – ibid., loc 4779.

'Hugely important to him, that adulation . . .' – *JN-T*, Richard Marson, p. 129.

'A crucial, sometimes controversial force within Northern Soul . . .' – *Discotheque Archives*, Greg Wilson, p. 58.

'Just remember – we'll still be here long after you've gone!' – *JN-T*, Richard Marson, p. 135.

'The budget was all but gone, and no amount of decent writing . . .' – *Is There Life Outside the Box?*, Peter Davison, p. 179.

'I was never very happy with my second series. I think it just got a little bit dull . . .' – *Doctor Who The Collection Season 20*, Limited Edition booklet, p. 31.

'I burnt my bridges and tried to imagine a life after *Doctor Who*. . .' – *Is There Life Outside the Box?*, Peter Davison, p. 186.

Chapter 8: The Target (1984–86)

1. Unfair Attacks

'A bit of bomb that, had I been sitting up . . .' – *This is Colin Baker*, Big Finish, August 2015.

'I was just a tosser who wore glasses. I acquired more . . .' – 'Exclusive: Colin Baker jokes he "was the only Doctor Who without a sonic screwdriver"', Bill Borrows, *Daily Mirror*, 12 November 2023.

'The BBC's senility' – ibid.

'Everywhere I went . . .' – *Doctor Who: A BBC Production* (DWM583 Supplement, October 2022), p. 25.

'My involvement in Doctor Who's attempted assassination will overshadow . . .' – *Doctor Who: The Wilderness Years*, Radio 4, 19 November 2023.

2. 'We Wanted It to Die'

'John was immediately someone you liked . . .' – *JN-T*, Richard Marson, p. 150.

'My memory is that whenever [Nathan-Turner] came into the office . . .' – ibid., p. 191.

'Here are the programmes we are making for you next year . . .' – ibid., p. 223.

'I thought it was horrible, awful. I thought it was so out-dated . . .' – Michael Grade interview, BBC Norfolk, 24 September 2014.

'It was terrible [. . .] What it needed was triple the budget . . .' – *JN-T*, Richard Marson, p. 224.

'Oh, I think absolutely, *absolutely* he was casting himself' – ibid., p. 188.

'Colin Baker did seem to be him . . .' – ibid., p. 189.

'In the first few chapters, you think he's a prig . . .' – *DWM: Find the 600* (DWM600 Supplement, February 2024), p. 13.

'Absolutely God-awful' – 'He eats, sleeps and breathes television – and at last he's got round to watching some', William Langley, *Sunday Telegraph*, 11 March 2007.

'I can only say that it wounds me . . .' – DWM503, August 2016, p. 21.

'Britain's top *Who* fan Ian Levine declared war on the BBC decision . . .' – 'Save Our TARDIS!', Phil Dampier, *Sun*, 1 March 1985.

'If they take the Daleks to the House of Commons . . .' – *JN-T*, Richard Marson, p. 230.

'I cringe because I hate it so much . . .' – ibid., p. 229.

'The people who make *Doctor Who* have got rather complacent . . .' – ibid., p. 216.

3. Peri

'While the character of Doctor Who is generally considered likeable . . .' – BBC Television Audience Research Report 1985, included as a PDF file in *Doctor Who The Collection Season 22*, Blu-Ray box, p. 1.

'I seriously think that the costume was the greatest mistake in the history of television' – *JN-T*, Richard Marson, p. 188.

'Said the wrong thing about the Doctor . . .' – 'Trials and Tribulations', *Doctor Who The Collection Season 23*, Blu-Ray box, disk 4.

'A couple of really nice English guys' – *Doctor Who, Planet of Fire*, part one, 23 February 1984.

'I'm sorry, Howard. I didn't mean it . . .' – ibid.

'Hellish wilderness' – *Doctor Who, The Twin Dilemma*, part one, 22 March 1984.

'Do try and use your brain, my girl . . .' – *Doctor Who, The Two Doctors*, part two, 23 February 1985.

'How could I ever let you go . . .' – *Doctor Who, The Caves of Androzani*, part two, 9 March 1984.

'Human ancestry'– *Doctor Who The Complete History*, Stories 136–8, p. 22.

'Oh, what a fine, fleshy beast . . .' – *Doctor Who, The Two Doctors*, part three, 2 March 1985.

'It's like [Peri] never got to put proper clothes on . . .' – 'Nicola Bryant in Conversation', *Doctor Who The Collection Season 22*, Blu-Ray box, disk 7.

'Can you slap her? She's gone blue . . .' – *Doctor Who: 60 Years of Secrets and Scandals*, Channel 5, 25 November 2023.

'Being stuck in a leotard and shorts – that's not normal clothes' – 'Nicola Bryant in Conversation', *Doctor Who The Collection Season 22*, Blu-Ray box, disk 7.

'It was a gay man's idea of what heterosexual men want' – *JN-T*, Richard Marson, p. 187.

'The reason they bothered me . . .' – ibid., p. 187.

'I did not answer back . . .' – 'Nicola Bryant in Conversation', *Doctor Who The Collection Season 22*, Blu-Ray box, disk 7.

'I think, at [that] stage in my life, I did seem to attract people who want to control me . . .' – ibid.

'Everybody wonders why I didn't do . . .' – ibid.

'JN-T came up to me, spat in my face . . .' – *JN-T*, Richard Marson, p. 210.

'There was a point when I said to Eric Saward, the script editor . . .' – Colin Baker speaking at the Visions convention, USA, 1992.

4. 'Doable Barkers'

'Although I did meet some people who felt that their treatment . . .' – *JN-T*, Richard Marson, p. 197.

'Have you ever had two up you?' – ibid., p. 193.

'When I left the BBC in the 60s and came back in the early 80s . . .' – ibid., p. 80.

'Grade didn't like what he saw as the "Gay Mafia" at the BBC . . .' – DWM503, August 2016, p. 22.

'John got Gary into the BBC and then kept him there . . .' – *JN-T*, Richard Marson, p. 63.

'Was wholly dominated by queer men of a bitchy nature' – *Blue Box Boy*, Matthew Waterhouse, ebook, loc 5982.

'Did not assume that absolutely every Doctor Who fan was gay . . .' – ibid., loc 6435.

'It's easy to draw a link between gayness and fandom . . .' – 'Russell T Davies on secrets, sex and falling for Doctor Who: "Something clicked in my head: I love you"', *Guardian*, 17 November 2023.

'Gays who failed to attend the Gay Switchboard Benefit at Hammersmith Town Hall . . .' – DWM Bookazine #32, *60 Moments in Time*, November 2023, p. 64.

'That's the one time I had to get fucked by him . . .' – *JN-T*, Richard Marson, p. 123.

'A Roman emperor. I had to have eight people in my house . . .' – ibid., p. 128.

'Gary held John back because there were so many people who couldn't abide Gary . . .' – ibid., p. 54.

'Away from Gary, he was a wonderful person who would do anything for you . . .' – ibid., pp. 55–6.

5. On Trial

'I think I may have based Sarah a little bit on Barry Letts' – *Elisabeth Sladen*, Elisabeth Sladen, p. 114.

'Right in front of me was a man who wore a leather jacket . . .' – *I Love the Bones of You*, Christopher Eccleston, p. 162.

'Just remember – we'll still be here long after you've gone!' – *JN-T*, Richard Marson, p. 135.

'The last eight or nine years have seen a very steep decline in the quality of the show . . .' – *Did You See . . . ?*, BBC Two, 1987.

'It hasn't improved that much since it went off the air . . .' – *Open Air*, BBC One, 8 December 1986.

'I was talking to my partner Jane Judge . . .' – *Trial of a Time Lord* part one 'making of' documentary, *Doctor Who The Collection Season 23*, Blu-Ray box, disk 1.

'I remember my first reaction to that was, "Ooh, risky . . ."' – ibid.

'There may have been . . .' – *JN-T*, Richard Marson, p. 251.

'Somehow lost credibility with myself . . .' – ibid., p. 250.

'I wanted an ending that clearly implied the show was back . . .' – ibid., p. 251.

'It was the one time in his life when . . .' – 'Trials and Tribulations', *Doctor Who The Collection Season 23*, Blu-Ray box, disk 4.

'Walk-down, happy pantomime ending' – 'Revelations of a Script Editor', *Starburst #97*, September 1986, p. 17.

'Very paranoid individual . . .' – ibid., p. 16.

'Shook with rage [. . .] How could someone I'd worked with for so long . . .' – *JN-T*, Richard Marson, p. 257.

Chapter 9: The Mystery (1987–95)

1. The Human Bomb

'That's when I realised that the English class system was really bananas . . .' – 'Sylvester McCoy in Conversation', *Doctor Who The Collection Season 24*, Blu-Ray box, disk 8.

'We got involved with the audience, directly and physically . . .' – ibid.

'I discovered I'd been handed one of the great television acting roles . . .' – 'Sylvester McCoy at 80: Doctor Who legend looks back on his career', *Radio Times* YouTube channel, 20 August 2023.

2. Mystery

'One man's life or death were but a small price to pay . . .' – *Frankenstein*, Mary Shelley, volume one, letter four, p. 29.

'The owls are not what they seem' – *Twin Peaks*, series two, episode one.

'There'll be a reckoning with the nameless Doctor . . .' – *Doctor Who, Silver Nemesis*, part one, 23 November 1988.

'It was like peeling an onion, stripping away the previous interpretations . . .' – *Script Doctor*, Andrew Cartmel, p. 7.

3. The Greatest Show in the Galaxy

'Although I never got to see the early days, I know it's not as good as it used to be . . .' – *Doctor Who, The Greatest Show in the Galaxy*, part three, 28 December 1988.

'Enjoying the show, Ace? . . .' – ibid., part four, 4 January 1989.

'A formidable, mysterious entity . . .' – *Script Doctor*, Andrew Cartmel, p. 123.

'How many people have you destroyed . . .' – *Doctor Who, The Greatest Show in the Galaxy*, part four, 4 January 1989.

'I've sent them so many things. *Everything* I've sent can't be rubbish . . .' – *JN-T*, Richard Marson, p. 329.

'I suppose you could question whether you can have an anniversary special . . .' – *Is There Life Outside the Box?*, Peter Davison, p. 241.

'I don't think he was necessarily the best producer for *Doctor Who*. . .' – ibid., p. 307.

'The last time I spoke to him . . .' – DWM Special Edition: 'Showrunners', March 2023, p. 59.

4. Going Underground

'Considered insane at the time. It was partly because . . .' – DWM556, September 2020, p. 34.

'Fan fiction trained me . . .' – ibid., pp. 33–4.

'In a way it was the apotheosis of the fan mentality . . .' – ibid., p. 36.

'I've got a friend out there. He might be able to help . . .' – *The Stranger: More Than a Messiah*, BBV Productions, 1992.

'I thought [Baggs] was bonkers to do it and risk being sued . . .' – *Downtime*, Dylan Rees, p. 29.

'It has quite an oppressive atmosphere, especially if you're working . . .' – ibid., p. 26.

'Cursed' – *Revenge of the Cybermen* 'making of' documentary, *Doctor Who The Collection Season 12*, Blu-Ray box, disk 5.

'It was just dialogue between him and me but . . .' – *Elisabeth Sladen*, Elisabeth Sladen, p. 168.

Chapter 10: The Romantic (1996–2003)

1. Daleks vs Time Lords

'You asked me to drop you a note to confirm . . .' – Memo from Mark Shivas to Jonathan Powell, BBC Archives, 13 October 1989.

2. 'Segal Couldn't Tell Us Apart'

'I am afraid I think a new series is premature . . .' – 'Seven Year Hitch', *Doctor Who the Movie Special Edition* DVD, Disk 1.

'It was, at the time, hated . . .' – ibid.

'Who's he? He's my Doctor! I want him!' – Paul McGann interviewed by Sophie Aldred, *Myth Makers #142*, 2019.

'I think that was because Segal couldn't tell us apart . . .' – ibid.

3. The Hero's Journey

'You're a beautiful woman, probably' – *Doctor Who, City of Death*, part two, 6 October 1979.

'She's my best friend!' – *Doctor Who, Seeds of Doom*, part three, 14 February 1976.

'I was at a convention in Chicago right after it first came out . . .' – *Doctor Who Am I*, dir. Matthew Jacobs and Vanessa Yuille, 2022.

'Once he kisses somebody, he no longer belongs to everybody . . .' – ibid.

4. Half-human

'Half-human on my mother's side' – *Doctor Who, The TV Movie*, 27 May 1996.

'See that? [. . .] That's the retinal structure of the human eye . . .' – ibid.

'Stupid apes' – *Doctor Who, Rose*, 26 March 2005.

5. Jackie Tyler and River Song Meet the Krotons

'As far as the BBC is concerned, these new stories . . .' – DWM275, March 1999, p. 4.

Chapter 11: The Survivor (2004–05)

1. 'God Help Anyone in Charge of Bringing It Back'

'The only thing I could really, really get excited about . . .' – *The Long Game*, Paul Hayes, p. 44.

'It was a great privilege. I loved it. I just couldn't believe it . . .' – ibid., p. 45.

'I was in the same room as *Doctor Who . . .'* – DWM594, August 2023, p. 11.

'Wrote a *Doctor Who* novel in which the six-foot blond, blue-eyed companion . . .' – 'Transmission was madness. Honestly', Russell T Davies, *Guardian*, 15 September 2003.

'Oh I'd love to do it, absolutely . . .' – DWM279, June 1999, p. 12.

'I wouldn't produce it . . .' – *The Long Game*, Paul Hayes, p. 84.

'Orwellian nightmare' – ibid., p. 22.

'I was the mad, passionate fan, and you can be a real bore if you are a fan . . .' – ibid., p. 180.

'We all suffer from fan shame . . .' – ibid., p. 217.

'Russell's version is so bold – ours was apologetic' – *T Is for Television*, Mark Aldridge and Andy Murray, p. 185.

'*Doctor Who* Ready to Come Out of the TARDIS for Saturday TV Series . . .' – *Daily Telegraph*, 26 September 2003, quoted in *The Long Game*, Paul Hayes, pp. 290–1.

'I think it's fair to say that absolutely nobody else . . .' – *Imagine . . . Russell T Davies: The Doctor and Me*, BBC One, 18 December 2023.

2. 'I Changed It'

'When I was a kid, *Doctor Who* had never really meant anything to me . . .' – *I Love the Bones of You*, Christopher Eccleston, p. 158.

'I knew how much I'd invested in TV as a child, how it had sparked my imagination . . .' – ibid., p. 161.

'That means he's travelling through time . . .' – ibid.

'I put a PS – just on instinct, really . . .' – *Doctor Who The Complete History*, Stories 157–9, p. 28.

'I would lose myself so thoroughly in my own imagination . . .' – *I Love the Bones of You*, Christopher Eccleston, p. 15.

'I'll carry the absolute shame of that to the grave . . .' – ibid., p. 12.

'A lifelong body hater' – ibid., p. 99.

'I was extremely body-conscious, and so what did I do . . .' – ibid., p. 110.

'I loved getting drunk . . .' – ibid., p. 115.

'I did something positive. The role – posh, received pronunciation . . .' – ibid., p. 168.

'Men in Time Lord collars shouting at each other . . .' – *The Long Game*, Paul Hayes, p. 193.

'Considering he's an alien, he's more human . . .' – *T Is for Television*, Mark Aldridge and Andy Murray, p. 187.

'If the Zogs on the planet Zog are having trouble with the Zog-monster . . .' – *Doctor Who The Complete History*, Stories 157–9, p. 31.

3. 'Images of Johnny B'

'I've learnt, over the years, that when the *Official History of Doctor Who*. . .' – DWM584, November 2022, p. 11.

'Wikipedia is truly sometimes . . .' – 'Sarah Sutton and Janet Fielding in Conversation', *Doctor Who The Collection Series 20*, Blu-Ray box, disk 4.

'Having been in the hot seat, I'm really sceptical of . . .' – Chris Chibnall interviewed by the author, 16 September 2023.

'He hoped viewers continued to enjoy the series . . .' – 'BBC admits Dr Who actor blunder', BBC News online, 4 April 2005.

'I was told by my agent at the time . . .' – 'Christopher Eccleston: "I gave *Doctor Who* a hit show and then they put me on a blacklist"', Gareth McLean, *Guardian*, 12 March 2018.

'My relationship with my three immediate superiors . . .' – 'Christopher Eccleston says he "lost faith and trust and belief" in *Doctor Who* bosses while filming', Huw Fullerton, RadioTimes.com, 19 March 2018.

'Sack Russell T Davies. Sack Jane Tranter. Sack Phil Collinson. Sack Julie Gardner . . .' – Christopher Eccleston & Billie Piper Doctor Who Panel, For the Love of Sci-Fi convention, Manchester 2023.

'I didn't agree with the way things were being run . . .' – Eccleston's comments are quoted online at http://badwilf.com/eccleston-explains-why-he-left-doctor-who/ [accessed 08/01/2025]

'It's amazing!' – Paul McGann interviewed by Sophie Aldred, *Myth Makers #142*, 2019.

'Twat' – *Sunday Brunch*, Channel 4, 26 November 2023.

'If I stay in this job, I'm going to have to blind myself...' – *Radio Times*, 19–25 June 2020.

'I found them extraordinary...' – *Doctor Who: The Inside Story*, Gary Russell, p. 13.

'I did spend the whole pre-production period...' – *T Is for Television*, Mark Aldridge and Andy Murray, p. 193.

'To be quite frank, there were no...' – *The Long Game*, Paul Hayes, p. 275.

'To everyone else, but not to me...' – DWM398, 20 August 2008.

'In 2004 we decided to reboot *Doctor Who* in Wales...' – 'New report finds *Doctor Who* regenerated creative industries in Wales', BBC Media Centre, 23 November 2023.

'I still find plenty of moaners complaining that...' – *T Is for Television*, Mark Aldridge and Andy Murray, p. 220.

'I think if it was now, it would be crossing the line...' – *Lorraine*, ITV, 13 December 2021.

Chapter 12: The Lonely God (2006–09)

1. Niche Construction

'Christopher Eccleston will not be returning as the Doctor...' – 'Doctor Who – new series confirmed', BBC Press Office, 31 March 2005.

'Good to have you back, Gordon...' – *The Quatermass Experiment*, BBC Four, 2 April 2005.

'It was extremely sweet...' – 'Bring Something Back' documentary, *The Quatermass Experiment* DVD, 2005.

'I saw Jon Pertwee turning into Tom Baker...' – *Imagine... Russell T Davies: The Doctor and Me*, BBC One, 18 December 2023.

'The cast of eighteen are uniformly excellent with the exception of...' – *A Life in Time and Space*, Nigel Goodall, p. 42.

'If there's any little walk-ons in *Doctor Who*, I'm very happy to...' – *Doctor Who Confidential: The Eleventh Doctor*, BBC Three, 3 January 2009.

'Frankly, I would say we got him at "hello"...' – ibid.

'I didn't realise he was regenerating...' – *Imagine... Russell T Davies: The Doctor and Me*, BBC One, 18 December 2023.

'*Doctor Who* made me a writer, it really did...' – 'Doctor appointment', David Winner, *Financial Times*, 25 March 2005.

'You go into edit suites and TV studios up and down the land . . .' – DWM596, October 2023, p. 30.

2. The Lonely God

'A child. Give the Doctor a child! . . .' – *The Writer's Tale*, Russell T Davies and Benjamin Cook, p. 35.

'I don't really like plays very much . . .' – DWM503, August 2016, p. 24.

'It's something to do with the Doctor . . .' – *Doctor Who, Rose*, 26 March 2005.

'I just love writing about it . . .' – *T Is for Television*, Mark Aldridge and Andy Murray, pp. 173–4.

'The truth is, old *Doctor Who* was an entirely sexless series . . .' – *Matt Smith*, Emily Herbert, p. 214.

'I resisted jumping his bones . . .' – ibid., p. 58.

'I love you . . .' – *Doctor Who, Doomsday*, 8 July 2006.

'Coming to terms with his own specialness . . .' – *T Is for Television*, Mark Aldridge and Andy Murray, p. 174.

3. The Content Avalanche

'Oh, it's God!' – *T Is for Television*, Mark Aldridge and Andy Murray, p. 20.

'Lost her mind . . .' – ibid., p. 10.

'Not allowed . . .' – 'Russell T Davies talks about Torchwood', BBC Radio Wales, 17 October 2005.

'I dread the day I leave the programme, because then . . .' – *Doctor Who: The Inside Story*, Gary Russell, p. 30.

'When filming begins in earnest next week . . .' – ibid., p. 6.

'The show's success is so mad that I don't think . . .' – *A Life in Time and Space*, Nigel Goodall, p. 172.

'Number One Gay' – *The Writer's Tale*, Russell T Davies and Benjamin Cook, p. 75.

'We decided that we'd have a fourth series . . .' – ibid., p. 59.

Chapter 13: The Time Traveller (2010–13)

1. Timey-wimey

'I think time travel is fascinating. I think the timeline of a story is fascinating . . .' – *Doctor Who: The Fan Show*, 17 January 2018.

'People assume that time is a strict progression of . . .' – *Doctor Who, Blink*, 9 June 2007.

'Look at you. Oh, you're young . . .' – *Doctor Who, Silence in the Library*, 31 May 2008.

'You know when you see a photograph of someone you know . . .' – *Doctor Who, Forest of the Dead*, 7 June 2008.

'Russell and I went through a phase of trying to work out . . .' – *Doctor Who: The Fan Show*, 5 January 2018.

2. 'Oh, That's Him'

'I don't think young, dashing Doctors are right at all . . .' – DWM279, June 1999, p. 12.

'He was just spot-on, right from the beginning. The way he said the lines . . .' – *Doctor Who Confidential: The Eleventh Doctor*, 3 January 2009.

'Matt Smith has got a fascinating face. It's long and bony . . .' – 'Dr Who? Big names lose out to Matt Smith, Caroline Davies and David Smith', *Observer*, 3 January 2009.

'His childhood was by and large uneventful . . .' – *Matt Smith*, Emily Herbert, p. 129.

'Matt sometimes seemed almost too normal to be an actor . . .' – ibid., p. 164.

'Yes, I was in a mess. Football was everything . . .' – ibid., p. 130.

'There are great disciplines from being a sportsman . . .' – ibid., p. 132.

'I think my dad instilled hard work in me . . .' – 'Matt Smith on friendship, fame and radical theatre', Rachel Cooke, *Observer*, 4 February 2024.

'I just wanted the mantle. I wanted to run things . . .' – *Matt Smith*, Emily Herbert, p. 136.

3. 'We're All Stories in the End'

'This song is ending . . .' – *Doctor Who, The End of Time* part two, 1 January 2010.

'We're all stories in the end' – *Doctor Who, The Big Bang*, 26 June 2010.

'A goblin, or a trickster, or a warrior . . .' – *Doctor Who, The Pandorica Opens*, 19 June 2010.

'For me, *Doctor Who* is a fairy tale . . .' – *Matt Smith*, Emily Herbert, p. 76.

'Human beings are story addicts . . .' – Chris Chibnall interviewed by the author, 16 September 2023.

'The poet with his words and phrases' – Plato, *Republic*, Book 3.

'There have been great societies that did not use the wheel . . .' – *The Language of the Night*, Ursula K. Le Guin, p. 15.

'The show that is on in the corner of the room . . .' – Chris Chibnall interviewed by the author, 16 September 2023.

4. 'Home. The Long Way Round'

'The weirdest thing about *Doctor Who* now is . . .' – DWM503, August 2016, p. 40.

'Here you can meet the people who make the show possible . . .' – *Doctor Who Official 50th Celebration* programme, p. 3.

'You're not going anywhere, you're just wandering about . . .' – *Doctor Who, The Day of the Doctor*, 23 November 2013.

'Periodically, *Doctor Who* must change a lot because . . .' – *Doctor Who: The Fan Show*, 17 January 2018.

5. Made of Some Sort of Steel

'We sign this petition to ask that the BBC remove Moffat . . .' – 'BBC: Remove Steven Moffat from Doctor Who', Change.org, 19 May 2013.

'Was an utterly awful piece of television . . .' – anti-moffat.tumblr.com/post/68322932504/the-day-of-the-doctor-reviewcritique-by-claudia/amp [accessed 08/01/2025]

'I have Emotional Intensity Disorder (otherwise known as Borderline Personality Disorder) . . .' – www.claudiaboleynofficial.com/about [accessed 08/01/2025]

'An impossibly small number of incredibly rude . . .' – *Doctor Who: The Fan Show*, 17 January 2018.

'Only one death threat, two demands for my immediate resignation . . .' – '*Doctor Who* boss Steven Moffat gets death threat', Bangshowbiz, Yahoo! News, 7 June 2011.

'Browsing Outpost Gallifrey to read how crap I am' – *The Writer's Tale*, Russell T Davies and Benjamin Cook, p. 59.

'Helen Raynor went on Outpost Gallifrey last month and . . .' – ibid., p. 76.

'The people who like it really like it and the people who hate it . . .' – RHLSTP (Richard Herring's Leicester Square Theatre Podcast) #490, 15 February 2024.

'Pains me to an extraordinary extent. Because the relationship . . .' – *Doctor Who: The Fan Show*, 17 January 2018.

'She wrote about that with some anger, but also with . . .' – *The Writer's Tale*, Russell T Davies and Benjamin Cook, p. 77.

Chapter 14: The Death and Resurrection Show (2014–17)

1. 'She Cares So I Don't Have To'

'Every single time I did a series of *Sherlock* I was running . . .' – *Doctor Who: The Fan Show*, 17 January 2018.

'I always sort of assumed that I would leave with Matt . . .' – ibid.

'I bumped into Steven Moffat at the Scottish BAFTAs . . .' – *Young Again with Kirsty Young*, BBC Radio 4, 13 February 2024.

'I knew he might say yes and the moment I thought of him playing the Doctor . . .' – *Doctor Who: The Fan Show*, 3 August 2018.

'He was showing me the TARDIS . . .' – *Young Again with Kirsty Young*, BBC Radio 4, 13 February 2024.

'Essentially there is something there that it's not good to . . .' – DWM Bookazine #32, *60 Moments in Time*, November 2023, p. 11.

'I have a very mythical and personal concept of Doctor Who . . .' – 'Would Peter Capaldi Return to Doctor Who?', io9 YouTube channel, 11 January 2024.

'We've had two quirky young men as the Doctor . . .' – *Doctor Who: The Fan Show*, 3 August 2018.

'Steven said that the new doctor would be brusque . . .' – Jamie Mathieson interviewed by the author, 15 February 2024.

'An ordinary man: that's the most important thing in creation' – *Doctor Who, Father's Day*, 14 May 2005.

'Human beings! You are amazing!' – *Doctor Who, The Impossible Planet*, 3 June 2006.

'In nine hundred years of time and space, I've never met anyone who wasn't important' – *Doctor Who, A Christmas Carol*, 25 December 2010.

'[Clara's] my carer. She cares so I don't have to' – *Doctor Who, Into The Dalek*, 30 August 2014.

'I asked Steven about this during the writing of the fiftieth . . .' – email from Richard Cookson to the author, 21 June 2024.

'I don't think there's any plot at all in the Doctor looking for Gallifrey . . .' – *Doctor Who: The Fan Show*, 3 August 2018.

'I'm not trying to win . . .' – *Doctor Who, The Doctor Falls*, 1 July 2017.

'It's a gas and a good thing in the world' – 'Peter Capaldi on "Criminal Record" and "Doctor Who" Being "Good for the World"', Simon Thompson, *Forbes*, 10 January 2024.

'You're going to die too, some day . . .' – *Doctor Who, The Doctor Falls*, 1 July 2017.

2. The Snow Globe

'I don't understand this autism thing, Pop . . .' – *St. Elsewhere, The Last One*, NBC, 25 May 1988.

'I now wish I'd put it somewhere more where you can see it . . .' – Ben Wheatley interviewed by the author, 5 June 2023.

'You sit at night there on the couch beside your partner . . .' – *Light of Thy Countenance*, Alan Moore, Felipe Massafera and Antony Johnston, 2009.

'This is BBC Television. The time is a quarter past five . . .' – *Doctor Who, Remembrance of the Daleks*, part two, 12 October 1988.

3. Death and the Doctor

'It was very well received and there was . . .' – Jamie Mathieson interviewed by the author, 15 February 2024.

'I've done whole jobs that have taken less time than . . .' – *Doctor Who: The Fan Show*, 3 August 2018.

'By the time I wrote [the end of Capaldi's last season] . . .' – DWM597, October 2023, p. 26.

'During the Capaldi years, I was always looking to do . . .' – ibid., p. 27.

'[With] *Doctor Who*, you've got to talk about monsters and it's a sort of circus . . .' – *Where There's a Will, There's a Wake, with Kathy Burke*, 15 January 2024.

'I tend to describe it as a meditation on grief, not death . . .' – @rtalalay Twitter account, 21 January 2024.

4. They Cross Generations

'Over the past 100 years, the Walt Disney Company has entwined itself with our families . . .' – 'The "Disney adult" industrial complex', Amelia Tait, *New Statesman*, 24 February 2024.

Chapter 15: The Foundling (2018–22)

1. Her Own Cupboard

'Someone, somewhere might be a little bit worried . . .' – '5 things the Doctor does in any worrying situation', BBC YouTube channel, 26 March 2020.

'The thing that you have to make a call on . . .' – Chris Chibnall interviewed by the author, 16 September 2023.

'The girl that's got bloody mascara running down her face . . .' – '"I were crap at school": Jodie Whittaker, the new Doctor Who', Jasper Rees, theartsdesk.com, 16 July 2017.

'I played on my own for hours. I didn't need anyone . . .' – ibid.

'The line between Jodie and Sylvester McCoy and Patrick Troughton . . .' – Chris Chibnall interviewed by the author, 16 September 2023.

2. 'It's about Time'

'I know there's this big debate about whether the Doctor should be a woman . . .' – *The Ed Doolan Show*, BBC Radio WM, 21 September 1984.

'If it's going to be a new Doctor . . .' – Chris Chibnall interviewed by the author, 16 September 2023.

'We found that negative words in news headlines . . .' – 'Negativity drives online news consumption', Claire E. Robertson et al., *Nature Human Behaviour* 7, 2023, pp. 812–822.

'I think it's a fantastic opportunity for her . . .' – '*Doctor Who* star Peter Davison "calls it a day" on Twitter after "toxicity" around female Doctor comments', Paul Jones, RadioTimes.com, 24 July 2017.

3. 'The Absence of a Set Destiny'

'I had a cancer diagnosis when I was 22 . . .' – DWM583, October 2022, p. 42.

'You have to pour yourself into it . . .' – Chris Chibnall interviewed by the author, 16 September 2023.

'I have a thing on my desk which somebody gave me . . .' – Chris Chibnall interviewed by the author, 16 September 2023.

'It is true to say that I attempted to imply that William Hartnell was not the first Doctor . . .' – *A History of the Universe*, Lance Parkin, p. 255.

'I loved what [the Cartmel-era writers] did in that era . . .' – Chris Chibnall interviewed by the author, 16 September 2023.

4. 'To Disrupt from a Place of Love'

'You felt that anything you did would be judged against your race . . .' – DWM589, March 2023, p. 41.

'What [the success of] *Broadchurch* gave me . . .' – Chris Chibnall interviewed by the author, 16 September 2023.

'24 per cent of the highest-rated modern *Doctor Who* episodes . . .' – '*Doctor Who*'s female directors have defied the odds', Rachel Talalay, RadioTimes.com, 8 March 2024.

'Let me take it from the top. Hello, I'm the Doctor . . .' – *Doctor Who, Fugitive of the Judoon*, 26 January 2020.

'Came in to disrupt in a positive way . . .' – Chris Chibnall interviewed by the author, 16 September 2023.

5. Bad Wolf

'How the BBC can become more representative of the people who pay the licence fee . . .' – 'BBC staffed by people "whose mum and dad worked there", says Nadine Dorries', Peter Walker and Heather Stewart, *Guardian*, 4 October 2021.

'Only one in 20 people under the age of 30 . . .' – 'If even my 89-year-old mum isn't watching, the BBC is in real trouble', Nadine Dorries, *Daily Mail*, 9 August 2023.

'This licence fee announcement will be the last . . .' – 'BBC licence fee to be abolished in 2027 and funding frozen', Jim Waterson, *Guardian*, 16 January 2022.

'The woman's an idiot, a big fucking idiot' – 'Russell T Davies: *Doctor Who* writer brands Nadine Dorries a "f***ing idiot" over BBC row', Harry Fletcher, *Metro*, 8 October 2021.

'Mortal enemy' – 'Dominic Cummings thinktank called for "end of BBC in current form"', Rowena Mason, *Guardian*, 21 January 2020.

Chapter 16: The Bridge (2023)

1. 'A Divine Right'

'I kind of do . . .' – 'Russell T Davies and Steven Moffat on life after *Doctor Who*', *Radio Times* YouTube Channel, 31 January 2019.

'Murderers, bastards, abusers and liars' – 'Russell T Davies slams Tories as "wounded dogs" that "bite everyone and spread rabies" in savage acceptance speech: "They're murderers, bastards, abusers and liars"', Meghna Amin, *Metro*, 14 July 2022.

'To cut out the "T" . . .' – '*It's A Sin* creator Russell T Davies blasts LGB Alliance: "To cut out the T is to kill"', *Attitude Magazine* YouTube channel, 13 October 2021.

'As I considered this show's future . . .' – DWM586, January 2023, p. 7.

'I have a divine right' – *Radio Times*, 16–22 December 2023, p. 13.

'It's like you're Charlie in *Charlie and the Chocolate Factory*. . .' – *They Like To Watch*, 26 March 2024.

'The most magnificent finale ever shot on planet Earth . . .' – '*Doctor Who* showrunner Russell T Davies details the heartbreaking backstory of Ncuti Gatwa's Doctor's companion Ruby', Darren Scott, gamesradar.com, 1 December 2023.

'I shouldn't say that we're confident . . .' – 'The Shocks and Scares Will Make You Scream', *Radio Times* 15–21 June 2024, p. 15.

'There's six-year-olds watching this show, and I'm not trying to educate them . . .' – 'When Caitlin Moran met Russell T Davies, the king of *Doctor Who*', Caitlin Moran, *The Times*, 21 December 2023.

'We will utilise commercial partners much more actively . . .' – 'A BBC for the Future', Tim Davie, Royal Television Society address, 26 March 2024.

'If the BBC ever had a heart it went into cardiac arrest . . .' – *From the Oasthouse: The Alan Partridge Podcast*, series 3, episode 3.

'You've got to look in the long term at the end of the BBC . . .' – *They Like To Watch*, 26 March 2024.

'Russell T. Davies has now caused the most massive backlash . . .' – @IanLevine Twitter account, 18 November 2023.

'Newspapers of absolute hate, and venom, and destruction . . .' – '"Doctor Who" Gets More Than 100 Complaints Over "Inappropriate" Transgender Character', Jake Kanter, Deadline.com, 8 December 2023.

'It's a new thing, it's the sixtieth – imagine how much fans love new things . . .' – *Doctor Who: Unleashed*, 60th Anniversary Specials: 3. 'The Giggle', BBC iPlayer, 9 December 2023.

Chapter 17: The Doctor (2024–)

1. 'In Case Either of You Have a Magic Wand'

'Something I remember as almost over our heads . . .' – 'The 15th Doctor Will See You Now', Roslyn Sulcas, *New York Times*, 18 June 2024.

'The only thing stopping me from being on the streets . . .' – '*Doctor Who*'s Ncuti Gatwa shares his delight over new London pad having previously battled "homelessness"', Lisa McLoughlin, *Evening Standard*, 2 February 2023.

'Probably filled a gap that religion left in me . . .' – 'Ncuti Gatwa on *Doctor Who*: "The Doctor is me"', Alison Rumfitt, *Rolling Stone UK*, August 2023.

'I'd love to play either Willy Wonka or Doctor Who . . .' – WhatsApp messages shared by Ncuti Gatwa on his Instastory, 10 December 2023.

'This person survived a genocide. This person fits in everywhere and nowhere . . .' – 'Ncuti Gatwa on *Doctor Who*: "The Doctor is me"', Alison Rumfitt, *Rolling Stone UK*, August 2023.

'I want a young audience watching, and they talk about their emotions . . .' – 'The 15th Doctor Will See You Now', Roslyn Sulcas, *New York Times*, 18 June 2024.

'I almost didn't even leave my house . . .' – 'A new (re)generation: Inside Ncuti Gatwa's *Doctor Who*', Devan Coggan, *Entertainment Weekly*, 16 April 2024.

'We were talking about the world. I was like . . .' – 'Ncuti Gatwa: *Doctor Who* reminds me that there is always hope', Adrian Lobb, *The Big Issue*, 4 December 2023.

'It became clear to me that there isn't a mould . . .' – 'The 15th Doctor Will See You Now', Roslyn Sulcas, *New York Times*, 18 June 2024.

2. Roughly Half

'I was brought back to bring in a younger audience . . .' – 'The Shocks and Scares Will Make You Scream', *Radio Times*, 15–21 June 2024, p. 14.

'I used to love, but they've completely ruined' – Nigel Farage campaigning for the Reform party ahead of the 2024 general election, 30 June 2024, see https://x.com/GuyLambertUK/status/1807456343118196823 [accessed 08/01/2025]

'Not afraid of Doctor Who' – Kemi Badenoch's X account, 1 September 2024, see https://x.com/KemiBadenoch/status/1830296975079842209 [accessed 08/01/2025]

3. 'There's Always a Twist at the End'

'We're in a very busy science-fiction/fantasy world now . . .' – DWM603, April 2024, p. 17.

'A children's story come to life' – *Doctor Who, Space Babies*, 11 May 2024.

'With all of my adventures throughout Time and Space . . .' – *Doctor Who, The Devil's Chord*, 11 May 2024.

'I was already saying to the production team, "You must cast Susan" . . .' – DWM605, June 2024, p. 16.

'You've seen my life. I bring disaster, Kate . . .' – Doctor Who, *The Legend of Ruby Sunday*, 15 June 2024.

'I pride myself that I am better than you . . .' – *Doctor Who, Empire of Death*, 22 June 2024.

ACKNOWLEDGEMENTS

Thank you to everyone who has enthused, conversed and ranted to me about *Doctor Who* over the years, both for this book and in general. They include Ben Wheatley, Chris Chibnall, Jamie Mathieson, Steven Moffat, Richard Cookson, Tom Baker, Jason Arnopp, Kermit Leveridge, Adam Peters, Alan Edwards, Richard Williams, Richard Selby, Tim Leopard, Stef Wagstaffe, Elizabeth Sandifer, Tommy Calderbank, Simon Guerrier, Robin Ince, Joel Morris and David Keenan. Special thanks and much love to those ranters who also gave their time to be the beta readers of this book – Joanne Mallon, Andrew O'Neill, Alister Fruish, David Bramwell and Lia Higgs.

Huge thanks to those who made this book real, the mighty Jenny Lord alongside Lily McIlwain, Ellen Turner, Jo Whitford, Ian Allen, Tom Noble, Paul Stark and Steve Marking. As always, thanks to my agent Sarah Ballard and all at her new home C&W, and thanks also to Liv Bignold, Eli Keren and Alison Lewis. Love to Eric Drass, Gilly Forrester, Matt Pearson, Chris Davies, Richard Norris, Andy Starke and all at the East Sussex Psychedelic Film Club.

And finally, love always to my family, Joanne, Lia, Isaac, Paul, Sue, Brice, Patricia, Helen, Maura and maybe Dennis.

INDEX